# Developments in
# Labour Market Analysis

*Other titles by John Shorey*

*The Allocation of Resources*, with K. D. George

*Other titles by Caroline Joll*

*Industrial Organisation*, 3rd edn, with K. D. George

# Developments in Labour Market Analysis

Caroline Joll, Chris. McKenna, Robert McNabb
and John Shorey

*University College, Cardiff*

London
GEORGE ALLEN & UNWIN
Boston          Sydney

**George Allen & Unwin (Publishers) Ltd**
**40 Museum Street, London WC1A 1LU, UK**

George Allen & Unwin (Publishers) Ltd,
Park Lane, Hemel Hempstead, Herts HP2 4TE, UK

Allen & Unwin Inc.,
9 Winchester Terrace, Winchester, Mass 01890, USA

George Allen & Unwin Australia Pty Ltd,
8 Napier Street, North Sydney, NSW 2060, Australia


First published in 1983

---

**British Library Cataloguing in Publication Data**

Developments in labour market analysis
    1. Labor supply – Mathematical models.
1. Joll, Caroline
331.12′0724        HD5707
ISBN 0-04-331089-3
ISBN 0-04-331090-7 Pbk

---

**Library of Congress Cataloging in Publication Data**

Main entry under title:
    Developments in labour market analysis.
Bibliography: p.
Includes index.
1. Labor supply.   2. Labor economics.   1. Joll,
Caroline.
HD5706.D43   1983       331.12       82-22740
ISBN 0-04-331089-3
ISBN 0-04-331090-7 (pbk.)

---

Set in 10 on 11 point Times by Preface Ltd, Salisbury, Wilts
and printed in Great Britain by Biddles Ltd, Guildford, Surrey

# Contents

# SECTION II

# Preface

Labour economics is a rapidly expanding part of economic analysis. Its theoretical framework is continually being refined. The stock of empirical evidence on the subject is continually being added to and improved. This text is aimed at second and third level students. It is therefore assumed that the reader is familiar with elementary labour market analysis. We have omitted any systematic analysis of the simple, utility-maximising work/leisure trade-off model of labour supply and of the marginal productivity theory of labour demand, principally because this analysis is now adequately covered in many introductory microeconomic, macroeconomic and labour texts. The section entitled 'Further Reading' refers the reader to some of these. This text builds upon the foundations of the basic labour market model, therefore we recommend that some time be spent in mastering its concepts. Considerable effort is required here, but will be well rewarded.

The objective of theoretical analysis is to provide insights into the functioning of the labour market by abstracting certain key variables and relationships from a complex real world. Theory should generate testable predictions by means of which those insights can be evaluated. This text is divided into two sections. Section I sets out what we consider to be important recent developments in labour theory. Each has been the result of work by many economists; the further reading recommended for each chapter consists only of writings which we feel will help the reader confirm her/his grasp of the subject under discussion. We therefore recognise here our great debt to the hereafter unacknowledged contributors to developments in labour theory. At no point in this text do we attempt to provide a full bibliography of relevant material. We concentrate on the ideas, and any interested reader will be able to follow up particular issues by tracing other sources from the references given here. Our objective in Section I is to help the reader to grasp the central ideas, issues, problems and possibilities of each theoretical development in turn, treating each chapter as an exercise in the techniques of abstraction and model-building.

Section II sets out to demonstrate how the ideas of Section I can, together, significantly improve labour economic analysis. We discuss various major topics of labour economics, in each case indicating how the different theoretical models of Section I might be used to investigate the labour market processes involved. Mixing models in this way is hard for any student. It is all too easy to pigeonhole certain theories as applying only to specific issues, to ignore the possible interrelationships and the need sometimes to integrate ideas, and to hold back from attempting to think through the issues as a whole. Much greater understanding of the labour market will be obtained if one is prepared to follow up the implications of the basic theoretical models into all areas of labour market analysis and at the same time to use every available theoretical device to analyse any specific issue.

Since labour economics is a branch of applied economics, improvements in empirical analysis are as important to the development of the subject as those in theory. In this text we do not attempt to provide a comprehensive review and critique of the empirical literature which tests the predictions generated by the theory of Section II. Our objective is to identify at each stage the principal research techniques involved and the problems confronted. We also try to indicate the direction of empirical research in each area and, where possible, broad conclusions so far reached. The further reading for each chapter contains pieces of research which we feel illustrate the methodological issues and provide a feel for the findings. Again we are indebted to many, hereafter unacknowledged, researchers who have improved our understanding of the topics in Section II.

C. J.
C. M.
R. M.
J. S.
*University College, Cardiff, 1982*

# Developments in
# Labour Market Analysis

# SECTION I

# Introduction

The six chapters of this section set out some of the most interesting and evocative developments in labour economic theory. For heuristic purposes we introduce each stage of our analysis against the background of what we shall refer to as 'the basic model of the labour market'. That model rests upon three theoretical foundations: the marginal productivity theory of labour demand; the utility-maximising theory of individual labour supply; and the competitive theory of market equilibrium. That model is simple, concise, powerful and the core of traditional neoclassical labour economics. Our objective therefore is to substantiate the relevance and insight of recent developments in labour theory by reference to the assumptions, analysis and predictions of the basic model. That model is comprehensively covered in many elementary textbooks dealing either with general microeconomic theory or with labour economics. The reader is thus strongly recommended to consult one of these texts, if he/she has not already done so, before embarking upon the present text. The principal features of the basic model are as follows.

Marginal productivity theory can be applied to the demand for any factor of production. It is a theory of derived demand. It assumes, in its simplest form, that firms are competitive in product as well as factor markets. They thus face a perfectly elastic labour supply curve. Firms are assumed to be profit maximisers, to possess perfect information upon the characteristics of all current and potential employees and to face a stable, known product demand. The only cost of employing labour is the hourly wage rate which makes labour a totally variable factor of production. Technology is given, and embodied in a production function where factors are imperfect substitutes for one another. The firm treats every worker of the same skill in exactly the same way because, within any skill, workers are perfectly homogeneous and the firm's only concern is with labour productivity. The firm employs different factors and skills of labour in the proportions defined by equality between their relative efficiencies and their relative prices. The firm employs additional units of labour until the extra cost of hiring more labour equals the extra benefit from selling the output produced by that labour. Diagrammatically this means employing the relative proportion of factors that emerges from tangency between the relative input price ratio and the appropriate isoquant at each level of output, and employing additional units of labour up to the point where the marginal labour cost curve cuts the marginal revenue product curve. Under competitive conditions the marginal revenue product curve is equivalent to the demand for labour curve. *Ceteris paribus*, a fall in wages will increase the demand for labour. This comes about because of substitution of labour for other factors as labour becomes relatively cheaper. There is also, however, a scale effect increasing labour demand (and all other factor demands) arising from the reduction in total costs following the fall in the price of labour. These effects may be offset, but not negated, if the increase in demand for labour drives up the market price of labour or if the prices of alternative factors fall because the substitution effect towards labour is particularly strong. The most important determinant of the wage elasticity of demand will consequently be the degree of substitutability between inputs in production.

The supply of labour in the basic model arises out of utility-maximising behaviour on the part of individuals who distribute the time available to them between work and leisure. They attempt to derive the most satisfaction possible from consuming the goods they purchase out of labour income and from leisure, subject to the wage rate they receive for market work. Workers have stable preferences governing substitution between goods and leisure. Workers are assumed to know every detail concerning the job opportunities open to them. The jobs at a given skill level are identical and offer exactly the same wage. Wages are the opportunity cost of leisure. Each individual supplies additional person-hours of identical productivity until the marginal rate of substitution between goods (and thus income) and leisure in the preference map equals the wage rate per hour. Diagrammatically the solutions for hours supplied lies where the highest possible indifference curve is tangential to the budget line. The tangency point could lie below the leisure axis in which case we have a corner solution at the point on the leisure axis measuring the total hours available: the worker supplies no hours, does not participate in the labour force.

A rise in the wage rate will increase the foregone earnings price of leisure time. A worker will thus, on the one hand, substitute towards work and consume more goods at the expense of leisure. On the other hand, the increase in the wage rate will have an income effect which, if the worker regards leisure as a normal good, will increase the consumption of leisure. The final result for labour supply is therefore unknown *a priori*: the substitution effect of a wage increase would increase labour supply, *ceteris paribus*; the income effect would reduce it. If the substitution effect is dominant, the result is the conventional upward-sloping supply curve. If the income effect becomes dominant at some higher wage level the result is the backward-bending supply curve. The higher the wage rate the more likely it is, *ceteris paribus*, that the tangency solution will lie above the leisure axis and thus the greater is the probability that the individual will participate in the labour market.

With the demand and supply curves of labour so determined, the final element in the basic model is the assumption that competitive market clearing forces prevail. The labour market is thus treated no differently from any other market. Consequently the equilibrium level of employment in any labour market is defined by the intersection of the aggregate supply and demand curves, each of which is merely a horizontal summation across the appropriate curves for individual workers or firms. Equilibrium is achieved and maintained by the pressure of excess demand and supply. Wages must be identical everywhere in the market and equal to the marginal revenue product at the equilibrium employment level. Every firm is thus subject to market forces for each type of labour it employs. The internal wage structure for the firm must be identical to the market wage structure. Deviations can only be temporary and transitional.

Though clearly the basic model represents a most severe abstraction from reality, it does provide some useful insights into the workings of the labour market. In the following six chapters we attempt to improve the model by respecifying in turn a number of its key assumptions. For the most part, however, our approach remains faithful to the neoclassical tradition. Two central interdependent themes in labour market analysis, as in every field of microeconomics, are technical efficiency and equity in resource allocation. We shall inevitably pursue these same themes as we focus upon various developments in labour theory.

## Further Reading

INTRODUCTION

B. M. Fleischer and T. J. Kniesner, *Labor Economics*, 2nd edition (Englewood Cliffs, N.J.: Prentice-Hall, 1980).

R. Perlman, *Labor Theory* (New York: John Wiley, 1969).

D. Sapsford, *Labour Market Economics* (London: George Allen & Unwin, 1981).

# 1
# The theory of individual labour supply

The basic model of labour supply outlined in the introduction to this section is, for its simplicity, rich in both predictions and insight. However, whilst this simplicity is valuable, especially in the preliminary stages of enquiry, it is clearly inhibiting when it comes to analysing working labour markets. In this chapter, and in the next two, we examine some of the more obvious limitations of the basic model. We attempt to show how relaxing certain assumptions improves its explanatory powers without unduly compromising its straight-forward, analytical rigour.

Throughout our analysis we retain the core exploratory device of utility-maximising decision makers operating with perfect information. In this chapter and in Chapter 2 we are concerned with short-run labour supply decisions, relating to participation in the labour market and hours worked. Long-run supply decisions, relating to labour quality, are considered in Chapter 3.

## 1.1  The basic labour supply model

The essential ingredients of the basic labour supply model are as follows: a utility function

$$U = U(G, L) \tag{1.1}$$

where $U$ is individual utility, $G$ are goods and $L$ is leisure; an income constraint,

$$P_G G = WH \tag{1.2}$$

where $P_G$ is the price of the goods, $W$ is the wage rate and $H$ the number of hours worked; and a time constraint,

$$T = H + L \tag{1.3}$$

where $T$ is total time available to the individual. Maximising equation

(1.1) subject to equations (1.2) and (1.3), with wages, prices and time fixed, produces the labour supply function for $H$ in terms of $W$. Diagrammatically this result is achieved by systematically altering the slope of the budget constraint and recording, for each wage rate, the hours worked at the tangency point between the budget line and an indifference curve.

Consider now some of the limitations of this model. First, the model recognises no institutionally determined limits to the individual worker's choice as to the amounts of work and leisure he undertakes. In practice individuals face both non-linear budget constraints and restrictions on hours which will have important implications for, amongst other things, the responses of labour to price signals. We consider these implications in Section 1.2.

Second, equation (1.1) presents a very naive view of the workers' true utility relationship. The only arguments in the function are the quantities of goods and leisure which are separately consumed and are always substitutes. This arbitrary distinction ignores entirely the fact that consumption activities involve time, as well as the purchase of goods, and that leisure involves the consumption of goods, as well as time. As such, the simple model fails to pick up the various substitutions between time and goods that may take place when relative prices change, not only between so-called leisure and consumption, but also *within* each of these two activities. Such further substitution effects have a direct bearing upon labour supply. This will only emerge from a theory of labour supply which focuses upon the allocation of time across various activities, each requiring different time inputs and in which labour supply is both the time left over after consuming activities and the means of financing the goods required for those activities. Such a theory is developed in Section 1.3.

Third, the model deals only with the supply decision of the individual. In reality, however, most labour supply decisions are taken by households. Necessarily, therefore, at any point in time there are two interdependent decisions to be made: what is to be the total labour supply of the household; and what is to be the division of that household supply amongst household members? The specific outcome of both these decisions will depend, amongst other things, upon the earnings potential of the different household members. Recognition of the household as the decision unit introduces the possibility, ignored in the basic model, of interdependence between the supply decisions of different workers and of substitution of work or leisure between members of the household. We consider household decision making in Section 2.1.

Recognition of the household as the decision-making unit makes it possible to consider the special labour supply behaviour of secondary workers – members of the household who earn significantly less than other members. Secondary workers are usually married women who constitute a growing proportion of the total labour force. Because the basic model makes a sharp distinction between goods and leisure it cannot easily accommodate decisions regarding domestic work. Decoration, building and general work connected with the home, childcare, housework and so on give considerable benefit to the family, use up non-working time but are not usually regarded as leisure activities. When domestic activities are undertaken the foregone earnings involved in doing-it-yourself must be compared with the costs of contracting the work out rather than with the lost utility from leisure given up. A model of the allocation of time would recognise domestic work as an activity in the workers' utility function that involves both time and goods, and that labour supply will thus depend *inter alia* upon the substitution effects arising from relative price changes between imported labour and goods used in domestic activities. Furthermore, a model of the allocation of time developed within the context of the household provides insights into the relationship between the demand for domestic activities and the labour supply of individual household members, particularly married women. Such an analysis is developed in Section 2.2.

Fourth, since the model as set out above is timeless, it implies that every future period is exactly identical to the present period, so that any labour supply decision taken today sets the pattern for all future decisions. This ignores the systematic changes through time, particularly as workers age, in the environment within which such decisions are taken. In reality therefore the labour supply decision relates not merely to the question of how much time should be supplied to the market but also to the question of when. Workers must decide on the distribution of their labour effort through their working lives. Such issues are discussed in Section 2.3.

Fifth, a model which is timeless cannot incorporate the fact that future consumption can be raised not only by foregoing present consumption and saving but also by foregoing present earnings to undertake education programmes. Education raises future earnings, and therefore future consumption potential. Thus, in reality, at every point in time each individual must allocate his time between work, leisure and education in order to maximise his lifetime consumption. The basic model incorporates education merely as one of many consumption activities in the preference map of individuals, and thus provides no way of analysing such a decision. In Chapter 3 we consider the implications for labour supply of workers' decisions regarding education.

We are unable to consider other limitations of the basic model in depth in this text. However, we can at least identify two of the most important.

First, the utility function given in equation (1.1) above does not explicitly take into account the possible utility/disutility effects of market labour over and above those arising from the loss of leisure time. The precise sources of the utility/disutility are disparate, but factors such as the amount of contact with other workers, the level of responsibility, and the exercise of skills must play some part. This implies that the supply of otherwise homogeneous labour to different jobs will vary according to the characteristics of the work, the utility/disutility attached to those characteristics and the pattern of preferences across workers. As Adam Smith recognised in his discussion of compensating variations, wage differentials normally ignored by competitive theory could result.

Second, because the basic model is timeless it cannot incorporate the cumulative and feedback effects arising from the labour supply decisions taken in any one time period on future decisions. An important instance of such dynamic effects involves marginal workers. These are workers with low wages when at work, unstable employment records and a very low attachment to the labour force. In practice marginal workers are usually women, young and old male workers and the least skilled prime age male labour.

The observed low wage level of, say, certain female workers is a vital element in explaining their limited labour supply. But it alone is not sufficient to explain their peculiar circumstances. In practice their current labour supply decisions are not independent of decisions taken previously. In particular, decisions to become inactive, or to switch jobs frequently, will have deleterious effects upon their future labour market opportunities. First, such decisions, perhaps perfectly rational in the circumstances, will lead employers to question the reliability of such workers when job vacancies occur. Second, movements between jobs and in and out of the labour force both impair the workers' skills, and usually prevent their further accumulation. Each worker's current labour supply decision will bear crucially upon the level of education and training expenditures by both the workers and the employer. Third, periods of inactivity may well reshape the individual's utility function and thus influence future supply decisions. A worker's preference for leisure may become stronger as she adjusts her life style to inactivity, the more so where other members of the household participate in the labour market. Work itself may become a negative factor in the utility function as she reacts adversely to the personal and social relationships to which work commits her. Fourth, low wages, inferior jobs and frequent job changes will tend in time to alienate workers from market work with the result that job instability becomes progressively more serious. Finally, finding a new job is an exacting process in pecuniary and non-pecuniary terms. Pecuniary costs will be relatively high for inactive marginal workers because they lose touch with market opportunities. They could be high for active marginal workers because they have to look harder, given that their continual turnover reduces the number of fresh openings. The non-pecuniary costs could also become more onerous over time. Each of the above factors will act in a cumulative way, so that the attachment of certain workers to the labour market falls through time to the detriment, in many instances, of the individuals concerned and of the aggregate supply of labour to the economy. To understand the phenomenon of the marginal worker one must therefore go beyond the current low level of the wages she is offered to consider why they are so low and why her labour supply responses to them are so limited. This necessarily involves consideration of workers' lifetime experiences in the labour market, particularly the very earliest experiences.

## 1.2 Institutional constraints upon labour supply

Few individuals in the labour market face a simple linear budget constraint like the one described by equation (1.2) above. For one thing, additional constraints exist in the form of restrictions upon the number of hours of work any worker is permitted to supply. For another, non-linearities in the budget constraint arise, primarily because of the existence of overtime premiums, taxes and transfers. In this section we consider what modifications might be made to the predictions of the basic labour model when such facts are recognised.

### NON-LINEAR BUDGET CONSTRAINTS

The most familiar case of a non-linearity in the budget constraint occurs because the individual possesses unearned income, $B$. The budget constraint then becomes

$$P_G G = WH + B \tag{1.4}$$

and the diagrammatic solution is shown in Figure 1.1. The existence of unearned income means that though the individual faces an *earned income budget constraint* XY his *full income budget constraint* becomes the kinked line XCZ. Any change in $B$ alters the line XCZ and will thus have an effect upon labour supply. Since there is no change in XY there is no relative price change and therefore the change in $B$ cannot involve conventional income and substitution effects. It has what will be referred to as an *unearned income effect* which, in Figure 1.1, is seen as the shift of the full income budget line to XC'Z' and of the optimum from b to c, as $B$ increases from XC to XC'.

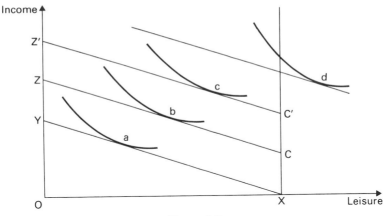

**Figure 1.1**

Whilst $B$ might be income from wealth, it could also be transfers from the state. In Figure 1.1 an increase in transfer income shifts the full income budget line upwards. Given that leisure is always treated as a normal good, higher transfers mean, *ceteris paribus*, fewer hours of work supplied and a greater probability of non-participation.

The unearned income case can be used to clarify the effects of less familiar non-linearities in budget constraints. In Figure 1.2(a) the worker again faces a kinked budget constraint, here XYZ. The wage rate, $W$, gives the wage line XYD, but income from work is taxed at the proportional rate $t$ above income level OA. In Figure 1.2(b) the kinked budget constraint arises because of the incidence of a higher

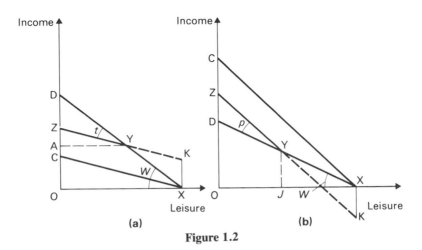

**Figure 1.2**

wage payment indicated by the mark-up, $p$, on hours worked above $J$. In both cases, for individuals optimising along YZ, the earned income budget line (the income constraint determined by the wage rate the worker actually receives) is given by XC. This implies from our previous analysis that in the taxation case the individual must derive positive unearned income to give him the full income budget line YZ. In the overtime case the individual appears to derive negative unearned income. These unearned income elements can be quantified by extending the line YZ to the intercept with zero hours worked at X. So in both cases the unearned income element is XK. These two cases are therefore very similar to the case of unearned income in Figure 1.1 if we regard unearned income XK in the tax and overtime cases as monetary estimates of notional benefits rather than as direct financial benefits. Unearned income again shifts the earned income constraint to become the full income constraint along which the individual optimises. As should now be clear, no individual really faces a kinked constraint like XYZ. Individuals optimising to the right of Y do so along the earned income constraint XY and have no full income constraint. Individuals optimising to the left of Y face the earned income constraint XC but optimise along YZ. The kinked line is thus an aggregate concept across different individuals.

Let us consider the tax-induced non-linearity first. Any change in taxes will not affect individuals whose optimum position in Figure 1.3 lies along XY. For individuals whose optimum lies along YZ the

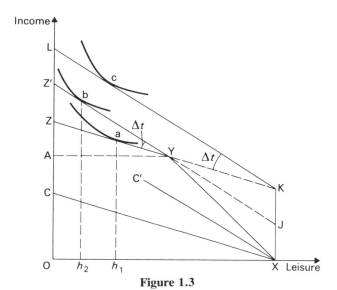

**Figure 1.3**

positive income element XK represents the notional or hypothetical value to them of the tax exemption below the income level OA. So, for the individual whose initial optimum is at a, supplying $Xh_1$ hours, the earned income budget line is XC. A reduction in the rate of income tax will mean that each individual now faces a full income budget constraint YZ'. Such a shift produces the conventional income and substitution effects. With non-linearities in the budget constraint there is a third effect, the unearned income effect, arising in this case from the increased value to the individual of his tax exemption. In Figure 1.3 the individual responds to the tax reduction by moving from an optimum at a to a new optimum at b and thus supplies $h_1h_2$ more hours. This movement can be broken down into three stages. The effect of the tax reduction, $\Delta t$, is first to raise the relative price of leisure. This will swing the earned income budget line from XC to XC'. The full income budget line, net of unearned income, changes from KZ to KL. As a result the individual's optimum shifts from a to c in the diagram with an increase in labour supply, given the assumption that the substitution effect dominates the earned income effect. The movement from c to b represents the result of a further shift, now downward, of the full income budget line from KL to JZ'. With a lower tax rate the individual derives less value from his tax exemption than he did previously. The monetary representation of this loss is indicated by the change in unearned income at zero labour supply. It falls from XK to XJ. It can be seen that this unearned income effect, assumed always to be negative, works here to increase labour supply. b will be somewhere to the left of c. The additional income effect in the non-linear case thus strengthens the prediction that lower taxes tend to increase labour supply.

A rise in the tax threshold (the obvious policy alternative to a tax cut) will raise rather than lower the value of the exemption and thus of the hypothetical unearned income. The relative price of leisure is unchanged in this case so the single unearned income effect leads unambiguously to a decrease in labour supply. The full income budget line for individuals optimising along YZ in Figure 1.4 shifts to Y'Z' as the monetary value of the notional unearned income measured at zero hours rises from XK to XS with a rise in the exemption level. The optimum position moves from a to d. Tax reductions and higher exemptions produce quite different labour supply responses.

A change in wages with no change in the exemption level cannot change the value to the individual of his tax exemption. Only the conventional income and substitution effects thus apply. The individual could, however, move from an optimum along XY to one along Y'Z' as his wage rises. Indeed with multiple non-linearities, introduced for example by a multi-tier tax system, one can imagine that as an individual's wage increases, *ceteris paribus*, his optimum may

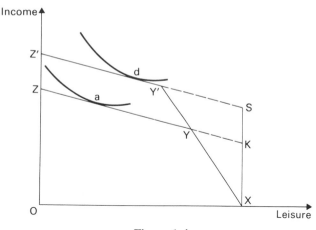

**Figure 1.4**

well move across segments of the full income constraint as it shifts upwards. There will then be unearned income changes, with consequent additional labour supply effects.

Consider now the case of an individual who works overtime. Here XK in Figure 1.5 represents the monetary value of the notional loss which the individual suffers because he is not allowed to benefit from the premium rate shown by XC for the hours he works up to X$J$. He therefore faces a full income budget constraint ZY and optimises at a, supplying X$h_1$ hours.

If the basic wage rate were now to rise the new full income budget constraint might be Y'Z'. The individual's labour supply response can again be broken down into two income effects and one substitution effect. Even if the individual were to face the same relative price of leisure after the wage change, i.e. even if the conventional income and substitution effects were to be removed, the individual would still react to the wage change because his full income has changed. There is still an unearned income effect because the increase in the overtime wage increases the hypothetical loss to the individual of not being able to work at such a rate for his entire labour supply.

The full income budget constraint holding the relative price of leisure constant shifts from KZ to QD as the non-pecuniary loss increases in monetary terms from XK to XQ. The individual shifts from an optimum at a to one at b, giving an increase in labour supply to X$h_2$ on the assumption of negative unearned income effects. When the change in the relative price of leisure is re-introduced, the full income budget constraint becomes QZ' and labour supply will increase further to X$h_3$. We now have even stronger reasons than

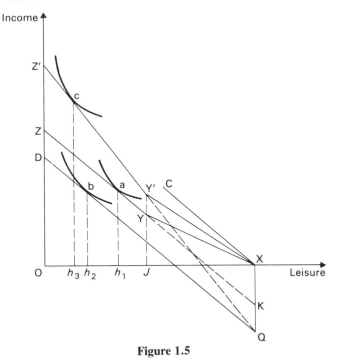

**Figure 1.5**

previously for expecting wage increases to increase the supply of labour. Any increase in the overtime premium, *ceteris paribus*, will have similar, even stronger, consequences.

State transfer payments also give rise to non-linear budget constraints and thus affect the supply of labour. We shall consider two cases which indicate the importance of the conditions of eligibility attached to transfers and the interaction between transfers and taxation.

Suppose, as in Figure 1.6, a lump sum payment, NB, is paid conditional upon non-participation. If any hours are worked, the transfer becomes zero. Given the wage rate $W_1$ the full income budget constraint is BNZ. It can be seen that the worker optimises at a zero hour supply or inactivity. He is then on a higher indifference curve, $I_1$, than any he can reach along NZ. Clearly the wage would have to reach a level $W_2$ before the rational individual would consider moving into the labour force. A higher transfer, say $NB_1$, which shifts the budget constraint to $B_1NZ$, makes inactivity more likely. The higher the transfer, the higher the market wage must be to induce entry to the labour force.

In practice, of course, state transfers are often not withdrawn in

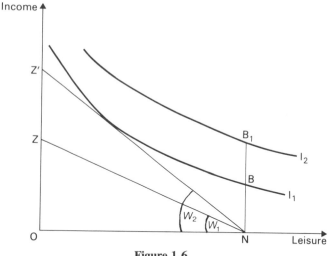

**Figure 1.6**

one go but are phased out. However, the effects of gradual withdrawal depend upon the way the receipt of transfers overlaps with the payment of taxes. One important example of this is the so-called poverty trap: the phenomenon of individuals paying very high effective marginal rates of taxation, sometimes close to or even above 100 per cent. Certain low-income individuals receive means-tested benefits and yet come within the lowest tax range. In such circumstances, if an individual were to earn only slightly more she would lose one or more of her transfers, in part or in total. She would also pay tax on her extra earned income. The result could be that the final net addition to income is small and the effective marginal rate of taxation is high. A given increase in wages will then have a much smaller effect upon the labour supply of this particular individual than upon that of others.

In Figure 1.7 the individual, given the wage $W$, faces the income opportunities XC. Means-tested benefits XK are available but are phased out gradually by income level R. At income level OS a proportional tax comes into force. The aggregate full income budget constraint XKYY'Z thus has three kinks in it. Suppose now that the tax and transfer systems overlap, i.e. income level S is below R, then between these two income levels the effective tax rate is high because both state fiscal systems apply simultaneously. This could come about during a period of inflation if tax exemptions are not increased in line with the rate of change of prices but transfers are. Consider the implications of this.

In Figure 1.8 two budget constraints are shown, derived from Figure

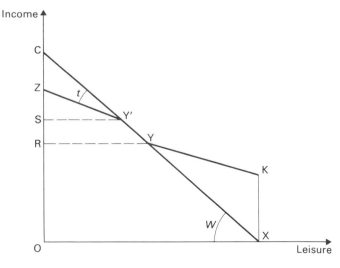

**Figure 1.7**

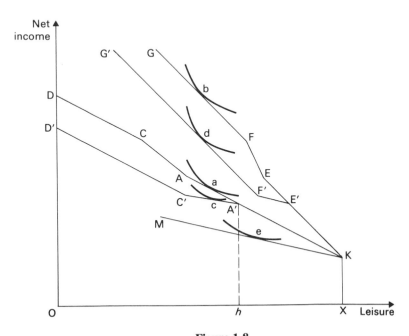

**Figure 1.8**

1.7. KACD is the constraint facing a low income individual, L, KEFG that facing a high income individual, H. L optimises at a, H at b. They have the same preference map. As a result of inflation the value of the tax exemption is reduced and the budget constraints shift to KA'C'D and KE'F'G'. The optimal solutions shift to c and d. Individual L optimises along A'C', the poverty trap, with a very high marginal tax rate. The increase in the tax rate between a and c reduces the relative price of leisure, inducing income and substitution effects which we assume on balance to *reduce* labour supply. The higher tax rate also generates an unearned income effect as it increases the notional value of the tax exemption. This further *reduces* the labour supply of L. Individual H, in moving from b to d, suffers only a fall in the value of the tax exemption, an unearned income effect, which leads to an *increased* labour supply. The different consequences for L and H follow from the differences noted earlier between a tax rate increase and a tax exemption level reduction, but it is the overlap of tax and transfer systems that makes the difference important.

In Figure 1.8 e represents the optimal solution for a very low income individual W, given the budget constraints KM and paying no taxes. As a result of a wage increase the budget line shifts to KA'C'D' (assuming inflation has caused the tax and transfer system to overlap) and the optimal solution becomes c. The wage increase alone has a positive effect on W's labour supply through the conventional income and substitution effects, but this is mitigated by the incidence of taxation and by the unearned income effect arising from the notional value of the tax exemption now received. The higher the marginal tax rate over the poverty trap range A'C' the smaller the response of supply to the wage increase. With a marginal tax rate above 100 per cent there would be a strong disincentive to supply more than $Xh$ hours.

## RESTRICTIONS ON HOURS WORKED

We turn now to consider the impact upon labour supply if utility-maximising individuals are not allowed to supply precisely the number of hours they would freely choose at the going market wage rate. There is every reason to expect *a priori* that workers (collectively) and employers will agree to a fixed hours contract as mutually beneficial. Such a constraint will guarantee workers a steady income and employers a steady output level. At the same time, however, such constraints will prevent certain individuals from achieving the levels of utility they would have achieved with a free choice.

To assist our analysis we introduce the concept of an individual worker's offer curve. This curve represents a locus of tangency points

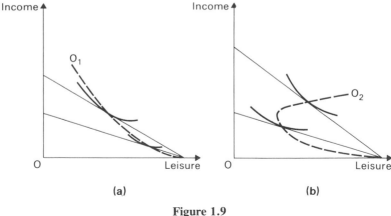

**Figure 1.9**

between the individual's indifference curves and the market wage rate as the latter increases from zero. In Figure 1.9 offer curve $O_1$ represents the conventional case, where substitution effects dominate income effects. Offer curve $O_2$, on the other hand, represents the case where the income effect becomes dominant, and gives the backward bending labour supply curve. We shall concentrate on the former case throughout our analysis.

In Figure 1.10 we introduce an hours constraint fixed at $J^*$ into the basic labour supply model. It can be seen from the diagram that individual A is unaffected by the adjustment. He is indifferent between a contract fixing his hours at $J^*$ and one giving a free choice of hours. Individual B is worse off with the constraint. She is forced to a lower indifference curve, from $I_1^B$ to $I_2^B$. She would prefer to work

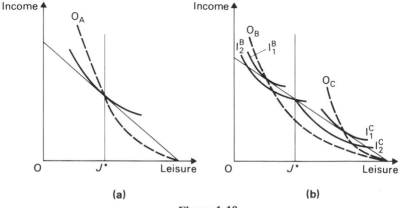

**Figure 1.10**

more hours and thus we refer to her hereon as an income preferer within the market context specified. Individual C is also clearly worse off with the hours constraint. He is forced to the lower indifference curve $I_2^C$ and would prefer to work fewer hours. We refer to him hereon as a leisure preferer under the going market conditions and his tastes for goods and leisure.

Consider the case of the income preferer in more detail and let us now suppose that overtime is available at a premium rate. We thus have a budget line XYZ′ as shown in Figure 1.11(a). Individual B is then in fact better off in two senses. First, she can work more hours and, second, she actually gets paid at a premium for doing so. She would be prepared to work more hours at the standard rate. How

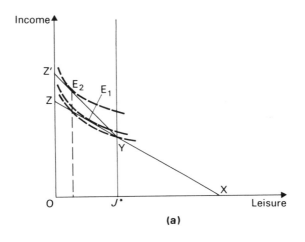

(a)

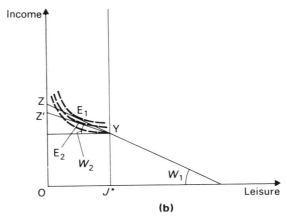

(b)

Figure 1.11

much better off she is will depend of course upon how much overtime is available. Given sufficient overtime and a large enough premium, B could be better off in the constrained case than in the unconstrained case. In practice, however, overtime is limited, so we can hypothesise the following.

First, income preferers will shop around for jobs that offer the highest overtime possibilities. Since different jobs, industries and firms do have different commitments to overtime (according to their technology *inter alia*), most workers should be able to mitigate the effects of hours constraints upon their income/leisure choice.

Second, income preferers who cannot obtain sufficient overtime in their principal task will consider taking on second jobs. Their income preference could be so strong that certain individuals take on second jobs at wages a good deal below those paid in their primary jobs, irrespective of any possibilities for tax and insurance evasion. This case is illustrated in Figure 1.11(b). Although the wage rate $W_2$ is lower than the wage $W_1$ of the principal employment, the worker can reach a higher indifference curve at $E_2$ than the one she is constrained to at Y. Such double jobbing or moonlighting, as it is called, will be more common amongst low income groups. If $J^*$ is common to all jobs, the incidence of income preference will depend upon the location of the optimum solution within each individual's indifference map, and this is determined not simply by tastes but also by the wage rate the individual faces. Lower income groups will normally prefer both a high $J^*$ and to be able to work overtime. Since there are, however, significant adjustment costs in holding two jobs the incidence of double jobbing will vary with such costs. Firemen, postmen and university lecturers are examples of workers whose principal employment makes double jobbing possible. Double jobbing of course provides an important source of cheap labour for the economy, which may benefit employers, but not perhaps alternative labour.

Third, union attempts to reduce normal hours below $J^*$ will be resisted by income preferers, especially by those who cannot get as much overtime as they would like. Since all workers benefit from an increase in basic wages, in general unions will be more active in pushing wages up than in pulling hours down. Income preferers will also not surprisingly be very active against union policies to reduce overtime work, even in order to increase employment.

Leisure preferers have two possible courses of action open to them. Some of them, as in Figure 1.12(a), enter the labour force at $J^*$ hours; others, as in Figure 1.12(b), choose to remain outside the labour force, despite an unconstrained preference to work a number of hours. Clearly, the outcome for any single worker depends upon the wage rate, the hours constraint and the slope of his offer curve.

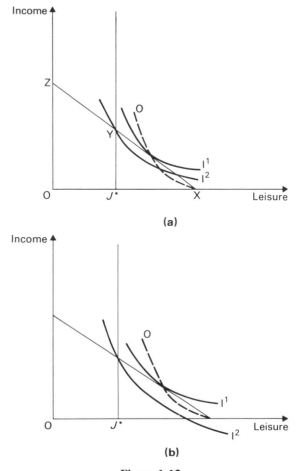

**Figure 1.12**

Either way, the worker is worse off as a result of the constraint. Any opportunity for part-time work, and indeed shift work if this allows more flexibility and therefore more choice over hours, will increase the individual's utility. In practice, such opportunities are limited. We can, however, predict, first, that leisure preferers are likely to gravitate towards areas where part-time or shift work is possible, where longer holidays are the norm, or seasonal factors apply. Increasing the supply and variety of such employment could add significant numbers of workers to the labour force as well as making the individuals concerned better off. The greater the opportunities the less restrictive the hours constraint becomes.

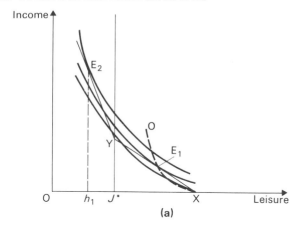

(a)

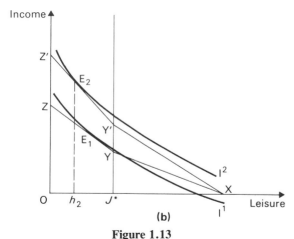

(b)

**Figure 1.13**

Second, it is very likely that leisure preferers will exact some of their preference for leisure by adopting appropriate working practices, such as systematic absenteeism. They might opt for jobs that have the greatest on-the-job leisure characteristics. They could regularly change their jobs, introducing precalculated periods of leisure in between. Leisure preferers will not surprisingly be a pressure group for shorter, more flexible hours within union deliberations.

Third, it is theoretically possible that the existence of overtime premiums makes leisure preferers better off in the constrained position than they otherwise would be. For example in Figure 1.13(a) the worker, given the constraint $J^*$ and no overtime, chooses to stay inactive. The overtime premium, however, induces him into the market. He works $J^*h_1$ overtime hours and is on a higher indifference curve at $E_2$ than at either $E_1$ or $Y$. Interestingly therefore the analysis predicts that some people might choose either very long hours or zero hours according to their access to overtime. Also we can see, as in Figure 1.13(b), that a decrease in taxation or a rise in the gross wage over some range will not induce the participation of certain individuals, but at some point a further change could lead immediately to a rise in hours to $J^*h_2$. The converse of course will be the case if taxes rise or wages fall.

## 1.3 The supply of labour and the allocation of time

The strict dichotomy between consumption and leisure in the utility function (1.1) of the basic model seems inappropriate, so consider the following model. Individuals derive utility from consuming activities $(Z_i)$. So

$$U = U(Z_i), \quad i = 1, \ldots, n \quad (1.5)$$

Each unit of activity involves quantities of various goods, $x_j$, and of time, $T$. The price of a unit of any activity, $P_i$, thus varies with the price of the goods involved, $p_j$, and the price of time, which here we identify with the wage foregone, $W$. The price of an activity also varies with quantities of the inputs – goods and time – involved. There are $k$ goods in the market. Let us denote the quantity of the $j$th good per unit of activity $i$, i.e. $x_{ji}/Z_i$, by $b_{ji}$ and the quantity of time per unit of activity $i$, i.e. $T_i/Z_i$, by $t_i$. Some activities are goods-intensive with a high goods content per unit of the activity and thus high $b_{ji}$ values at current levels of $p_j$ and $W$. Others are time-intensive, having a high time content per unit of the activity, and thus a high value for $t_i$. So

$$P_i = \sum_{j=1}^{k} b_{ji} p_j + t_i W \quad (1.6)$$

Each individual has a maximum time available of $T$, of which he distributes some amount $T_c$ across the available activities:

$$T_c = \sum_{i=1}^{n} t_i Z_i \quad (1.7)$$

Each individual has a resource constraint in the form of a maximum potential income level from working all available hours $T$. This income is partly expended by reducing work time to consume activities. Expenditures on goods cannot exceed the income derivable from the time remaining for work. Thus we can write the *resource constraint* as

$$\sum_{i=1}^{n} Z_i \sum_{j=1}^{k} b_{ji}p_j = TW - W \sum_{i=1}^{n} t_i Z_i \qquad (1.8)$$

Thus if there were two goods M and N and two activities $A$ and $B$, the budget constraint would be

$$A(p_M b_{MA} + p_N b_{NA}) + B(p_M b_{MB} + p_N b_{NB}) = TW - Wt_A A - Wt_B B$$

Following normal maximising procedures we derive the result that an activity will be consumed until its marginal utility, $U_i$, is equal to its price. So

$$U_i = \sum_{j=1}^{k} b_{ji}p_j + t_i W \qquad (1.9)$$

Some activities will be of the kind conventionally thought of as 'leisure' activities, e.g. playing squash. But though $t_i$ may generally be high, such activities will have varying time intensities and could indeed have lower time intensities than certain 'consumption' activities, e.g. having a five star meal.

We can derive the following predictions for labour supply from the above model by analysing the effects of changes in each of the independent variables in equation (1.10). First, consider the derivation of the labour supply curve. If the wage rate rises, *ceteris paribus*, the price of each activity will rise (eqn 1.7). Those activities that are time-intensive (have a high $t$ value) will, however, rise in price relative to other activities. Individuals will, consequently, switch their consumption towards less time-intensive activities. This *consumption substitution effect* increases time at work. It must of course be set against the income effect arising from the shift in the resource constraint outwards with the wage increase (eqn 1.9), which, if we assume that all activities are normal, increases consumption and reduces the time available for work. The novelty of the present approach, however, lies in the prediction that the increase in wages will induce individuals to use more goods and less time in each and every activity. This constitutes a second substitution effect, which we call the *input substitution effect*, working again towards an increase in labour supply. All activities, including 'leisure' activities, will become less time intensive, to a degree which depends upon the level of input substitutability, i.e. upon the production technology of activities.

Wage increases through time, therefore, might be expected, *ceteris paribus*, to induce a substitution, for example, of entertainments such as the theatre for gardening as individuals move closer to city centres to reduce travel-to-work times. They will also substitute goods for time in their choice of mode of travel. Of course the final effect on labour supply remains unknown *a priori*.

Second, following on from above, high wage groups face higher prices for all activities than low wage groups. Prices will, however, be relatively higher for time-intensive activities inducing a consumption substitution effect. There will also be substitution of goods for time in each activity. This will often involve goods of a higher quality (i.e. with more desirable characteristics per unit) than those consumed by low income groups because the higher price of time justifies the expense of these goods if they release sufficient time to alternative uses. Both effects raise the labour supply of high wage groups above that of low wage groups. On the other hand the income effect leads to higher consumption of all activities and thus a lower labour supply. High wage groups might be expected *ceteris paribus* to have fewer children, spend more on them and their rearing, and purchase higher quality but less time-consuming family activities.

Third, if the prices of all goods, $p_j$, fall in the same proportion, the effect will be the same as if wages had increased: in particular an input substitution of goods for time in activities and a consumption substitution towards goods-intensive activities. Thus a country experiencing steady increases in industrial productivity and falling prices would expect an increase in labour supply if the substitution effects are dominant.

Fourth, if the prices of only those goods used in time-intensive activities fall, *ceteris paribus*, the prices of those activities will fall relative to others. The result will be to induce both income and substitution effects. We shall continue to assume here that all activities are normal so that the income effect leads to a fall in labour supply. The input substitution of goods for time in time-intensive activities has the opposite effect. This further increases the fall in the relative prices of time-intensive activities brought about by the fall in the prices of the goods involved. There will follow a consumption substitution towards time-intensive activities and a fall in labour supply. Income and consumption substitution effects here complement each other against the input substitution effect. Though the final effect is indeterminate *a priori*, the factors determining the labour supply response are clear enough: the marginal rate of substitution between activities in consumption, the marginal rate of substitution between the inputs goods and time in the production of activities, and the income elasticities of the activities. The analysis therefore predicts that following significant relative price reductions in sporting facilities and equipment, *ceteris paribus*, there would be an increase in sporting activities, a growth in relatively expensive but low time content sports, and possibly a fall in labour supply. We have assumed that all activities are normal so that the income effects upon labour supply are negative. In fact the strength of the income effects will vary considerably across activities. The consumption of *activities* with negative income elasticities (not so unlikely as *goods* with negative income elasticities) will fall with an increase in income. If those activities were time-intensive, labour supply would rise. The outcome for labour supply of the income effect thus depends upon the distribution of income elasticities across activities, the size of those elasticities, and the time intensities of those activities, as well as upon the size of the real income change.

Fifth, advances in the technology of producing certain activities, which reduce their time intensities, will also induce labour supply responses. *Ceteris paribus*, the fall in $t$ reduces the relative price of the activities concerned. This induces a consumption substitution effect as usual, but no input substitution effect since the relative prices of inputs are unchanged. If the activities involved are goods-intensive, the consumption substitution effect leads to increased labour supply. There is no money income effect of the conventional kind here. There is, however, a relaxation of the resource constraint (1.4). The technological change releases time which the individual allocates between market work and the consumption of activities. Clearly the final increase in labour supply must be sufficient to cover the increased demand for goods. More domestic activities, more gadgetry and greater labour supply *simultaneously* are a feasible outcome of developments in the do-it-yourself industry.

Finally, and following on from the last point, if certain groups of people are more efficient than others of the same income, in the sense that they produce the same quantities of all activities with lower time and goods inputs (lower $b$ and $t$ values) then they will face lower prices for all activities. If $b$ and $t$ are lower to the same degree, the relative prices of different activities to each group remain the same; there will be no consumption substitution effect. There will be no input substitution effect since the relative prices of inputs are unchanged. There will be a relaxation of the resource constraint releasing both money income and time. If most activities consumed have high positive income elasticities and are significantly time intensive then even with identical tastes it follows that the labour supply of the efficient groups could be less than of other groups. We might anticipate, *ceteris paribus*, that highly educated people consume a lower quantity of food, though of both a high quality and a high time content, but buy more books and records and in the end supply less labour than less educated people of *identical income and tastes*.

The model outlined above is distinctive in three respects. First, and theoretically most interesting, each individual in the model is assumed to be both a producer and consumer. Before applying his consumer preferences across activities subject to his resource constraint, he first constructs the range of activities over which he will choose. In this he attempts, like producers, to combine the inputs, here goods and time, in ways which minimise costs, expenditures plus foregone earnings, for given outputs of the different activities. The individual's production frontier depends upon both his own efficiency and the technology of producing activities. This important insight leads directly to the identification of input substitution effects for consumers alongside the conventional consumption substitution and income effects. Secondly, the model avoids the sharp, untenable distinction between goods and leisure of the basic model. Time and goods are substitutes in the production and consumption of activities. Since all activities involve different amounts of goods and time, even switching expenditures between different consumption or leisure activities generates changes in labour supply; indeed the distinction between consumption and leisure activities loses any analytical value. Finally, though some of the predictions on labour supply set out here are derivable from the basic model, the present approach extends the number of predictions before us. Further predictions will emerge when the analysis is applied in the next chapter to household decision making.

Further Reading: see page 47–8

# 2
# The theory of household labour supply

In this chapter we reconstruct the basic model of labour supply on the assumption that the decision-making unit is the household. This allows us to analyse interdependence between the labour supplies of different workers, and introduce secondary workers and domestic activities. It also provides an appropriate platform upon which to develop life-cycle models of labour supply decision making.

## 2.1 Household labour supply

In practice labour supply decisions are often taken not by individuals, as the basic model assumes, but by households. This suggests a relationship between the labour supply decisions of members of the same household which the basic model cannot accommodate. We consider two models in this section. The first contains restrictive assumptions on the nature of the household's utility function and the budget constraint but makes it possible to illustrate interdependence diagrammatically. The second is the general case.

Imagine a representative household made up of two individuals of working age, the husband and the wife, though the model can be generalised to include additional household wage earners. Let us propose, first, that the household utility function has the form

$$U = U(G, L_H + L_W) \qquad (2.1)$$

where $L_H$ is the husband's leisure and $L_W$ the wife's. For ease of exposition, in this section we maintain the dichotomy between goods and leisure in the utility function, but this will be revised in Section 2.2. The level of household utility is assumed in equation (2.1) to be independent of the distribution of goods and leisure between its members. Second, let us assume that the husband's market wage rate, $W_H$, exceeds that of the wife, $W_W$, so that the wife is the secondary worker. The household's income constraint is

$$P_G G = W_H H_H + W_W H_W + B \qquad (2.2)$$

where $H_H$ and $H_W$ are the hours supplied to the market place by the husband and wife respectively, and $B$ is non-labour income. Third, let us specify the household's time constraint, given both members have $T$ available time units, as

$$2T = L_H + L_W + H_H + H_W \qquad (2.3)$$

Fourth, in order to focus, initially at least, upon the participation decision, let us assume that the jobs available are all offered at fixed hours $H^*$ so that $H_H$ and $H_W$ can only equal zero or $H^*$. The model can then be set up diagrammatically as in Figure 2.1, where $XJ = JK = H^*$.

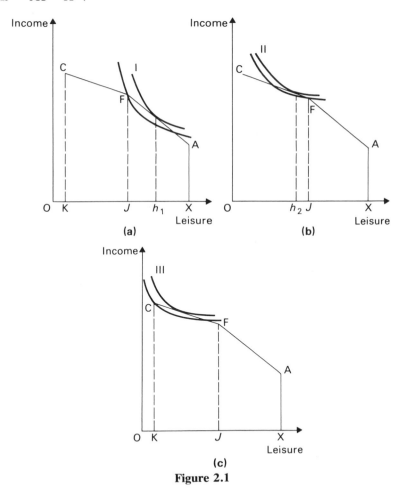

**Figure 2.1**

The household budget constraint AC is non-linear. XA (OX = $2T$) represents the value of the non-labour income. Because of the assumptions of the model, the first member of the household to participate is the husband, so that the slope of AF measures the wage rate $W_H$. Only after $H^*$ of his available hours, $T$, have been expended will the wife participate. So the slope of FC measures the wage rate $W_W$. Given the hours constraint the choice is between the three points A, F and C. If the indifference map for the household is as in Figure 2.1(a), then the optimum unconstrained solution, i.e. with no hours constraint, would involve the husband's participation, but not the wife's, the former supplying $Xh_1$ hours. With the hours constraint the household chooses F, the husband participates at $H^*$ hours

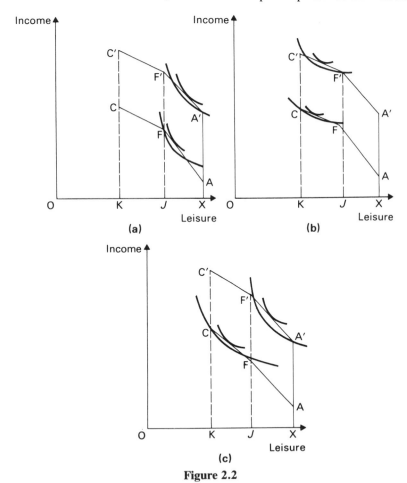

**Figure 2.2**

but the wife does not. If the indifference map is II, as in Figure 2.1(b), the unconstrained solution for the wife, given that the husband is constrained to $H^*$, involves the participation of both household members, the husband supplying $H^*$ hours, the wife $Jh_2$ hours. When both parties are constrained however, the optimum solution will again be at point F with the wife inactive. With indifference map III in Figure 2.1(c) the constrained optimum solution would be at C, where both members of the household supply $H^*$ hours.

The following predictions follow from the above analysis. First, if household non-labour income, $B$, rises, the whole budget constraint AC shifts upwards as in Figure 2.2. This will move the unconstrained equilibrium down the budget constraint if leisure is a normal good. The final location of the optimum solution will depend upon the nature of the household's indifference map. In principle the constrained optimum solution could therefore shift from F to A' or from C to F' or even from C to A', as in Figure 2.2(a), (b) and (c) respectively. We can define this as an increase in the *probability* that the secondary or both workers become inactive.

Second, if the husband's wage rises, the budget line shifts to AF'C' in Figure 2.3. If previously the household's unconstrained optimum involved the supply of $Xh_1$ hours by the husband, the effect of the wage increase, if the substitution effect dominates, is to increase his hours. Therefore $h_1$ in Figure 2.3(a) moves towards J, and this means that the constrained solution is more likely to be F' and less likely to be A. If the household's unconstrained optimum, as in Figure 2.3(b), involved the supply of $Jh_2$ hours by the wife, the husband's wage increase pushes $h_2$ towards J. The constrained solution is more likely

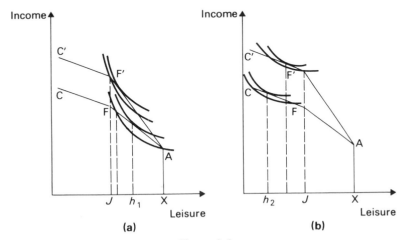

(a)                    (b)

**Figure 2.3**

therefore to be F' and less likely to be C'. The general result of an increase in the husband's wage is an increase in the probability of the husband's participation and a reduction in the probability of the wife's participation. The exact outcome depends upon the shape of the indifference map and the extent of the wage change.

Third, an increase in the wife's wage shifts the budget line to AFC' in Figure 2.4. If, as in Figure 2.4(a), the household's unconstrained optimum involves a supply of $Xh_1$ hours by the husband and its constrained optimum is at A or F, the wage change has no effect upon the constrained outcome. In Figure 2.4(b) the household optimum, with the husband constrained but not the wife, involves a supply of $Jh_2$ hours by the wife. If both are constrained the optimum is F. The effect of the wage increase is to shift $h_2$ towards K and to increase the probability that C' will be the outcome in the constrained case. In other words, the wife's wage increase leaves the probability of the husband's participation unchanged but increases the probability of the wife's participation.

Fourth, if the husband is the secondary worker, or becomes the secondary worker because of a significant increase in the wife's wage rate, any wage increase paid to the wife reduces the likelihood of the husband's participation, whilst it increases that of the wife.

Since household utility functions and earnings opportunities differ, households' optimal allocations of time will be distributed along budget lines similar to AFC. What we have referred to as changes in the probability of participation will mean, in reality, that any given change in non-labour income or wages will cause a change between inactivity and activity for some household members and no change

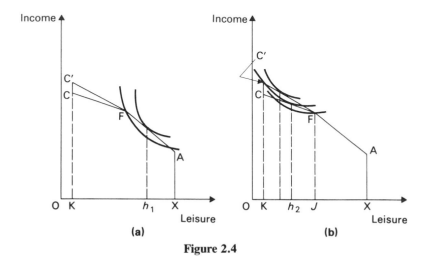

**Figure 2.4**

for others. The aggregate effect, however, is that, for example, an increase in $W_H$ will increase the married men's aggregate *participation rate* and reduce that of married women, whilst a rise in $W_W$ will increase the participation rate of married women, and possibly lower that of married men. The participation rate for any group within the population is the proportion of that group which is economically active.

The interdependence between household members' labour supply decisions is evident from the above model. Though the broad conclusions hold up in less restrictive circumstances, the model is limiting in at least two respects. Whilst it assists diagrammatic exposition of interdependence between participation decisions within the household, the assumption of fixed hours precludes a detailed analysis of the interdependence between the household members' hours decisions, and between hours and participation decisions. Furthermore, the assumption that the household's utility is independent of the distribution of leisure between the husband and wife is patently unrealistic. When deciding how to reallocate time in response to wage changes the current leisure consumption of individual members will not be a matter of indifference. No household would contemplate the absolute exhaustion of the husband's leisure time, as the model implies, before the wife enters the labour market. The marginal utility which the household derives from the consumption of leisure by each member ($U_{LH}$ and $U_{LW}$) will decline, i.e. $\partial^2 U / \partial L_H^2$, $\partial^2 U / \partial L_W^2 < 0$. The utility the household derives from its total consumption of leisure will thus vary with how that leisure is distributed across members of the household. In equilibrium we would expect that the relative marginal utilities of leisure between household members will reflect relative foregone earnings, i.e. $U_{LH} / U_{LW} = W_H / W_W$. Therefore every change in relative wages must simultaneously alter the labour supply outcome for all members.

Consider now the general model. The utility function is

$$U = U(G, L_H, L_W), \qquad \frac{\partial^2 U}{\partial L_H^2} < 0, \qquad \frac{\partial^2 U}{\partial L_W^2} < 0 \qquad (2.4)$$

and the hours constraints are $H_W \geq H_W^*$; $H_H \geq H_H^*$. Solving for optimal hours, $H_H^e$ and $H_W^e$, it can be shown that the solution will produce hours equations, imposing linearity, of the form

$$H_H = H_H^e = a_1 + b_1 W_H + c_1 W_W + d_1 B \quad \text{for} \quad H_H^e \geq H_H^* \, (2.5)$$

$$H_W = H_W^e = a_2 + b_2 W_W + c_2 W_H + d_2 B \quad \text{for} \quad H_W^e \geq H_W^* \, (2.6)$$

When $H_W^c < H_W^*$ then $H_W = 0$ or $H_W^*$. When $H_H^c < H_H^*$ then $H_H = 0$ or $H_H^*$. Clearly then we could derive two relationships for the participation decision by the husband and the wife, $P_H$ and $P_W$. The higher $H^c$, *ceteris paribus*, the more likely is participation. Therefore

$$P_H = a_3 + b_3 W_H + c_3 W_W + d_3 B \qquad (2.7)$$

$$P_W = a_4 + b_4 W_W + c_4 W_H + d_4 B \qquad (2.8)$$

It is clear that the hours and participation decisions of the husband and wife are determined simultaneously inside the household labour supply decision. The independent variables acting upon the household decision enter each of the equations (2.5)–(2.8). Any change in one or more of these variables will affect all four outcomes simultaneously. Household members' supply decisions are interdependent in that the parameters of (2.5)–(2.8) are all determined by the same things: the hours constraints and the marginal utilities of $L_H$, $L_W$ and $G$ in the household's utility function.

The following arguments can be put forward relating to these equations. First, assuming leisure is a normal good, an increase in the household's non-labour income, *ceteris paribus*, always has a pure income effect, and reduces labour supply. The coefficients $d_i$ in each equation above will therefore be negative. Second, an increase in each household member's *own* wage, *ceteris paribus*, induces both income and substitution effects on his/her own labour supply. As always the latter will have a positive effect, but, since the income effects involved are negative, each of the parameters $b_i$ in the four equations is of unknown sign *a priori*. Third, an increase in the *other* member's wage similarly produces both income and substitution effects for each member's labour supply. The so-called cross-substitution effects can be of either sign, but a common restriction imposed upon the utility function is that these effects should be equal, so that an income-compensated change in the husband's wage always has the same effect on the wife's labour supply as an income-compensated equal change in the wife's wage has upon the husband's labour supply. The income effects will be negative, but the sign of each of the parameters $c_i$ above will again be unknown *a priori*.

## 2.2   Household labour supply, secondary workers and domestic activities

The labour supply decision of married women is of particular interest to labour economists, for any future growth in total labour supply to the market place is likely to come primarily from increased participation and hours of married women. It is clear from the previous sections that the labour supply decision of married women must be analysed within the context of the household's decision-making process in which married women are generally secondary workers. Their earnings potential and leisure consumption are also treated differently to that of the husband in household decision making and this has important implications for wage elasticities and the parameter values of equations (2.5)–(2.8).

In so far as the changing labour supply of married women is a response to economic forces, two possible broad relationships suggest themselves. The discouraged worker hypothesis argues that a fall in economic activity will reduce the labour force participation and hours of married women. The added worker hypothesis argues that a fall in economic activity will lead to higher participation rates and hours.

In fact, as will be evident from a review of the household model of labour supply, these hypotheses are not inconsistent. They represent two opposing forces working simultaneously upon the household labour supply decision. The nature of that decision has been formalised in equations (2.5)–(2.8) of Section 2.1 above. Let us, however, concentrate upon the participation decision, as represented by

$$P_W = a_4 + b_4 W_W + c_4 W_H + d_4 B \qquad (2.8)$$

As we have previously noted, the signs on the coefficients $b_4$ and $c_4$ are, *a priori*, indeterminate. Conventionally, however, it is assumed that the own wage substitution effect outweighs the related income effect so that the coefficient $b_4$ is positive. The income effect on the wife's labour supply arising from a change in the husband's wage is conventionally assumed to be negative since leisure is treated as a normal good. Furthermore, if the cross-substitution effect is negative, i.e. the husband's and wife's time are substitutes, the coefficient $c_4$ would clearly be negative.

If both the husband's and the wife's earnings potentials fall during a business contraction, the effect on the wife's participation depends upon the relative size of the two wage changes and the relative size of the coefficients $b_4$ and $c_4$. If the coefficient $b_4$ exceeds the coefficient $c_4$, given identical reductions in male and female earnings during the contraction, the discouraged worker effect will be dominant. The two hypotheses would therefore appear to be complementary, describing different forces acting *simultaneously* upon the wife's labour supply decision through four income and substitution effects, the outcome of which can only be determined empirically. Empirical work must first verify that $b_4$ is indeed positive and $c_4$ negative to substantiate the existence of the two opposing effects. The relative size of the two coefficients can then be assessed.

This analysis uses the household model as developed in Section 2.1. But that model was directed towards a world in which changes in the wife's and husband's incomes were permanent. However, labour supply responses may require a modified analysis if wage changes are regarded as transitory rather than permanent, as is likely with cyclical variations in economic activity. Let us continue with the participation decision for married women but respecify equation (2.8) as

$$P_W = a + bW_W^P + cW_H^P + dW_W^T + eW_H^T + fB^P + gB^T \qquad (2.9)$$

where the superscripts indicate whether the variable captures permanent (P) or transitory (T) changes. The signs on the coefficients $b, c, d$ and $e$ on the wage variables are again indeterminate, *a priori*, being made up of both income and substitution effects. But if now we assume that over short-term movements in business activity permanent changes in wages and income are zero, our attention is directed towards the coefficients $d$, $e$ and $g$. Let us further suggest that over short-term movements in economic activity transitory changes in income are recognised by households as likely to cancel out. What is more the household anticipates all cyclical variations in income, and will thus take them into account in making its labour supply decisions. Labour supply responds to the underlying long-term movements of income potential not current income. This implies that the income effects of transitory wage movements will be negligible. In equation (2.10) we are therefore left with short-term variations in participation arising from the compensated own substitution and cross-substitution effects $s_W$ and $s_H$. The former is known *a priori* to be positive; the latter seems likely to be negative.

$$P_W = a + s_W W_W + s_H W_H, \qquad s_W > 0, s_H < 0 \qquad (2.10)$$

In this case whether the added or discouraged worker effect is dominant therefore depends on whether $s_W$ is greater or smaller than $s_H$. It seems plausible to anticipate, furthermore, that both substitution effects of transitory wage changes will be less than those of permanent wage changes simply because of the costs to the household of rearranging labour supply for relatively short periods so that husband's and wife's leisure can be switched. However, though we have reduced the number of indeterminacies, the nature of the final relationship between short-term variations in participation and economic activity remains an empirical issue.

Further insights into the determinants of labour supply of married women are possible if we reintroduce the analysis of the allocation of time from Section 1.3, but with the household as the decision-making unit. Such an approach allows us to consider the impact of domestic activities. These, like any other activity, are 'produced' by the household, subject to the available technology, by combining goods and the time of household members. There are therefore, following our earlier analysis, production functions for each domestic activity with the conventional properties of diminishing rates of substitution between inputs. The household produces a hypothetical set of alternative combinations of activities by combining inputs as efficiently as possible. In doing so the household, like the individual, takes into account the following: the production technology, particularly the goods and time intensities of activities and the substitutability between goods and time; the price of goods; the cost of time; and the amount of time available. In the case of the household, however, the final form of the efficient activity set will also depend upon the relative productivities of different household members in producing activities, which in turn depend upon biological and social factors, and the relative costs of those members' time. Once the household has 'produced' the efficient set, it then chooses between the various combinations of activities according to its utility function.

Our model therefore has the household utility function

$$U = U(Z_i), \qquad i = 1, \ldots, n \qquad (2.11)$$

where $U$ is household utility and $Z_i$ are activities. The price of any activity, $P_i$, varies with the price of goods, $p_j$, and the price of time, which is $W^H$ if the time is the husband's and $W^W$ if it is the wife's. The price per unit of activity also varies with the quantities of inputs involved; goods $x_j$, wife's time $T^W$ and husband's time $T^H$. As in Section 1.3, we use $b_{ji}$ to indicate the goods intensity of each activity $(= x_{ji}/Z_i)$ at current prices and wages. The time intensity of each activity is again measured as $t_i(= T_i/Z_i)$, but we now distinguish activities which are wife's time intensive, with a high $t_i^W$ $(= T_i^W/Z_i)$, from activities which are husband's time intensive, with a high $t_i^H(= T_i^H/Z_i)$. We thus have

$$P_i = \sum_{j=1}^{j=k} b_{ji} p_j + (t_i^H W^H + t_i^W W^W) \qquad (2.12)$$

for each activity $i$. The household has a maximum time available of $2T$, $T_c$ of which it distributes across activities consumed, so

$$T_c = \sum_{i=1}^{i=n} (t_i^H + t_i^W) Z_i \qquad (2.13)$$

Each household has a resource constraint in the form of a maximum potential income level from working all $2T$ hours. This is partly expended by using time in the consumption of activities. Income from using the remaining time for market work must cover the expenditures on goods associated with that consumption. Thus

$$\sum_{i=1}^{i=n} Z_i \sum_{j=1}^{j=k} b_{ji}p_j = T^H W^H + T^W W^W$$

$$- \left( W^H \sum_{i=1}^{i=n} t_i^H Z_i + W^W \sum_{i=1}^{i=n} t_i^W Z_i \right) \qquad (2.14)$$

Let us define the activities $1-d$ as domestic activities and assume that they are, like leisure, though of varying time intensity, generally time intensive. They have high $t_i$ values.

If we were to assume that the wife were universally more efficient in producing domestic activities than the husband, and has a lower wage, the wife would clearly specialise in such activities and in the household's efficient activity set

$$\sum_{i=1}^{i=d} t_i^H Z_i$$

would be zero. Even if the husband is more efficient in some activities, the principle of comparative advantage might lead to the same·result. However, we shall assume that under these conditions normally both members produce domestic activities, each specialising in those where their productivity is greatest. It will be possible for both members to participate in each activity if each member's marginal productivity in producing any domestic activity falls with the amount of time devoted to it; and/or household members' time are complementary inputs; and/or the household's utility varies with the amounts of time each member devotes to domestic activities and to market work, perhaps first increasing but then after some point decreasing. On such assumptions we hereon define $t_i^W$ and $t_i^H$ both to be greater than zero for domestic activities, though in general $t_i^W$ will be much larger than $t_i^H$. In equation (2.14) $b_{ji}$, $t_i^H$ and $t_i^W$ represent the goods and time intensities of activities for the efficient set of $Z_i$ combinations across which the household chooses. *Ceteris paribus*, the more productive the wife is in producing domestic activities and the lower her market wage the larger will $t_i^W$ be, the more domestic activities the household will consume and the lower the wife's supply of labour.

The model of the household's allocation of time enables us to extend our predictions on the labour supply of married women in the following ways. First, consider the implications of a rise in the wife's wage $W_i^W$. *Ceteris paribus*, this will raise the relative cost of all the wife's time-intensive activities, i.e. all $Z_i$ with a high $t_i^W$ in (2.14). This will induce three substitution effects, all leading to an increase in the wife's labour supply. The first will be a consumption substitution effect as the household switches towards a decrease in the wife's time-intensive domestic, leisure and consumption activities and, on our assumptions, away from domestic and leisure activities as a whole. The result will be an increase in the wife's labour supply, the size of which will depend upon the household's preferences for domestic activities and their time intensities. The second substitution effect of the increase in $W^W$ will be an input substitution effect as the household attempts to replace the wife's time by goods in each activity, particularly in domestic activities. This will sometimes involve the introduction of more expensive, higher quality goods into domestic activities because of their time-saving properties. The degree to which such input substitutions are carried through, and therefore the increase in the wife's labour supply, will depend upon the degree to which goods and wife's time are substitutable in producing domestic activities in particular. The third substitution effect involves the replacement of the wife's time by the husband's time in all activities, but particularly in domestic activities because they are wife's time-intensive. The outcome of this substitution effect for the increase in the wife's labour supply depends upon the sensitivity of household utility to the increase in the time the wife devotes to market work and the husband to domestic work. These substitution effects will be offset as usual by the income effect. The increase in $W^W$ will mean that, consuming the same activities as previously, the household will have surplus income. It will thus increase its consumption of all activities but must reduce its time commited to market work to generate the time to go into producing these additional activities. The final impact of the increase in $W^W$ on the wife's labour supply is again indeterminate, *a priori*, but the above analysis strengthens the expectation of a positive relationship. Such an analysis is consistent with a rise in women's wages leading to the following: a shift in the production of domestic activities from making to shopping for the families clothes; a shift in household consumption towards eating out more frequently and fewer coffee mornings; the use of domestic paid help, childcare services and electric powered domestic aids; husbands taking a greater part in shopping; and an increased supply of labour from married women.

Second, a rise in the husband's wage $W^H$ can induce opposing substitution effects upon the wife's labour supply. There will be a consumption effect away from all the husband's time-intensive activities. To the extent that this involves a move away from household time-intensive activities such as leisure activities the wife's labour supply will rise. To the extent that it involves a shift towards the wife's time-intensive activities, such as domestic activities, the wife's labour supply will fall. The input substitution effect will involve the introduction of more goods and wife's time for husband's time in all activities, particularly in leisure activities. This will reduce the wife's labour supply. The income effect will also act to reduce her labour supply. On the whole therefore the present analysis supports the expectation of a negative cross-substitution term in labour supply equations like (2.8) and thus a negative parameter $c_4$. We have been assuming that the wife's and husband's time are substitutes in producing activities. In fact many leisure and domestic activities require joint participation. This will nullify the input substitution effect upon the wife's labour supply and at the same time strengthen the consumption substitution effect, increasing the wife's labour supply. Joint participation is one argument therefore for a positive cross-substitution term and uncompensated wage effect.

Third, a fall in the relative price of all goods used in producing domestic activities will also induce a series of substitution effects upon the wife's labour supply. The input substitution effect releases the wife's time in particular as goods are introduced into domestic activities. The consumption substitution effect works to reduce the demand for time-intensive domestic activities and increase that for goods-intensive domestic activities. Both effects lead therefore to an increase in the wife's labour supply. On the other hand there will be a consumption substitution effect towards domestic activities as a whole as their relative prices fall. Given their high values of $t_i^W$ this will constitute a factor leading to a reduction in the wife's labour supply, as does the income effect that arises out of the price reductions. The wife's labour supply is more likely to increase the greater the technological possibilities for substituting goods for time in domestic activities, the more favourably inclined the household is towards consuming more goods-intensive domestic activities, and the less favourably inclined it is towards consuming more domestic activities at the expense of other activities. If the price reductions are concentrated upon goods used primarily in producing domestic activities with high $t_i^H$ values, such expectations are so much stronger. We might therefore anticipate that following technological advances that reduce the prices of diverse forms of gadgetry used in domestic activities more gadgets are used; more domestic activities are consumed, but particularly those that use mechanical aids, and the labour supply of married women rises.

Fourth, a change in the technology of producing domestic activities which effectively lowers the time inputs required – $t_i$ and $t_i^W$ – will reduce the relative price of domestic activities. The consequent consumption effect will lead to a higher demand for domestic activities. The fall in $t_i$ will also generate a resource effect, in that consuming the same activities as previously leaves the household with unused time.

This will lead to an increased demand for all activities. Part of the available time will be devoted to producing the additional activities but some must be devoted to market work to generate the income necessary to finance the additional goods required. Some of the time will have to be devoted to cover the substitution towards domestic activities. The resource effect increases labour supply. Normally one would expect a fall in $t_i$ to increase the wife's labour supply. But it is possible that the household's tastes for domestic activities could be so strong that the consumption effect requires that all of the time released be devoted to additional domestic activities and, furthermore, some of the goods released by the move away from goods-intensive activities be forfeited for additional consumption time. The latter would constitute a fall in labour supply.

To the extent that more educated households have lower $t_i$ and $t_i^w$ values, normally one would anticipate a higher labour supply from the wives in more educated families, even for identical earnings potentials and tastes.

Finally, a shift in preferences towards domestic activities will, *ceteris paribus*, reduce the wife's labour supply since she now has to devote more time to producing activities and the necessity for income is reduced. The precise extent of the reduction in her labour supply will depend upon the goods and time intensities of the activities across which tastes change.

The household's preferences for domestic activities are likely to differ at different stages of the household life cycle. Let us for ease of exposition assume that the household derives utility from goods and domestic activities. Let us propose that the household divides the wife's time between market work for goods and the collective domestic activity D. In this case we can define the value the household sets upon the wife's time spent in producing domestic activities as the shadow wage of her market work. The shadow wage will presumably decline with the amount of the domestic activity undertaken and consumed in any period. In Figure 2.5 the line $SW_1$ defines the shadow wage. The opportunity cost of the domestic activity is the market wage, so domestic activities will only be undertaken if the shadow wage exceeds the market wage. Domestic activities will be undertaken until the shadow wage equals the market wage, until $N^1$ domestic activities are produced in Figure 2.5. Labour supply will be $(T - tN^1)$ where $t$ is the time intensity for the collective domestic activity. The faster the decline in the shadow wage the greater is the wife's labour supply.

The shadow wage will presumably be high when there are young children in the household, but will decline as the children grow up. Such a decline will shift the curve $SW$ inwards with time and thus increase the wife's labour supply, in Figure 2.5 by $t(N^1 - N^2)$. With

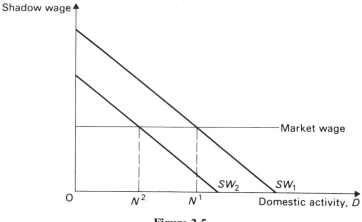

**Figure 2.5**

many different domestic activities there will be many curves like *SW*. The household will increase its production of each until each curve intersects the market wage line. The same is true if we inject non-domestic activities. At the margin the shadow wage of market work, defined in terms of any alternative activity, must equal the market wage rate. The general point holds, however, that at certain stages in the household's life cycle the *SW* curves for many domestic activities will shift systematically. Married women's labour supply will display similar systematic variation.

The last paragraph suggests that labour supply in period $t$ will differ from that in period $t + n$ if household consumption requirements differ between the two periods. But if the household knows in $t$ what its consumption requirements will be in $t + n$, the labour supply decisions for the two periods will be interdependent. Labour supply in $t$ will depend in part upon the household's consumption demand in $t + n$ because purchasing power can be accumulated in advance. It will then also be related to labour supply in $t + n$, because the latter will in part depend upon consumption requirements in $t + n$. Since this is true for every $t$ and $t + n$, there is a strong case for developing labour supply analysis on the basis of a life-cycle model of household decision making.

## 2.3   A life-cycle approach to labour supply

The basic model of individual labour supply is timeless. It therefore implicitly assumes that the individual faces the same wage offer and has the same preferences across goods and leisure throughout his lifetime. Once the optimal labour supply is determined it remains constant through time. Whilst the effects of changes in wages are analysed in the model these are once-for-all changes. In practice, however, an individual's earnings potential varies systematically over his lifetime and so too will preferences across goods and leisure. Furthermore, since it seems more realistic to consider household decisions about the allocation of time, we must recognise the existence of systematic variations over time in households' preferences across domestic and other activities. No household will calculate its current optimal labour supply without taking into account the future pattern of earnings potential and preferences. This leads us naturally therefore to formulate a life-cycle model of labour supply. A central feature of such a model is the interdependence of labour supply and consumption at each point in time and through time. Life-cycle labour supply decisions and life-cycle consumption decisions are clearly interrelated.

The labour supply model of either equation (2.1) or (2.4) gives labour supply relationships for the household. But of course the same utility-maximising procedure gives the demand for goods relationship:

$$D_G = f(P_G, W^H, W^W, B) \qquad (2.15)$$

relating the composite good, G, to its price, $P_G$. If we used single products and their respective prices, we could derive individual product demand curves. In any period consumption and labour supply decisions are thus simultaneously determined. Strictly speaking therefore, equations (2.5)–(2.8) should contain the prices of goods as independent variables.

Since the income received by supplying labour in any one period can be saved or anticipated by borrowing, consumption and labour supply decisions can be related *through time*. They will be related if earnings potential and/or consumption requirements change through time. Consider first variations in the earnings potential of a household consisting of husband and wife and dependent children. Suppose productivity changes with age as shown in Figure 2.6. Initially earnings rise with increasing experience but then decline with deterioration of skills. In this case, even if the household's utility function is the same in every period, with time preference current consumption will depend upon lifetime rather than current income as long as borrowing and lending are possible. The larger future income the greater the scope for bringing income forward at given interest rates. When the husband and wife are young the household consumes out of an average lifetime income which exceeds its current income. The marginal propensity to consume out of current income will therefore be high,

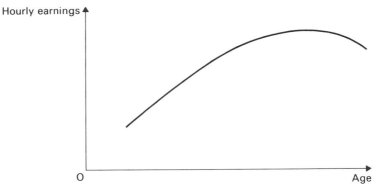

**Figure 2.6**

necessitating perhaps extensive borrowing. In their middle years, the household consumes out of a lifetime income which is less than its current income. The marginal propensity to consume will be relatively low and lending high. In later years the same household again consumes out of a lifetime income above its current income, drawing off past savings. *Ceteris paribus*, the lifetime consumption profile is thus flatter than the lifetime earnings profile if labour supply is exogenously determined.

Figure 2.6 implies that the cost of leisure is relatively high for any household in middle years, which creates a strong incentive to forego leisure during this period. The pattern of household lifetime labour supply, if it is determined by the household, will reflect the pattern of earnings potential, for this indicates the relative cost of leisure through time. If market goods are substitutes for leisure, then the household would substitute in middle years additional goods for the loss of leisure. There would then be a tendency for both labour supply and consumption to duplicate the pattern of Figure 2.6. However, given that households prefer present consumption to future consumption and that money markets exist, then those households whose rate of time preference is less than the interest rate have an incentive to delay consumption and increase their labour supply and earnings when their members are young. Other households whose rate of time preference exceeds the interest rate will have an incentive to borrow and consume more early on in the working life, and increase their labour supply later on. In aggregate therefore a life-cycle approach predicts that the pattern of consumption and of labour supply will be flatter than that of earnings potential through time. However, in any one period consumption and labour supply depend on lifetime earnings potential.

The above analysis assumes so far that the only systematic variation in the household's circumstances over the life-cycle is in productivity and therefore in market wages. But requirements vary too, as pointed out at the end of Section 2.2. As workers age the value they attach to leisure alters. Family responsibilities change: if children are produced they must be reared and supported. Household composition changes: the husband and wife may have to support ageing parents, children grow up and leave the household. The household's valuation of consumption activities therefore varies systematically through time, and this has an independent effect on the lifetime pattern of labour supply. The increased utility of leisure with age, for example, shifts labour supply earlier in the life cycle. Childcare responsibilities will also shift labour supply towards the early part of the working life cycle. In general, therefore, in any one period the household's consumption and labour supply will depend on the lifetime pattern of consumption requirements, as well as on the lifetime pattern of earnings potential.

The lifetime earnings profile drawn in Figure 2.6 is not in practice exogenously determined. By undertaking educational programmes the household can shift its income profile upwards. During the programme its labour supply will normally fall. This will reduce its income and thus its consumption possibilities out of current income. The higher the earnings potential at any point in time the greater the income and consumption foregone. Similarly the greater current household consumption requirements the greater the welfare loss if household members take up education. If any household member does take up education there will be an incentive for other members to compensate, again illustrating the interdependence of labour supply decisions of household members. It is clear that individual labour supply decisions through time will be taken simultaneously with education decisions, both depending, amongst other things, upon the following: the lifetime pattern of household consumption requirements; the shape and level of each household member's earnings profile; and the effect of education upon those profiles. Although we cannot deal with these particular interdependencies in this text, in the next chapter we consider the important question of educational decision making.

## Further Reading

CHAPTERS 1 AND 2: THE THEORY OF LABOUR SUPPLY

G. S. Becker, 'A theory of the allocation of time', *Economic Journal*, Vol. 75 (September 1965).

W. G. Bowen and T. A. Finegan, *The Economics of Labor Force Participation* (Princeton, N.J.: Princeton University Press, 1969).

C. V. Brown, *Taxation and the Incentive to Work* (Oxford: Oxford University Press, 1980).

G. R. Ghez and G. S. Becker, *The Allocation of Time and Goods over the Life Cycle* (New York: Columbia University Press, 1975).

J. Mincer, 'Labor force participation of married women; a study of labor supply', in *Aspects of Labor Economics* (Princeton, N.J.: Princeton University Press, 1962).

L. Moses, 'Income, leisure, and wage pressure', *Economic Journal*, Vol. 72 (June 1962).

# 3
# Human capital theory

This chapter considers decisions to take up and provide educational opportunities. In the basic model of the labour market education is treated like any other consumption good. Educational decisions are formulated in terms of the utility derived during the process of learning, the costs of provision, and prices. This approach, however, assumes that the benefits of education are exhausted immediately, neglects the significant impact of education upon labour rewards and produces an unsatisfactory model of occupational choice. In this chapter we trace the consequences for educational decision making, occupational choice and thereby the workings of the labour market of treating education as an investment good within the traditional utility/profit-maximising paradigm.

Since our analysis is a perfectly general one across the many forms of educational opportunity, we use the term education throughout to embrace all forms. However, since post-compulsory schooling, state training schemes and employer-provided on-the-job training are particularly important to the operation of the labour market, these opportunities are discussed individually in the final section.

## 3.1 The concept of human capital

According to conventional economic theory, if education is regarded as a consumption good, it follows from maximising procedures that the quantity and form of education undertaken will depend on educational programmes' endowments of desired characteristics compared to other goods, individuals' preferences across these characteristics, and the relative price of education. If, simultaneously, education is the principal mechanism whereby productive abilities, or skills, are acquired, and the principal delineator of occupations, it follows that each individual's choice of occupation and his rewards are merely the residual outcome of his consumption decisions on education. An increase in rewards to occupation $i$ therefore, following say an increase in the demand for its outputs, would increase the supply of labour to that market (leaving participation and hours aside) only to the extent that labour already in possession of the appropriate skills in other occupations chose to transfer. It would not affect the total stock of those skills since it leaves education decisions unaffected.

This makes changes in the supply of labour to each occupation depend upon exogenously determined changes in individual consumer preferences and in the characteristics of educational programmes. Clearly these are predictions that can only be evaluated empirically. However, through this and the following sections, we develop an alternative set of predictions based upon the assumption that each individual is aware of, and responds to, the fact that labour rewards vary systematically with skills so that his choice of education significantly affects his lifetime profile of rewards.

Let us begin by considering the nature of labour skills. The first obvious feature to note is that skills can take considerable time to acquire. Some educational programmes span years rather than months. Secondly, the pecuniary and non-pecuniary rewards of possessing skills often come through only over significant periods of time. Third, skills deteriorate with time because of failing memory, under-utilisation, or simply as the worker ages. Fourth, since skills embody the productive knowledge of the time the education is undertaken, they become obsolete with technical change. In principle, therefore, continuous re-education is required to offset both deterioration and obsolescence. What should by now be apparent from this discussion is that labour skills have essential characteristics in common with physical capital such as plant and machinery. It is for this reason that skills merit the title of human capital. It follows that, if education is the mechanism by which human capital is increased, education is, in part at least, an investment good. This extension of economic jargon can be justified if the application of traditional physical capital and investment theory to education decisions provides new, interesting predictions on the workings of labour markets which are supported by empirical evidence.

Of course labour skills are not entirely analogous to physical capital. The most obvious difference is that skills are inseparable from the human body. In the absence of slavery, there can therefore be no market place for skills comparable to those for physical capital. There are no conventional entrepreneurs specialising in producing, accumulating and selling skills. There are, however, markets for skills where the suppliers are individual workers who hire out their productive talents, under very specific conditions, and upon whom therefore the responsibilities of entrepreneurship fall. A second difference between human and physical capital is that, in certain circumstances, skills can be acquired, or at least extended, without any capital outlay. Practice and imitation are central to 'learning by doing' as a mechanism for enhancing productive abilities.

All decisions to undertake education involve, to different degrees, some element of consumption and some element of investment decision. In this chapter, however, we shall assume that the rational maximizing individual regards education as purely an investment good. This abstraction makes possible some simple model building from which a clear, interrelated set of predictions can be obtained. The extent to which this simplification is valid and useful must again emerge from the empirical content and robustness of the predictions.

## 3.2 The human capital model

Suppose an individual at the start of year A already possesses educational qualifications up to and including level $i$, and has to decide whether to continue for a further $S$ years of education to attain the next level $j$ associated with a given occupation N, or enter employment M now. The simple human capital model analyses this decision with the aid of the following assumptions. First, all individuals aim to maximise lifetime utility and, if utility derives solely from consumption and consumption depends on income, it follows that they aim to maximise lifetime income. Second, educational levels are uniquely related to earnings streams (because education is related to skills, skills to marginal productivity, and productivity to earnings). Therefore levels $i$ and $j$ are associated with future earnings profiles $Y^i$ and $Y^j$ as shown in Figure 3.1. Third, these earnings streams and the costs of education are known with certainty. Fourth, there are no restrictions on the supply of places on the programme leading to level $j$. Fifth, all

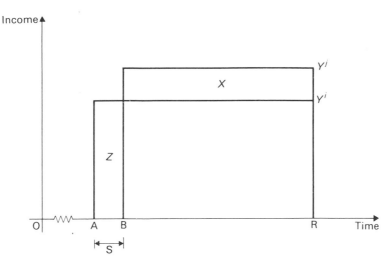

Figure 3.1

individuals have the necessary ability to undertake this programme. Sixth, there are no income constraints on individual choice.

In Figure 3.1 it is also assumed that age–earnings profiles are linear, which means that no further education is undertaken and that no learning-by-doing effects exist. We assume the individual starts work in occupation N at the beginning of year B, and stops working at the beginning of year R. These assumptions are made purely for simplification.

Our representative individual makes her decision on the basis of normal investment appraisal methods: she compares the benefits from undertaking further education with the costs, and if the benefits outweigh the costs she enrolls in the programme for level $j$. The benefits are of course increased earnings: area $X$ in Figure 3.1, which is the increase in earnings due to the increment in education, $(Y^j - Y^i)$, multiplied by the number of years, $n (= \text{RB})$, for which the increase is received. The costs of undertaking education are of two kinds: direct and indirect. Direct capital costs are tuition fees net of grants, $K$, here assumed to be paid in a lump sum at the beginning of the course. Direct running costs are expenditures (e.g. on books and materials) which would not otherwise be incurred, $C_t$, net of grants (here assumed to be constant over the $S$ years of the course). Indirect costs consist of earnings foregone during the $S$ years of the programme under consideration. Our individual could be earning $Y^i$, therefore her foregone earnings amount to $SY^i$ or area $Z$ in Figure 3.1.

Costs and, *a fortiori*, benefits clearly extend over a period of years. In order to compare costs and benefits satisfactorily it is essential to take account of their distribution through time because £1 of extra earnings in 10 years' time will not compensate for £1 of foregone earnings this year. In general people prefer consumption sooner rather than later, i.e. the value attached now to £1 decreases the further into the future the £1 is to be collected or spent. This is the phenomenon of time preference, which exists independent of changing money values and market opportunities for borrowing and lending. It arises because of declining marginal utility of income, because of risk aversion and possibly because of naive myopia. An individual's rate of time preference measures her marginal rate of substitution between consumption in two periods. Figure 3.2 shows an individual's indifference curves between consumption in periods $t$ and $t + 1$. The slope of the indifference curve at any point measures $-(1 + \delta)$, where $\delta$ is known as the rate of time preference. The value of $\delta$ at the point where an indifference curve cuts the 45° line, i.e. where the individual has equal amounts of consumption in periods $t$ and $t + 1$, is called the rate of time preference proper.

A valid comparison of the costs and benefits of education then

Consumption in
next period

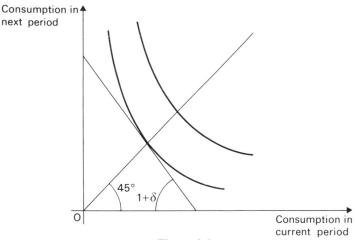

45°

1+δ

O

Consumption in
current period

**Figure 3.2**

must allow for time preference by *discounting* future costs and
benefits more heavily the further into the future they accrue. Let us
now consider the position of an individual faced with the choice represented in Figure 3.1. In year A ($t = 0$) she faces running costs
of $C_0$ and foregone earnings of $Y_0^i$. In the next year ($t = 1$) she
faces running costs of $C_1$ and foregone earnings of $Y_1^i$. Even if, as
assumed here, both running and indirect costs are the same in these
two years, the individual will regard the costs as less onerous in the
$(A + 1)$th year. Specifically, costs of $(C_1 + Y_1^i)$ next year are equivalent to costs of $(C_1 + Y_1^i)/(1 + \delta)$ this year. Similarly, costs of
$(C_2 + Y_2^i)$ in the $(A + 2)$nd year are less onerous again, being valued
as equivalent to $(C_2 + Y_2^i)/(1 + \delta)^2$ this year. The *present value* of the
costs incurred over the $S$ years ($S = 3$) of the educational programme
leading to level $j$ is given by:

present value of cost (PVC)

$$= K + C_0 + Y_0^i + \frac{C_1 + Y_1^i}{(1 + \delta)} + \frac{C_2 + Y_2^i}{(1 + \delta)^2} \qquad (3.1)$$

$$= K + \sum_{t=0}^{t=S-1} \frac{C_t}{(1 + \delta)^t} + \sum_{t=0}^{t=S-1} \frac{Y_t^i}{(1 + \delta)^t} \qquad (3.2)$$

The benefits from education begin in year B ($t = S$). In this year
the individual earns $(Y_S^j - Y_S^i)$ more than she would have earned
without the education. Because she has to wait until year B to receive
this sum, it is worth less to her than if she received it in year A.
Specifically, the present value at A of this sum received in year B is
equal to $(Y_S^j - Y_S^i)/(1 + \delta)^S$. Similarly, the present value of the whole

stream of earnings increments due to the educational investment is given by:

present value of benefits (PVB)

$$= \frac{Y^j_S - Y^i_S}{(1 + \delta)^S} + \frac{Y^j_{S+1} - Y^i_{S+1}}{(1 + \delta)^{S+1}} + \cdots + \frac{Y^j_{n+S-1} - Y^i_{n+S-1}}{(1 + \delta)^{n+S-1}} \quad (3.3)$$

$$= \sum_{t=S}^{t=S+n-1} \frac{Y^j_t - Y^i_t}{(1 + \delta)^t} \quad (3.4)$$

Now the individual can make her decision systematically, taking into account the time pattern of costs and benefits by comparing the present value of costs with the present value of benefits.

The investment up to level $j$ is worthwhile if the present value of benefits of the educational programme exceeds that of costs; that is if

$$\sum_{t=S}^{t=S+n-1} \frac{Y^j_t - Y^i_t}{(1 + \delta)^t} > K + \sum_{t=0}^{t=S-1} \frac{C_t}{(1 + \delta)^t} + \sum_{t=0}^{t=S-1} \frac{Y^i_t}{(1 + \delta)^t} \quad (3.5)$$

This expression can be simplified if we recognise that in a more general version of our model the indirect costs each year of the educational investment will be $Y^i_t - Y^j_t$. We have assumed in our model that $Y^j = 0$ during the programme. In the more general model the investment is worthwhile if

$$\sum_{t=S}^{t=S+n-1} \frac{Y^j_t - Y^i_t}{(1 + \delta)^t} > K + \sum_{t=0}^{t=S-1} \frac{C_t}{(1 + \delta)^t} + \sum_{t=0}^{t=S-1} \frac{Y^i_t - Y^j_t}{(1 + \delta)^t} \quad (3.6)$$

that is if

$$\sum_{t=0}^{t=S+n-1} \frac{Y^j_t - Y^i_t}{(1 + \delta)^t} - K - \sum_{t=0}^{t=S-1} \frac{C_t}{(1 + \delta)^t} > 0 \quad (3.7)$$

that is if the *net present value* (NPV) (= PVB–PVC), of the investment is positive.

An alternative method of appraising an educational investment is to calculate the *internal rate of return* (IRR) to the investment. This method uses the same discounting approach as the present value method, but instead of discounting by $\delta$ and seeing whether the resulting NPV is positive or negative, we solve equation (3.8) below to find the rate of discount which makes the NPV equal to zero:

$$\text{NPV} = \sum_{t=0}^{t=S+n-1} \frac{Y^j_t - Y^i_t}{(1 + \rho)^t} - K - \sum_{t=0}^{t=S-1} \frac{C_t}{(1 + \rho)^t} = 0 \quad (3.8)$$

The resulting discount rate $\rho$ is the internal rate of return on the educational investment leading to level $j$. If it exceeds the individual's rate of time preference, this investment is worthwhile for our individual. The internal rate of return is analogous to the marginal efficiency of capital for a non-human investment.

In the model above, where the human capital decision to be taken is the simplest possible, i.e. whether one single programme is worthwhile or not, the net present value and internal rate of return are equally satisfactory decision criteria. A programme whose internal rate of return exceeds the relevant rate of time preference will also have a positive NPV.

Let us now extend our model by introducing the following: first, the existence of many investors; second, the availability of alternative programmes for reaching educational level *j*; third, alternative education 'subjects' within each level and the existence of many different educational levels; and fourth, the existence of money markets.

First, the *net return*, calculated above either as an IRR or as a NPV, measures the *ex ante* return for one individual if no-one else undertakes the investment to reach educational level *j*. If other people also enroll on the programme, when they reach occupation N earnings in N would fall, and area *X* in Figure 3.1 would contract. The net return then overestimates the benefit that the individual derives from her education. Entry into occupation N may take many years in view of the long gestation period for setting up and undertaking educational programmes. The first new entrants will therefore lower wages slightly and subsequent entry will continue this process. The net return for each annual group of new students will thus decline and the *marginal net return* to each year's entrants will be lower than the *average net return* over all those currently investing in the programme. Depending upon current and past levels of educational costs this average net return could be higher or lower than that calculated for the existing members of occupation N. The marginal net return to any individual in year A therefore depends upon the number of people who also invest in year A, the number of people ahead of her in the education pipeline and the speed with which people enter after her. If individuals fail to take these considerations into account, overinvestment in education could result and also, if demand for skills varies over time, cobweb cycles in wages and labour deployment.

Second, suppose that there are several different educational programmes which all lead to level *j* and occupation N, each with its own peculiar structure of costs and benefits. Suppose also that our decision maker has alternative non-educational uses for her funds. In this case, since the educational investments are mutually exclusive, they must be ranked in some way. This could be done in order of NPV; she would then choose the programme with the highest NPV, assuming that this is positive, and compare this programme with all other non-educational programmes again using the NPV criterion. Alternatively, the ranking and selection of the education programmes could be made on the basis of the IRR criterion. Unfortunately the ranking of educational programmes and other projects may differ according to which criterion is used. NPV rankings vary with the rate of discount used, which makes sense; IRR rankings do not. The IRR ranking, on the other hand, is sensitive to the size of the initial outlay and to the distribution of benefits through time, and this is undesirable. For these and other reasons the NPV criterion is generally to be preferred. So far we have assumed that the decision maker has a limited amount of funds available for investment; the problem therefore is to find the best possible combination of the projects available, including the best educational programme, which exactly uses up her funds. In these circumstances the NPV criterion must be reformulated, because the use of NPV ranking would bias the decision towards projects with large outlays and returns. The available projects should be ranked according to their *NPV ratio*, NPVR, which is given by PVB/PVC. All projects in the final listing will therefore have an NPVR greater than one. The decision maker first undertakes the project with the highest NPVR, then that with the next highest and so on until her budget is exhausted.

Third, for our individual at the start of year A, level $j$ is merely one of the many levels she can reach from $i$. There will be an educational programme to take her from level $j$ to level $k$, one to take her from $k$ to $l$, and so on, each programme requiring satisfactory completion of the preceding programme. If she attains level $j$ she will then have to decide whether to go on to the next level, $k$, immediately or at some time in the future. For each individual, *ceteris paribus*, the net return earned on successive stages of education, which we call the *incremental net return*, is likely to decline so that the incremental return on the next possible programme is below the average return on all education undertaken to date. There are two reasons for this: each successive level of education involves higher indirect costs than the one before because each completed programme increases earning power and therefore foregone earnings, and also every extension of education reduces the number of years over which the benefits of education, i.e. the increased earnings, can be enjoyed. It follows from our analysis above that the incremental net return on any programme to our individual at year A depends upon the number of other investors in that programme.

In moving between levels $i$ and $j$ the individual will also be faced with a choice of 'subject' matter. There will be a wide range of subjects to choose from and an educational programme associated with each subject. The individual thus calculates the marginal net return for each subject to make a rational investment decision.

Each possible combination of subject-related educational programmes, each programme from a different educational level, constitutes an *educational path*. Such paths will differ in terms of educational content, length, costs and returns. Each will have a net return calculated at the start of year A. Each occupation will require specific educational paths, each defining both the subject matter at each educational level and the level to be reached. Each occupation therefore defines the number and the content of educational programmes the individual is required to complete. The individual will thus calculate marginal net returns to each of a restricted set of educational paths and choose at A the path with the highest net return. In doing so the individual is not committing herself irrevocably to a given occupation because having achieved level *j* she can reassess her position in the light of any changes in costs or benefits that may have taken place in the meantime. Of course the fact that she has reached *j* following a certain subject will influence her decision whether to continue along the previously determined path because many alternative options will involve returning to level *i*, taking a different subject and thus incurring additional costs to get back to *j*. The further along any path she gets the more costly a change of direction is likely to be because of the number of education levels she will have to repeat. Nevertheless, all individuals will be taking and reassessing education decisions throughout their lives.

Fourth, we have so far assumed that our decision maker is able to finance educational investments entirely out of her own funds. Let us now introduce perfect capital markets and a rate of interest *r*. This will affect decisions about educational investments according to the relationship for each individual between *r*, her rate of time preference *δ*, and the returns to the programme she is considering. Let us consider first people for whom the investment is worthwhile, i.e. *IRR* > *δ*. Some of these people will have a rate of time preference higher than the interest rate, and they can now borrow funds at *r* if necessary to finance their educational investment. Those whose rate of time preference is lower than the interest rate will undertake the educational investment if the IRR is greater than *r* and they have enough funds. They would not borrow money to finance it. For other people for whom educational investment is not worthwhile, i.e. *IRR* < *δ*, the existence of capital markets provides an alternative use of funds: if *r* is greater than their rate of time preference, any funds will be lent out at *r*. At the current interest rate, therefore, because of the distribution across individuals of time preference rates, some people will want to borrow and some to lend. If aggregate demand for funds exceeds supply, the rate of interest will go up so that some people who were previously borrowers and investors in education will become lenders, and this process will continue until a market-clearing rate of interest is reached.

Consider now the case of an investor faced with a given educational path who can borrow or lend. As noted earlier the incremental rate of return on successive stages along the path will fall. The investor enrolls on successive programmes until the incremental rate of return falls to the level of the interest rate. At the same time the individual will borrow or lend until her rate of time preference in consumption is also equal to the market interest rate. Therefore, at the margin, each individual's rate of time preference will equal the rate of return to education.

This can be illustrated diagrammatically if we make the simplifying assumption that the whole educational path can be completed in one period. In Figure 3.3, with no further educational opportunities and no money market, the individual is at point A on indifference curve $I_0$. The existence of the educational path means that, by foregoing consumption in the current period and investing in education, consumption in all future periods can be increased. The investment possibilities of the educational path are shown by curve AB. If the individual invested in the whole path, her income in each future period would be M. The slope of AB at any point measures the incremental rate of return to a further unit of educational investment, which declines as the individual proceeds along the path.

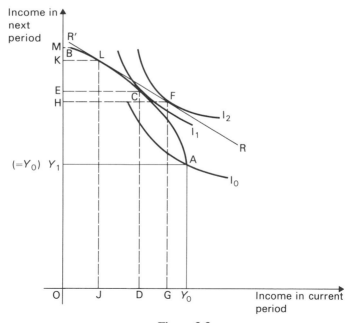

**Figure 3.3**

With no money market this individual will choose to invest an amount $DY_0$ in the current period. Her income in all future periods will be E and she attains a higher indifference curve $I_1$ at point C. Now let us introduce the market clearing rate of interest, $r$, which gives the slope of the line RR'. The individual now optimises at point F where RR' is tangential to the higher indifference curve $I_2$. Consumption in the current period is G and in all future periods is H. Optimal investment is now given by point L where RR' is tangential to the investment frontier AB An amount $JY_0$ is invested in education in the current period and thus future income is raised to K. This investment is financed by borrowing amount JG in the current period. Repayment is shown by HK $(= JG (1 + r))$.

At point F the slope of the indifference curve $(- (1 + \delta))$ equals the slope of RR' $(- (1 + r))$. Therefore the rate of time preference equals the rate of interest when the individual is at an optimum consumption point. The implication of this analysis is that on certain assumptions the market rate of interest is an appropriate proxy for the unobservable and variable rate of time preference, and can therefore be used as the discount rate in calculating the net present value of educational programmes.

## 3.3  Predictions of the human capital approach

The simple model of the preceding section can be used to generate predictions about the relationship between educational decisions and the labour market.

First, the human capital approach provides the basis for a model of occupational choice. In choosing between alternative educational paths according to their marginal net returns investors are also choosing between occupations. The long-run supply of labour to an occupational labour market will increase, *ceteris paribus*, with the wage offered because this will raise the marginal net return to the associated education path. This is a long-run relationship because the supply response will take time depending partly on the length of the education involved. The long-run supply of labour to an occupational labour market will also rise, *ceteris paribus*, if fees or the duration of educational programmes fall or grants rise at any given wage rate. A fall in the general level of time preference, and thus of interest rates, will also increase the marginal net returns to all educational investments but will increase most the supply of labour to those occupations which require the longest educational investment.

Second, individuals will normally choose to acquire their education while they are young because indirect costs (foregone earnings) increase with age if earnings profiles are non-linear and because delaying education reduces the length of time over which outlays on education can be recouped by higher earnings. An exception to this rule will be provided by groups whose expected participation in the labour force is intermittent, such as married women. If skills depreciate they may prefer to acquire their education prior to re-entry to the labour force after child-rearing.

Third, the number of applications to any particular educational programme will vary directly with the marginal net return to the path or paths of which it forms a part.

Fourth, in the long run, for any prospective investor the marginal internal rate of return to all educational paths will equal the rate of interest. In the short run, if paths have different rates of return, investors will choose those offering the highest return. This will increase the supply of labour to the associated occupations and lower their relative wages. This in turn will lower the marginal and incremental rates of return and bring them back into line with returns to other human and non-human investments.

In the long run there must be equality of marginal net returns between different programmes to achieve a given educational qualification, as well as between different paths to the same occupation. This implies that the longer of two alternative courses for the same qualification (which necessarily involves higher foregone earnings) must have lower direct costs to compensate.

Fifth, the following prediction about the occupational distribution of earnings follows directly from the equalisation of marginal net returns to all educational programmes. The discounted difference in earnings between occupations requiring educational levels $i$ and $j$ will exactly compensate for the costs at the margin of acquiring the extra education. If the earnings differential were to rise above this, the marginal net return to the investment would go up, more people would apply for the educational path, the supply of labour would increase, and relative wages – and hence the earnings differential – would decline.

It also follows that differences in earnings across individuals will be related to differences in education undertaken and, in equilibrium, must exactly compensate for the costs of those differences in education.

## 3.4   Limitations of the human capital approach

The simple human capital model outlined in Section 3.2 has been seen to give rise to a large number of interesting and important predictions, but is also open to a number of serious objections, to which we now turn.

We may question, first of all, whether individuals (or their parents as the case may well be), even if they are aware of some link between education and future earnings, approach their decisions in anything resembling the systematic fashion outlined above. Information on educational opportunities is often limited, future earnings streams only vaguely identifiable, and individuals are often neither consistent nor rational but myopic about their own best interests.

Second, the model takes no account of differences in educational abilities across individuals. If, as assumed above, people have identical abilities then, given any initial distribution of wages between occupations, they will all have exactly the same marginal net return to any educational investment and will therefore all aim for the same occupation, i.e. whichever offers the highest marginal return. This is clearly unrealistic so let us introduce differing abilities. *Ceteris paribus*, a more able person can achieve a given education level at lower cost (i.e. in less time), and therefore receives a higher marginal net return than a less able person from any educational path. It follows that people of different abilities will choose different educational paths and occupations. If, at the initial distribution of wages across occupations, demand for labour exceeds supply in some occupations, then the net returns to the associated educational paths will rise to induce increased investment in the appropriate skills. Investment will increase by some people extending their education and by others choosing to enter these particular paths until both the marginal and the incremental internal rate of return equal the interest rate. Net returns must be equalised everywhere because there are individuals at different educational levels. If demand and supply are still not equal in all occupations, wages will adjust accordingly and further investments will be induced. This process continues until equilibrium is reached. In this model investors will be distributed across occupations according to their marginal and incremental net returns which in turn depend on their costs of education and therefore on their ability. The ablest people will enter the jobs which require most education, involve the highest costs of education and therefore pay the highest wages.

This model is an improvement on the assumption of identical abilities in that it explains why people choose different occupations, and who will end up in the best-paid jobs. It also predicts that able people in high-education occupations may get very high wages indeed if their abilities are scarce. In this case their earnings will depend upon the costs of training a sufficient number of less able people to equate supply with demand. The wages of any occupation in excess demand must rise in order to induce more people to train for the job. The wage rise must cover education costs and is therefore higher the less able are the new entrants. Once wages have adjusted and demand and supply are equal, all the people in this occupation will earn the same wage, but the most able workers are better off in welfare terms since they incurred the least cost in training for the job. On this argument, therefore, we could predict that the average rate of return to a given educational path is lower for the last entrants into the associated occupation than for the earlier ones. If abilities are scarce then the high wages earned by people with these abilities do not merely compensate them for educational costs but will also contain a possibly significant element of scarcity rent.

Third, if we extend the model as above to include differences in ability, it predicts that all people with the same ability will achieve the same educational level. This prediction results from the assumptions that there are no supply restrictions, no capital market imperfections and no extra-market impediments to competitive behaviour. In practice, people may not be able to follow the education programme of their choice because insufficient places are available. This occurs partly because of lags in supply responses, partly because of the difficulties facing private suppliers in a market as sensitive as education, and partly because of the extensive intervention, both directly and indirectly, of the government in this sector. Severe financial constraints exist because it is generally impossible to borrow money for human capital investments on anything like the same terms as for physical capital investments. At the same time individual and family financial resources are limited. Equality of opportunity in education is unlikely even for those of identical abilities. Social circumstances place many people at a disadvantage in the competition for places.

Fourth, the model assumes that the only benefit to the individual from education is the increased earnings resulting from increased productivity, while in fact many educational programmes have other effects such as promoting individual development or social awareness and are also enjoyable in themselves. Therefore the net return to education calculated as above underestimates the true benefits of education to the individual and this should be allowed for in decisions about the provision of – or demand for – education.

Fifth, the prediction that marginal net returns to educational programmes will be equalised and earnings differentials between occupations will exactly compensate for their differential training requirements ignores non-pecuniary differences between occupations. Recognition of these differences implies that the net returns to training calculated as above for occupations in which non-pecuniary benefits are high (such as teaching, or the clergy) will be lower than others in equilibrium.

This list of problems obviously constitutes a serious qualification to the simple human capital model. The value of the model must, however, be determined empirically; are the predictions outlined in Section 3.2 substantiated by the actual workings of the labour market? If the model's predictions were empirically supported, the model would have a significant impact on our view of how labour markets work. We might then consider whether the introduction of more realistic assumptions yields increased insight worth the cost of complicating the model.

## 3.5 Social rates of return

The preceding analysis has considered how human capital investment decisions are taken from the point of view of the individual concerned. How should such decisions be viewed by society as a whole? Society will view an individual's educational investment favourably if the total benefit to society exceeds the total social cost, both discounted at the social rate of time preference (SRTP), or alternatively if the social internal rate of return to the investment exceeds the SRTP. Calculations using social net returns differ from those using private returns both because of a wider definition of costs and benefits and because the appropriate discount rate is different.

Social benefits include private benefits, i.e. increased earnings, though these should be measured gross, rather than net of tax, as the whole differential measures society's gain in total product. Also included, however, are externalities – benefits from the investment which affect people or firms other than the individual concerned. The list of potential external benefits from educational investments includes increased income for other people; increased income for future generations from a better educated present generation; benefits from increased flexibility of the labour force; encouragement of research and development; increased social responsibility; increased political awareness; and so on.

Social costs include private costs without deduction for grants plus all costs borne by the state which are not covered by fees: expenditure on buildings, teaching staff, equipment and materials.

Since social costs and benefits are spread over time, society will discount future values according to its preference for consumption in different time-periods, as measured by society's rate of time preference. The SRTP is likely to be lower than individual rates of time preference because the government is less myopic than individuals, or more likely to consider the needs of future generations. It follows that, at least for marginal investments, the SRTP is lower than the market interest rate, which means that the latter is not an appropriate proxy for the unobservable SRTP. Some proxy must be found, however, if society is to assess educational investments. The rate of interest on long-term government bonds is one proxy that is used.

The inclusion of capital and other costs of education not borne by the student means that, *ceteris paribus*, the social NPV and IRR will be lower than the private NPV and IRR calculated for the same investment. The inclusion of the social benefits of education, *ceteris paribus*, will have the opposite effect. If, at the same time as we include all costs and social benefits, we use the social rather than a private rate of time preference then, because the former is lower, the social NPV for the investment will generally be higher than the private NPV. The social IRR will be compared with the lower time preference rate in making the decision as to whether the investment is worthwhile. On either criterion, therefore, the investment is more likely to be undertaken on the basis of a social calculation. On those occasions when the private NPV exceeds the social NPV it may be socially optimal to restrict the supply of education to a level where the private NPV is permanently and significantly above zero. In practice, however, calculations of the social NPV and IRR must always be treated with some caution because it is impossible to value many of the social benefits associated with education and also because the measure employed for the SRTP will always be suspect.

Social net returns provide a basis upon which governments can determine whether the allocation of resources to education is efficient. It is socially optimal that all individuals should pursue their education up to the level at which the social internal rate of return to education equals the SRTP. The government should therefore see that enough places are available for this objective to be attained and additional places should first be provided on those programmes which offer the highest social net return. If the social net return were higher than the private return, the government should take action to increase private investment in education to the socially optimal level by increasing the private net return, say by providing or increasing grants.

The resource allocation implications of the human capital model depend on the existence of direct causal links running from education to productivity and from productivity to earnings. Under certain circumstances either of these links can be weakened or actually destroyed. These circumstances constitute further objections to the model.

It can be argued that the link between education and earnings is not one of direct causation but works through ability, i.e. more able people both acquire more education and earn more. This would not remove the incentive to acquire education if employers recognised the relationship and used educational qualifications as a way of selecting able employees. But in this case, since education does not increase productivity, it can have no effect on the aggregate supply of labour to the economy. We shall return to this issue in Chapter 4 when we consider uncertainty in labour markets.

The second direct causal link identified above, i.e. from productivity to earnings, will function fully in profit-maximising, competitive firms. Under other circumstances, however, the relationship between earnings and productivity will depend on the internal workings of the firm. As we shall see in later chapters, we may find the relationship distorted by discrimination or by the workings of internal labour markets. Distortions in the labour market on either side (arising from monopsonistic firms or trade union entry restrictions) will also break the link between earnings and productivity and impair the extent to which disequilibrium wage differences are translated into educational enrolments and occupational supply changes. Rates of return are unlikely to converge, nor, since the link between productivity and earnings is broken, will they represent valid indicators of efficiency in resource allocation.

## 3.6 The decision to invest and the nature of skills

We have assumed above that each individual acts as the entrepreneur for her own abilities, calculates rates of returns, procures funds and invests in education. The returns to education, the individual's investment decision and whether the optimal amount of investment in aggregate takes place all depend crucially on the extent to which the contemplated skills can be switched from one use to another in the labour market. This is because transferability, which depends to a large extent upon the nature of the skills involved, influences the earnings profile which the individual can expect.

We suggested in Section 3.1 that human capital is different from physical capital in that the former is attached inextricably to the human form, and, since this cannot be purchased, human capital can only be hired, not purchased and owned as can physical capital. This prevents entrepreneurship, in particular by employers, since without ownership or at least very long-term binding contracts, returns to any human capital investment cannot be appropriated. This generalisation, however, depends upon the nature of the skills in question. In principle there are circumstances in which employers will provide and finance workers' education.

Let us first of all distinguish two types of skills: general and specific. General skills increase the workers' productive capability in any firm. Specific skills, on the other hand, can only be employed in a single firm. Let us assume that there are two types of education distinguishable by the fact that one produces only general skills whilst the other produces only specific skills. We can therefore identify them as general and specific educations. Let us propose that before education the worker's marginal product and wage are $MP$ and $W$, during training they are $MP_T$ and $W_T$, after general education is completed they are $MP_g$ and $W_g$ and on the completion of specific training they are $MP_s$ and $W_s$. Conventional analysis suggests that $W = MP$. Workers have an incentive to finance their own general education. Because general skills can be employed in any firm the worker can be confident that by undertaking general training he can shift his whole earnings profile upwards and that $W_g$ will always equal $MP_g$. Our previous analysis of educational investment decisions still applies: the worker decides whether to undertake training according to whether the discounted difference between $W_g$ and $W$ outweighs the costs of the training. There may be under-investment in general skills if workers are myopic or have difficulty in procuring funds, and the market's ability to provide educational programmes may be impaired by the variability of investments. There may, therefore, be a need for government intervention to stimulate investment by paying grants and also to provide educational facilities. Is there any chance that this intervention could come from firms rather than from the government?

At first glance it would seem that firms will not finance general education. Firms, like other sources of finance, will be reluctant to lend money for educational investments because of the probability of dropout or failure, the risk of default on payment and the difficulty of collecting debts on such socially sensitive loans. Nor, given the costs involved and the unpredictability of demand, will they want to supply educational facilities. There may, however, be some conditions on which firms would find it profitable to be involved in the provision of general training.

A firm would be able to earn a return on financing its own workers' education if it could pay $W_T < MP_T$ during the education period. Since after general training the wage must equal $MP_g$, the whole cost plus any profit must be earned while training is going on. The firm in this case acts as a capital market for its own workers and will be prepared to finance education up to the point at which the IRR equals the interest rate. There are problems associated with such an arrangement. First, if the education is expensive and short the wage would have to be so low that applicants would be discouraged, and might even be negative. Second, even if workers stand to reap considerable benefit from the training (i.e. $W_g$ is much bigger than $W$), if they have a high rate of time preference they will be unwilling to accept a low $W_T$ during education. Third, union rules on differentials may cover trainees so that the firm's ability to determine $W_T$ is limited. Fourth, if workers drop out during training the firm will lose some part of any fixed costs of providing the training.

On the other hand, there are ways in which it can become more worthwhile for a firm to provide general training. First, if the firm can reduce the costs of education by providing it itself, then $W_T$ could be higher. Costs might be lower if economies of scale in training can be reaped in large firms, or if firms can combine training (and teaching) with production activities and thus raise $MP_T$. Second, the value to the firm of having trainees would increase if the training programme had benefits additional to that of increased productivity of trainees, such as prestige and government approval or technical improvements emanating from training departments. The additional benefit could be the satisfaction of an option demand: the firm knows that if the labour market gets tight and skills are scarce its own 'graduates' will provide it with a cushion. Providing education also has the advantage that the firm acquires a lot of knowledge about its trainees so that the costs and uncertainty of hiring and promotion decisions later are reduced. All of these factors work to increase $MP_T$ and make it possible for the firm to recoup its outlay on general training without having to pay trainees prohibitively low wages.

Let us turn now to specific education. There is a strong disincentive for workers to finance their own training in specific skills. If a worker is discharged by the firm to which his skills are specific there is no way in which he can recoup his costs. Workers will therefore under-invest in such skills to an extent which depends on job security in the relevant occupations, which in turn depends on technical change and the stability of product demand. Even when jobs are secure workers with specific skills may receive a wage lower than their marginal product $MP_s$ because their dependence on a single firm to use the skills they have financed gives the firm leverage in bargaining. The gap between $W_s$ and $MP_s$ represents a monopsony rent for the firm. In the case of specific skills, therefore, our earlier analysis of the worker as entrepreneur for his own skills is inappropriate. Even with perfect capital markets and rational workers there will be under-investment in specific skills.

Again we may ask whether firms will play a part in financing education, and in the case of specific skills it appears at first that they will do so. As with general skills the firm will only train its own workers and will get a return on its outlay by adjusting wages. In this case, however, the firm can pay $W_T = MP_T$ during training to encourage enrolment and discourage dropout, and recoup its costs by paying $W_s$ less than $MP_s$ when training is completed. The firm is willing to finance the education because the possession of specific skills is a strong disincentive to mobility, and therefore specifically trained workers are likely to stay with the firm long enough for the firm to get a return. This return, costs plus surplus, is given by the discounted difference between $MP_s$ and $W_s$ over the post-training period. The worker has an incentive to undertake specific training as long as $W_s$ exceeds $W$.

Does this analysis suggest that firms will provide the optimal level of specific education so that no government intervention is necessary? There are factors which limit the amount of education firms will provide. First, and crucially, the incentive for any firm depends on its expected level of quits. Although specific skills are not transferable, some workers with specific skills will quit both during and after education, for a variety of reasons. In these cases the firm loses at least some of its outlay. The firm could discourage quits during education by paying $W_T$ above $MP_T$ if $MP_T$ is considerably less than $MP_s$. But this will have to be matched by a bigger discounted difference between $W_s$ and $MP_s$ after education. The firm has to decide how to spread this difference over time: whether to recoup its outlay quickly by paying $W_s$ significantly below $MP_s$ for a short period or more slowly with a smaller gap between $W_s$ and $MP_s$ for a longer period. The effect of each strategy on quits will be a paramount consideration. Second, the incentive to invest will depend on the importance the firm attaches to its specific skills; if education is given low priority then in times of financial stringency education investments will be very vulnerable. Third, in firms whose product demand varies considerably, the fact that employment contractions occur regularly will discourage educational investment.

Nevertheless, the incentive for firms to finance education is much stronger for specific than for general skills. Furthermore, the arguments above concerning the possibility of cutting the costs of education by providing the facilities and concerning the indirect benefits from education apply to specific education more strongly than to general education. By its very nature specific training has to take place within the firm and at the same time as production. The likelihood of technical spillovers is higher. The probability of market shortages of specific skills is obviously greater. Firms will devise a number of means to increase the stability of their labour force so that they can reap their return on educational expenditure. Promises of more education and of promotion and agreements with unions on job protection will tie the worker more closely to the firm. The costs involved enter the firm's investment calculation but increase the probability of earning returns oh the investment.

The distinction set up here is extreme. In practice every education programme is likely to provide the worker with both specific and general skills and therefore has a certain degree of specificity which lies between our two extremes. An example of an education programme with high specificity is that producing stainless steel welders, who are a relatively rare and expensive manufacturing input. An example of a programme with low specificity is that producing motor vehicle fitters, workers who are useful in any of the numerous areas where combustion engines are produced and used. Most university courses involve a low degree of specificity.

What does this discussion imply about whether the optimal amount of investment in education will be undertaken? First, the amount of investment will be closer to the optimal level in education programmes with either very high or very low specificity since these provide the greatest incentive for investment by firms and workers respectively.

Second, there are strong *a priori* reasons for expecting under-investment in programmes with a large element of general skills, given the unequal distribution of income and wealth and market imperfections, because the level of investment in such programmes depends on the entrepreneurial performance of individual workers. It is unlikely that firms will compensate for this under-investment and therefore there is a strong case for government involvement in the provision of general education.

Third, whether there is optimal investment in the provision of specific skills is likely to depend crucially on firms' successes in restricting turnover and on their ability to impose a wage structure on specifically trained workers which will enable costs to be recouped. Wage movements elsewhere in the economy may be important here. The suitability of applicants to receive and repay specific training will become an important element in firms' hiring decisions.

Fourth, the disincentive for a worker to invest in education programmes with a high specific skill content will be reduced by factors such as trade union involvement, high business expectations and skill shortages, all of which increase workers' job security.

Fifth, investment in human capital would be higher if arrangements could be made for employers and workers to share the costs of education and thereby the risks and rewards of entrepreneurship. This could be achieved by collective bargaining agreements which guarantee continuous training by the firm and job security for graduate trainees and also stipulate the payment of a wage less than marginal product both during and for some period after education is completed. The more general the education the lower the wage might be during training, and the nearer the wage might be to marginal product on completion.

Sixth, changes in educational programmes which give them more of a slant towards general skills will make them less attractive investments to firms. The balance between general and specific skills in available programmes is critical to whether investment reaches the optimal level.

## 3.7  Alternative forms of education

Until now we have discussed education in general terms. In this section we briefly consider the three most important forms of education:

post-compulsory schooling, government training and on-the-job training.

The model of Section 3.2 clearly fits most closely the formal educational programmes of schooling beyond the minimum leaving age, universities and colleges. It is worth noting, however, that because such schooling contains a very high element of general education, as well as social education, there may be a strong case for government intervention of some kind to prevent under-investment by individuals. Second, if state intervention takes the form of payment of fees and partial maintenance grants, foregone earnings can represent nearly 100 per cent of total costs. If under-investment in education persists, the government would have to consider offsetting students' indirect costs by increasing grants still further.

Government training principally involves provision of training facilities and programmes for adults who are either unemployed or attempting occupational mobility. Human capital analysis has the following special features in this context. First, foregone earnings may be very low or even zero. Therefore, unless the trainee has earnings from the black economy or values his leisure highly, private net returns are substantial. Second, social net returns will be high if there is a low displacement effect and a high vacuum effect. A displacement effect arises if a retrained worker gets a job but makes someone else unemployed. The gain in total product is then zero. A vacuum effect arises if the job from which the trainee comes is filled by a formerly unemployed worker and the trainee himself later finds suitable employment. Third, both private and social net returns depend critically upon whether the worker gets a position at the higher skill level, how quickly he gets it and how long he keeps it after he completes his training. If he simply returns to his former position, either unemployment or his old job, there is no increase in output. Fourth, the workers involved in government training schemes could include, by self-selection, a high proportion of people with labour market difficulties which would seriously limit the returns to their retraining. Fifth, the government's control of supply is much more noticeable in this area than in that of schooling; the quantity provided varies more. Sixth, the drop-out rate from government training schemes is likely to be higher than that from formal education. Allowing for the probability of trainees dropping out will therefore have a significant impact on calculated net returns.

In principle the drop-out rate, displacement and vacuum effects can be integrated into the calculation of net returns. For instance, suppose that after training a worker will either find an appropriate skilled job or return to his previous job. In the former case his earnings would go up by £1000 a year and the probability of getting such a job is 0.6. In this case the *expected* private benefit from undertaking the training is (for the first year after completing the course) $0.6 \times 1000 + 0.4 \times 0 = £600$, and this figure should be used to calculate an *expected* net return. In fact uncertainty about future earnings and employment characterises all human capital investment decisions and therefore in principle our whole analysis should be conducted in terms of expected values.

On-the-job training comes in a multitude of forms, but basically involves training provided by the firm, a significant specific skill element, and some degree of financing by workers through payment of wages below marginal product during training. The workers may be trained by state agencies on a day release system, by internal training departments, by studying at home, and by imitation. For human capital analysis the main points of note here are, first, the importance of labour turnover in the firm's investment appraisal. For each instance of on-the-job training the firm will calculate an expected net return using the appropriate probability of keeping the trained worker. Second, the amount of investment in training depends crucially upon whether firms in a particular skill market can tacitly or overtly reach a joint decision to invest for the market, i.e. each firm trains more than it currently needs so that if workers are unexpectedly lost they can be replaced from the market by workers trained elsewhere. Third, there is strong pressure from firms to make training programmes as specific in skill terms as possible. Fourth, the long gestation period for much training holds special significance here. The investment decision will be whether to invest, and how much to invest, now for *m* years' time. Expectations of demand will therefore be very important. Furthermore, the decision to make a big investment must often be taken when the firm can least afford the capital outlay. The long gestation period suggests the need for a strong counter-cyclical pattern in training. However, to the extent that demand changes are not anticipated or financial considerations overshadow economic efficiency, decision lags will produce both training cycles that duplicate the business cycle and more or less permanent under-investment in training. Fifth, the strong possibility of under-investment by individuals and the vagaries and specialisation of companies' human capital requirements severely limit the potential for a prosperous private market in training programmes.

## Further Reading

CHAPTER 3: HUMAN CAPITAL

G. S. Becker, *Human Capital*, 2nd edition (New York: National Bureau of Economic Research, 1975).

M. Blaug, *An Introduction to the Economics of Education* (Harmondsworth, Penguin, 1970).

M. Blaug, 'The rate of return on investment in education in Great Britain', *The Manchester School*, Vol. 33 (September 1965).

G. E. Johnson and F. P. Stafford, 'Social returns to quantity and quality of schooling', *Journal of Human Resources*, Vol. 8 (1963).

A. Ziderman, 'Costs and benefits of adult retraining in the UK', *Economica*, Vol. 36 (November 1969).

# 4
# Uncertainty, screening and signalling

Elementary models of the labour market, like the one outlined in the introduction to this section, assume that workers and firms have perfect knowledge of the market environment within which they operate. In this chapter we consider the implications of relaxing this assumption, for it is clear that in reality labour markets are characterised by severe deficiencies in information. Decision makers are uncertain about the options open to them and the consequences of their actions. Risks are calculated, and errors are made. Agents can of course acquire additional information, but only at a cost. In modelling decision making under uncertainty we shall incorporate the information-gathering procedures available to workers and firms. Since the accumulation of labour market knowledge can sometimes be mutually beneficial, workers and firms will both attempt to transmit as well as to gather information. We therefore consider the nature and consequence of such behaviour for decision making under uncertainty.

## 4.1 Information in labour markets

Elementary models of the labour market assume that each worker knows precisely the pecuniary and non-pecuniary rewards attached to each job, where all relevant jobs are, and where vacancies exist. Each employer knows what rewards other firms are offering for specific tasks, and what each available worker has to offer in terms of total productive capability. In reality of course both sets of agents (and all other agents in the economy) have only sketchy knowledge of these and other relevant facts. The resulting gaps in information generate uncertainty, by which throughout our analysis we mean that agents know all the possible outcomes but can only attach probabilities to their occurrence. Since the lack of information normally prevents the realisation of maximum utility or profits, there is an incentive for economic agents to try to acquire more information than they already have. However, as we will see, there is no incentive for agents to acquire *complete* information. The search for information brings both

**Table 4.1**

| Information sought by | Observable by inspection | Observable by experience |
|---|---|---|
| workers | wage offer, hours, overtime availability, holidays, recreation facilities | promotion prospects, supervision, safety, fringe benefits |
| firms | wage demand, age, employment record, qualifications | performance at tasks, reliability, flexibility, punctuality, creativity |

benefits and costs – it is the existence of costs which limits the amount of information gathering undertaken by an agent. The question we must thus attempt to answer is, 'How much information should an agent acquire?'

The information sought by workers and firms can relate to very different characteristics of the working environment. Such characteristics can be divided into two categories: those which are readily observable and those which are not. Table 4.1 provides an illustration of how this classification might be made. Those characteristics that can be readily observed are termed *inspection characteristics* and those that are not are termed *experience characteristics*. Generally inspection characteristics can be discovered by enquiry or from advertisements. Experience characteristics can be discovered by probation schemes, trial periods and by formal tests. References or recommendations from experienced third parties may reveal experience characteristics at less cost than these methods, but may be less reliable. The various procedures adopted by labour market agents to acquire information are referred to as *screening*. Screening for inspection characteristics will be referred to as *search* in order to distinguish it from screening for experience characteristics which will be referred to as *prospecting*.

Our analysis of uncertainty in the labour market must perforce be restricted to limited, specific decisions. Accordingly we focus, firstly, upon the problems facing a worker looking for a job with inadequate information on available opportunities. Secondly, we focus upon the problems facing a firm possessing inadequate information on the available labour looking for new recruits. Workers are assumed to lack information on wages in Sections 4.2 and 4.3, which are therefore concerned with worker search. Firms are assumed to lack information on worker quality in Section 4.4, which is therefore concerned with employer prospecting.

## 4.2 The worker search model

Let us consider a representative worker in a given labour market deciding whether to move to a more rewarding job. We assume, first, that workers in this market are homogeneous in all respects, and that the worker faces, not a single market wage offer for his labour services as in the basic labour market model, but a variety of offers as summarised in the frequency distribution of Table 4.2, columns (1) and (2). We assume that all characteristics of the jobs other than wages are known and identical. Second, we assume that the worker knows the exact form of the wage distribution, including the minimum and maximum values, the mean and the variance, etc. Uncertainty arises because the worker does not know which firms are offering each wage; for example, which 14 of the 155 firms are offering £130 per week. Third, we assume that the individual can begin to discover which firms are offering which wage by search, i.e. by selecting a firm at random from the distribution and making a job application. We can imagine the worker, after randomly selecting a firm from the names in the telephone directory, then goes to the personnel office of the firm to enquire about the wage offer. Fourth, the worker is assumed to prefer a higher wage to a lower wage, and to have an infinite life span over which he searches for the highest wage offer.

Under these conditions, if there were no cost constraints, search would be undertaken to locate the maximum wage no matter how long it took. If all workers were totally unconstrained, high wage firms would be overwhelmed with applicants and low wage firms would have difficulty filling vacancies. The former group would lower their offers and the latter group would increase their offers, so that

### Table 4.2

| *(1)* *Weekly wage,* *W (£)* | *(2)* *Nos of* *firms* | *(3)* *Probability of obtaining* *each wage, P[W]* |
|---|---|---|
| 120 | 2 | 2/155 = 0.0129 |
| 125 | 7 | 7/155 = 0.0452 |
| 130 | 14 | 14/155 = 0.0903 |
| 135 | 28 | 28/155 = 0.1806 |
| 140 | 40 | 40/155 = 0.2581 |
| 145 | 26 | 26/155 = 0.1677 |
| 150 | 20 | 20/155 = 0.1290 |
| 155 | 15 | 15/155 = 0.0968 |
| 160 | 3 | 3/155 = 0.0194 |
| | 155 | |

eventually all firms would offer the same wage. In this case the distribution can be said to 'degenerate' and our search problem disappears. However, we now introduce the crucial assumption that each application imposes a significant cost upon the worker. We shall use the term search costs at this stage in a very general way to include travel expenses, opportunity costs (foregone leisure or earnings from the time expended in writing letters and going to the firm) and so on. We shall assume that search costs are known, constant, lump-sum payments incurred each time an offer is sampled from the distribution and an approach made to a firm, whether the offer is accepted or rejected. Thus we refer to the marginal cost of search as the cost of one more selection. We now proceed to model the worker's decision-making process and his search behaviour under these assumptions.

Search brings a benefit to the worker in that the more units of search he undertakes, the more likely it is that a high wage firm will be discovered. However, each additional unit of search imposes a cost. Therefore, search will continue only whilst the marginal benefit of search exceeds its marginal cost. To model the worker's decision formally we must define precisely the benefits from search. These can then be compared with the costs to derive the optimal amount of search to undertake.

Since information is imperfect, the worker must calculate the *expected* benefit to search. This is derived in the following manner. First, the worker calculates the probability of obtaining each wage offer $P[W]$. This can be estimated directly from the frequency distribution of wages in Table 4.2. The probability of obtaining a wage offer of £130 is thus $P[W = 130]$, i.e. $14/155 = 0.0903$. The full probability distribution is shown in column (3) of Table 4.2.

The worker calculates the expected wage, $E[W]$, for a single random selection across the firms as the sum of the product of each wage and its probability. This is simply the average wage of the distribution, viz.

$$E[W] = \sum_{i=1}^{i=9} W_i P[W = W_i]$$

$$= (120 \times 0.0129) + (125 \times 0.0452) + \cdots + (160 \times 0.0194)$$

$$= 141.2225 \tag{4.1}$$

This particular wage is not available in the market place but the calculation implies that our worker can expect to receive a first offer of £140. There is of course no certainty that he will receive such an offer. Any wage in the distribution of Table 4.2 is a possible offer. The actual offer could therefore be more or less than £140. How should the worker proceed? Should he make his first random selection and first application? When the first offer is received, how does he decide whether to stop searching and accept the offer or to continue the search? Clearly any model of uncertainty must specify precisely the decision rule to be adopted. In our analysis we introduce two possible procedures.

(a)  The worker decides before search begins to calculate the maximum expected wage offer for each sample size $n$ and to choose that number of firms, $n^*$, to be sampled which maximises the difference between expected maximum wage and search costs.
(b)  The worker decides before search begins upon the lowest wage offer that is considered acceptable and to stop searching when an offer is received which is greater than or equal to that acceptable wage. The wage in question is that which maximises expected income net of search costs.

We will refer to the first as the Stigler decision rule and the second as the sequential decision rule.

## THE STIGLER DECISION RULE

This is sometimes referred to as the fixed or optimal sample size rule. Let us state the procedure involved first, then go through the details more slowly. The individual worker calculates the number of search units (applications), $n^*$, which maximises expected wages net of search costs. He makes precisely $n^*$ selections and accepts the largest wage offer from the $n^*$ received, if this represents an improvement upon his present position.

The first step is for the worker to calculate the highest wage likely to be encountered over $n$ units of search, where $n$ represents all integers from 1 upwards. What would be the highest expected wage offer received if two firms were simultaneously chosen? What would it be if 10 firms were chosen? Consider Table 4.2 again. The wage distribution has already given us, in equation (4.1), the expected wage $E[W]$ for the single random selection. This can be rewritten as

$$E[W] = E[\max \{W_1\} \mid n = 1] \equiv E[R \mid n = 1] \qquad (4.2)$$

The expected wage from a single random selection is equal to the expected maximum wage from a sample of size one. Denote the maximum wage of the sample by $R$. What then can be said of $E[R \mid n = 2]$? What happens to $E[R \mid n]$ as $n$ increases?

To answer the first question the worker produces a list of all possible pairs of wages which could be drawn from Table 4.2. There are 81 such pairs, (120, 120) (120, 125) and so on. For each pair he calculates the probability of drawing that particular pair at random, assuming replacement. For example, the probability of drawing £120 and another £120 is $P[W = 120] \times P[W = 120] = 0.0129 \times 0.0129 = 0.000\ 166\ 41$. The probability of receiving offers of £120 and £125 is $P[W = 120] \times P[W = 125] = 0.000\ 583\ 08$. Thus for each pair of wages he takes the highest of the two numbers and multiplies it by the probability that that particular pair occurs. A few of the necessary computations are shown in Table 4.3.

The expected maximum wage from a sample of size 2 is therefore the sum of the alternative maximum possible wages times their probabilities of occurrence, i.e. $E[R \mid n = 2]$ = [maximum $\{W_1 W_2\} \mid n = 2]$ is formed from the sum of all the numbers in the fourth column of Table 4.3. This is in fact £146.045 12. The procedure is the same for all $E[R \mid n]$ for larger $n$. This will produce an array of expected maximum wages for the worker for all possible values of $n$ – the first four of which are shown in Table 4.4, column (2). We are now able to answer the second question – $E[R \mid n]$ increases as $n$ becomes larger, but at a decreasing rate. There are in this case continuously diminishing marginal returns to search.

However, the searcher has solved only part of his problem – he knows the benefits of search. To calculate the expected *net gain* to search over a sample size $n$, $E[G \mid n]$, he must subtract from $E[R \mid n]$ the total cost of sampling. $E[G \mid n]$ is shown in column (4) of Table 4.4 on the assumption that the cost of each selection, $c$, is £2. Each item in column (3) is therefore the total cost from a sample of size $n$. It can be seen from column (4) that the *optimal* sample size, $n^*$, is 3 since this maximises expected net gain, $E[G \mid n]$.

Having calculated $n^*$ as 3, if the expected net gain from search,

### Table 4.3

| *(1)*<br>*Wages in a*<br>*sample of*<br>*size 2 (£)* | *(2)*<br><br>*Probability of*<br>*each sample* | *(3)*<br>*Maximum wage*<br>*of each sample,*<br>*R (£)* | *(4)*<br><br>*= (2) × (3)*<br>*(£)* |
|---|---|---|---|
| 120,  120 | 0.000 166 41 | 120 | 0.019 969 2 |
| 120,  125 | 0.000 583 08 | 125 | 0.072 885 0 |
| 125,  130 | 0.001 164 87 | 130 | 0.151 433 1 |
| 160,  160 | 0.000 376 36 | 160 | 0.000 217 6 |
|  |  | $E[R \mid n = 2] =$ | 146.045 120 0 |

**Table 4.4**

| (1) Sample size, n | (2) E[R \| n] (£) | (3) Search cost, cn (£) | (4) E[G \| n] (£) |
|---|---|---|---|
| 1 | 141.222 5 | 2 | 139.22 |
| 2 | 146.045 12 | 4 | 142.05 |
| 3 | 148.472 40 | 6 | 142.47 |
| 4 | 150.009 74 | 8 | 142.01 |

$E[G \mid n = 3] = £142.47$, is greater than $£\overline{W}$, the value to the worker of remaining in his present state, he would begin search. He would draw three names randomly from the list of firms in his labour market and apply to each for a quotation on wages. When the three replies come back, the searcher would accept the best offer of the three, if it exceeded $£\overline{W}$. This offer could of course be more or less than £148, the expected maximum wage $E[R \mid n = 3]$ from column (2) of Table 4.4. But no more than three selections would be made even if the highest offer were to be considerably less than £148. If either $E[G \mid n = 3]$ or the highest of the three offers is less than $£\overline{W}$ the worker would remain in his present state.

The outcome of the Stigler decision rule can be seen diagrammatically if we move away from the discrete distribution of Table 4.2 to a continuous distribution, i.e. to a distribution where there are probabilities on every conceivable monetary value between £120 and £160. We therefore allow the number of possible wage offers to be very large. This allows us to draw smooth continuous expected benefit and total cost curves, as $cn$ and $E[R \mid n]$ in Figure 4.1. The

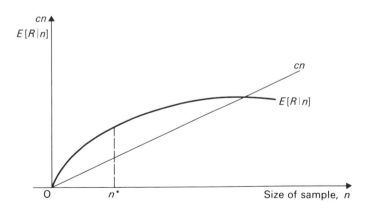

**Figure 4.1**

former increases uniformly with $n$ and the latter is concave in $n$. The optimal solution for $n$ maximises the distance between the expected return and cost curves, i.e. the point at which marginal cost and marginal expected returns are equal.

## THE SEQUENTIAL DECISION RULE

Under this rule the individual does not decide in advance upon the number of searches to be made, but rather upon a minimum acceptable wage offer known as *the reservation wage*. The worker begins to search if the reservation wage exceeds £$\overline{W}$, which is the value to him of his present state. Firms are then selected from the relevant list, at random, one at a time. All wage offers lower than the reservation wage will be rejected and search resumed. The first wage offer at least as large as the reservation wage is accepted. The manner in which the reservation wage is calculated is illustrated in the following simple example which again uses the data of Table 4.2.

Imagine that the worker is searching for a wage which will be earned for just one week, after which he 'dies'. Imagine also that the worker searches sequentially but that the process takes no time. Under these strange but useful assumptions if the individual always turns down an offer below wage $r$ the expected net return to his search, $V(r)$, is given by

$$V(r) = E[W \mid W \geqslant r]P[W \geqslant r] + V(r)\{1 - P[W \geqslant r]\} - c$$

(4.3)

The expected net return is equal to the return should the worker accept a wage offer plus the return to further search if he does not accept the offer, minus the cost of obtaining that offer (which is paid whether or not the offer is accepted). The return should the worker accept a wage offer, which must be because it is equal to or greater than $r$, is

$$\sum_{W \geqslant r} W_i P[W_i], \quad \text{which can be written as} \quad E[W \mid W \geqslant r]P[W \geqslant r]$$

The offer is not accepted, however, if it is below $r$. This has a probability $\{1 - P[W \geqslant r]\}$ of happening. Once the worker resumes search the expected net return will then again be $V(r)$. But the anticipated return to the worker prior to any search being undertaken, should he not accept the offer, is

$$V(r)\{1 - P[W \geqslant r]\}$$

Solving for $V(r)$ from equation (4.3) we have

$$V(r) = E[W \mid W \geq r] - \frac{c}{P[W \geq r]} \qquad (4.4)$$

The worker's problem is to choose $r$ before search begins so as to maximise expression (4.4). Search costs, $c$, are again assumed to be £2 per unit. All the other information required is contained in Table 4.2. Table 4.5 summarises the appropriate calculations. Column (2) records the expected wage given that it is greater than or equal to $r$ for each value that $r$ can take. $E[W \mid W \geq r]$ is derived from

$$\frac{\sum\limits_{W \geq r} W_i P[W_i]}{\sum\limits_{W \geq r} P[W_i]}.$$

So when $r = 120$, $E[W \mid W \geq r] = £141.2225$, which is simply the mean of the distribution since *all* available wages are greater than or equal to 120. We can see that as $r$ assumes higher values $E[W \mid W \geq r]$ becomes larger. When $r$ is £155 we have

$$E[W \mid W \geq 155] = \frac{\sum\limits_{W \geq r} W_i P[W_i]}{\sum\limits_{W \geq r} P[W_i]}$$

$$= \frac{(155 \times 0.0968) + (160 \times 0.0194)}{0.968 + 0.0194}$$

$$= 155.8003$$

**Table 4.5**

| (1)<br>r<br>(£) | (2)<br>$E[W \mid W \geq r]$<br>(£) | (3)<br>$c/P[W \geq r]$<br>(£) | (4) = (2) − (3)<br>$V(r)$<br>(£) |
|---|---|---|---|
| 120 | 141.2225 | 2.0000 | 139.2225 |
| 125 | 141.4998 | 2.0261 | 139.4737 |
| 130 | 142.2916 | 2.1234 | 140.1682 |
| 135 | 143.5950 | 2.3485 | 141.2465 |
| 140 | 145.9083 | 2.9806 | 142.9277 |
| 145 | 149.6016 | 4.8438 | 144.7678 |
| 150 | 152.7488 | 8.1566 | 144.5922 |
| 155 | 155.8003 | 17.2117 | 138.5886 |
| 160 | 160.0000 | 103.0928 | 56.9072 |

Column (3) records the expected cost, $c/P[W \geq r]$, associated with each wage $r$. It is an *expected* total cost because the total number of selections is uncertain and depends on $r$. Column (4) gives the expected *net* return associated with each wage, $V(r)$, as column (2) minus column (3). The searcher chooses the *optimal* wage $r^*$, the reservation wage, which maximises the value in column (4). In this example, $r^*$ is £145. The worker should accept the first offer at least as great as £145 and reject all others.

As with the Stigler strategy, the sequential strategy has an analogue in the continuous distribution case. The wage distribution is defined as $f(W)$, say, as in Figure 4.2(a). The probability of any wage up to a level $r$ is thus the sum of the frequencies under the distribution up to $r$, described by the cumulative frequency $F(W)$. The probability of a wage less than $r$ is $F(r)$. Since the expected wage is $W$ times the probability of $W$, there exists a series of expected wages given by $Wf(W)$. We may thus write

$$V(r) = \int_r^\infty Wf(W) \, dW + V(r)F(r) - c \qquad (4.5)$$

where the first term is the expected wage over all wages greater than $r$ times the probability that $W$ is greater than $r$; the area to the right of $r$ in the expected wage series. From this expression we derive

$$V(r) = \frac{\int_r^\infty Wf(W) \, dW}{1 - F(r)} - \frac{c}{1 - F(r)} \qquad (4.6)$$

which is the equivalent in the continuous distribution case of equation (4.4) in the discrete distribution case. The reservation wage $r^*$ is the value of $r$ which maximises (4.6). Since this is derived by setting the derivative of the equation equal to zero and solving for $r$ we can show the solution diagrammatically. In Figure 4.2(b) the curve $mb(r)$ is the derivative of the first term on the right hand side of equation (4.6). The curve $mc(r)$ is the derivative of the second term. The two curves in the figure are based upon the information from columns (2) and (3) of Table 4.5 to approximate the continuous case. The intersection of the two curves gives the reservation wage, $r^* = £145$.

Before we consider the predictions and extensions of our model of worker's job seeking under uncertainty, it is instructive to compare the two strategies described above. In each case the searcher is maximising the expected return to search; only the decision variable differs. In each case the sampling takes no time, so by construction

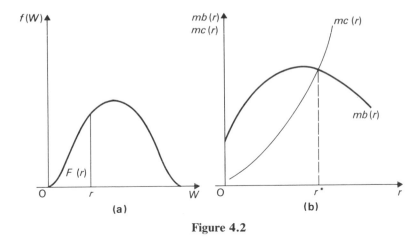

**Figure 4.2**

there is perfect recall, and therefore the possibility of selecting any one of the offers received. However, in the first case the individual chooses the number of selections to make (in our example the searcher will make exactly three selections). In the second case the individual chooses a minimum acceptable wage, leaving the number of selections to be determined by the 'luck of the draw'. Under both strategies, however, the wage which is eventually received is uncertain *ex ante*.

## 4.3 Predictions and extensions of the worker search model

In the very simple model derived so far, a central feature of the worker's decision-making process is the interplay between search costs and the distribution of wage offers. Our initial set of predictions therefore concerns changes in these two parameters.

The effects of an increase in unit search costs on both strategies are illustrated in Figure 4.3. In each case, the implication is clear – an increase in search cost, *ceteris paribus*, lowers the (expected) duration of search. In the case shown in Figure 4.3(a) it does so directly, while in that of Figure 4.3(b) it does so indirectly by lowering the reservation wage, making searchers less 'choosy' and thus increasing the chance of finding an acceptable wage. This is probably the most fundamental result of search theory, generating a number of predictions. First, since an increase in search costs reduces $n^*$ and $r^*$, the costs of search could become so high relative to the benefits that $n^*$ and $r^*$ fall so far that no search is undertaken. Second, in so far as governments reduce the cost of search by supplying information on

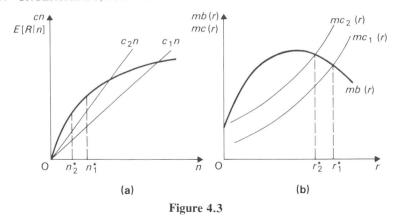

**Figure 4.3**

job opportunities, workers will be able to sample more firms than otherwise and to hold out for higher offers. Such intervention will be justified on efficiency grounds if information has public good characteristics, the costs of gathering information are smaller for the government, or workers are myopic. Third, more search will be carried out by workers living in urban areas because firms are less dispersed and transport networks better in urban areas, so search costs are lower. Fourth, since search costs are higher for unskilled than for skilled labour due to the greater efficiency in search of the latter, the unskilled will search less.

The effects of changes in the distribution of wages are rather more difficult to identify, since a distribution can change in any number of ways. However, suppose the whole distribution shifts to the right by a uniform amount, search costs remaining constant, then under our assumptions the searcher will calculate a new $n^*$ or $r^*$. If the distribution shifts in this way, then both will in fact increase. (This can be seen by working through the two strategies using the second column in Table 4.2 as before, but replacing the first column with the column of wages {125, 130, 135, 140, 145, 150, 155, 160, 165}. This gives a uniform shift in the distribution of +£5.) The effects of changes in the variance of the distribution upon $n^*$ or $r^*$ are more complex and little can be said in general. However, it can be shown that, under the Stigler rule, if the distribution of wage offers is normal, then

$$
\begin{aligned}
E[G \mid n] &= E[\max\{W_1, \ldots, W_n\} \mid n] - cn \\
&= 0.65 n^{0.37} \sigma_w + \bar{W} - cn
\end{aligned}
\tag{4.7}
$$

where $\bar{W}$ and $\sigma_w$ are the mean and standard deviation of the wage offer distribution. Equation (4.7) clearly shows that for this particular case an increase in the dispersion of the distribution increases the expected gain from each sample size, so that, *ceteris paribus*, $n^*$ will increase.

Our analysis of workers' job search has brought us a long way, but further progress requires that we relax some of its more restrictive assumptions. Most progress can be made if we employ the sequential decision rule. Perhaps the most serious omission from the model is an explicit treatment of time. Search uses up time and thus involves foregone earnings. The benefits accrue over time. Suppose, initially, that the searcher has an infinite lifespan in which case the expected return to search must include *all* future discounted weekly wages. Discounting has been discussed in Chapter 3, so let us here denote the single period discount factor, $1/(1 + i)$ by $b$. If a job is accepted paying a wage $W$, it has a discounted present value of

$$W + bW + b^2W + \cdots = W \sum_{t=0}^{\infty} b^t \approx \frac{W}{1 - b} \tag{4.8}$$

Hence we can redefine $V(r)$ as the expected *discounted* returns to search and rewrite equation (4.3), assuming each unit of search is equivalent to one period of time, as

$$V_t(r) = \frac{1}{(1 - b)} E[W \mid W \geqslant r] P[W \geqslant r]$$

$$+ bV_{t+1}(r)\{1 - P[W \geqslant r]\} - c \tag{4.9}$$

Equation (4.9) reads as follows: the expected net discounted return to search is equal to the present value of the accepted wage earned in each week forever, plus the expected discounted return to search next period if the current wage offer is unacceptable, minus the costs of search. Because an infinite horizon and constant cost and timeless search are assumed in the model, $V_t(r) = V_{t+1}(r) = V(r)$ so (4.9) can be solved for $r^*$ precisely as before, but now $r^*$ also depends on the discount term $b$. An increase in $b$, *ceteris paribus*, leads to an increase in $r^*$. The increase in $b$ represents a shift of intertemporal preference away from present earnings towards future earnings; a reduced impatience for earnings. The increase in $r^*$ means that the worker will search longer. Furthermore, for groups with a higher $b$, such as those who have undertaken more education, we would expect to find longer search duration.

What happens, however, if the worker's time horizon is finite? Fortunately the search model is quite robust to changes in assumptions. With an infinite time horizon $r^*$ is constant because delaying acceptance and continuing search imposes no costs due to a fore-shortened earnings stream. With a finite time horizon, $T$, workers will maintain a constant $r^*$ only if they have perfect recall of previously rejected offers. In this case, since all previous offers are available, and in particular the maximum of the previous offers, the worker is able to stop searching either by accepting a current offer or by accepting the previous maximum. However, if individuals have limited recall, the reservation wage falls with each unit of search because as time runs out the stream of expected benefits in the workers discounted present value calculation shortens:

$$V_t(r) > V_{t+1}(r) \quad \text{so} \quad r_t{}^* > r^*_{t+1}$$

We can predict therefore that, given limited recall amongst workers searching at any point in time, those who have searched the longest will have the lowest reservation wage. Similarly, workers with the shortest time horizons will be least choosy and search the least. This will be relevant to older workers and married women. If a worker has searched for so long that the value of his reservation wage has fallen to £$\overline{W}$, search will be terminated and the worker will remain in his present state.

The model above fails to distinguish the different circumstances in which the worker's decision to seek out a job is made. In reality the worker could be unemployed, he could be employed but considering whether to become unemployed to seek a new job, or he could be employed and intending to stay employed whilst he assesses the alternatives. The model so far is perfectly general. To allow for these different circumstances, as we shall have cause to do in Section II, requires only that we specify carefully the relevant costs of search to derive the reservation wage and the relevant alternative rewards £$\overline{W}$. If state assistance is conditional on search, search costs for an unemployed worker will consist of transport and material costs less state assistance. Costs for the continuously employed worker will arise from the opportunity cost of leisure foregone during search. Costs for those intending to enter unemployment will be foregone earnings less unemployment benefit received during search. The unemployed worker will begin to search if his reservation wage exceeds the value he derives from the leisure associated with unemployment. The currently employed worker has to decide both whether and how to search: he will search on the job if his reservation wage exceeds his current wage plus any job transfer costs; he will search via unemployment if his reservation wage for unemployed search (which will be different since both gains and costs are different) exceeds his current wage (job transfer costs appear relatively less important in this case). If both methods of search are worthwhile he chooses that which offers the greatest gain over his current wage. Search continues until either an acceptable offer is received or the reservation wage falls to the level of the value of leisure, for unemployed workers, or to the level of the current wage plus transfer costs, for employed workers.

Our analysis suggests therefore that state unemployment assistance can act as a subsidy to search. The higher is the benefit level the higher the reservation wage for unemployed searchers and therefore the more searchers there will be and the longer they will search.

Our model assumes that every time a job sampling is made a wage and a vacancy are simultaneously offered. This clearly is not the case for often workers are given attractive wage quotes but no jobs are available. One way of introducing this possibility formally into our analysis is to treat samplings that produce no vacancies as zero wage offers. Alternatively one could introduce the worker's expectation of finding a job opening as a determinant of the expected maximum wage. The fewer expected vacancies there are the lower $r^*$ and the shorter the search duration, whether or not search is successful.

Our model assumes that workers have only one means of gathering information. In fact all economic agents simultaneously use a variety of information channels to acquire, improve and confirm information. It is useful to categorise these sources as formal or informal. By and large formal sources tend to be more costly and more reliable than informal sources. Formal methods of search for workers include the use of government and private employment agencies, trade unions, advertisements in the press, the notices of firms, and so on. Informal methods include the recommendation of friends and relatives and visits to the firm. The method of search chosen will depend upon the nature of the information sought. Informal methods are likely to be much more productive than formal methods in eliciting experience characteristics.

We have assumed that marginal search costs are constant. However, costs may well fall initially because of economies of scale, although eventually they are likely to rise. Workers will search first in areas with low search costs, e.g. local industrial estates. If these prove unfruitful they will be driven to areas where search costs are higher.

Finally, the search theory presented above is rather characterless – all individuals are alike and jobs differ only in terms of the wage offer. This is unsatisfactory in at least three respects. Firstly, if workers form an entirely homogeneous group in terms of age, sex, market experience and so on, they will all set the same reservation wage. Consequently, firms with wage offers below that reservation wage will have unfilled vacancies. Under the assumption that firms revise wages according to the number of applications, such firms will raise their wages. The reservation wage will then increase because the benefits to search go up. Firms with wages below the new reservation wage will have to raise their wages. Eventually all firms must come to offer the same wage; as they would if there were no search costs. However, heterogeneous workers, facing different search costs, will set different reservation wages and this may be sufficient to ensure continued wage dispersion – even the lowest wage firms will be able to capture a share of the workforce. We can predict that in general the higher the search costs the less search takes place in any given market so the greater will be the dispersion around the value of the marginal revenue product.

Secondly, if jobs differ in characteristics other than wages but workers have limited information on these non-wage elements, then they must engage in job prospecting as well as job search. Can our model be respecified to include both search and prospecting? In one respect there is no problem about doing this. If we redefine the distribution to be over utilities, $f(U)$, rather than wages, $f(W)$, the worker becomes an expected utility maximiser and searches using a reservation utility level. The job characteristics entering the worker's utility function include hours, conditions, safety, incentive payments and so on. However, defining screening costs when jobs are heterogeneous is rather more problematic. In our simple model, information upon wages is obtained by direct application; a visit to the firm. Information on other readily observable job characteristics may also be acquired by search. Information on certain *experience* characteristics could be obtained indirectly through other workers, union sources and so on. Such prospecting could fit into our model. But wherever personal experience is required our approach will prove inadequate. We must think of search as just the first stage in seeking a job. A possible sequence of events might be as follows: a worker searches for an acceptable wage offer and certain job characteristics. When he takes up a job at the end of a period of search he does so not for ever, as before, but for just long enough to discover the previously unobservable benefits and costs attached to that particular job. Then, and only then, is the individual in a position to decide whether or not to take up the job permanently. If the non-pecuniary benefits are found to be inadequate, the worker may begin the search process again. In any labour market, therefore, there will be an element of mobility between jobs for those individuals prospecting as part of their optimal screening process. Since young people presumably have least knowledge about the quality aspects of jobs, we can expect that they will be disproportionately represented in the group of workers engated in so-called 'job shopping'. A further prediction is that, since both tastes across non-wage characteristics and prospecting costs vary across workers, a distribution of characteristics levels, characteristics mix, and wage/non-wage elements will persist across firms.

Thirdly, if searchers are identical, firms have no need to choose between applicants. Given the heterogeneity of the labour force, workers have an incentive to *signal* their suitability for the job to the employer and employers have an incentive to screen applicants. We turn to these issues in the next two sections.

## 4.4 Workers' signalling

Consider a market in which workers of the same technical skill differ in productive performance or quality. They differ in ingenuity, reliability, consistency, independence, patience and so on. Firms are aware of the heterogeneity and prefer higher quality, but do not know where in the distribution of qualities any worker is located. Each firm is again assumed to be a passive agent in workers' decision making, undertaking no systematic screening but simply declaring wages and offering vacancies, if they exist, to enquiring workers according to some arbitrary rule. Every worker with the appropriate skills who approaches a given firm has the same probability of being made an offer.

Consider now the position of a high quality worker in this market. Given the uncertainty under which we have assumed firms operate, she could well be overlooked in favour of a much inferior fellow applicant. This could be expensive because further search might generate a lower though still 'acceptable' offer. Consequently it might be in the interest of a high quality worker to identify herself to employers and thus increase her probability of recruitment even at some expense to herself. Such signalling will in principle be worthwhile up to the point where the marginal cost of her communications equals the marginal benefit in terms of a higher probability of recruitment.

As noted earlier, quality is an experience rather than an inspection characteristic. It is not itself observable or communicable during the job-seeking process. The worker must therefore identify a personal characteristic which is controllable, readily observable, communicable, and conveys information on quality to firms. Indices are certain personal characteristics such as age, sex and colour which do not meet all of these requirements. Personal characteristics such as education, personal presentation, punctuality do meet these requirements and are therefore referred to as *signals*. The best signals will be those that are consistently the most difficult for low quality people to acquire. Educational qualifications are the obvious candidate here because low quality workers are the least likely to be able to achieve the required standards, or alternatively are those who find it most expensive to achieve those standards. Higher quality people will accordingly devote more time and resources to acquiring qualifications than lower quality people simply because of education's value as a signal. It follows from this analysis that, firstly, employers will recognise and rely upon certain signals as they come to associate the performance of their workers with the related personal characteristics. If previously reliable signals ever become misleading, in that the expected productive potential does not materialise, firms will disregard them and high quality workers will have to find alternative signals.

Second, workers will prefer those signals to which firms attach most importance, that is signals most closely related to the qualities firms are looking for. In choosing between educational programmes workers will therefore decide not according to the educational content of the courses but according to how they test for such qualities; for example diligence, perseverance and consistency. The function of the education is then merely to provide the qualification; the firm can and will provide the worker with all the necessary productive skills once he is employed. Studying part time whilst employed will therefore effectively signal the possession of certain desirable qualities. Third, social activities may also serve a signalling function: leadership qualities are indicated by holding senior positions in social organisations; social skills by participation in sporting and other leisure activities, resourcefulness by the pursuit of an independent life style. Fourth, certain qualities firms value, such as obedience, passivity and conformity, may be in conflict with the traits valued and fostered by educational institutions. Fifth, educational establishments and not just individual courses will come to acquire a reputation among both workers and firms as good signallers, in that qualifications from these establishments are particularly strong indicators of desirable qualities so that graduates from these establishments will be preferred by firms. Workers' demand for places will rise and the signalling function becomes self-generating.

Access to signals depends on social position as well as the possession of certain abilities and qualities. Some workers will therefore find it easier to signal than others of equal ability. To the extent that there is unequal opportunity to invest in education, educational qualifications will be of less value as signals.

How much should be spent by workers upon signalling? Even if the costs of acquiring a particular signal are known, considerable uncertainty surrounds the benefits. But expectations can be formed. An additional year's education will be undertaken if the expected benefit exceeds the cost. In general therefore the worker will continue to acquire signals until the marginal cost of so doing equals the expected marginal benefit.

## 4.5 Employer Prospecting

Consider the activities of a single firm in a given labour market seeking to fill a vacancy. Let us assume, as in Section 4.4, that though labour in this market is all of the same technical skill there are significant differences in quality. Second, we assume, at least initially, that there is a single market wage for the skill in question so the profit-conscious firm has an incentive to recruit workers of the highest quality. Third, we propose that when the vacancy is announced the firm receives a large number of suitable applications of varying quality. The firm knows precisely the distribution of qualities, and thus of marginal revenue productivities, across the list of applicants, but does not know where in the distribution any particular applicant is located. Fourthly, we assume that if the firm calls a worker for interview, the worker's true quality is revealed, but that each interview imposes a fixed, lump-sum cost upon the firm. Finally, we assume that workers play a purely passive role, in the sense that they engage in no systematic screening or signalling. All firms with vacancies then face the same distribution of qualities.

It should be apparent that this model is the direct counterpart, for employer's prospecting, of the model for worker's search set out in Section 4.2 above. To maximise expected profit the firm first determines the reservation quality from the known distribution of qualities and the costs of interviewing. If the reservation quality offers the firm a return, net of wages, greater than the cost of leaving the vacancy open the firm will randomly select its first interviewee. Having ascertained the quality of that worker, if it equals or exceeds the reservation quality, the firm will hire that first interviewee. If the quality is lower than the reservation quality, the firm will continue prospecting. The firm continues random sampling and interviewing until it finds a worker with a quality at least as great as the reservation level.

Given the parallel with the worker's search model it is unnecessary to pursue the present model formally. There will of course be parallels in the predictions and extensions of the two models. Most important, the model predicts a negative relationship between prospecting costs and the amount of prospecting undertaken by firms. An increase in costs lowers the reservation quality and makes firms less particular in choosing a recruit. They interview fewer applicants, which in general implies a lower quality appointment. There are obvious ways in which firms can reduce unit prospecting costs. Interviewing in batches brings economies of scale, whilst at the same time reducing any problems arising from limited recall. However, unit costs may well rise after some point as the capacity of existing production management to handle prospecting duties is exceeded, so that specialised inputs or even outside agents have to be used. The relationship between prospecting costs and the amount of prospecting undertaken by the firm generates the following predictions. First, because unit costs are lower in large firms than in small firms due to specialisation and economies of scale in prospecting, large firms can be expected to prospect more than small firms. Second, the model predicts that firms will engage in more prospecting, *ceteris paribus*, amongst groups of workers who impose lower prospecting costs, for example amongst internal as opposed to external candidates. If for certain jobs conventional prospecting techniques are less effective at identifying quality in workers belonging to certain groups than in others, the costs of prospecting to acquire the same amount of information will be higher for those workers. The firm might thus prospect to fill certain jobs only amongst men and only amongst white native workers, which constitutes discrimination in the labour market. Third, the fact that the costs are likely to be higher for skilled workers than for unskilled workers would on its own lead us to expect that firms will prospect less for skilled labour. However, the greater variability of quality within the skilled category increases the benefits to search and thus generates the opposite prediction. Fourth, the model predicts that, if prospecting costs are sufficiently large, no prospecting will be undertaken and the post will remain unfilled. This will be more likely the smaller the costs of alternative adjustment mechanisms, such as holding stocks.

As with the worker's reservation wage, the firm's reservation quality will fall if we assume that each unit of prospecting is associated with a period of time, no recall is possible, and the firm considers each post it attempts to fill to have a finite life. Delaying hiring therefore reduces the value of the hire. The firm thus becomes less choosy the longer it takes to fill the post. In the last resort, if the reservation quality falls sufficiently, the firm will stop prospecting.

This particular outcome is more likely if we recognise that not every worker of the required skill could do the particular job the firm offers. A certain minimum quality might be required for technological reasons and the reservation quality cannot then fall below this level. This means that, having interviewed several applicants, the firm could have found no worker with the required standard despite the reservation quality having fallen to the minimum level. The vacancy must remain unfilled. The shorter the firm's time horizon, the shorter the life of the post, the faster the reservation quality will fall because the cost of leaving the post vacant at each stage is higher. Less prospecting will be undertaken and the greater is the likelihood that the post will not be filled. Similarly, for any given job life, the greater the output required the less prospecting is undertaken and the greater the likelihood that the post will not be filled.

We have assumed in the model that there is a single market wage for each skill. This implies that high quality labour everywhere receives the same rewards as low quality labour. It leaves the firm with no means by which it can persuade high quality labour to take up its offer in preference to those of other firms, or by which it can retain good people in its employment. Under competitive conditions, wage offers to high quality people will be bid up, particularly by those firms which value high quality labour most. If there are sufficient numbers of firms requiring labour of each quality, competition will eventually mean that wage offers will approach the marginal revenue product *at each quality level.* Hence, assuming each firm requires a particular quality as well as particular skills, each firm will be offering one of a range of wages for each skill that it employs and firms with relatively low prospecting costs will be able to afford high quality labour. This therefore explains in large part why in their search activities workers face a distribution of wages, not a single wage, and why certain firms will be high wage, high quality labour employers. However, given that workers do not have perfect information on where high quality, high wage firms are, and given that firms do not have perfect information on which workers are of high quality, there will also be a distribution of wages at each quality level.

Finally, not all offers need be accepted by workers once prospecting has been carried out. The firm must thus include in its expected benefit the probability of acceptance. This will depend upon the firm's knowledge of its own place in the net rewards hierarchy and of the availability of alternative openings. It follows that firms located in large urban and industrialised areas and firms recruiting in times of tight labour markets will have lower reservation qualities, undertake less prospecting, and generally make a lower quality recruitment.

Despite the above analysis, it is by no means obvious that a variant of the worker search model is an appropriate device through which to study firms' prospecting behaviour. The model embodies two limiting assumptions about employers' prospecting techniques that require special consideration; first that employers have only one method of acquiring information – interviews, and second that this method is perfectly accurate in revealing the quality of sampled workers. In view of the heterogeneous nature of quality these assumptions tax the credibility of the model. In fact, employers' methods of acquiring information are almost as numerous as the different dimensions of labour quality. Since quality is never an observable characteristic, prospecting must be carried out indirectly via intensive questionnaires, simulation exercises, medical reports, references from past employers and relevant third parties (teachers, unions, staff agencies, etc.) Such methods vary considerably in cost to the firm and also in reliability and completeness. In principle, these screening techniques come within the framework of our model. We can imagine firms employing some cost-effective package of different information-gathering techniques to screen each applicant. Even so, there are important quality characteristics which are difficult to isolate by such a package and effective screening will require a probationary period. This will be very accurate and complete in revealing quality, but relatively expensive because any production loss, and any supervision or assessment outlays, must be added to the cost of initial selection. It is possible therefore that the initial selection of a worker is merely the first step towards filling a vacancy. The final decision is not taken until the end of the probation period, when the firm either ratifies the candidate's appointment or dismisses him and begins prospecting again. Probationary periods serve the same purpose for prospecting employers as trial periods do for prospecting workers. As noted earlier, however, they cannot easily be fitted formally into the framework of screening models. The problem is that although the firm may calculate an optimum length for its probationary period, this must be accepted by job applicants who will independently set an optimal duration for their trial period. In other words, the period must be negotiated and contracts must lay down a specific duration before the initial hire. Each worker can then calculate the probability of a satisfactory performance in his probationary period, knowing his own aptitude and firms' screening mechanisms. He can calculate the probability of being offered the job permanently before he accepts any initial contract and thus can calculate the expected return to search before search begins. Similarly firms can calculate the expected return on prospecting across workers taking into account the probability that workers on probationary periods will come up to the required standards. Our simple search model might be extended to incorporate these interdependent calculations if the length of the probationary or trial period were exogenously given.

## 4.6   Advertising, signalling and credentialism

Contrary to our assumption that each firm gets a random sample of applicants, in reality the number and quality of applicants considered by any firm is partly determined by the firm's own activities. In particular, it is in the interest of employers, up to some point since costs are involved, not to leave applications to chance. Firms can influence workers' screening activities by advertising their position in the market, i.e. identifying themselves, recording the existence of a vacancy, notifying the wages paid, the skills and quality of labour required, the pecuniary and non-pecuniary rewards of the work, and so on. As with workers' information channels during search, we can characterise employers' advertising as formal or informal. Which of these is chosen depends upon the nature of the information to be transmitted. So we might anticipate, for example, more advertising in labour markets where workers and firms are geographically dispersed and where there is excess demand for labour. We would also expect more advertising, particularly of an informal kind, for skilled vacancies because non-pecuniary characteristics which are costly to communicate formally are relatively important. As well as trying to increase the number and quality of applicants, firms will provide job counselling at interviews, visits to the shop floor and introductions to unions and supervisors, in order to encourage workers to take up offers without trial periods.

Prospecting costs will be lower if the firm is able to identify certain personal characteristics in workers that convey accurate information about quality. Such characteristics may then serve workers as effective signals. However, it is possible that the firm chooses characteristics, for example age, race or sex, that are not associated with quality. Time should reveal to the firm its error. But until this happens certain groups of workers will be at a disadvantage in applying for jobs; uncertainty again generates discrimination in the labour market.

In principle firms, like workers, would like to communicate their unobservable qualities by means of appropriate signals. But if signals are to be recognised by workers, they must be highly correlated with the quality characteristic involved and more expensive for low quality firms than for high quality firms. In practice, these conditions are much harder to meet in the case of firms than in the case of workers. For example, consider a firm whose managers are skilful, resourceful yet fair, responsible and responsive to the labour force. How can firms signal this fact?

Expenditures upon signals such as donations to charities, to the local community, to local and national worthy causes, to sports and to recreation activities are all highly correlated with such qualities. But these signals are no more costly in pecuniary terms for low quality firms than for high quality firms. The money to pay for such signals might come from the rents to expertise for high quality firms, but merely, perhaps, from monopoly and/or monopsony rents for low quality firms. The result is that workers will come to distrust these signals after a few false moves. The argument here is really no different to the point made earlier on the limitations of education signals in a world where there is a maldistribution of resources between individuals.

We have now reached the point where we can imagine a labour market in which workers are systematically searching and prospecting across firms. Firms for their part will assist as well as respond to workers' screening. Simultaneously, firms will search and prospect across workers, who will respond by signalling their quality. The greater the efficiency of firms' screening and signalling the less the uncertainty for workers and the less workers' screening will be required. The more efficient workers' screening and signalling the less will be the uncertainty for firms and the less firms' screening will be required. In general, therefore, the benefits both sides derive from screening depend upon each side's cost of communicating information. Screening decisions will be interdependent in that the more screening outlays by one side, the more information available to the other.

Education signals sent by workers and accepted by firms as indicators of quality raise rather special issues for the analysis of the labour market, so let us consider such signals in more detail. Suppose, for the purposes of exposition, that education adds nothing to the productivity of workers but is highly correlated to quality and is more expensive or difficult to obtain for lower quality workers. It follows that education will be a valuable human capital investment for individual workers because as a good signal its possession will increase the workers' lifetime earnings by more than the capital outlay. All the usual investment analysis follows: workers will invest in signals as long as the net discounted present value is positive, there will be rates of return to the acquisition of signals, and so on. But note again that we have assumed that education does not raise the worker's productivity at all. Each worker goes on investing until the incremental private internal rate of return equals the interest rate, which will happen at different education levels for different workers according to their qualities. We would then, for illustration, expect the following labour market behaviour. First, firms will advertise jobs indicating both the skill classification and the educational requirements. Second, screening by firms will involve the collection, synthesis and verification of educational qualifications, at a much lower cost than conventional screening. Finally, firms will devote resources to familiarising themselves with the educational value of different education programmes, attempt to establish stable, continuous relationships with educational establishments and focus their advertising, signalling and screening upon those establishments.

So far, such predictions could be derived from the human capital model of Chapter 3, despite the very different premises upon which the two models are based. But the model of workers' educational signalling, or *credentialism* as it has become known, provides further predictions which clearly run counter to the human capital approach to education. Credentialism implies that the value of education programmes to the economy lies in their signalling properties, not in their educational content *per se*. Improving the efficiency of educational

provision means improving its signalling value, that is finding programmes that best fulfill the criteria for good signals. Credentialism
further implies that the value of educational programmes to the firm
is large because of their superior cost-effectiveness over other
information-revealing methods. These predictions, however, raise
two important questions. First, should the content of educational
programmes be determined merely by the requirements of firms,
especially when these may well be inconsistent with improving the
educational content of these programmes? Second, is the education
service, involving considerable sums of state money, the most cost-
effective way of eliciting information on quality from society's point
of view? Is it consistent with collective welfare criteria that the state
should, effectively, pay a large part of the costs of firms' information
gathering?

## 4.7 Models of screening and signalling: an evaluation

The models presented in this chapter to describe worker and firm
decision making under uncertainty may appear to be excessively
mechanistic and unrealistic. Our treatment of 'uncertainty' still
requires that economic agents possess a vast amount of information.
The agents have to know the distributions of wage offers and qualities, to know the effect of signals on hiring probabilities and applications, and so on, in order to calculate the expected returns to their
screening activities. In practice information is much more limited,
even though the means, both formal and informal, of acquiring
information are many and varied. A more plausible picture might be
of workers and firms learning during rather than prior to the process
of search. They then begin screening with an estimated distribution of
wages and qualities. Each unit of screening and the information
obtained leads to some revision of that distribution. Screening
behaviour will then in part depend upon the decision rule by which
agents revise their estimated distributions.
    The model is neoclassical in that it assumes vigorously rational
behaviour on the part of workers and firms, who optimise in the face
of significant search costs. Nobody thinks that economic agents do in
practice behave quite like this. But if in the course of their decision
making they respond to search costs, try to anticipate market
opportunities, and try to anticipate the gains from search even in a
casual way, then our model will have something to say about labour
market behaviour. Ultimately the significance of search costs and the
validity of the assumption of rationality can only be determined by
empirical analysis of the model.

# Further Reading

CHAPTER 4: UNCERTAINTY, SCREENING AND SIGNALLING

K. J. Arrow, 'Higher education as a filter', *Journal of Public Economics*, Vol. 2 (1973).

J. D. Hey, *Uncertainty in Microeconomics* (Oxford: Martin Robertson, 1979), Chapters 13 and 14.

S. A. Lippmann and J. J. McCall, 'The economics of job search: a survey' (in two parts), *Economic Inquiry*, Vol. 14 (June and September 1976).

A. Rees, 'Information networks in labor markets', *American Economic Review*, Vol. 56 (May 1966).

G. J. Stigler, 'Information in the labor market', *Journal of Political Economy*, Vol. 70 (October 1962).

# 5
# Non-competitive behaviour

In the preceding four chapters we have relaxed, one by one, a number of the assumptions of the basic labour market model. We have retained, however, the assumption of competitive behaviour everywhere. In this chapter we consider the nature and consequences of non-competitive behaviour. Due to the variety and complexity of such behaviour we are forced to include only a limited number of topics and, despite their theoretical and practical importance, to deal with them in only a cursory way. We consider four topics: firms' monopsony power in labour markets; trade unions' activities in the wage determination process; the operation of the labour market inside the firm; and the impact of extra-labour market non-competitive pressures upon labour market outcomes.

## 5.1 Monopsony

The basic model assumes that there are many firms operating independently in each labour market. Every firm has a labour demand curve equal to its marginal revenue product curve. Competition for labour between firms means that each of them faces a horizontal labour supply curve. Wages will be the same everywhere and equal to the marginal revenue product, MRP (= marginal product × marginal revenue), in each use and to the value of the marginal product, VMP (= marginal product × price), since product markets are assumed to be competitive. The distribution of labour between uses will reflect the pattern of MRP curves. This is shown in Figure 5.1. The aggregate demand curve for market $i$, $MRP^T$, is the horizontal sum of all the firms' demand curves. The demand curves for two firms are shown as $MRP^1$ and $MRP^2$. $SL$ is the labour supply curve to market $i$, the result of goods/leisure choices by individual workers.

Let us now, however, assume that there is only one firm in market $i$, with a marginal revenue product curve $MRP^T$. Since that firm faces the upward sloping supply curve for labour, $SL$, it has monopsony power: it can control the market wage and thus vary the number of applications it receives from workers. The labour supply curve to the monopsonist measures the average cost of labour to the firm (ACL), given that it pays one standard wage. There must therefore be a

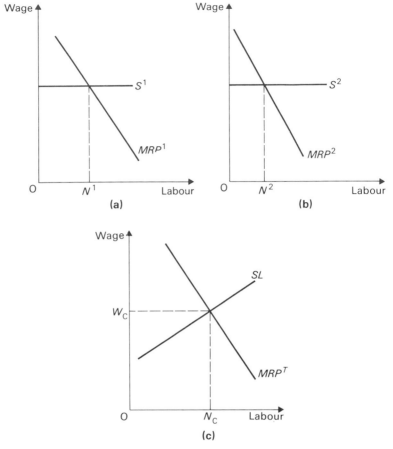

**Figure 5.1**

corresponding marginal cost curve, *MCL*. As shown in Figure 5.2(a) this lies above the *ACL* curve because the monopsonist has to pay a higher wage to attract each additional unit of labour. Employers recruit additional labour until the marginal cost equals the marginal benefit, which for the monopsonist means employing labour up to $N_M$, where $MRP^T = MCL$. To obtain this labour the firm pays a wage $W_M$. The demand for labour at any wage can thus only be derived once the supply curve is known, so there can therefore be no labour demand curve of the conventional kind under monopsony.

In practice, monopsony is unlikely to arise in the extreme form of a single buyer of labour, though local labour markets may sometimes come close to this if the transaction costs for workers of having a job

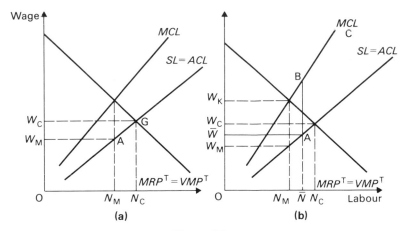

**Figure 5.2**

further away are prohibitive. Monopsony power is more likely to arise from collusion between firms or where information gaps and search costs effectively subdivide the labour market. Firms will also achieve monopsony power as a result of financing specific human capital investments which tie workers to their employment.

The monopsony model yields the following observations. First, if the government were to introduce a minimum wage, $\bar{W}$, above the going wage in this market, contrary to the usual predictions, wages and employment could rise. Under competitive conditions a minimum wage displaces labour because that labour has a marginal revenue product less than the minimum wage. Under monopsony conditions a minimum wage may not displace labour because the MRP is significantly everywhere above the going wage and thus perhaps above $\bar{W}$. In Figure 5.2(b) the minimum wage makes the marginal cost curve of labour $\bar{W}$ABC. Following profit-maximising rules the firm optimises at the higher employment level $\bar{N}$ and at the wage $\bar{W}$. Only if the minimum wage were set above $W_K$ would the level of employment fall.

Second, the existence of monopsony can have significant implications for the efficient allocation of resources and thus for welfare. The level of employment under monopsony, $N_M$, is lower than that under equivalent competitive conditions, which would be $N_C$ in Figure 5.2(a). The monopsony level of output will thus be lower than the competitive level which indicates a consumer welfare loss. This is reflected in the fact that at $N_M$ the value consumers place upon additional units of output from additional units of labour exceeds the costs of employing that labour.

Monopsony involves the exploitation of labour in the sense that the wage, $W_M$, is less than the marginal revenue product, i.e. less than the value at the margin that the firm receives from workers' output. If the employer has the power to discriminate across additional units of labour beyond $N_M$, i.e. pay them according to their transfer earnings or supply prices, it will pay the monopsonist to expand the input of labour to $N_C$, the competitive level. The monopsonist then extracts an additional producer surplus $W_C W_M AG$ in Figure 5.2(a). Put another way, workers can induce the monopsonist to expand employment to the competitive level if they allow it to extract their economic rent.

Where the monopsonist is also a monopolist in product markets the welfare implications are stronger. The firm then has a product price greater than its marginal revenue and therefore a MRP curve below its VMP curve. In Figure 5.3 the firm equates $MCL$ and $MRP^T$ at employment $N_{MM}$, and pays the wage $W_{MM}$, according to the supply curve $SL$. The figure shows that $N_{MM} < N_M$ and $W_{MM} < W_M$. Consumers suffer a welfare loss associated with the restriction of output that reduces employment from $N_C$ to $N_{MM}$, a restriction which is larger than if the firm had only monopoly power. The level of exploitation is higher than in the previous monopsony case.

A further welfare loss may arise from monopsony because the transfer of labour to other markets may either reduce wages elsewhere or produce unemployment. The distributional effects of monopsony may be particularly important if the monopsony power is greater for certain groups of workers than for others. Those groups with low elasticities of labour supply will suffer a relative disadvantage in terms of wages, employment and unemployment. Monopsony is therefore likely to figure strongly in the analysis of discrimination.

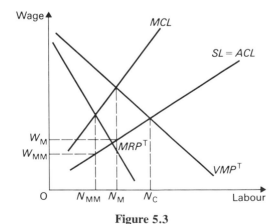

**Figure 5.3**

In theory, therefore, both labour market outcomes and the efficiency with which markets operate are affected significantly by the introduction of monopsony powers into the basic model. The prevalence of monopsony in actual labour markets is thus an important empirical issue. The monopsonist's ability to pay a wage below $W_C$ arises because the firm's labour supply curve is upward sloping. Trade unions could, by setting a single wage demand, re-establish the perfectly elastic supply curve of the competitive model. Presumably, if raising employment is one objective of unions, the union wage will be set closer to $W_C$ than to $W_M$. Trade unions might, therefore, be seen as countervailing power, establishing higher welfare for both consumers and workers by mitigating firms' monopsony powers. However, in practice the trade unions' role in the wage determination process is much more positive than this and it is to an analysis of this role that we now turn.

## 5.2 Trade union activities

In the basic model of the labour market, firms in any market collectively face an upward sloping supply curve of labour but individually face identical horizontal supply curves, as curves $S^1$ and $S^2$ in Figure 5.1(a) and (b). Such an analysis is clearly limited. Let us therefore assume that a trade union is formed amongst workers in a market to monopolise the supply of labour to all firms operating therein. The union is concerned to increase the welfare of its members, which varies with the level of wages $(W)$ and the level of employment $(N)$. The union's utility function is thus

$$U = U(W,N), \qquad U_W > 0, U_N > 0 \qquad (5.1)$$

which can be represented by an indifference map, as in Figure 5.4(b).

Let us assume that the firm plays a passive role in its dealings with the union; it accepts the supply of labour emerging from union deliberations, and maximises profits subject to that additional constraint. We assume furthermore that the union accepts that the demand for labour will always be given by the market's aggregate downward sloping marginal revenue product curve, $MRP^T$ in Figure 5.4(b). This curve is the same as the VMP curve since to begin with we assume competitive product markets. The union maximises equation (5.1) subject to this constraint at the tangency point M in Figure 5.4(b). In negotiations with each firm the union states that the wage will be $W_u$. Firm $j$ responds by stating that the level of employment will be $N^j$. Total employment across all firms is then $N_u$. All firms

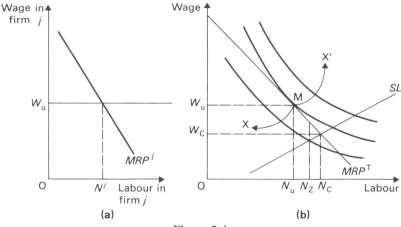

**Figure 5.4**

make normal profits. Wages will be generally higher and employment lower than under competitive supply conditions (i.e. $W_u > W_C$ and $N_u < N_C$).

It is implicit in our analysis so far that the wage, $W$, is the money wage. If the union optimises with respect to the real wage or, more realistically, the expected real wage, then in Figure 5.4(b) there will be a different indifference curve map for every value of expected prices, $P^e$. The higher is $P^e$ in general the higher up the $MRP^T$ curve will be the union's optimum $(W, N)$ combination. Higher prices will also perhaps shift the $MRP^T$ curve upwards.

Several important observations follow from this very simple trade union model. First, the precise outcome for wages and employment depends upon the form of the union's utility function, in particular the trade-off (or marginal rate of substitution) between wages and employment. In practice this will no doubt emerge from political processes within the union and will therefore vary across unions according to the personalities of the union leadership and the composition of the membership. The trade-off will also vary through time. This could arise because, as the MRP curve moves upwards through the utility map, the shapes of the indifference curves alter. Alternatively it is possible that the utility function itself changes through time. For example it could be that once any wage is reached the utility function assumes an asymmetry above and below that wage. If therefore a cyclical recession shifts the $MRP^T$ curve to the left, the union prefers to take this increasingly as a fall in employment. If, on the other hand, the $MRP^T$ curve shifts temporarily to the right, the union prefers to take this increasingly as a rise in wages. The locus of tangency points would therefore resemble XX' in Figure

5.4(b). If the union prefers to take more of each business expansion as additional wages than it takes of each contraction as reduced wages, through time the level of wages will rise and that of employment will fall.

Second, the union must control labour supply effectively if it is to maximise utility. In practice, such control will take many forms since labour supply has many dimensions. The union must control the quantity and distribution of overtime, using quotas and rotas where necessary. Job content, the speed of machinery, normal output expectations must all be supervised within a precise effort contract. Training must be regulated. But of course the main control variable will be the employment level. The optimal level $N_u$ can be achieved by closed shops and union vetting of potential entrants. Unions will try to influence the firm's selection and recruitment procedures and particularly the rules governing minimum entry qualifications. Labour markets where educational qualifications are relevant provide an obvious example of this practice. Indeed professional workers' unions have a genuine advantage over other unions, particularly where, as is sometimes the case, they are a strong force within the agencies providing the qualifications. The more effective the union's control of supply, the greater the incentive to use its monopoly position. An ineffective control of supply could in principle give workers only marginally better wages than the competitive outcome, as for example if labour supply were to be $N_z$ in Figure 5.4(b), but might impose significant organisational costs.

Third, any restriction upon labour supply displaces union members. The union's utility function will presumably include some allowance for the losses imposed upon those workers forced to leave the market, and indeed the losses to the union (in terms of workers and funds) as well. The losses to displaced labour will depend upon other markets' ability to absorb them and the wage adjustment required to do so. Wage increases achieved by the union will induce a queue for membership (and entry). This queue must also be controlled, perhaps by setting entry qualifications which, by raising the cost, reduce the net gain from entry to market $i$.

Fourth, though in the long run firms are no worse off as a result of union activities, consumers of course are. The increase in wages raises the price of all products using unionised labour, even after all profitable input substitution has taken place. There will therefore be a loss of consumer surplus. Consider a world of only two products, product 1 uses only labour from market $i$, product 2 initially uses only labour from market $k$. The wage is assumed to be the same in each market under competitive conditions $(W_0)$ and in Figure 5.5 the labour demand curves are assumed to be parallel. Following unionisation of market $i$, the wage there rises to $W_1^i$. $\Delta N$ labour transfers to product

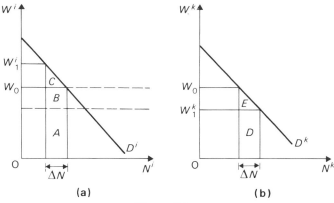

**Figure 5.5**

2. The price of labour in $k$ falls to $W_1^k$. It can be seen that the welfare loss for consumers of product 1 is given by the area $A + B + C$, the area under the labour demand curve. The gain to consumers from purchasing extra units of good 2 is $D + E$. Since by assumption $A = D$ and $C = E$, the net loss is the area $B$; the consumer welfare loss as measured in the labour market. This loss will be the greater, the less feasible it is for workers from $i$ to switch to producing good 2.

Firms will not lose by the union's control of supply in the long run. But some might do so in the short run. Market output must contract and, depending upon cost conditions across firms, this may involve a reduction in the number of firms as their profits fall permanently below the normal level.

Fifth, the union will be able to achieve a larger wage increase for any given reduction in employment the more inelastic the demand for union labour $i$. That elasticity in turn depends upon the four Marshallian conditions. Thus the union will be able to reach a higher indifference curve: the lower the elasticity of substitution in production between inputs; the lower the elasticity of demand for the products produced using labour $i$; the smaller the expenditures on $i$ in the total costs of firms using labour $i$; and the less elastic the supply of other inputs to firms where labour $i$ is used. The more difficult it is to substitute inputs the smaller will be the input substitution effect away from labour $i$ and thus the smaller the fall in $N^i$ as wages rise. The less important labour $i$ is in total costs the smaller will be the increase in costs, the smaller the scale effect decreasing the demand for labour $i$ and thus the smaller the fall in $N^i$ as the wage increases. The less responsive product demands are to price increases, the less the consequent reduction in demand as firms pass on a wage increase. The greater the input price increases as all firms attempts to replace labour $i$ by other inputs, the less the reduction in demand for labour $i$.

It will, of course, be in the interests of the union in the longer term to *shift* the demand curve for labour in its favour. So, the union will favour import restrictions, tax changes and any other measure which reduces the elasticity of product and labour demand. The union will favour demarcation lines and resist technical change to reduce substitutability. It will arrange with other unions to restrict the supply of substitute labour to areas where labour $i$ is important and also to place, through them, controls upon material inputs. Small unions in capital-intensive industries will seek to maintain their distinct, independent smallness.

Sixth, if the buyer of labour $i$ is a monopsonist, the union could act as countervailing power to establish the competitive solution as indicated in the previous section. But, even given that the firm accedes to the union's supply decision, this would be a special case. The final outcome of our model depends upon the form of the union's utility function. With the indifference map I in Figure 5.6 the outcome is indeed the competitive one, but with map II the wage is set at $W_u$. Note that, as with the competitive solution, the wage here equals $MRP^T$, so there is no exploitation. It is the union which determines the extent of the misallocation of resources, and reaps the benefits therefrom. It is possible of course that the union prefers a *higher* employment level than the competitive outcome. In this case it must supervise the additional supply above $N_C$.

Seventh, if any of the firms employing labour $i$ is a monopolist in product markets, then the restrictive output and employment effects associated with monopoly are compounded by the introduction of a union. A monopolist maximises profits by equating the marginal cost of labour to its MRP. In so doing it will restrict inputs. Since the

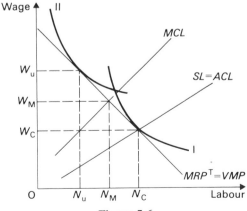

**Figure 5.6**

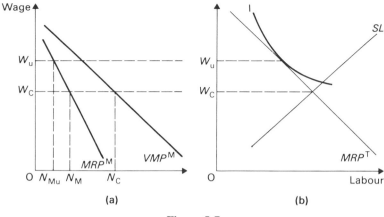

(a)                          (b)

**Figure 5.7**

union itself maximises subject to the $MRP^T$ curve, this will lead to a further restriction. In Figure 5.7 employment for a competitive firm is $N_C$ at wage $W_C$. The effect of monopoly power is to restrict employment to $N_M$ at wage $W_C$. The firm's demand curve for labour is $MRP^M$. The demand for labour for the market is $MRP^T$. Union activities will, given indifference map I, raise market wages to $W_u$ and reduce employment to $N_{Mu}$ in the monopoly firm. The restriction of output and the loss of consumer welfare are thus additive.

The above analysis assumes that the whole of the $i$th market becomes unionised. If only a part of the market becomes unionised a wage differential will emerge between identical units of labour. Our analysis is relevant if we redefine market $i$ as the unionised sector of some wider labour market. The difference in wages between unionised and non-unionised firms and the welfare loss will depend upon the elasticity of demand for labour and, since labour in $i$ is identical to labour outside $i$, upon the union's ability to control entry to the unionised sector.

The analysis also assumes that the union maximises utility subject to the market labour demand curve $MRP^T$, and thus identifies a single optimal wage across all firms in the market. But suppose that the market embraces a number of firms (perhaps in different industries) each with a different product demand elasticity and that the union can effectively divide the market. It could then discriminate across firms, and maximise utility in each firm separately. If it chose to do this the wage/employment solution would differ across firms according to the position of each firm's MRP curve in the union's indifference map. This would pose the union a difficult dilemma: if there are differences in wages for identical labour within the same union, internal political repercussions are likely to follow. Alternatively, if it maximises utility in the market as a whole, and sets a single wage, it restricts the utility gains of some of its members.

The simple union model outlined above has obvious limitations. The union is treated as a cohesive entity maximising a well defined utility function whose only two arguments are economic variables. This contrasts sharply with the institutionalist view of the union as an amorphous entity operating in a political environment. Furthermore, even viewed on its own terms, the model involves four assumptions which are hard to reconcile with working labour markets. First, both sides have perfect information. Second, each side accepts the other's maximising behaviour as an exogenously given constraint upon its actions. Third, the model does not develop the implications of firms having monopsony power. Fourth, the simple model ignores the ability of each side to impose costs upon the other to achieve its objectives. Let us consider these in turn.

First, the union is assumed to have perfect information about the MRP curves of all firms in the market. In practice this is very unlikely to be the case. The result is that the union may determine its optimal wage according to a false view of its market constraints. Consequently the labour required by firms at the union wage will not be that anticipated by the union. Even if the union perceives market opportunities correctly, the firm might not. This would again result in the union anticipating employment incorrectly. Since such an outcome cannot arise in the simple model, the model offers no indication of how it is resolved. The implications are that any union model should concentrate upon the mechanisms by which the two agents acquire information, should set up any maximising procedures in expected not exact terms, and should identify the decision rules which agents follow under conditions of uncertainty.

Second, in a world of imperfect information, each side will try to influence the other's perceptions of market opportunities. In particular firms will not be passive observers when unions set their wage target. Since the union's decision could be based, in the firm's opinion, upon an over-optimistic view of market potential, the firm will try to improve the union's calculations of the MRP curve. Moreover, if the firm can induce the union to believe that the MRP curve is $MRP^2$ in Figure 5.8 rather than the true curve $MRP^1$, the union will opt for the wage/employment combination that gives the firm the surplus $XYZW_2$. Simultaneously the union, aware perhaps of the conservative nature of the management, will attempt to swing the firms perceived MRP curve to the right. There are clear limits to what either side can achieve of course. To be credible their arguments must be consistent with the available data. But negotiations will nevertheless inevitably involve bargaining, which may take the form of

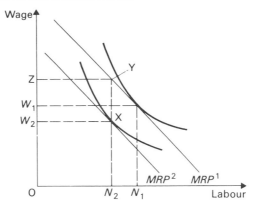

**Figure 5.8**

exchanges of genuine information, debate, misrepresentation, the introduction of irrelevant facts and arguments, feigned ignorance and so on. Each side will no doubt seek to persuade the other as much by the vehemence as by the cogency of its arguments. A more realistic union model would thus embody a statement of how and how far the two agents' perceptions of market opportunities are influenced by bargaining behaviour. Third, our simple model assumes that the union faces many firms employing its members. No firm can influence the market outcome, which becomes the union's prerogative. If the union faces a monopsonistic firm in a bilateral monopoly relationship, however, the firm has countervailing power. Thus according to Figure 5.6 when the union enters negotiations and states that the wage will be $W_u$ the firm responds by stating that it will be $W_M$. The model is indeterminate. Since firms often have some degree of monopsony power, a union model should specify how they use this power, and how the conflict with the union is resolved.

Fourth, in working labour markets each side possesses, in the form of industrial action, the means to impose significant costs upon the other for disagreeing. Such action takes many different forms, the strike being the most obvious, and can be precipitated by either side. However, since industrial action invariably imposes costs upon the instigator, any decision on whether to use it must weigh up benefits and costs. *Ceteris paribus*, the greater costs any action imposes upon the other side the higher the benefits to the decision maker. In a totally rational world of perfect information each side would know precisely the pattern of costs and benefits to themselves and to the other side so that the principal sufferer would concede immediately in order to avoid the costs of a struggle. The wage would be set at $W_u$ or

$W_M$ depending upon who concedes. In a world where information is imperfect, each side will threaten industrial action. Some of these threats will be real, some bluff, some counterbluff. A union model should therefore analyse wage determination and industrial action simultaneously and embody both mechanisms by which agents can evaluate the costs of industrial action and decision rules by which they then proceed.

To extend our simple union model to incorporate simultaneously uncertainty, bargaining behaviour, monopsony and industrial action would be a daunting task and economists have certainly been slow to take up the challenge. It could be argued that the task is impossible with the tools of analysis available to economists. Bargaining compounds the uncertainty that agents work under. Rationality gives way to obstructionism. The basic social conflicts of interest inherent in the work relationship produce highly emotive negotiations in which both sides aim to exploit and see themselves as exploited. Irrationality actually becomes a negotiating weapon. Breakdowns are frequent, acrimonious and unpredictable. The implication is that the wage determination process can be modelled, if at all, only in very general terms, concentrating upon institutional procedures and precedent, and by research within specific circumstances. However, in the rest of this section we do attempt to extend the simple union model. Whether this is ultimately worthwhile depends upon whether the additional predictions are supported in empirical tests.

Consider the following model. We assume, first, that the union deals with single firms in a series of bilateral monopsony relationships. There are three distinct agents to each relationship – management, unions and workers – but only the first two are actively involved in negotiations. The utility function of the union differs from that of workers, in that it includes the status of the union as an organisation and the political interests of union leaders. Second, the model incorporates a workers' wage decay function. At the start of negotiations, the union establishes the minimum wage increase $\Delta W^A$ acceptable to its members, $\Delta W_0^A$. If this is not forthcoming negotiators are instructed to terminate negotiations and industrial action will begin. But once that action begins the minimum acceptable wage increase $\Delta W^A$ falls with the duration of the action ($s$), so

$$\Delta W^A = \chi(s) \qquad (5.2)$$

(Fig. 5.9). $\Delta W^A$ declines because the longer the action lasts the more costly it becomes for workers. Savings are depleted and the pressure of regular fixed expenditure commitments, such as hire purchase, rises. Third, we assume that the union reveals the form of the wage decay function to management during negotiations. Union officials are con-

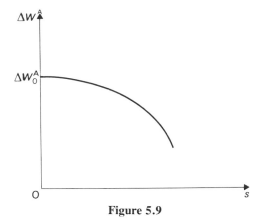

**Figure 5.9**

cerned about the impact of disagreements upon the union and their own status. It therefore makes the information available to the firm to rule out any possibility that the firm might miscalculate the workers' mood. If the workers stand by a claim in excess of the firm's best offer, union leaders will prefer a strike to concession since they are then seen to stick by their membership.

Under these assumptions management knows precisely the change in costs it will incur if it terminates the action at each duration. These costs are made up of an addition to the wages bill and the expenses of the completed industrial action. The longer the firm holds back its offer the lower the wage costs but the higher the costs of the industrial action. The profit-maximising firm calculates its optimal duration for the action (which could be zero) as that for which a marginal increase in duration adds as much to the costs of industrial action as it reduces wage costs. Exactly how much to offer and when to offer it are thus simultaneously determined *during* negotiations.

The firm minimises the change in costs, $\Delta C$:

$$\Delta C = (N\Delta W + sCS) \tag{5.3}$$

where $N$ is the labour force and $CS$ industrial action costs per period. Given that the firm's offer will always be equal to $\Delta W^A$ and given equation (5.2) we have

$$\Delta C = (N\chi(s) + sCS) \tag{5.4}$$

The firm calculates the value of $s^*$ by minimising (5.4) and uses (5.2) to derive $\Delta W^{A^*}$. If the wage change has repercussions for prices and therefore labour demand and/or the unit costs of industrial action rise with the duration, (5.4) can be further solved out to introduce

$$N = f(\Delta W^A) \quad \text{and} \quad CS = g(s) \tag{5.5}$$

The above model is limited in that it assumes rather peculiar behaviour for trade unions. This effectively removes all uncertainty from the model, makes workers entirely passive agents in wage setting and obviates the need for bargaining behaviour. A strike is absolutely inevitable if the claim $\Delta W_0^A$ is not met. Since workers are outside the negotiation process, there is no possibility that a wage increase less than $\Delta W_0^A$ could be agreed to by negotiation (say in the light of the costs of industrial action) nor that claims and offers will subsequently be revised.

The model is, however, valuable in four respects. First, by introducing the wage decay function the model incorporates industrial action directly in the wage determination process. It can be shown that the flatter is the decay function in Figure 5.9 the larger is $\Delta W^{A*}$ and the less likely industrial action. Second, the model recognises that unions are political institutions wherein union leaders pursue personal and organisational objectives. It also recognises that union leaders, given their access to information, may well see the logic of the firm's case but nevertheless pursue industrial action vigorously both to preserve internal unity and in order to force the membership to come to terms with market opportunities. Third, the model recognises the importance of negotiations as the means by which information is exchanged between the two agents. Fourth, the model recognises the monopsony position of the employer who does not accede to the union's labour supply decision despite collective action.

However, in view of its limitations consider the following further extension of the basic model. First, we make no distinction between union and workers in the bilateral monopoly relationship. The union is aware that its actions have consequences for employment. Therefore during negotiations it formulates its perceived MRP curve for the firm, taking into account any monopoly power the firm has. It optimises subject to a *perceived* wage elasticity of demand for labour which also takes into account its experience of how the firm has in the past used its monopsony power and the extent to which general monetary demand is expanding (since this would offset some of the price repercussions of its claim). Thus

$$\Delta N = N^u(\Delta W) \tag{5.6}$$

Given the collective utility function

$$U = U(W, N) \tag{5.1}$$

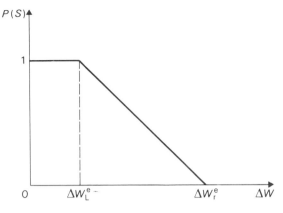

**Figure 5.10**

the union's utility-maximising claim, solving equations (5.6) and (5.1), is $\Delta W_u$. It recognises, however, that any increase which is less than $\Delta W_r$ will cause internal problems and generate pressures for industrial action. The further the wage increase is below $\Delta W_r$ the greater the likelihood of internal dissent and therefore the more likely it is that the union will have to initiate collective action. Second, we assume that management estimates the probability that workers will strike, $P(S)$, for each wage offer it might make. In Figure 5.10 management *expects* that, if it offers any wage increase below $\Delta W_L^e$, $P(S)$ is unity. Between $\Delta W_L^e$ and $\Delta W_r^e$, $P(S)$ is less than unity and is lower the higher the offer:

$$P(S) = \phi^e(\Delta W) \tag{5.7}$$

Equation (5.7) embodies the management's best estimate of both $\Delta W_r$ and the workers' likely reaction to a wage below $\Delta W_r$. Third, we assume that if industrial action takes place the costs thereof induce unions to reduce their minimum acceptable wage increase. Management is assumed to formulate expectations as to the nature of the workers' wage decay function:

$$\Delta W = H^e(s) \quad \text{or} \quad s = \lambda^e(\Delta W) \tag{5.8}$$

Equation (5.8) thus indicates the offer which the firm expects will terminate any industrial action. Fourth, if industrial action takes place, the union is well aware that the firm, having made a final offer of $\Delta W_1$ in negotiations, will then be calculating the profit-maximising wage offer to end the action. Knowing the basis of this calculation,

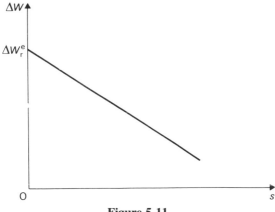

**Figure 5.11**

the union anticipates the revised wage offer $\Delta W_0$ for each duration of the action as

$$\Delta W_0 = J^u(s) \quad \text{or} \quad s = \Omega^u(\Delta W_0) \tag{5.9}$$

This function does not necessarily rise continuously above $\Delta W_1$. At some $s$ the offer could fall below $\Delta W_1$. To the union this function records the expected minimum duration necessary if any claim it makes is to be accepted by the firm.

On the above assumptions the wage determination process can be modelled through five steps:

*Step* 1    The union formulates the wage claim $\Delta W_u$. In fact it makes a claim considerably higher than this because it recognises that negotiations will involve compromise and it requires something to give away. Also it can only estimate the elasticity of demand for labour and a high claim will cover it, to some extent, for overestimation.

*Step* 2    Having arrived at an estimate of $\Delta W_r^e$ and the wage decay function (5.8), the firm calculates its optimum strategy. If industrial action were to take place, the additional costs it would face, $\Delta C$, would be given by

$$\Delta C = N\Delta W_2 d + s_2 \pi V \tag{5.10}$$

where the first element is the increased wage bill and the second is the costs of the industrial action. $N$ is the size of the labour force; $\Delta W_2$ is the wage change that terminates the industrial action and $d$ is $\{1 + [1/(1 + r)]\}^{-1}$, an approximation to the present value of an infinite stream of a single monetary unit discounted at the rate $r$.

$s_2$ is the completed duration of the action; $\pi$ is profits per unit of sales; $V$ is the value of all sales lost per period as a result of the industrial action. $V$ thus depends, for example, upon the nature of the action and the ability to operate from stocks. Given (5.8) we can rewrite (5.10) as

$$\Delta C = N\Delta W_2 d + \lambda^c(\Delta W_2)\pi V \qquad (5.11)$$

For a constant labour force the firm can calculate $\Delta W_2$ to minimise equation (5.11). This gives $\Delta W_2^*$ and, from (5.8), $s_2^*$. The firm thus decides in advance that *if* a strike occurs it will offer $\Delta W_2^*$ after $s_2^*$ periods.

*Step* 3   The firm decides upon its final negotiation wage offer, $\Delta W_1$. For any such offer there are two possible outcomes: agreement or industrial action. The firm thus formulates an expected cost function, $E[\Delta C]$ for $\Delta W_1$, as

$$E[\Delta C] = [1 - P(S)] \text{ (cost of agreement) } +$$
$$P(S)(\text{cost of industrial action}) \qquad (5.12)$$

which from (5.7) and (5.10) becomes

$$E[\Delta C] = [1 - \phi^c(\Delta W_1)][N\Delta W_1 d] +$$
$$\phi^c(\Delta W_1)[N\Delta W_2 d + s_2\pi V] \qquad (5.13)$$

and given that the firm has calculated $\Delta W_2^*$ from (5.11),

$$E[\Delta C] = [1 - \phi^c(\Delta W_1)][N\Delta W_1 d] +$$
$$\phi^c(\Delta W_1[N\Delta W_2^* d + \lambda^c(\Delta W_2^*)\pi V] \qquad (5.14)$$

The firm maximises profits by choosing that value for $\Delta W_1$ which minimises (5.14). The firm makes a final offer of $\Delta W_1^*$ to end negotiations.

*Step* 4   Faced by the offer $\Delta W_1^*$ the union's expectations about how this offer will be revised during the industrial action come from (5.9). The union will proceed with industrial action if its expected benefits, $\Delta U^{**}$, exceed those of accepting $\Delta W_1^*$, $\Delta U^*$. $\Delta U^*$ can be written from (5.1) and (5.6) as

$$\Delta U^* = U(\Delta W_1^*, \Delta N^u(\Delta W_1^*)) \qquad (5.15)$$

If the union calls a strike the expected gain, $G$, is

$$G = \Delta W_0 N d - s_2 CS \qquad (5.16)$$

where $CS$ are the costs per period to the workers of industrial action. This becomes, through (5.9),

$$G = \Delta W_0 Nd - \Omega^u(\Delta W_0)CS \qquad (5.17)$$

The union therefore maximises its gain from industrial action by finding $\Delta W_0$ to maximise (5.17) – say $\Delta W_0^{**}$. If industrial action took place the union would thus offer $\Delta W_0^{**}$ after $s_2^{**}$ periods (from eqn 5.9) which it expects will be accepted. The union will reject the offer $\Delta W_1^*$ if the increase in utility expected from a settlement at $\Delta W_2^{**}$ exceeds $\Delta U^*$, i.e. if

$$\Delta U^{**} = U[(\Delta W_0^{**} - s_2^{**}CS), N^u(\Delta W_0^{**})] > \Delta U^* \quad (5.18)$$

*Step 5*  The employer's offer $\Delta W_1^*$ is either accepted or rejected. If it is rejected industrial action begins. Assuming no change in their expectations the action will continue until $s_2^*$ or $s_2^{**}$ (whichever is sooner) when either the firm or the union will put forward their settlement offer $\Delta W_2^*$ or $\Delta W_0^{**}$. If the union has been reasonably accurate in predicting the firm's decision function (5.9) and the firm has come close to assessing accurately both $\Delta W_r$ and the workers' decay function, then $\Delta W_2^*$ and $\Delta W_0^{**}$ will be close together and so will $s_2^*$ and $s_2^{**}$, so that the chance of a settlement is high. If the firm revises its expectations during the industrial action so that $\Delta W_2^*$ rises and $s_2^*$ falls, then clearly the chances of a settlement increase. The union could get a better offer sooner than it had anticipated. Continual revision will no doubt take place throughout any action. Given that the information underlying these revisions is valid the chances of a settlement increase. The model predicts that the wage settlement (approximately $\Delta W_2^*$ if industrial action takes place, $\Delta W_1^*$ if it doesn't) will be higher *inter alia* the higher $\Delta W_r^e$, the higher the rate of discount $r$ the firm uses, the higher the profit on sales $\pi$ and the flatter is the wage decay function $\lambda^e$.

The above model prompts the following general observations. First, the role of negotiations as a medium through which both sides obtain information and thus reduce the uncertainty inherent in their relationship is crucial. The better the information, the greater will be the common ground, and the more likely a smooth adjustment, with or without industrial action, to a final settlement. In practice information gathering is likely to be highly effective. Negotiators on both sides are highly skilled at eliciting the information they require. Acquiring reliable information often involves revealing information. Second, the model plays down the importance of bargaining behaviour in determining wages. This could be justified as follows. Bargaining certainly takes place but the two sides have a common interest in settling negotiations reasonably amicably. There has to be a settlement. Theirs is a continuous relationship. To sour it by excessive pressure could jeopardise the future returns to their relationship. Gains and losses are soon evident and introduce pressures into later negotiations. Ultimately neither side can afford to risk damaging the position of the other by deliberate misrepresentation of their circumstances. Firms may contract; good workers may leave. Bargaining serves as an initial protective device, a display of activity for outsiders to the negotiations and a playing out of roles. In practice each side is inevitably only too familiar with the style of the other, since negotiations involve long-term personal relationships between certain individuals.

Third, the model embodies the idea of industrial action as one means by which both sides become reconciled to the final settlement, whether or not any action actually takes place. The action itself may not be acrimonious. It becomes an institutionalised adjustment mechanism, negotiators on both sides recognising it as a means of bringing round their respective clienteles. If the information exchanges are highly effective and the cost of industrial action is significant for both sides, most negotiations will reach agreement without any industrial action proving necessary.

Fourth, the model puts great emphasis upon the monopsony power and maximising behaviour of the firm. In contrast to the simple union model the union here, though assumed to follow maximising procedures, merely responds to the firm's offer of $\Delta W_1^*$. The various initial claims and $\Delta W_r$ have only a secondary role in the process. As a description of bilateral monopoly the model is asymmetrical. The firm evaluates the *exogenously* given workers' wage decay function. The union predicts the firm's wage responses during industrial action, which are *endogenously* determined, in part by the workers' wage decay function.

Fifth, the model has no unique solution. It assumes that settlements will be reached if the negotiating positions of the two sides are brought close together. The closer they are, implicitly, the more acceptable are compromise solutions. Given that negotiations can be emotional, a compromise can sometimes be long in coming.

Finally, the union is assumed to determine its optimum wage increase $\Delta W_u$, and by implication $\Delta W_r$, in part according to its perception of the firm's elasticity of demand for labour and its utility function across employment and wages. This ignores the fact that in reality the size of $\Delta W_u$ and the probability of industrial action will depend in part upon what other workers have been awarded. We consider this and related issues in the next section.

## 5.3 Non-competitive behaviour within the firm

There are several arguments predicting non-competitive internal labour market behaviour by firms. Probably the most important relates to discrimination, which we shall consider in the next chapter. Of the other arguments we mention three here, each a development of the critique of the profit-maximising theory of the firm and a consequence of non-competitive behaviour in product markets. The first argument is that in a world of imperfect information, and therefore of extreme uncertainty, profit maximisation becomes an unrealisable objective. In consequence the firm adopts rules of thumb upon which to base all its decisions, including those relating to labour. Satisfying behaviour will encompass adherence to fairly rigid wage structures across different grades of labour and the maintenance of some slack for long periods. External market forces will not therefore directly affect wages, hiring, training or labour deployment within the firm.

Second, it can be argued that the sheer complexity of internal wage structures will reduce the firm's ability to respond to market forces. There are significant information costs in keeping up with market signals and also transaction costs to altering internal rates of pay. This is especially true where overtime, bonus and shiftwork systems multiply the possible earnings combinations. Once again the firm will wish to adhere to fairly rigid wage structures, which are sticky through time and idiosyncratic, in which case the internal allocation of labour resources could differ considerably from that predicted by conventional economic analysis.

The third argument sees the exchange relationship between the employer and workers inside the firm as dominated by a lopsided power relationship. A pure exchange relationship would be based upon a specific contract guaranteed by exogenously prescribed, impartial laws and rules. A contract for labour would define an obligation for workers to supply a certain labour effort in a specific way to a defined production process in return for a specified wage. A lopsided power relationship exists if either side to the exchange possesses the ability to deviate from the contract with impunity, despite which the other has limited opportunity to cancel the contract. The exchange relationship for labour is not well defined. Employers can alter the terms of the relationship unilaterally. Workers' ability to prevent this through individual or collective bargaining is limited. Unions have limited resources. A worker can leave but getting alternative employment is not easy and always involves transaction costs. Acquired skills, seniority rights and established positions in promotion structures all increase the costs of leaving. The power relationship is thus biased in the employer's favour. This in turn allows the employer to shape contracts, institutions and wage structures both to improve his position in the exchange relationship and to strengthen his power base. The firm uses wages to devalue lower skill grades and to divide workers; it institutionalises promotion by seniority to create an internal hierarchy whose occupants are sympathetic to its leadership; it uses access to training to favour sympathetic and amenable workers; and it uses relativities to undermine union solidarity. This implies that the allocation of labour within the firm reflects, not market forces, but the power structure within the firm and, in particular, the firm's strategy to maintain its dominance.

A full analysis of these arguments cannot be pursued here since it would take us far beyond a discussion of the labour market. Suffice it to say that none offers specific predictions as to how internal labour markets work, which would require explicit formulation of the decision rules under satisfying behaviour, the historical origins of wage structures before they become sticky, or of the precise form in which wage structures best serve the firm's political objectives. Without such statements non-competitive models of the firm cannot be empirically evaluated against the competitive model. In that respect the worker's side of the internal labour market, to which we now turn, is rather more interesting.

In the union models of Section 5.2 the union's optimum wage for sector $i$ (either a market or a firm), $W_u$, is determined solely by the union's utility function and the perceived demand for labour function:

$$U = U(W, N) \tag{5.1}$$

$$N = N^u(\Delta W) \tag{5.6}$$

i.e. only by current market characteristics within $i$. However, external factors may well influence $W_u$, and thereby $\Delta W_r$, in the bargaining model, if the utility function contains not only the money wage and employment levels but also a *reference wage*, $W^R$, reflecting workers wage expectations:

$$U = U(W, N, W^R) \tag{5.19}$$

where the reference wage is determined either by $i$'s past wages record or by current wage payments elsewhere.

Consider first a sector in which workers evaluate any wage they receive against a target real wage level $w^T$. The union's utility function therefore embraces not only $w^T$ but also the union's expectations regarding prices, $P^e$:

$$U = U(W, N, P^e, w^T) \tag{5.20}$$

The wage $w^T$ is determined by the union's perceptions of the underlying growth rate of the economy. So, for any period $t$,

$$w_t^T = w_{t-1}^T(1 + g) \qquad (5.21)$$

where $g$ is some fraction measuring the union's perception of the long-term growth rate of the economy over past periods. Price expectations are fixed by recent price movements:

$$P_t^e = P_{t-1} + (P_{t-1} - P_{t-2}) \qquad (5.22)$$

Any wage $W$ received by the union will be valued less highly, *ceteris paribus*, the higher are $P^e$ and $w^T$. Consequently, faced by the labour demand function, the union will opt for a higher wage to maximise utility, $W_u$, the higher is $w^T$ at that moment in time. $\Delta W_r$ will also be higher, which increases the likelihood of industrial action, and implies a higher settlement wage and a lower level of employment. Such effects will, however, be mitigated by any shifts in the demand for labour function following demand or productivity improvements. The final outcome for wages and employment depends crucially therefore upon the relative magnitude of the expected and actual growth rates of the economy. *Ceteris paribus* a fall in the underlying growth rate will in the short run, before expectations are adjusted, induce a period of higher levels of industrial action and of wage settlements that reduce employment and, possibly, raise prices.

Alternatively, consider a sector of the labour market in which the reference wage, $W^R$, depends upon wage payments awarded elsewhere. In the union models of Section 5.2 the union's utility-maximising wage, $W_u$, in sector $i$ might be related to wages elsewhere indirectly through competitive market forces. An increase in the demand for goods produced by $j$ labour will raise the wage, $W_j$, of $j$ labour. If labour $i$ is also used to produce these goods, the demand for it will also increase. If $i$ labour produces goods competitive with those produced by $j$ labour the demand for $i$ labour will fall. In the first instance to maximise utility the union in $i$ will opt for a higher wage; in the latter case it will have to accept a lower wage. The existence and nature of the relationship between $W_i$ and $W_j$ will depend upon the relationship between the outputs of $i$ and $j$ labour. It can be argued, however, that wages, and therefore the allocation of resources, are the subject of strong political and social forces working partly through wage relativities, administrative rules and custom and practice. Wages in sector $i$ may then be related to wages elsewhere in the labour market through the action of non-competitive market forces.

Suppose that the utility function of the union in sector $i$ were

$$U_i = U_i(W_i, N_i, W_j), \qquad i \neq j; j = 1, \ldots, n; U_{W_j} < 0 \quad (5.23)$$

where $W_j$ stands for the wages paid in the $n$ sectors which the workers in $i$ identify for bargaining purposes. Such a utility function might be justified on the following grounds. Workers and their unions conceive of an optimal hierarchy of jobs and rewards in which their own jobs and rewards can be clearly located. This hierarchy provides workers with a means of determining, in a stratified society, their position in the social order and thus their structural relationship to others. It provides, that is, a measure of status. The hierarchy also provides the union with a mark of its position in the economic and social power structure. The optimal hierarchy will embody workers' notions of fairness rather than of scarcity, so it will be based upon criteria such as physical effort, danger, dirtiness, inconvenience and training required and, very importantly, historical precedent. The hierarchy will thus be stable and will reflect historical practice.

Workers and the union in $i$ will therefore be conscious of the wage increases going to workers elsewhere in the hierarchy because, if such increases seriously disturb the structure of rewards, they will be seen as lowering $i$ workers' status and their union's prestige and as conflicting with established notions of fairness. Any wage $W$ offered to $i$ workers will therefore be evaluated in the light of the wage structure arising out of awards currently being made elsewhere. The union's optimal wage, $W_u$, will be higher the higher are these external awards. Wage changes in any sector will thus be transmitted to other sectors: there will be spillover effects. This means that the employment and allocation in labour market $i$ will be partly determined by events elsewhere, with perhaps important consequences for allocative efficiency and consumer welfare.

In certain circumstances wage negotiations will produce wage leadership. If the union in $i$ uses a specific sector for reference purposes and if many other sectors attach themselves to that same reference sector, then wages across a wide area of the labour market will be tied together very effectively. Any increase in a *key wage* will precipitate several similar wage adjustments. The increase in wages overall will then be determined largely by conditions in the key sector. Employment will be determined by the conditions governing that sector in relation to those in the key sector. If, for example, productivity rose rapidly in the key sector and so, as a result, did wages, there would be pressure for wages to rise elsewhere even in sectors where local conditions were unfavourable. Adverse output, product price and employment adjustments would then no doubt follow.

Even if workers in sector $i$ use only sectors close to $i$ in the wages hierarchy for reference purposes, given the continuous nature of the hierarchy, the entire structure will be bound together. A change in the wage of any one sector will set in motion a ripple effect up and down the hierarchy to restore customary differentials. To the extent that negotiations take place at different points in time this ripple effect will appear as a sequence of similar wage adjustments through time: a wage round. The explanation for any given wage change must then be seen in terms of changing economic conditions elsewhere in the labour market in some past period.

The two models of reference wage effects are intuitively appealing and seem to be consistent with casual observation. However, economic analysis of such effects is both limited and *ad hoc*. There is no well developed theory to explain how unions formulate their perceptions of the underlying growth rate of the economy, $g$, how these perceptions adjust with time and to unanticipated events, to explain why unions in $i$ should be concerned with the growth of the economy rather than that of their own sector and so on. It is impossible in the spillover model to predict *ex ante* which sectors $i$ will choose as reference points or to explain any linkages that appear to exist. Such facts make the reference wage models difficult to test in any rigorous way. However, they do have important implications. In Chapter 11 we shall have cause to return to the real wage target model when we consider inflation. The spillover model has considerable significance for the analysis of internal labour markets to which we now turn.

The basic model of the labour market entirely ignores firms' internal organisations. Each firm is assumed to be open at every grade of labour to market forces. Wages are the same for any grade in every firm, so that differentials between grades are identical too. Wage offers in the external market are everywhere identical to those paid inside the firm. The firm, as an institution, poses no barrier to competitive pressures. Specific institutional arrangements are irrelevant. Firms continuously compete to retain and attract labour, and workers compete to retain their current jobs and for jobs elsewhere. The internal labour market is therefore perfectly integrated into the external labour market; no distinction or separate analysis is required. In reality, however, internal labour markets may operate rather differently.

If we now interpret 'sectors' in our analysis of spillover effects as being different occupations within firms, we would predict the emergence of a rigid wage structure *within* the firm. Consider a firm, F, in which one particular wage is determined by reference to an external key wage, but which itself acts as the key wage within the firm. External market forces will have little impact upon internal wage differentials. If the internal key wage rises, all internal wages inside F will rise accordingly. Once established, in time internal wage relativities become institutionalised; a part of the firm's custom and practice. Relativities will eventually bear little relationship to relative skill scarcities. Wages can no longer act as signals for the efficient allocation of resources within the firm or as measures of productivity. The firm operates simultaneously with excess demand for some skills and excess supply of others. The labour market as a whole displays misallocation of resources.

Why does the firm permit events to reach such a point? Why does it accept relativities into negotiations? First, to some extent it has no choice: the firm must sometimes maximise subject to constraints set by union objectives. No doubt in negotiations firms will attempt to inform unions of the consequences of an inappropriate choice of external key wage and of an excessively rigid internal wage structure. No doubt unions will also learn from their experience of industrial conflict and employment contraction. Nevertheless, if reference bargaining is widespread and monetary demand is increasing, firms will not suffer unduly. Second, the firm may accede to the introduction of relativities into negotiations as an expedient to forestall further union penetration into its activities. Third, in a world where the firm does not know the final impact of any wage change on product demand, agreeing to match wages with those paid by competing firms may not be an inappropriate course of action as long as conditions are attached that guarantee similar productivity changes across firms. The extent of misallocation of resources then depends upon the identity of the external reference sector and on the rigidity of the comparisons and does not arise from reference bargaining *per se*. Indeed the outcome of reference bargaining could differ little from that of the basic union model except that the indirect links between sectors are institutionalised.

Negotiations based upon comparabilities which are insensitive to market forces may give the internal labour market a rigid wage structure; but may impinge upon the firm's other allocation decisions to produce a *structured internal labour market*. The internal wage hierarchy will be as important to workers and unions as is the external wage hierarchy, and for the same reasons. Unions will thus want to impose a well-defined job hierarchy within the firm, with promotion criteria based upon age and tenure, since such characteristics will invariably describe those with the most voice in union affairs. If unions achieve this, internal candidates will be preferred to external candidates, even to the exclusion of more able applicants. This could lead to a position where only jobs at the bottom of the hierarchy were open to outsiders, which would greatly assist the union in controlling total labour supply to the firm. Since training is often the mechanism by which promotion is achieved, a structured promotion system will include internal training geared to the needs of internal applicants.

Such training will take place even when trained labour exists outside the firm. Access to training will also be determined by age and tenure. Certain firms will be much more likely to accept such practices than others. Clearly an effective trade union presence will be necessary to enforce relativities. Firms producing in large units will be more likely to have both monopoly power and the technology that can justify elaborate promotion hierarchies and permanent training programmes and to be able to absorb the resource misallocation. A high stable level of product demand is essential if rigid wage structures are not to break down. Similarly, where technological change is slow, firms are more likely to tolerate a structured internal labour market, for in such circumstances promotion and training practices not based exclusively upon ability will be less expensive.

## 5.4 Extra-market forces

The basic model of the labour market assumes a competitive world in which each individual has equal opportunities on entry to the labour market. Each faces exactly the same constraints on his/her choices. As we have seen in Chapter 3, differences in innate ability will play some part in determining occupational choice. If such differences are relatively minor, the competitive labour market appears at first sight to be a suitable instrument for maximising social welfare, for the competitive model predicts a distribution of income with no significant skew. This, however, ignores two basic realities of working labour markets. First, the total resources individuals bring to the labour market differ considerably. The advantages some individuals possess in terms of income, wealth and social capital extend their range of choice by relaxing the institutional constraints they face. Productive abilities vary according to education, training, information and work orientation, each of which is itself to a large extent the outcome of social advantage rather than innate ability. Second, once in the labour market, some individuals possess important advantages in their transactions: they can, for example, borrow more easily. Labour market outcomes are therefore very different for individuals of the same innate abilities and tastes. It is therefore unlikely that the distribution of final output will be socially acceptable since inevitably, under competitive conditions, it reflects the distribution of initial resources. Thus, whilst the labour market itself may be competitive, market outcomes will reflect external non-competitive forces.

Labour market outcomes can only be analysed on the basis of some understanding of the wider society in which labour markets operate. Any analysis of extra-labour market advantage or disadvantage therefore necessarily leads us to consider social stratification. Society is stratified according to each individual's membership of class, status and power groups. Class refers to a group of individuals with similar amounts of material resources. Status groups contain individuals of similar ranking in society's hierarchy of social esteem. Power groups contain individuals with similar abilities to control their own and other people's decisions. To the extent that primary stratification by class, status or power determines access to the output produced by society, it will generate secondary advantages and disadvantages, for example in access to health, housing and so on. For the purposes of exposition let us outline two very different models of the relationship between social stratification and extra-labour market noncompetitive forces. Throughout we maintain the assumption of competition within labour markets.

In our first model the division of society's material resources dominates all other considerations. Status and power thus follow directly from wealth and earnings potential. Society is stratified primarily along class divisions. There are essentially only two classes and the upper class has historically the major share of society's resources. The membership of elites (groups of individuals who occupy positions of authority in society) operating in every sphere of social life come from the upper class. Entry to any elite is restricted. Elites are bound together by common values, and the power they possess is centralised and wide-ranging. Attached to the upper class is a stratum of society which administers the economic, political and social system, and from which the ablest are recruited to the upper class when social organisations expand beyond the capacity of the existing upper class to provide sufficient numbers of officers. The system persists through the control which the ruling class has over the means of socialisation and communication. The dominant ideology is therefore the ideology of the ruling class. Institutions, organisation, attitudes and so on all favour the interests of that class. In particular the ideology substantiates the existence and continuation of a freely working capitalist competitive economy. This ideological dominance makes overt coercive action rarely necessary and prevents the alienation of the lower class becoming aggressive class consciousness. Trade unions become institutionalised into the system, so that the lower class remains disorganised and distracted.

Some of the implications of this model of society for labour market analysis are as follows. First, their high levels of income and wealth give members of the ruling class, and of the administrative stratum, a considerable advantage in the acquisition of productive skills. Second, the all too apparent restriction on entry to many areas of social life is a strong disincentive for individuals from the lower class to invest in human capital. Third, the dominant ideology and the socialisation process, substantiated by the realities of life, give members of the upper class the motivation, expectations, information and technique to deal successfully with economic and social life in a free market system. Fourth, upper class individuals enter the market place with the economic and social resources of their families and class behind them, and whilst in the market continue to benefit from this advantage. Fifth, in the market such individuals benefit from the structuring of the market place and of economic and social organisations to suit the interests of members of the upper class.

Upper class individuals enter the competitive labour market with considerable resources and inevitably occupy jobs offering high rewards. Lack of qualifications, social capital and market leverage crowds the lower classes into bad jobs, bringing down wages there whilst producing high rents in goods jobs. The result is that upper class individuals occupy jobs which offer both high material and non-material rewards contrary to the Smithian prediction of compensating differentials.

The process is moreover cumulative. Lack of income, status and power not only limits lower class individuals' access to goods markets; it also produces poor housing, a poor environment (for example confinement to decaying city centres), poor health and poor leisure. Bad jobs provide few opportunities for further training and self-improvement. Low income makes individual initiative impossible. The nature of the work performed is a strong dispiriting factor. The result is that productive performance may well deteriorate rather than improve with time. Since the normal market processes operate in the reverse way for privileged groups, differentials in rewards will in fact widen with age. Cumulative forces may also have an inter-generational dimension. Secondary disadvantages, restricted social capital and unsympathetic attitudes within the family will further restrict the pre-market resource acquisition of lower class children and therefore, later, limit their effectiveness in market activities. Extra-market non-competitive forces will thus assign lower class families permanently to a disadvantaged position.

In our second model the nature of social stratification is very different. Class, status and power produce separate hierarchies within society. In turn each is made up of many segments. So, for example, there are many classes each defined and bound together by the degree and nature of their resource ownership. Elites in every area of social life are open in recruitment and operate within decentralised power structures, with a narrow range of influence. They are relatively loose groups, with only a limited amount of shared ideals and values. Membership of elites is not confined to any particular class or status group. There are therefore a multitude of elites each with a different membership brought together by a particular interest. The relationship between elites can be competitive and is defined within a pluralist framework, wherein elites interact within democratic processes, where rules are laid down, agreed to, and adhered to in order to resolve differences through consensus and compromise. The state and the elites themselves exist and operate on the basis of a legal, rational, authoritative power base rather than coercion or propaganda. The economic system contains a mixture of private and public activities reflecting rational decisions to maximise efficiency and output, taking equity and the preferences of social agents into consideration. The market economy as a whole, the state and the social system exist because they are seen by the community as a whole to serve a clear function in maintaining and increasing the welfare of individuals in society. The mixed market economy in particular provides incentives and rewards for effort without gross inequalities, and signals for resource allocation without relying too greatly upon centralised decision making. The whole system is very flexible in accommodating changes in social, political and economic realities.

The implications for labour market analysis of this second model are as follows. First, given that innate ability differences are not significant, the labour market requires and produces wage and income differentials between individuals, but of a fairly limited kind, especially after tax and government expenditures are taken into account. Second, since there are no impediments other than productive ability to entry, and since access to training, education and so on is open due to state intervention, considerable occupational mobility takes place. Preferences (temperament, interests, etc.) can play a considerable part in determining an individual's occupational choice and therefore economic position. Third, socialisation processes encourage individual development, foster differences in interests and therefore encourage utility-maximising, varied choices in labour markets. The education system equips individuals with information, social capital, productive skills and motivation, and compensates for any disadvantages of children from low income family backgrounds. Fourth, as an important employer itself and through legislation, the government ensures that access to jobs is fully competitive, so that higher social strata have no special advantages. Fifth, ideologies vie with one another for public support, but within a framework endorsing and propagating the rational consensus approach to the organisation of society.

Extra-labour market differences in resources exist in this model and produce differences in material outcomes. The differences in material outcomes are seen as acceptable in that they are minor, with limited intertemporal or inter-generational consequences. They often result from choice and increase both social and, in the long run, every individual's economic welfare. The divorce of ownership and control in industry, the growth of trade unions, joint representation and consultation, and the activities of government all give workers insight into and involvement in their daily work. Technology reduces the physical labour in many jobs and permits workers to choose significant amounts of leisure time. However, some workers have very strong preferences for goods so they choose bad but highly paid jobs. Other workers have a strong preference for leisure provided that they attain a basic living wage level, so they choose to do poor jobs with good social contacts, low responsibility and effort, and abundant leisure on and off the job. Workers who become dissatisfied in bad jobs have every opportunity to improve their position and many of them do just that.

Of course these are by intention two very different and somewhat naive characterisations of social stratification and its labour market implications. However, working through them as we have serves to indicate the following: that the way in which the labour market functions is critically dependent upon the structure of society; that to model the labour market successfully therefore requires us to make assumptions about the wider social organisation; and that to ignore this is simply to build in assumptions implicitly which may well lead us to make incorrect predictions. It will not be an easy task to construct such social models nor to integrate them with economic analysis. Economists have certainly been reluctant to undertake such a task. The real world presumably lies somewhere between the two extremes described above. It is not, however, very like the second extreme, which is much like the world implicitly assumed in the basic model of the labour market. Extreme social disadvantages do exist. In the remainder of this text we have no formal social model to offer. However, whenever appropriate we shall consider the possible impact of social advantage and disadvantage upon the labour market processes under discussion.

## Further Reading

CHAPTER 5: NON-COMPETITIVE BEHAVIOUR

A. M. Cartter, *Theory of Wages and Employment* (Homewood, Ill.: Irwin, 1959).

P. Doeringer, 'Determinants of the structure of industrial type labor markets', *Industrial and Labor Relations Review*, Vol. 20 (January 1967).

P. B. Doeringer and M. J. Piore, *Internal Labor Markets and Manpower Analysis* (Lexington, Mass.: Heath, 1971).

J. Johnston, 'A model of wage determination under bilateral monopoly', *Economic Journal*, Vol. 82 (September 1972).

I. McDonald and R. Solow, 'Wage bargaining and employment', *American Economic Review*, Vol. 71 (December 1981).

C. Mulvey, *The Economic Analysis of Trade Unions* (Oxford: Martin Robertson, 1978).

A. Rees, *The Economics of Trade Unions*, revised edition (Chicago: University of Chicago Press, 1977).

# 6
# Discrimination in labour markets

In the basic model of the labour market, labour at each skill level is homogeneous. This implies that the same wage and employment opportunities are open to, and equally likely to be taken up by, any unit of similarly skilled labour. In this chapter we consider ways in which this model might be modified to generate discriminatory behaviour, which occurs when equally productive workers are treated differently. Labour market discrimination may take the form of either assigning equally productive workers to jobs of different skill levels (employment discrimination) or paying them different wages for doing the same job (wage discrimination). Groups of workers may be discriminated against on the basis of race, age, sex or religion, but our theoretical analysis is intended to be perfectly general and we make no attempt in what follows to distinguish between these types of discrimination.

The neoclassical approach to micro-economic theory assumes that each economic agent aims to maximise a utility function which records the agent's preferences for different goods and activities. In the case of firms, the usual assumption is that their utility functions contain only profits:

$$U = U(\pi) \tag{6.1}$$

Individual workers decide how much labour to supply on the basis of utility functions which contain market goods and leisure time:

$$U = U(G, LT) \tag{6.2}$$

Such utility functions generate the prediction that equally productive units of labour will receive the same wage. Our modification is to introduce a new argument into the utility functions, a 'taste for discrimination', and analyse the effects of this taste upon the wages and employment of different groups of workers.

In Section 6.1 it is employers who have a taste for discrimination; in Section 6.2 it is employees who are the discriminators. We assume throughout that there are two groups of workers, A and B, and that it is the B group which is discriminated against.

## 6.1 Employer wage discrimination

Consider a single employer with a taste for discrimination against B workers. This means his utility depends not only upon the level of profits but also upon the number of B workers employed:

$$U = U(\pi, B), \qquad U_\pi = \frac{\mathrm{d}U}{\mathrm{d}\pi} > 0, U_B < 0, U_{BB} > 0 \qquad (6.3)$$

Since there are two arguments to the utility function, it can be represented diagrammatically as a set of indifference curves. In Figure 6.1 imagine to begin with that the firm earns a profit of $\pi_1$ with zero B workers employed. Since the marginal utility of employing B is negative, the indifference curve through $\pi_1$ will be upward sloping: the employer will have to be compensated for taking on more B workers with higher profits if he is to remain at the same utility level. Since we are concerned solely with the compensation for employing more B people, we can think of the indifference curve as drawn on the assumption of a given total employment level, $L^j$. The horizontal axis thus records both the number and the proportion of B workers. If we now imagine a second profit level, $\pi_2$, we can derive a second indifference curve, and so on to complete the indifference map.

The slope of each indifference curve at any point measures the amount of profit the employer requires to employ one more B worker: it is the marginal rate of substitution of profits for B

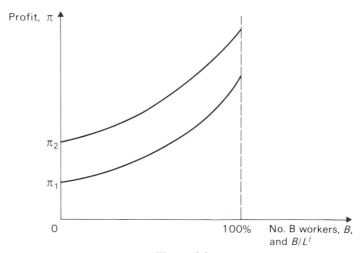

**Figure 6.1**

employment, known hereafter as the *discrimination coefficient*, $D_B$. This coefficient measures the strength of the employer's taste for discrimination. A strongly discriminatory employer will have steep indifference curves and hence a high value of $D_B$ at each level of $B$. In Figure 6.1 the indifference curves become steeper going left to right. This follows from the positive second order differential of the utility function in equation (6.3), which implies that a higher amount of compensation is required for each extra B worker employed as the proportion of B workers in the labour force rises.

The objective of the firm is to reach the highest possible indifference curve subject to the constraints it faces in the form of its demand and production functions. Let us imagine a competitive firm facing a given price $P^*$ for its product. Assume the firm were to produce $Q^1$ output. Given that the production function is of a short-run nature, we can ignore capital. Assuming A and B workers are perfect substitutes we have the production relationship

$$Q = Q(L) = Q(A + B) \qquad (6.4)$$

and the profits relationship

$$\pi = P^*Q(A + B) - W_A A - W_B B \qquad (6.5)$$

where $W_A$ and $W_B$ are exogenously given and constant. For the output $Q^1$ there will therefore be an efficient labour force $L^1$.

Imagine the firm employs only A workers, then the profits will be

$$P^*Q^1 - W_A A = \pi_A$$

where $A = L^1$; if the firm employs only B workers, profits will be

$$P^*Q^1 - W_B B = \pi_B$$

where $B = L^1$. We can use these two profit levels to define the range of employment opportunities facing the firm. In Figure 6.2 the line MN summarises the market constraint facing the profit-maximising firm at the price $P^*$, the value of $\pi$ at M given by $\pi_A^1$ and at N given by $\pi_B^1$. If $W_A = W_B$ the line MN must be horizontal and $\pi_A^1 = \pi_B^1$. If $W_B < W_A$ then the line will be upward sloping, as in MN'.

We can now put our indifference curves and profits constraint together. The firm will try to reach the highest indifference curve consistent with the constraint MN. In Figure 6.3(a) the line MN is horizontal ($W_A = W_B$), so the firm optimises by employing only A

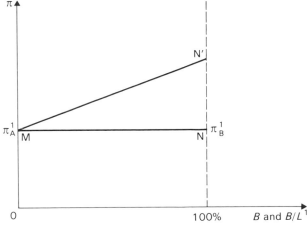

**Figure 6.2**

workers. But in Figure 6.3(b), given $W_B < W_A$, the solution involves a tangency point at X and B employment of $B^1$. This illustrates the general principle that, apart from corner solutions as in Figure 6.3(a), the profit-maximising equilibrium involves equality between the slope of an indifference curve and the profits constraint, i.e. between $D_B$ and $(W_A - W_B)$, both of which are positive. For each output level $Q^j$ there will be a unique value for $L^j$ and an optimal value for $B$, each subject to the same equilibrium condition. The firm will finally choose that level of output $Q^*$, and thus $L^*$ and $B^*$, which takes it to the highest possible indifference curve, given $P^*$.

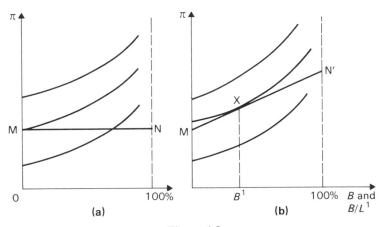

**(a)**        **(b)**

**Figure 6.3**

The same results can be derived mathematically as follows. The firm maximises the utility function

$$U = U[\pi, B] \tag{6.6}$$

which can be rewritten, using equation (6.5), as

$$U = U[(P^*Q(A + B) - W_A A - W_B B), B] \tag{6.7}$$

Differentiation gives

$$\left.\begin{array}{l} \dfrac{\partial U}{\partial B} = U_\pi(P^*Q' - W_B) + U_B \\[3mm] \dfrac{\partial U}{\partial A} = U_\pi(P^*Q' - W_A) \end{array}\right\} \tag{6.8}$$

where $Q'$ is the marginal product of labour. To maximise utility both first order derivatives must be equal to zero, so

$$\left.\begin{array}{l} U_\pi(P^*Q' - W_B) + U_B = U_\pi(P^*Q' - W_A) = 0 \\[3mm] Q' = \dfrac{W_B}{P^*} - \dfrac{U_B}{P^*U_\pi} = \dfrac{W_A}{P^*} \end{array}\right\} \tag{6.9}$$

Since the discrimination coefficient $D_B$ is the slope of the indifference curve it measures $-U_B/U_\pi$ (which is positive since $U_B < 0$), thus

$$\frac{W_B}{P^*} + \frac{D_B}{P^*} = \frac{W_A}{P^*} \tag{6.10}$$

and thus

$$W_A = W_B + D_B = P^*Q' \tag{6.11}$$

Equation (6.11) implies that the firm will hire A labour up to the level, $A^*$, at which its marginal revenue product equals the wage $W_A$, and B labour up to the level, $B^*$, at which its marginal revenue product equals $(W_B + D_B)$. The employer behaves as if B workers cost more than their wage cost. The optimal output level, $Q^*$, then follows from the production function $Q^* = Q(A^* + B^*)$.

At the given price and output, if we now systematically altered the

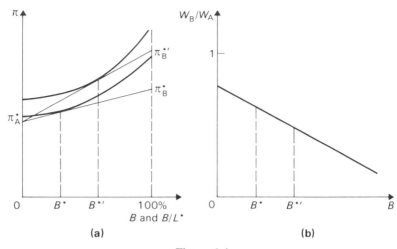

**Figure 6.4**

wage differential between A and B workers to the firm by reducing the wage of B labour, with $L^*$ constant we can trace out the number of B workers employed and the proportion of B workers in its labour force. In Figure 6.4(a) the lower $W_B$ relative to $W_A$ the steeper the profits line and the more advantageous it is to employ B workers. The substitution effect leads to an increase in the number and proportion of B workers employed by the firm. We assume that this dominates the income effect which, if the dislike of B workers is a normal taste, will lead to fewer B workers being employed. When $(W_A - W_B) = 0$ then $W_B/W_A = 1$ and, as shown earlier, only A workers are employed. In Figure 6.4(b) the demand for B workers becomes positive when $(W_A - W_B)$ increases sufficiently to produce a tangency solution in Figure 6.3. As $(W_A - W_B)$ increases, $W_B/W_A$ falls below one and the demand for B workers increases. In Figure 6.4(b) the demand curve will be steeper and lower the stronger the taste for discrimination at any level of B employment.

If of course the wages of B labour fall, then the firm's total and marginal costs fall and the firm will thus be able to expand output and increase profits. This increases $L^*$ and its demand for all labour. How far the demand for B labour therefore increases depends on the cost reduction as well as on the disutility attached to employing extra B people. Furthermore, substituting B for A workers, if all firms face the same wage change, will drive down the price of A labour whilst the cost reduction effect above will drive it up. The final effect upon $W_A$ is thus unknown *a priori*. It could add to or subtract from the initial substitution towards B labour. From hereon we shall in fact

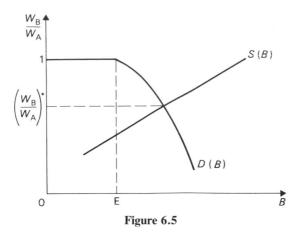

**Figure 6.5**

ignore these scale and secondary input price effects and assume that
the firm produces a given output, $Q^*$, so that the final demand curve
for B labour is as shown in Figure 6.4(b).

The shape of the aggregate demand curve for B workers, $D(B)$, a
horizontal summation across firms, will depend upon the pattern of
tastes for discrimination across firms. In Figure 6.5 the horizontal
section of the curve represents the demand for labour by non-
discriminatory employers. Beyond E, $W_B/W_A$ falls below 1 because
jobs are offered only by discriminatory employers (i.e. employers
with positive values of $D_B$) who require a wage differential. The curve
becomes steeper because each additional offer to B people requires a
larger fall in their relative wage. This follows, firstly, because as the
proportion of B workers in its labour force increases each firm
becomes more discriminatory and, secondly, because as more B
workers are employed the least discriminatory firms come to employ
close to all-B labour forces so that additional job offers must be
obtained from the most discriminatory firms. Given the supply curve
of B workers, $S(B)$, competitive forces will determine an equilibrium
market wage differential $(W_B/W_A)^*$. The predictions of the employer's discrimination model are as follows.

First, the model elicits pure wage discrimination. Equally productive A and B workers must accept different wages for absolutely
identical jobs if they are both to be employed.

Second, *ceteris paribus*, a general increase in the strength of employers' taste for discrimination against B workers amongst discriminatory firms, represented by a steepening of the aggregate demand
curve will lower the relative wages of B workers. If the number of
non-discriminating firms declines, the curve will shift leftwards.

Third, it also follows that an increase in the supply of B workers

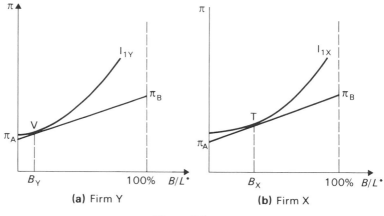

**Figure 6.6**

will, *ceteris paribus*, lower their relative wages as $S(B)$ shifts to the right. At the previous wage differential there will be unemployment of B workers. In order for full employment to be restored the relative wages of B workers must fall, and this will lead to the offer of jobs for B workers from employers at higher values of $D_B$, i.e. further down the demand curve.

Fourth, with convex indifference curves most employers will end up employing both A and B workers, though in different proportions. Segregated (all-A, or all-B) workforces will be the exception rather than the rule. The slope of an indifference curve between profits and B employment at any point measures the value of the employer's discrimination coefficient at that point. This varies across employers. Stronger discriminators have higher values of $D_B$ at any level of $B$, and steeper indifference curves throughout therefore. In Figure 6.6 firm Y is more discriminatory than firm X, but identical in all other respects. Suppose that the full employment market-clearing wage differential results in the constraint shown as $\pi_A\pi_B$ in Figure 6.6. Firms X and Y will choose to employ that percentage of B which brings their own subjective discrimination coefficient into line with the market discount on employing B workers. The highest in-difference curves firms X and Y can reach are $I_{1X}$ and $I_{1Y}$ at the points T and V respectively. At T and V, firms X and Y have the same value of discrimination coefficient, $D_{BX} = D_{BY}$, but the less discriminatory firm, X, employs a higher proportion of B workers ($B_X > B_Y$).

With the given constraint $\pi_A\pi_B$, firms X and Y reach tangency solutions employing both A and B workers. However, as indicated earlier, this need not be the case and corner solutions with segregated workforces are possible. In Figure 6.7(a) firm Z is an extreme

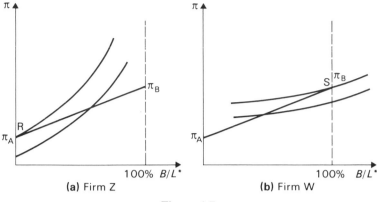

**Figure 6.7**

discriminator, whose discrimination coefficient $D_{BZ}$ is always higher than the market coefficient shown by the slope of $\pi_A \pi_B$: accordingly firm Z reaches its highest indifference curve possible by employing no B workers, at point R. Firm W has a very weak taste for discrimination, and thus employs 100% B workers at point S.

Fifth, if indifference curves are linear rather than convex, then segregated workforces will be the rule rather than the exception. Linear indifference curves imply that employers' discrimination coefficients are constant over varying amounts of B employment, so that the marginal disutility of employing B workers does not increase with the percentage of B employed.

In Figure 6.8 firm Y is again more discriminatory than firm X, but both have straight-line indifference curves and constant discrimination coefficients, $D_{BY} > D_{BX}$. With the market-clearing wage

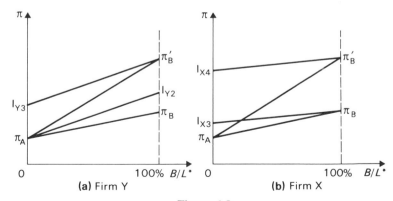

**Figure 6.8**

differential as shown in the slope of $\pi_A\pi_B$, firm X reaches its highest indifference curve ($I_{X3}$) by employing all B workers, and firm Y ($I_{Y2}$) by employing no B workers. The distribution of (constant) $D_B$ values across employers will divide firms into all-B and all-A firms according to whether their value of $D_B$ is below or above the market value. Only those firms with $D_B$ exactly equal to the market discrimination discount (i.e. where demand and supply intersect in Fig. 6.5) will be indifferent between A and B workers. In this case the aggregate demand curve will slope downwards because increased B employment requires that increasingly discriminatory employers switch from an all A to an all B labour force. The slope will depend upon the distribution of discrimination coefficients across employers.

If under these conditions the supply of B workers increases, in order to restore full employment the relative wages of B workers must fall and the slope of the constraint will increase say to $\pi_A\pi_B'$ in Figure 6.8. This will enable both firms to reach higher indifference curves but now the market discrimination coefficient is higher than that of firm Y as well as of firm X, so Y will maximise utility by switching from employing only A workers to employing only B workers.

We can predict from the above analysis that wage differentials between A and B workers doing the same job will be associated with labour force segregation between high-wage (all-A) employers and low-wage (all-B) employers. This contrasts with the earlier analysis where wage differentials between A and B workers doing the same job were associated with an integrated labour force within each firm.

Sixth, the introduction of equal pay will not prevent discrimination but will lead to unemployment of B workers. If A and B workers have to be paid the same wage, the mechanism of adjusting relative wage rates to ensure full employment is destroyed. All employers with a positive value of $D_B$ will maximise utility by employing only A workers (in terms of Fig. 6.6 the constraint becomes horizontal) and so B workers will only be offered jobs by non-discriminators.

Seventh, the employment of B workers can normally be encouraged by any policy which makes discrimination more costly, i.e. steepens the constraint in the diagrams above. This can be achieved by taxing the employment of A workers or by subsidising the employment of B workers. The introduction of an employment subsidy or its increase (movement from $\pi_A\pi_B'$ to $\pi_A\pi_B''$ to $\pi_A\pi_B'''$, in Fig. 6.9) will increase the employment of B workers, if the substitution effect dominates. It is possible, however, that, if the taste for discrimination is normal, the income effect of a subsidy could outweigh the substitution effect so that the employment of B workers falls. This can be avoided if the subsidy is payable only on increments in B employment.

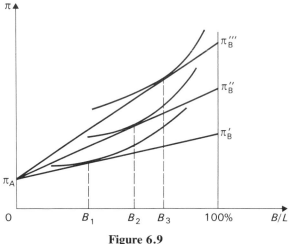

**Figure 6.9**

## 6.2   Worker discrimination

The second model of discrimination we consider is one in which A workers have a taste for discrimination against B workers. This would initially seem more promising because fellow workers, unlike employers, are in close contact with B employees. As we shall see, however, such a model does not actually predict discrimination if it involves merely altering the standard utility function for workers.

In this model employers have no taste for discrimination. The worker's utility function contains not only market goods $G$ and leisure time $LT$, but also the number of B people employed. So

$$U^A = U(G, LT, B), \qquad U_G > 0, U_{LT} > 0, U_B < 0, U_{BB} > 0 \tag{6.12}$$

The marginal utility $U_B$ is negative because A workers dislike having to associate with B workers. We can derive indifference curves for A workers, which are upward sloping, between wages and the percentage of B employed in exactly the same way we earlier derived the employer's indifference curves. Assume A workers receive a wage $W_1$ with no B workers employed. They must then be compensated for working with increasing numbers of B people by being paid a higher wage if they are to be as well off as previously. The indifference curve becomes steeper at higher levels of $B$ because of the assumption above of a positive second order partial derivative. A set of indifference curves is obtained by altering the wage at the zero B employment level. If it were so arranged that most A workers worked

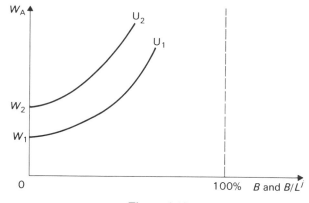

**Figure 6.10**

in all-A firms and most B workers in all-B firms, the wages for A and
B workers would converge to the market equilibrium rates $W_A^0$ and
$W_B$. If now B workers were introduced into previously all-A firms in
place of A workers, for any firm to maintain its level of employment
the wage offered to each remaining A worker must be higher the
higher the proportion of the labour force made up of B people. If A
and B are perfect substitutes, a non-discriminatory employer chooses
the level of A and B to minimise the costs, $C$, associated with the
labour required to produce output $Q^1$ at the product market price $P^*$.
So, formally, he minimises

$$C = W_A(B/L)A + W_B B \qquad (6.13)$$

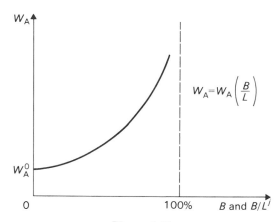

**Figure 6.11**

subject to $(A + B) = L^1$, where $L^1$ is given by $Q^1 = Q(L^1)$. Under no circumstances will the employer choose an integrated labour force. Whether all A or all B workers are chosen will depend upon the market established relative wage between A and B workers, in particular upon $W_B$ compared to $W_A^0$. Given the options for the firm its costs are as follows:

(a)  $W_B(B) = W_B(L^1)$ for an all B workforce.
(b)  $W_A^0(A) = W_A^0(L^1)$ for an all A workforce.
(c)  $W_A(B/L^1)(L^1 - B) + W_B B$ for a mixed workforce.

If $W_B < W_A^0$ clearly an all-B workforce will be hired since (a) is less than (b) and any possible variant of (c). If $W_B > W_A^0$ an all-A workforce will be hired. If $W_B = W_A^0$ then each firm will employ *either* an all-A *or* an all-B workforce, but which it chooses is indeterminate *a priori*. This is true for any $L^j$.

As constructed the model cannot predict wage discrimination. If for some reason $W_B > W_A^0$, all firms would employ an all-A labour force and no B workers would be employed. The shape of the worker's wage curve in Figure 6.11 and differences in tastes for discrimination are unimportant. Very quickly the wage of B workers would fall and that of A workers would rise. The equality of wages would eventually be established. The resulting segregation does not constitute discrimination. No wage difference between A and B workers in similar jobs exists. A and B workers of equal productivity have equal chances of being appointed to any job.

In order for workers' tastes for discrimination to generate wage discrimination the model must specify the conditions under which $W_B$ and $W_A^0$ are different, the conditions under which $W_B$ and $W_A^0$ will not converge, and the conditions necessary for firms to employ different proportions of A and B people. Consider the following variant on the model. Imagine that there are two skill levels, X and Y, which are complementary, X being the higher level. Assume there are A and B workers in both categories and A workers of grade X have a taste for discrimination against B workers.

If certain firms cannot find sufficient B workers of grade X to fill their requirements, they will appoint only A workers. Having once appointed these people at grade X, cost minimisation procedures will lead them to appoint only A grade Y workers. This will persist even if employers have no preference for A workers, even if B workers of grade X offer their services at the same wage as A workers, even if there is a plentiful supply of B grade Y workers, and even if A grade Y workers have no taste for discrimination. If the wage rate for all B workers then falls this will compensate employers with the least discriminatory A grade X workers sufficiently for them to take on B grade X workers and B grade Y workers, even though the wage of A grade X workers rises. In this case tastes for discrimination would give rise to wage discrimination rather than segregation. It is only in such a case that the slopes of workers' indifference curves become important. Different firms would employ different proportions of B workers according to the strength of the taste for discrimination of their A workforces.

An alternative scenario might arise where A workers have higher productivity than B workers in grade X. Once again an all-A grade X, and therefore grade Y workforce, will be employed if grade Y wages are the same for A and B workers and even if A and B grade Y workers are equally productive. The fall in the wages of B workers to achieve full employment must be sufficient to compensate employers for the lower productivity of B grade X workers and the additional costs of forcing the wages of A workers in mixed units upwards. Once again wage discrimination will occur rather than segregation and the employment of B people in each firm will be determined by the strength of the tastes for discrimination of its A workforce.

## 6.3   Discrimination and competitive forces

It is a fundamental weakness of each model set out above that it predicts discrimination to be a transitory phenomenon. In the long run, either because of competitors' or workers' actions, discriminatory firms will make losses. Discrimination thus becomes a preference that cannot be exercised, except in the form of segregation.

Consider first the employer's wage discrimination model. Here the more discriminatory employers will employ a higher proportion of A workers and therefore face higher wage bills than less discriminatory employers who employ more B workers at $W_B < W_A$. Therefore low-discrimination, low-cost firms will make higher profits than strongly discriminatory firms at going market product prices. These profits will encourage more low-discrimination firms into the market. This will drive down the price of the product towards that giving the normal profit level. Highly discriminatory firms must either employ more B people or go out of business. As they employ more B people, the wages of A and B workers will converge to equality. As long as any firm continues to discriminate, there is always an incentive for a non-discriminatory firm to enter. At the end of this process therefore firms with a taste for discrimination will either have gone out of business or will have had to swallow their preferences, operate at a lower utility level, and employ both types of worker. A small number of firms with a taste for discrimination might be able to exercise that taste by employing only A people, providing they can get hold of them. A certain element of segregation across firms might then persist, but no wage discrimination will be associated with this segregation. Discrimination will only persist in the long run, therefore, if the competitive mechanism, a basic element in neoclassical tastes models, fails to operate. The model, as so far developed, is either unrealistic or incomplete. There are a number of possible reasons why, in fact, the competitive process will not work. Appropriate additional and more restrictive assumptions might thus be built into the model.

First, discrimination can persist if the discriminating firm is in an imperfectly competitive industry, in which the pressure to behave as a profit maximiser is less than total. Firms with market power may maximise a utility function which contains arguments other than profits, for instance discretionary expenditures on staff, offices and perks. There is no reason why such discretionary expenditure should not include the indulgence of the employer's taste for discrimination, and the employment of an expensive all-A workforce, provided that the other firms in the industry do not face significantly lower costs as a result. Therefore, we can predict that employer wage discrimination may persist in concentrated industries, and the higher the concentration the greater the discrimination, *ceteris paribus*.

Second, if employers' utility functions show only a narrow range of tastes for discrimination, they will face only small differences in cost levels and the functioning of the competitive mechanism will take a long time. It will be speeded up if there are completely non-discriminatory employers in the market, who will employ all B workers and face significantly lower costs, but cultural factors and social pressures may prevent any A employer from acting as a total non-discriminator.

Third, members of the B group are the obvious candidates to become non-discriminatory employers who could enter the market and grow at the expense of discriminators. However, this will not happen if B people have little capital of their own, and/or are discriminated against in capital markets. This is a serious problem in capital-intensive industries. Capital requirements will then create a barrier to the entry of non-discriminating firms and protect existing high-cost discriminators. This reinforces the above prediction that discrimination is most likely to persist in concentrated industries, and also suggests that positive encouragement of non-discriminatory, B-led firms would be an effective policy measure against discrimination.

Fourth, the competitive erosion of discrimination will be at least delayed by the action of adjustment costs. Instantaneously changing A employees for B employees to reduce wage costs would be rational behaviour only if turnover were costless. But in practice employers face significant costs of recruiting and training new workers.

With non-competitive elements or adjustment costs built into the model, employer tastes will generate persistent wage discrimination. The relevance of the model then depends critically upon the prevalence of these factors in working labour markets.

In so far as the worker tastes model generates wage discrimination, we have seen that it depends upon the assumption of an inadequate supply and/or inferior quality of B grade X workers. This might be valid in the short run if discrimination and social disadvantage in pre- and extra-labour market education processes are presumed. But what of the long run?

If any firm employs A workers in the X grade who have little or no taste for discrimination, then that firm will have lower costs and higher profits than other firms. There is a strong incentive therefore for existing firms and new entrants to employ non-discriminatory A grade X people. The relevance of the worker tastes model in the long run depends upon the number of such people available in the market place. If the numbers are limited, the firms employing those available will make higher profits. Two things might then happen. First, the wages of non-discriminatory A grade X workers will be bid upwards, putting pressure upon discriminatory A grade X workers to temper their preferences. Secondly, firms will train B grade Y workers and non-discriminatory A grade Y workers up to the X level to compete with existing A workers. Both processes will continue until the wage discrimination crumbles. If the model is to predict persistent wage discrimination, it must thus be extended to embrace assumptions indicating the widespread prevalence of strong tastes for discrimination amongst A workers, restrictions on the wage differential between discriminatory and non-discriminatory A workers and substantial costs of training. Of course, as with the employer model, the introduction of these more restrictive assumptions tends to limit the applicability of the model whilst, at the same time, shifting attention away from tastes *per se* to non-competitive behaviour, non-labour market forces and institutional constraints.

Widespread discrimination is perhaps more likely to persist under conditions of less than full employment. Inadequate demand in product markets is likely to be a strong deterrent to potential entrants into markets where discrimination takes place. On the other hand, if product prices actually fall, this may put some pressure on the marginal (most discriminatory) firms to check their actions and employ more B people. Insufficient demand is also likely to deter firms from training or bidding up the wages of non-discriminatory workers. Whilst an economy may operate reasonably close to full employment for some, perhaps considerable, period of time, inadequate product demand may well characterise certain regions of the country, certain industries and certain grades of labour. On the whole therefore one would anticipate that without the assumption of full employment the discrimination predicted by tastes models will not everywhere be a transitory phenomenon.

## 6.4  The limitations of taste for discrimination models

We have seen that neoclassical models in which employers or employees have a taste for discrimination yield a number of predictions concerning the labour market position of minority workers. However, this approach has considerable theoretical limitations, some of which we outline below.

First, even within the framework of discrimination as a taste, worker and employer models are not the only possibilities. Discrimination could reflect the tastes of consumers. If consumers prefer to buy goods and services produced by A rather than by B workers, the latter will command a lower price and this will reduce the value of B workers to the employer. This will produce wage differentials between equally productive A and B workers. We would expect on this argument that B workers will be concentrated in industries where there is least contact between workers and consumers, e.g. in manufacturing rather than service industries.

Second, both the tastes models developed here predict wage discrimination. Nothing has been said of employment discrimination, which appears to be much more relevant to the experiences of B people in working labour markets. However, in principle tastes models can be developed to predict employment discrimination.

Assume that each firm contains a hierarchy of jobs each of which requires a certain productivity of the workers who fill it. Each job, $i$, has a wage attached to it, $W_i$, commensurate with its minimum productivity requirement $MP_i$. The employer with a taste for discrimination only hires B workers for jobs in the skill structure where the marginal productivity $MP_B$ is more than the wage paid for the job by an amount no less than his discrimination coefficient $D_B$. In other words B workers are placed in jobs so that

$$W_B = W_i = MP_i = MP_B - D_B$$

Every B worker will thus always be employed some steps in the job structure below his potential; the number of steps depends upon the strength of the employer's taste for discrimination. B workers must maintain their productivity to a $MP_i + D_B$ level, otherwise they will be demoted. They must therefore always work to higher standards (in all senses) than the A workers alongside whom they operate. Within each job level A and B workers will be paid exactly the same. Equally productive A and B workers are, however, assigned to different jobs and receive different rewards.

The process of displacing the B workforce downwards in the job hierarchy will mean that certain jobs at the top will have only A workers in them, the number of jobs again depending upon the size of $D_B$. Workers at the lowest productivity levels will fall below the firm's job hierarchy. Either they remain unemployed or they bid down their wages to encourage the firm to create a new lower level job. The consequence will be that there will be all-B jobs at the lowest level, and/or unemployment of a group of B workers who are as productive as their employed A counterparts.

The model of employment discrimination as stated so far predicts discrimination to be a purely transitory phenomenon. The process of shifting B workers downward will create shortages at the highest job levels and drive up the wage of A workers there. Despite the fact that the firm's unit costs would fall as it gets more returns from the output of B workers than it pays them in wages, on the whole discrimination will raise the costs of discriminating firms above those of non-discriminating firms. The usual competitive processes will then work to encourage entry and force discriminating firms to temper their behaviour. Non-discriminatory entrants will expand as B workers realise that by moving to non-discriminating firms they can improve their earnings. The joint pressures of falling prices and profits, and voluntary mobility, force firms to adjust their treatment of B workers.

As with the tastes models of wage discrimination, therefore, additional or alternative assumptions are needed if the employer discrimination model is to have any relevance to the real world where discrimination is patently not transitory. Central to the demise of employment discrimination in the model above are, first, the entry of less discriminatory firms and, second, the mobility of B workers.

The failure of non-discriminatory entrants to appear could be justified on the basis of the non-competitive arguments put forward above, but there is an alternative justification in the employment discrimination model. If the distribution of jobs across skills is much more positively skewed than the distribution of workers across skills, then discrimination acts as a convenient rationing device. Discriminating firms may then experience no labour shortages from displacing B workers downwards. They might indeed have lower costs and higher profits than non-discriminatory firms because they pay B workers significantly less than the value of their output. Potential non-discriminatory entrants will then be positively discouraged. Furthermore, competitive forces here work to *increase* discrimination because existing firms with lower tastes for discrimination will have to match the most discriminatory firms in their market. Second, the level of discrimination will not diminish even if jobs exist elsewhere, if B workers are subject to severe immobility. Workers suffer from acute information shortages and face significant search costs. The transactions costs of mobility are also significant, especially if geographical mobility is required. There may be psychic costs inhibiting quits, an aversion to the risks involved and to the penalties of failure. These factors may be more severe for B workers than for workers generally. Essentially, the immobility of labour, particularly of B labour, gives firms monopsony power. It is this, and not the strength of tastes for discrimination, which in the end will determine the extent of employment discrimination. A firm with a strong taste for discrimination may be constrained by the extent of its monopsony power, while a firm with a low taste for discrimination will be induced to discriminate to the full extent permitted by its monopsony power. Again, therefore, the tastes models can be criticised in that, although they generate the prediction of persistent discrimination, here employment discrimination, this is subject to very restrictive assumptions about the nature of the labour market, here the existence of monopsony.

The third limitation of the tastes model of discrimination is that the employer approach assumes a distaste for associating with B workers. This would appear to be a weak concept on which to build a model, both because employers or even top managers need have very little personal contact with their workers, and because to jeopardize their long-term survival in order not to employ B workers is behaviour uncharacteristic of neoclassical firms. One way round this difficulty is to interpret 'employers' to mean personnel in charge of setting the rules of recruitment, for whom profits enter into utility functions because their salaries are geared to profit levels. Alternatively one might suppose that the taste for discrimination arises not from employers but from lower level management (e.g. foremen and supervisors) who do have direct contract with workers but who are not so directly interested in profits. The following model contains supervisors, S, and shopfloor workers, L, and it is the supervisors who have a taste for discrimination.

A supervisor's utility function is

$$U_S = U_S (W_S, B), \qquad U_{WS} > 0, U_B < 0 \qquad (6.14)$$

The model is intermediate between those of employer and employee discrimination and has some of the features of each. If A supervisors are employed in A-only firms, then their wage would be market level $W_S^0$. They will then have to be paid a higher wage in any firm which

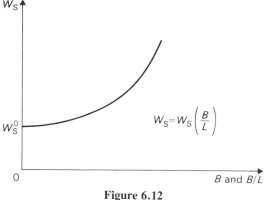

**Figure 6.12**

begins to employ B workers. In the diagram the curve indicating the wage required is steeper the stronger the taste for discrimination.

If A and B workers are again perfect substitutes in production, the firm's profit function is given by

$$\pi = P^*Q(L, S) - W_S S - W_B B - W_A A \qquad (6.15)$$

The employer's choice of profit-maximising levels of A and B employment will depend on their relative wages. If $W_A = W_B$, costs will be minimised by hiring only A workers because hiring B workers will increase costs by raising $W_S$. Therefore B workers will only be hired at a wage sufficiently below their marginal product to offset increased supervision costs and an equilibrium wage differential will be established in order to maintain full employment as in the employer model.

This model is clearly a variant of the earlier model of worker discrimination with two grades of labour; here it is assumed that grade X (supervisors) are all A workers. Discrimination is costly and firms whose supervisors have a weaker or no taste for discrimination will face lower costs than those with more discriminatory supervisors. Thus, as in the employee model, in the long run whether or not discrimination is eroded by competitive forces depends upon the supply of non-discriminatory supervisors, the level and pattern of tastes for discrimination and the costs of promoting non-discriminatory A people and B people. However, one may object to the nature of tastes assumed in the supervisors model. Discriminatory A supervisors might actually receive positive rather than negative satisfaction from overseeing B people. Alternatively, it would seem reasonable to model discrimination on the assumption that A workers resent working under B supervision.

Fourth, the persistence of discrimination in tastes models has been shown to depend upon the existence of specific labour market characteristics. This limits the applicability of such models. If these characteristics are not widespread, when discrimination does appear to be widespread, then much discriminatory behaviour remains unexplained. Tastes models without additional assumptions predict segregation. Widespread segregation does of course characterise the real world but, since it is invariably associated with discrimination, segregation models are incomplete or inappropriate.

Fifth, the differentials that emerge in the short run in models of wage discrimination are the direct result of the taste for discrimination and therefore (given the size of A and B workforces) measure the strength of this taste. This result, however, depends on the assumption that A and B workers are perfect substitutes – if this is not the case then the existence and extent of wage differentials cannot be seen as evidence for and measures of discrimination respectively. If A and B are not perfect substitutes, the firm's profits are given not by (6.5) but by

$$\pi = P^*Q(A, B) - W_A A - W_B B \qquad (6.16)$$

and the first order conditions for utility maximisation become

$$U_\pi(P^*Q'_A - W_A) = 0 \quad \text{and} \quad U_\pi(P^*Q'_B - W_B) + U_B = 0 \qquad (6.17)$$

Therefore

$$\left.
\begin{aligned}
P^*Q'_A - W_A &= P^*Q'_B - W_B + \frac{U_B}{U_\pi} \\[2ex]
(W_A - W_B) &= P^*(Q'_A - Q'_B) - \frac{U_B}{U_\pi}
\end{aligned}
\right\} \qquad (6.18)$$

but $-U_B/U_\pi = D_B$, so

$$(W_A - W_B) = P^*(Q'_A - Q'_B) + D_B \qquad (6.19)$$

This shows that when $Q'_A \neq Q'_B$, the wage differential has two components: one due to the taste for discrimination $D_B$, and the other due to the difference in marginal productivities $(Q'_A - Q'_B)$. If the difference in productivities is significant, discrimination may be of little relevance in explaining wage differentials. Instead we must concentrate on the causes of the productivity difference, for example on the factors lying behind differences in human capital possessed by A and B workers. Productivity differences may result from discrimination before entry into the labour market. The relative importance of pre-entry and labour market discrimination can, however, ultimately only be assessed empirically.

Sixth, and fundamentally, the neoclassical approach has obvious limitations arising from the concept of a taste for discrimination. The idea that an individual's tastes or preferences are central to the explanation of economic behaviour is familiar and acceptable to economists, but there are strong reservations to a theory founded upon tastes for discrimination. To say that wage differentials, for instance, are due to a taste for discrimination is not much of an explanation – where does this taste come from, and why? This is a general problem of the preference approach but is particularly important in the tastes for discrimination models because in the long run the discriminator may not benefit in economic terms from discrimination. The discriminatory employer and supervisor eventually price themselves out of the market and the discriminating employee merely achieves separation from equally well-paid B employees. We therefore need an explanation of tastes for discrimination which differentiates such tastes from tastes for other goods and services. Discrimination is, furthermore, a social and not an individual phenomenon. It is one group in society which discriminates against another. Although there is a distribution of discrimination coefficients, tastes for discrimination models depend on such tastes being widespread enough to have significant effects on the employment of B workers.

There are several possible explanations of why one group in society should have a taste for discriminating against another group, although all of them contain elements which do not fit comfortably into the models developed in this chapter. The first explanation associates tastes with social stereotyping. If employers believe that on average B workers are less productive than A workers, they will only hire B workers at a lower wage than A workers. Alternatively, A workers may feel their jobs threatened by the entry of B workers prepared, perhaps, to work for lower wages than the current level. Such social stereotypes arise partly from imperfect information on the labour market characteristics of workers and can lead to discrimination whether or not the stereotypes are accurate. The second explanation of tastes for discrimination is based on status, which is itself closely related to image of self. If members of the A group are concerned with status as well as income, and either employing or being employed alongside B workers reduces status, then A employers or employees will be motivated to exclude B workers. Particularly for certain (notably skilled) occupations economic reasoning suggests that such exclusion actually maintains high wage levels and thus status levels. Thirdly, discrimination is invariably practised against labour market minorities. This suggests that the taste for discrimination might in fact be a taste for dominance and the exercise of power which affords utility independent of any monetary benefits which it may yield. Finally, tastes for discrimination models generate seemingly rather limited policy prescriptions. If discrimination is due to a taste, the basic prescription is surely to change that taste. But we get little guidance from theory as to how this can be done. The recommended policy options (equal pay legislation, anti-discrimination laws, employment quotas and so on), though valuable, seem to be directed at the effects of discrimination – wage differentials and segregation – rather than at their cause.

## Further Reading

### CHAPTER 6: DISCRIMINATION

K. J. Arrow, 'The theory of discrimination', in O. Ashenfelter and A. Rees (eds), *Discrimination in Labor Markets* (Princeton, N. J.: Princeton University Press, 1973).

K. J. Arrow, 'Models of job discrimination', in A. H. Pascal (ed.), *Racial Discrimination in Economic Life* (Lexington, Mass.: Heath, 1972).

G. S. Becker, *The Economics of Discrimination*, 2nd edition (Chicago: University of Chicago Press, 1971).

R. Marshall, 'The economics of racial discrimination – a survey', *Journal of Economic Literature*, Vol. 12 (September 1974).

# SECTION II

# Introduction

The basic model of the labour market defined in the introduction to Section I of this text has been modified and extended through the six straight theory chapters of that section. At each stage the procedure was to present and develop new ideas by reconsidering one at a time key assumptions of the basic model. The result was a number of distinct, independent, sometimes abstract theoretical structures. The chapters of Section II are also primarily concerned with labour theory. In each of its six chapters we analyse a different issue or problem in labour market analysis, bringing together the various insights developed in Section I. This approach sometimes makes the analysis complex, but also perhaps brings it closer to the real world and at the same time generates a series of relevant and testable predictions. Section I has therefore provided us with a set of analytical tools. In Section II we illustrate how economists have sought to apply these tools to topics, like unemployment, that are at the forefront of labour market enquiry. It is intended that this section will not only add to our understanding of these specific topics but also improve our grasp of theoretical tools, and confirm their usefulness.

It is, however, only the empirical tests of the predictions we derive that can ultimately validate our theory. In this section we will be pointing out some of the principal empirical tests that can be applied to each topic and the problems involved. Where possible we will indicate some of the central findings. But this text does not set out to provide a comprehensive treatment of the empirical dimension of developments in labour economics. Instead we refer the reader at each stage to studies which illustrate the issues involved. The empirical literature is a vital accompaniment to this text.

The research methodology employed by labour economists is shared with all social scientists. We are concerned with understanding how social mechanisms work and, possibly, thereby finding out how to influence those mechanisms towards desired ends. The first step in a research programme is to define interesting and important aspects of the labour market to the researcher. These are then analysed by simplifying a highly complex real world down to a series of models each of which highlights specific phenomena and decision-making processes. Such models embody a series of underlying assumptions about how economic agents behave, hypotheses suggesting causal relationships and theoretical arguments in support of these hypotheses. So, for example, the basic model of labour supply involves the underlying assumption that individuals maximise utility, the theory of goods/leisure choices and the hypothesis that wage increases raise the level of labour supply. Each model generates predictions: from our example above emerges the prediction that a business contraction which induces a fall in wages will, *ceteris paribus*, brings about a fall in labour supply. Such model building was the rationale for Section I. Section II continues the process by attempting to integrate various models.

Once a set of predictions is derived the logical next step in our scientific approach is to subject them to the test of consistency with observed reality. Theory must thus generate testable, falsifiable predictions. Increasingly in labour economics testing uses econometric techniques. The basis of this approach is to formulate our models in mathematical terms, that is as a series of equations. Our predictions thus emerge also as equations. Using data collected by the government or by the researcher the coefficients of each equation are 'estimated' by various statistical techniques. The simplest kind of estimation process, least squares regression, involves finding the value of the coefficients that produces the closest 'fit' of a particular function to the relevant scatter of data. Our predictions are then assessed by how well the estimated function fits the data. The size and sign of the various coefficient estimates can be used to indicate the nature and importance of each causal link contained in the function. Estimation techniques used in applied economics are becoming increasingly sophisticated. The size of the empirical literature on labour economics is growing very rapidly indeed. There is therefore a lot for the reader of this text to look forward to. We proffer only the following guidelines. First, much statistical analysis is about correlation (related variations). It does not necessarily indicate causation so such statistical analysis should always be treated with caution. There is a very real danger of exaggerating the precision of empirical results. Second, although data in labour economics are more plentiful and of higher quality than in most areas of applied economics, there is always a gap between how we would ideally like to set up our tests and how, because of data limitations, they actually emerge. Finally, empirical work can in the end only be as good as the theory that goes to produce it. The next six chapters indicate the manner in which labour economists have refined their theoretical frameworks with this fact in mind.

# 7

# Labour supply adjustments

Labour adjustments mean changes in the stocks of labour in one or more sectors of the economy. Often stocks increase in one sector at the expense of others and involve a flow of people through the economy. So, an increase in hours per worker to a particular firm usually involves an increase in labour time to that firm at the expense of non-market activities. An increase in participation involves an increase in the size of the labour force and usually a flow of people from inactivity to certain sectors of the labour market. An increase in the stock of some particular skill in the whole labour market could

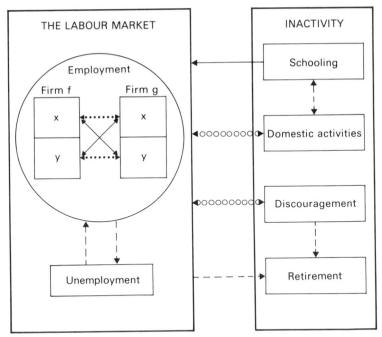

**Figure 7.1** *x* and *y* are two skill levels.
The dotted lines ⟨○○○○⟩ indicate net participation adjustments; the dotted lines ⟨····⟩ indicate skill adjustments as job mobility; the continuous lines ⟨——⟩ indicate skill adjustments as new entry and occupational mobility.

involve a flow of people from education or a flow from other skills, which would in turn involve a flow of people through the job structure, either within firms or across them. An increase in the stock of a particular skill in a firm could in addition result from a flow of people within a skill between firms. The basic model of the labour market provides only a very partial explanation of workers' decision making behind such adjustments and therefore of labour supply as a whole. In this chapter we employ the decision models of Section I to further the theoretical analysis of labour supply adjustments and thus of flows through the labour market.

Labour supply is multidimensional. In reality several different labour supply adjustments are the outcome of a single household decision. Various stock adjustments and flows are therefore interdependent. However in this chapter, to assist exposition, we consider only four supply adjustments and analyse them largely independently. In Section 7.1 we consider hours supply adjustments; in Section 7.2 participation adjustments, and in Sections 7.3 and 7.4 the two forms of skill supply adjustment. Figure 7.1 locates the flows discussed in this chapter within the economy.

## 7.1   Hours supply adjustments

Chapters 1 and 2 described how the basic model of labour supply founded upon utility-maximising behaviour should be modified to encompass household decision making; decisions regarding the allocation of time; institutional constraints on hours; and factors such as taxes, state benefits and domestic activities. Let us for summary and reference purposes express the main ideas in functional form. The forces acting upon individual $i$'s decision to adjust his supply of hours to his employer $j$ can be expressed as

$$H_{ij}^{s} = f(W_{ij}^{o}, W_{i}^{s}, t_{i}, B_{i}(SP_{i}), p_{j}, T_{i}^{d}, P^{gd}, \bar{H}_{j}) \qquad (7.1)$$

His hours supply will adjust to any change in his own wage $W^{o}$; the wage of his spouse $W^{s}$; taxes $t$; non-labour income $B$, including state, payments $SP$; the overtime premium $p$; his household's tastes for domestic activities $T^{d}$; the price of goods used in domestic activities $P^{gd}$; and the level of normal hours $\bar{H}$.

Investigating these important relationships has been the central point of much empirical work on labour supply. But how might this model be extended to accommodate human capital analysis? First, consider specific human capital formation. Since specific education raises the workers productivity, and thus earnings potential, in only firm $j$ (firm-specific) or one industry (industry-specific), it must act to restrict moonlighting. Furthermore, if the returns to the investment are to be recouped to the full, additional labour will be offered to firm *j* in the form of additional hours. Specific skills lead the firm to deter quits by offering the worker a significant non-pecuniary element in total rewards. This can usually be consumed only at work, and therefore provides an additional incentive to the skilled worker to offer more hours. In the most extreme case institutionalised hours can be abolished so that the worker sets his hours supply unconstrained. On such arguments we would expect that, *ceteris paribus*, each worker will adjust his supply of labour upwards as his specific human capital increases.

Second, training usually permits workers to enter higher quality jobs. Contrary to the assumptions of the simple utility-maximising model, workers can derive utility or disutility from performing their tasks at work. Low quality jobs involve extensive division of labour, repetition, physical exertion, boredom and thus some degree of alienation. In contrast, high quality jobs bring workers satisfaction from the performance of their skills and the value of their output. One would therefore expect that, for given wages, the hours offered by those with few or no skills will be significantly less than the hours offered by those with skills. In the former case more hours involve some disutility; in the latter case more hours mean greater utility.

Third, increased skills are often associated with increased technical and supervisory responsibilities. Both increase the hours expected of the worker. But both also increase the worker's willingness to supply hours, partly as a response to the higher job satisfaction available, partly through a natural desire to discharge any responsibility well. Hours supplied also increase, however, because the worker wants to continue his rise within the job hierarchy to higher incomes; which explains why so often workers accept promotion that appears to bring limited financial gains but much longer hours.

Fourth, the decision to acquire human capital involves the calculation of a stream of benefits through time which are then compared with a set of costs. Because of the discounting process and the deterioration or obsolescence of skills the sooner any benefits can be achieved the higher are net returns. By adjusting the time profile of his hours supplied to the firm a worker can, to a degree, reshape his earnings profile, bringing forward the returns. One would thus expect, *ceteris paribus*, any newly trained worker to adjust his hours supply upwards.

Fifth, and most obviously, because work and education often compete for workers' time, workers must adjust their hours downwards to accommodate education programmes. This will generally take place when the worker is young and foregone earnings are lowest. If access to finance is restricted workers may have to increase their hours to generate funds prior to education. For similar reasons one family member may have to increase his hours of work to finance other members' education.

So let us now consider the impact of uncertainty. Income preferers search across firms not only for higher wages, but also for greater access to overtime. Given a sufficiently wide distribution of the availability of overtime across firms most workers will in time be able to circumvent institutional hours restrictions. Firm $j$ will find that the hours of overtime it is offered will be closely related to the hours it has demanded in the past. Only if search costs are significant will the hours constraint bite; marginal adjustments to hours will not be possible for worker $i$. Second, any worker contemplating adjusting his labour supply to increase his income could either change his job or increase his hours. A move would involve search costs, as well as pecuniary and non-pecuniary transfer costs. The higher are such costs the more workers will adjust by increasing the hours they offer to their current employer. Third, in the process of changing jobs under uncertainty, prospecting mistakes will be made. Jobs will be taken that do not have the characteristics the worker seeks. In such an event the worker might adjust his hours downwards. Fourth, one would expect, *ceteris paribus*, some increase in hours before and after the move to meet the financial outlay.

Workers seeking promotion, training and higher earnings must indicate to their employers the superior quality of their labour. They signal this primarily of course by performing their current tasks efficiently. But they can also signal through good timekeeping, reliability and by a willingness to take on additional work: in the latter case partly a willingness to offer additional hours. One would thus expect a greater supply of hours from workers at the lower levels of the job hierarchy.

Labour market discrimination will affect the hours offered by B workers (the group discriminated against), even if they are paid the same as A workers. First, whatever form the discrimination takes, it makes work less attractive for B labour because it produces an unfavourable atmosphere in the workplace. This will result in a desire for part-time work, for jobs with shorter hours and in a reluctance to offer overtime. Second, discrimination by employers or managers could limit the access of B labour to those parts of the labour market where the choice of hours is less constrained. Where overtime and shiftwork are allocated at management's discretion, B workers will not receive the same opportunities as A workers. Discrimination by A workers will have much the same effect as employer discrimination if unions participate in screening hires and allocating overtime. Third, to the extent that discrimination confines B labour to poor quality jobs, their supply of hours will be reduced.

Whilst analysis of human capital, uncertainty and discrimination extend our model of labour supply adjustments in interesting ways, the most important modifications to the approach summarised by equation (7.1) probably arise from the activities of trade unions and non-competitive forces within the firm. To raise their members' wages unions will have to control the total supply of labour to the firm. At the same time the union will be concerned to maintain a high level of employment. On both counts, therefore, the union will seek to influence the level of normal hours and the supply of overtime. Normal hours are usually subject to national agreements and change only at discrete intervals. But the supply of overtime is a day-to-day matter for local union officials.

The introduction and maintenance of normal hours restricts the scope for supply adjustments by individual workers. But for the union such regulation is vital if it is to guarantee the continuity of income at a satisfactory level for its members. For the same reason the union will want to limit the supply of part-time and short-time work, despite costs to certain individuals.

Union influence upon the supply of overtime will invariably embrace not only restrictions on the amount supplied but also measures to guarantee the continuity of supply and demand. To restrict supply to a level consistent with employment objectives and normal hours decisions the union will have to devise rules to allocate supply across its members. A worker could in principle, therefore, find his ability to adjust hours restricted more by his union than by his employer. In practice the union will seek to avoid this by trying to increase the overtime premium. Whilst this benefits those workers who work overtime, it restricts the firm's demand. The firm is then seen to set the limit to hours and the union simply has the task of allocating those hours. The restrictive methods employed will invariably conform to the 'ethics of the queue' since this method of rationing is as well rooted in unions as in other social institutions. Each worker joins a continuous queue and works a specified number of overtime hours when his turn comes round.

In attempting to create an internal labour market closed to external forces workers will seek to establish a code of custom and practice governing internal labour adjustments. One part of that code will govern hours. The union will guarantee the firm a supply of hours which always responds to variations in demand in order to obviate the need for the firm to hire and fire. But the general level of hours will be limited to maintain high employment levels. At the same time it will establish limits to overtime at the higher skills to ensure training and promotion from lower levels.

Summarising the above arguments in equation form we have:

$$H_{ij}^s = f(SK_i, D_i, TU_i, SC_j, \mathbf{X}_{i,j}), \quad f_1 > 0, f_2 < 0, f_3 < 0, f_4 > 0 \quad (7.2)$$

where $SK$ represents the worker's skill level, $D$ the amount of discrimination against him, $TU$ his trade union status, $SC$ search costs and $\mathbf{X}$ other independent variables, including of course wages. No distinction has been made so far between the occupational classifications manual, non-manual, supervisory and so on, but clearly they can be distinguished through the variables identified in equation (7.2). Managerial, professional and supervisory workers will supply more hours than manual workers, *ceteris paribus*, primarily because of their higher skills. Clerical workers will supply fewer hours than manual workers primarily because of their participation in internal labour markets.

Observed hours adjustments will of course be the outcome not only of workers' supply decisions but also of decisions taken by firms. In practice therefore how much choice over the hours they work do workers really have? Is there a demand for overtime? Do firms require much part-time work? Is there a variety of demands across firms? We shall have cause to consider such questions in Chapter 8.

## 7.2  Participation adjustments

In the utility-maximising model of Chapters 1 and 2 participation and hours supply decisions are taken simultaneously. Therefore a functional relationship indicating the main factors bearing upon any participation decision taken by worker $i$ will look much like equation (7.1). A change in each independent variable brings about adjustments to participation either because it alters $i$'s preferences across different uses of time or because it alters the relative costs, pecuniary and non-pecuniary, of different uses of time. Most of the empirical work on participation has in fact been concerned with investigating various elements of this preference model. Nevertheless the theory of labour markets under uncertainty is of considerable value in understanding movements between inactivity and the labour market because it provides an explicit analysis of flows, introduces adjustment costs and identifies the role of job opportunities and demand in the participation decision. In this section we analyse flows in and out of the labour market as follows. The net flow from the labour market into inactivity, $N$, is made up of the net flow from unemployment into inactivity, $N^{UI}$, plus quits into inactivity $Q^I$, plus involuntary separations, $K$:

$$N = N^{UI} + Q^I + K, \qquad N \gtrless 0 \qquad (7.3)$$

Below we look at the components of this equation in turn.

First, then, let us consider flows between unemployment and

inactivity. Consider the position of worker $i$, currently jobless, who is deciding whether to enter employment. She must first consider whether or not to search. If she calculates a reservation wage, $r^*$, that exceeds $\bar{W}$, the value to her of inactivity, she will begin search. If $\bar{W} > r^*$ she does not search and either becomes or remains inactive. If she searches but fails to find an acceptable offer before $r^*$ falls to $\bar{W}$, she stops searching and becomes inactive. The likelihood that worker $i$ will decide not to participate therefore will be higher, *ceteris paribus*, the lower her expectations of finding an opening amongst acceptable job slots, the higher are screening costs, and the lower the quality of her labour and thus the likelihood of a job offer after firms' prospecting and probation. It also follows that the higher is un-conditional state assistance to the jobless the less likely it is that individual $i$ will begin search, the shorter the duration of search and thus the greater the likelihood of inactivity. On the other hand, the higher are search-conditional state unemployment benefits the more likely is search and the longer it will last, the more likely it is she will find an acceptable offer and thus participate. The precise effect of state benefits upon the flows into and out of inactivity is thus ambiguous in search theory and depends crucially upon the form the payments take.

Screening and preference models complement one another. For example, search costs explain why people remain outside the labour force despite the availability of acceptable jobs. The value people attach to domestic activities is an important determinant of $\bar{W}$, whilst taxes and overtime are both determinants of the rewards to search. But bringing together the screening and preference models also generates fresh insights into the participation decision. Contrary to the assumptions of screening theory, workers do not have unlimited resources and do have continuing financial commitments. To become or remain inactive or to persist in search workers must use up their savings or borrow. With limited personal wealth and imperfect capital markets inevitably their labour supply decisions will be constrained. The existence of family resources, however, allows the worker either to opt for inactivity or to pursue search as circumstances warrant. Family resources cover the outgoings that would otherwise reduce $\bar{W}$ and remove the possibility that search costs could not be covered. The likelihood that any individual will enter inactivity will thus be greater if other members of her household are economically active, both because, as the preference model suggests, there is a positive income effect on the demand for domestic activities, but also because there is a negative income effect upon search. However, for those who begin search, family income support permits more search and thus makes it more likely that an acceptable job will be found and inactivity avoided. The effect of household resources upon the flow into inactivity, as with state assistance, is thus strictly speaking unknown *a priori*. Greater family commitments, other things being the same, will unambiguously reduce the likelihood of inactivity, particularly for primary workers.

Our representative individual *i* could previously have been either in a job or inactive. These two possibilities give rise to different supply adjustment decisions because they correspond to different ends of the flow between unemployment and inactivity. Let us consider each in turn and in the process introduce human capital, discrimination and non-competitive behaviour into the analysis.

Consider first, then, the case of a worker now jobless but previously in employment. Her decision is whether to remain in the labour market or become inactive, and any resulting flow will be from unemployment to inactivity. We note, first, that because skills deteriorate and become obsolete with time, and especially with under-utilisation, the more skills a person possesses, *ceteris paribus*, the less likely it is that she will choose to become inactive. Such a course would severely reduce her wage in future market work. Second, the possession of under-utilised market skills must make inactivity less intrinsically valuable. Third, firms could use inactivity as a signal of low quality, especially in those areas where job stability and commitment are seen as essential. Inactivity will reduce the worker's chances in future job applications. All three arguments suggest that $\bar{W}$ will be lower for skilled workers, that flows into inactivity will be more important for the unskilled and that to become inactive is a more difficult decision than that to remain inactive. Fourth, any discrimination suffered by individual *i* in the labour market will discourage her, and others like her, from participating. It will reduce the value to her of work, the productivity of her search, and $r^*$. Moves into inactivity will therefore be more likely for B workers and the duration of their inactivity will be longer. Fifth, union members are less likely than non-members to become inactive. They may lose some of the wider benefits of their membership if they leave the labour force. They have access to union apparatus in their search and thus have lower search costs. They also face a wider choice of job opportunities because various areas of employment are open only to union members. Sixth, workers who enter unemployment involuntarily are more likely than other unemployed workers to become inactive. Those made redundant due to lack of work will face few job opportunities, and those dismissed because of unsatisfactory work will find many employers unwilling to offer them jobs. Redundancy payments allow workers to meet the costs of inactivity. They also extend the period of search and thus increase the likelihood of finding a job.

Now let us turn to the second case identified above: that where individual *i* is currently inactive. Her decision is whether to remain inactive or enter unemployment, and any resulting flow is from inactivity to unemployment. For her, many of the disadvantages of inactivity identified above will have materialised already: the attachment to non-market activities, the deterioration in information and in productive and screening skills, and perhaps also a decline in confidence. Clearly, the duration of the period of inactivity will be crucial: the longer the worker has been inactive *ceteris paribus* the less likelihood there is that search will be initiated. However, over the period of inactivity the ability to sustain inactivity will decline. Accumulated financial resources and stocks of clothing and durables will be run down. State aid may be inversely related to the duration of inactivity. The earnings of other family members will therefore be a vital factor in deciding whether to remain inactive. The demand for domestic activities will also change over time and may encourage re-entry to the labour market. But declining market potential will inevitably lock some people permanently into inactivity. This shows the importance for the individual of her participation decision: a move into inactivity, particularly at certain points in her career, e.g. when training is available, could have serious implications for her income over her whole lifetime.

Moves from unemployment to inactivity and vice versa have been analysed above as the outcome of workers' labour supply decisions. Let us now consider the role played in these decisions by demand-side factors. Search theory stresses the role played in the participation decision by the worker's expectation, $EO$, of finding an opening amongst acceptable job slots. For worker $i$ this will depend upon the expected number of vacancies for jobs using her skills or related skills, $V^e$, the competition from other searchers for these jobs, $U$, and the expected level of market entry, $N^e$, which $i$ realises is positively related to the number of job openings. So:

$$EO_i = f(V_i^e, U, N_i^e(V_i^e)), \quad f_1 > 0, f_2 < 0, f_3 > 0 \qquad (7.4)$$

From this we can see that the flows into and out of the labour market depend on firms' employment adjustment decisions as well as on supply-side factors. Any increase in labour demand which increases actual job openings, $V$, will increase $V^e$ by some amount and therefore both reduce flows into inactivity and increase flows out of inactivity into unemployment as more people search. The increase in $V^e$ will increase planned search duration as it increases $r^*$, making participation for any worker more likely. But, to the extent that actual exceed expected vacancies, that workers overestimate competition for jobs from the unemployed and re-entrants, and that the demand increase has more effect on job openings than it does on the number of searchers and their reservation wages, higher demand will reduce the actual duration of search and could thus reduce unemployment. Therefore, for the economy as a whole, the following relationship for participation decisions working through the net inflow from unemployment to inactivity, $N^{UI}$, is indicated:

$$N^{UI} = f(V, U, RR, SC, RC, DD),$$
$$N^{UI} \gtrless 0, f_1 < 0, \quad f_2 > 0, \quad f_3 \gtrless 0, \quad f_4 > 0, \quad f_5 > 0$$

(7.5)

The role played by state benefits and by workers' search costs, $SC$, has already been noted. In this equation the effects of state benefits are captured by $RR$, the replacement ratio, which measures the ratio of state benefits received when not working to the worker's wage when in employment. The distribution of demand, $DD$, and firms' recruitment and training costs, $RC$, are important in determining the match between the skills of jobless workers and those required for available jobs and the ability of workers and firms to overcome any mismatching.

The above analysis predicts that some jobless workers will opt out of the labour force because of lack of opportunities. Such discouraged workers may turn to domestic work or remain idle. Such decisions are perfectly rational. The model does not assume that non-participants' tastes across different uses of time are in any way different to those of participants. The analysis also indicates the importance of government policy, and not only in determining total effective demand. Government policy to increase the minimum wage, for example, will reduce participation. Some firms paying low wages who would previously have declared job openings will not now do so. The level of vacancies will be lower, search will be discouraged and the numbers inactive will be higher. The analysis predicts a strong counter-cyclical pattern in flows into inactivity and a strong pro-cyclical pattern in flows out and in the level of participation. Finally, the analysis indicates that participation decisions cannot be considered separately from firms' employment decisions.

Let us turn now to consider $Q^1$, the flow of workers moving directly from employment into inactivity. Any individual in employment remains in her job as long as her current wage $W$ exceeds $\bar{W}$ and $r^*$. When wages are low many workers will consider whether to leave the labour force. The low returns to search represent a strong market discouragement effect. Against this, however, there are strong pressures for workers not to leave their jobs. There are the costs noted previously in the discussion of unemployed workers. In addition an employed worker must take into account the costs of search she will have to incur if she ever re-enters the labour market. She must also recognise that quitting a job for inactivity will discourage future prospective employers who will see her decision in terms of the lost outlays on training for her previous employer. She will also take into account the social contacts she foregoes by leaving her job. It seems likely, therefore, that in practice quits into inactivity will arise primarily as a result of strong pull forces from outside the labour market, for example from additional demands for domestic activities. This implies that variations in the level of $Q^I$ will primarily be due to changes in the age structure of the population, in social *mores* and so on. It also implies that $Q^I$ will not be seriously affected by the usual demand-side factors even though firms do attempt to control the level of quits. $Q^I$ could, however, be affected significantly by longer-term policies that produce more flexibility in hours, encourage additional educational investments, and make domestic activities less time-intensive.

Finally we must recognise when discussing participation that there are certain flows into inactivity which do not arise from utility-maximising decisions by workers or firms. Such involuntary moves from unemployment or employment into inactivity, $K$, are primarily due to retirement and sickness, the level of which, as with $Q^I$, depends largely on structural factors.

Since $Q^I$ and $K$ are determined by structural factors they can be regarded as constant. Therefore $N$, the total net flow from the labour market into inactivity, varies through time according to the factors which determine $N^{UI}$ as shown in equation (7.5). The flow $N$ represents the outcome of workers' participation decisions; for each individual worker participation also depends on her personal characteristics and on a vector of variables $\mathbf{X}$ which includes those of equation (7.1). So:

$$P_i = f(SK_i. D_i, TU_i, \mathbf{X}_i), \qquad f_1 > 0, f_2 < 0, f_3 > 0 \qquad (7.6)$$

## 7.3 Skill supply adjustments and job mobility

Let us now turn to labour supply adjustments that bear upon the flow of workers within a particular skill classification between firms. Job mobility can most usefully be investigated at the flow's point of departure, since the cause of exit from a firm will influence workers' decision making and thus the nature of the adjustment. Workers can leave jobs either voluntarily (quits) or involuntarily (redundancies and dismissals). Either kind of flow might involve a period of unemployment between jobs.

We have referred to the position of those discharged workers who become unemployed in the section on participation. They are more likely to become inactive and more likely to have to pursue extensive search than quitters. On both counts therefore their period between jobs will be longer. For many discharged workers unemployment will not be transitional, so their experience cannot be described as job mobility.

If discharged workers receive enough advance warning they will be able to carry out on-the-job search and move directly into new jobs. Some workers will take almost any job, intending merely to use it as a basis for future search. Some of them will even quit before the period of advance notice of discharge elapses, though this will be less likely for those eligible for redundancy awards. But, in general, advance warning of discharge makes the supply decisions of the workers involved more like those of quitters.

Since job mobility within a particular skill takes place in a world where heterogeneous labour possesses only limited information on market opportunities, we structure our theorising on quits upon the model of workers' search developed in Chapter 4. It follows from that model that whether a supply adjustment across jobs takes place depends upon whether the worker decides to search or not. Each worker is continually assessing the value of a move and begins formal search when $r^*$ exceeds $\bar{W}$, the value to him of his present position which is made up of his current wage plus $LC$, the transactions costs of changing jobs. Search will be more likely and will be longer, and thus a quit more likely: the higher the level and the greater the variance of external wages, the lower search and transactions costs, and the lower the worker's current wage. The worker is engaged in on-the-job search so his search costs are made up of foregone leisure time, expenditures on applications and visits, time off work, and any aggravation at work caused by applying elsewhere. Flows between jobs will therefore be more significant the more extensive and the more efficient are the available information channels, state or private. Job mobility will be more significant over limited geographical distances.

It is apparent that the outcome of each worker's search calculation depends in part upon human capital considerations. First, if the human capital possessed by the worker and required by alternative jobs contains a high general skills element, most of the job openings with higher wages he uncovers will be open to him. If on the other hand his human capital and that required contain significant industry-specific skills, he will be excluded from many of the available job opportunities. This must reduce his expectations of an offer and thus $r^*$. Second, since some part of the worker's current wage is a return to his specific skills, the more of such skills he has, the less likely it is that wages paid elsewhere for general skills alone will exceed his current wage. And, since rewards elsewhere also contain a return to specific skills, the worker must calculate his expected maximum wage offer, not from observed wages, but from the wages he expects his transferable skills to warrant. Third, workers may be required to contribute towards the costs of specific training needed for the new job, generally by receiving a wage below marginal product. This will increase transactions costs. Fourth, in calculating the expected maximum wage the worker will make a present value calculation over future job rewards. Income profiles will depend, *inter alia*, upon promotion and training opportunities, technological and demand prospects. Any worker who has acquired skills and a place in the promotion hierarchy in his current work unit will have to assess openings in terms not only of their current wage levels but also of the effects a move will have on his long-term prospects. The further up the hierarchy the worker is, the greater the immediate disadvantage of moving. Fifth, to the extent that higher skill jobs involve more non-pecuniary as well as more pecuniary rewards, the higher skills a worker possesses the less likely it is that he will quit his current employment for any given wage difference. Non-pecuniary rewards are specific to the firm; workers become strongly attached to the non-pecuniary aspects of their own jobs and cannot easily transfer their attachment. Moreover, workers derive benefits from job stability itself, directly and, for skilled workers, indirectly through the status it confers. Sixth, when calculating the net benefit stream from any move each worker must consider the likelihood of dismissal or redundancy from his current and prospective jobs. Firms in markets where demand conditions make employment hazardous will experience higher quit supply levels. Finally, since the benefits and costs included in the quit investment calculation should, in principal, be in utility terms, quit probabilities will vary with not only the pecuniary but also the non-pecuniary costs of transferring jobs. These non-pecuniary costs – the uncertainty, the embarrassment of quitting and of making applications, the loss of friends – will vary in importance with the worker's personal characteristics but also perhaps with market demand conditions. A number of the above arguments suggest that willingness to quit will be higher for unskilled than for skilled workers, particularly those with significant specific skills. In firms and industries with important specific skill requirements, job mobility will be lower than in other areas.

The quit decision of any worker will be influenced by non-competitive forces in the labour market, arising from the activities of trade unions or from structured internal labour markets. A strong trade union presence reduces quits to the extent that it succeeds in raising wages. But its effects go beyond this. A worker with a particular grievance at work has two options: he can join some form of collective action or he can quit. When unions are relatively weak the former course is difficult to organise and of limited effectiveness. The worker must then rely upon individual industrial action in the form of quitting or at least threatening to quit. Grievances can be resolved, and sometimes prevented, if systematic means of communication and negotiation procedures within the work unit exist. Collective action and quits represent two such means, the former based upon 'voice' the latter upon 'exit'. Trade unions are a very effective form of 'voice' through which difficulties can be anticipated and dealt with rapidly. Quits as a form of 'exit' do communicate grievances but not very informatively and only at some cost to firms and workers. Such arguments suggest that the level of trade union involvement in the worker's current location and the probability of a quit will be negatively related.

The particular strategy adopted by a union in its dealings with employers will depend in part upon the pressure put upon it by its members. Certain members, for example those who have been with the firm some time, will have more 'voice' through their unions than other workers because they have more influence inside the union. They will thus have low quit rates. Moreover, unions will tend to follow strategies which suit these influential groups. So, for example, since senior people do not favour quits because of their difficulties in finding alternative employment, the union will exert pressure upon the firm to adjust employment to demand changes by hiring and firing, on last in first out rules, rather than by wage adjustments designed to vary quit levels. Workers will be much less willing to quit any work unit which has a protected structured internal labour market. They are attached to their jobs because of the job security, promotion ladders and the opportunities for income advances through internal training. No worker will want to forego these benefits without a very good reason. Internal labour markets are also characterised by wage-bargaining structures which keep workers' wages in line with established relativities and real wage targets. Internal labour markets may arise out of the imposition by workers of custom and practice and other institutional processes. In principle long-established firms, firms with monopoly power, firms with a strong union presence and firms dominant in local labour markets are most likely to encompass such non-competitive behaviour so their workers will have the lowest quit levels.

Workers experiencing discrimination in their current jobs will have a stronger motive than others to quit. However, a move could in fact make their position worse. Indeed if discrimination is widespread, workers might find themselves continually moving from one job to another unsuccessfully trying to avoid discriminatory practices. We would expect, *ceteris paribus*, to observe fewer quits amongst B workers employed in areas where there are large proportions of B labour on the presumption that this indicates a lower level of discrimination.

The preference models of Chapters 1 and 2 also have implications for job mobility. First, progressive taxes reduce the attractiveness of any job move. For those near the poverty trap the incentive is to quit the labour force rather than to change jobs. Second, marginal wage gains become particularly valuable for income preferers faced by overtime restrictions. They will move jobs not only, as noted in Section 7.1, to find more overtime, but also to achieve higher wages. Third, belonging to a family with other income earners and collective resources affords the worker the opportunity to search longer. On the other hand, family expenditure commitments are likely to make the worker more cautious about changing jobs. The costs involved, the possibility of some initial income reduction, the uncertainty about the future value of a new job will all act to encourage the worker to seek longer hours, better paid tasks and promotion within his current workplace rather than to change jobs.

Let us now reconsider the search approach to quits, and in particular its treatment of time. To justify the model for a world of continuous time we might imagine that each worker periodically (say at the end of every month) recalculates $r^*$ to decide whether to search over the next month. Each unit of search represents a smaller time period, say a day. If the worker decides not to search he simply continues in his current employment until the next reassessment. If he searches we assume that he either quits or gives up search before the month is up. What is being decided, therefore, is the level of quits and the flow between jobs in each month. But this raises a number of questions. Do workers make continual reassessments of their position in this way? If not, what exactly provokes the beginnings of search: a recent internal wage settlement, say, or a well publicised external settlement? Perhaps, alternatively, workers have a predetermined view about the length of time they should remain in one job. The answer could well influence the time pattern of quits and job mobility.

Second, if workers do continually evaluate job moves, there may be no good reason why they should go on searching until they find an opening with a wage greater than or equal to $r^*$. A wage above his current wage by enough to cover transactions costs may be enough to inspire a quit, in the knowledge that a further period of search and another move are possible. One might imagine, therefore, the worker moving to an acceptable job, not directly, but via a series of moves where each intervening job is held only for a short period. The limiting factor in such job hopping will be transaction costs. But such behaviour may well be worthwhile if there is limited recall in the current search period, if the worker is risk averse, and if search costs or market opportunities are expected to be more favourable in the future.

Third, the model assumes that all units of search are exactly alike. In fact, however, search may be more costly or more productive in some circumstances than in others. For example workers contemplating job mobility have to decide whether to quit their current job and search from a position of unemployment, or to search on the job as we have assumed so far. A worker therefore calculates two reservation wages, one for on-the-job and one for unemployed search, and follows the search strategy with the highest $r^*$. Search costs will generally be higher in the unemployment case because they include foregone earnings equal to the worker's current wage, though offset by any state unemployment assistance and the value to the worker from additional leisure while unemployed. Therefore if anyone is to enter unemployment to search it must be the case that unemployed search has higher benefits. Unemployed workers can search more intensively than employed people who have limited leisure time available for search; they can approach firms during working hours, spend more time on promising openings and follow up leads immediately. If these factors outweigh the extent to which an unemployed worker is less likely than an employed worker to be offered an available job because firms use unemployment as an index of quality, then unemployment will increase the probability of getting a job offer. $r^*$ for unemployed search could therefore be higher than for search on the job, and some people will quit into unemployment to search. One can predict, therefore, first that any increase in the replacement ratio, following an increase in state assistance to the jobless, will increase the total number of quits because it encourages quits into unemployment. Second, better facilities and arrangements to allow workers to search whilst employed will increase job to job quits and reduce quits into unemployment. State information and counselling services, interviews outside normal working hours, mass media information services and reimbursement of lost income for interviews and tests would all have this effect. Third, since it is the additional time available which in particular generates the extra benefits to unemployed search, the less time-intensive search activities become, the less likely are quits into unemployment. Fourth, workers will be discouraged from entering unemployment to search by a high level of existing unemployment because this increases competition for jobs and lowers the returns to search.

A worker who enters unemployment to search will have a higher reservation wage than other unemployed workers because his search costs are higher. Therefore he will search less long and is more likely to become inactive. The search model therefore predicts that employed workers will chose to leave their job and search from unemployment if this offers the highest $r^*$ even though this strategy carries a, possibly significant, risk of dropping out of the labour market and ending up with no wage at all, dependent on state transfer payments to inactive workers. Search through unemployment, unlike on-the-job search or search by those already unemployed, can lead to the worker becoming significantly worse off. Therefore it seems likely that workers will only choose this strategy if unemployed search is very much more productive than employed search, so that the gap between $r^*$ for the two strategies is big, or if they are risk lovers, or if the costs to them of inactivity are small, for instance because of a very high level of family income from other sources. For an ordinary risk averse worker with limited family resources and fixed expenditure commitments a quit into unemployment is not likely to be an acceptable way of changing jobs, particularly if unemployment brings social stigma and psychological problems. Search through unemployment is especially unattractive for workers who may be discriminated against in job applications and skilled workers who need to remain employed to keep their skills in good condition and signal their continuing productive value to employers.

In the final analysis, quits and job mobility will depend upon demand as well as supply-side forces. We shall have cause to consider firms' responses to workers' quits in detail in the next chapter. The importance of general demand conditions has already been indicated in the previous section where we considered search by the unemployed. In their calculation of the reservation wage, workers considering a change of job will take into account the likelihood of finding a job opening when they identify an acceptable employer. Their estimate of this likelihood will depend upon their perception of the number of existing openings for their skills. Since the worker's perceived number of vacancies and his success in search vary with the actual number of vacancies, the number of quits will be strongly positively related to the number of vacancies. In any economy vacancies will arise continuously from involuntary separations (deaths, retirements, illness, etc.). Furthermore quits will generate their own vacancies. But the most important sources of vacancies will be changes in total labour demand. We therefore expect quit levels to be strongly pro-cyclical.

To summarise our discussion, consider the following functional relationships. For any skill, both the level of quits directly into jobs, $Q^j$, and those into jobs via unemployment, $Q^u$, will vary through time with changes in the wage structure, $WS$, the level of vacancies, $V$, search costs, $SC$, and transaction costs, $LC$. Flows between jobs via unemployment will in addition vary with the replacement ratio, $RR$, and the level of unemployment, $U$. For the whole economy we have:

$$Q^j = Q^j(WS, V, SC, LC, DD) \qquad (7.7)$$

$$Q^U = Q^U(WS, V, U, RR, SC, LC, DD) \qquad (7.8)$$

where $DD$ captures the distribution of demand and vacancies across different skills.

For any individual $i$, the likelihood of a quit during any period, $P(Q_i)$, is given by:

$$P(Q)_i = f(SK_i, D_i, TU_i, \mathbf{X}_i), \qquad f_1 < 0, f_2 > 0, f_3 < 0 \qquad (7.9)$$

where $\mathbf{X}$ is a vector of variables that includes those from equation (7.1).

Taken with the previous section the analysis here suggests that increased aggregate demand raises flows into unemployment from both inactivity and employment whilst it increases flows out of unemployment by shortening search. The same increase in demand raises the flow out of employment to begin search whilst it raises the flow into employment because search becomes more successful as the number of actual vacancies increases.

## 7.4 Skill supply adjustments and occupational choice and mobility

The flow of labour into a particular skill changes as a result of decisions taken by entrants to the labour market on the quantity and content of their education, and as a result of decisions taken by current market participants to change occupations. Let us consider these two adjustments in turn.

### OCCUPATIONAL CHOICE

In Chapter 3 we saw that human capital theory provides a model of occupational choice for individuals preparing to enter the labour market. Each individual makes a rational assessment of the future benefits of different education paths against their costs. Skill adjustments therefore arise out of changes in any of the elements that go into the investment calculation of successive groups of students: any change therefore that alters the private net return to each skill and its associated education path. The supply of a particular skill will increase after the following: a rise in its wage, due perhaps to an increase in demand for some good it produces; a fall in the costs of the education required; an increase in the non-pecuniary or consumption benefits of the skill or its education path, or in the valuation of those benefits.

In the present context educational programmes represent post-compulsory schooling and initial formal training, such as apprenticeships. Investment decisions are therefore taken by young people and their parents, in consultation with schools and colleges and in relation to alternative uses of family funds. Foregone earnings will form the largest part of schooling costs. Future promotion, training and job security will all be part of the net return calculation. That calculation may lack the completeness of the stylised model in Chapter 3 but it will be a serious, conscious attempt at an investment decision for all that. The duration of the educational programme will be of particular importance.

In practice education programmes, even for similar qualifications and of similar duration, vary in quality with the staff involved, the facilities, the course structure and so on. Each individual must allow for this in her calculation in so far as it affects costs and future income. Given the lifetime implications of initial educational investments, the non-pecuniary rewards associated with education programmes, and even more with occupations, will play an important part in shaping educational choices. To the extent that certain occupations, say in industry in contrast to government and the professions, involve disutility (for example from industrial conflict and unfavourable physical working conditions), and to the extent that wages or state assistance to students do not offset such differences, supply will always be more sensitive to price signals in favoured occupations, producing both excess demand for educational places and excess supply of labour.

Investment levels vary across individuals with the rate of time preference used to discount future net benefits. In a world in which future income streams cannot be known with certainty, the discount rate will depend upon each individual's attitude towards risk. However, in practice, the risk associated with any future income will be less if occupational mobility is possible in the future. Since the worker can influence her future potential for mobility now, risk is in fact endogenous to the education decision. One would expect that workers will prefer to invest heavily in general skills during schooling and initial training because they enhance the scope for future profitable mobility. They will certainly not want to invest in specific skills immediately because of the possibility of losing their jobs. Specific skills make mobility difficult, and costly to the extent that new skills must be acquired. Workers will therefore choose to spread their investment in specific skills through their working lives as and when their inclination and scope for mobility declines. Supply adjustments will be greater for occupations where risks of future income instability are smaller, the education required is more general and mobility is easier.

The private return to any educational programme is higher for more able people. They will therefore gravitate towards education-intensive occupations. But a worker may not know the quality of her own productive efforts with certainty before she enters the labour market – it will be revealed only through work experience. Certain occupations admit greater variability of quality and thus of income than others. They hold greater risk for new entrants, but also greater opportunities for high quality people. Lower quality market entrants may choose such occupations whilst lower quality market participants, because they know their own quality, will choose less risky occupations. The implication of this is that supply adjustments by market entrants will be more sensitive to market signals emitted by heterogeneous occupations.

The human capital model assumes perfect information and competition in both education and labour markets. In a market place characterised by limited information, education decisions must be made on the basis of expected values, taking into account the individual's expectation of finding a job opening, the wage distribution and screening costs. Labour supply to any particular occupation will therefore depend upon the expected number of job openings, the variability of earnings, screening costs, and the extent and efficiency of information channels available to students. Schools, colleges, firms and the state all operate extensively in this area. Students will use informal more than formal channels because of their labour market inexperience and the importance of job experience characteristics. Family labour market knowledge will assume some significance. Some occupations no doubt have more effective information systems than others.

Because rewards become increasingly complex at higher skill levels, involving fringe benefits, training, promotion hierarchies and so on, information mechanisms will come under increasing pressure. This implies that workers will want to undertake trial periods and must expect to be mobile early on in their careers. This in turn implies some degree of instability in supply adjustments as recent entrants move across educationally similar occupations. However, decreasing occupational substitutability at higher levels will limit any tendency for transitory inflows to be positively related to skills.

The net return to any educational investment and therefore supply adjustments to a particular skill may be restricted by trade union activities. In order to control total supply, unions may raise the education qualifications required for entry. This increases the costs of entry and delays returns to investments. As a result the union deters entry by people with limited resources or lesser abilities or high discount rates. Alternatively the union might control entry by stipulating entry age levels. If entry to an educational programme is restricted to people of 16, no older individual can alter her decision not to acquire the associated skills, whatever market signals might indicate. Again, the union might regulate the form and content of the educational programme or training leading to an occupation; entry can be restricted by making it abstract, narrow and complex. Of course control of the pass criterion gives the union ultimate control over entry.

If entry to an occupation requires union membership the procedures for acquiring membership can act to restrict entry. The union may operate a controlled queue, and exclude certain groups as part of its rationing. In general unions will require that existing, particularly jobless, union members are given preference over new entrants. Support for structured internal labour market will certainly require this. These arguments suggest that supply adjustments to occupations where unions are strong will be both restricted and controlled.

The human capital model in Chapter 3 recognises differences in ability between individuals but not the existence and importance of differences in resources. The model assumes that there are no significant financial constraints impeding the efficient development of human skills. In fact the capital market is far from an effective instrument where human capital is concerned. It is often simply impossible to borrow money, except at excessively high interest charges, to finance human investments, even though the rate of return may be much higher than for competing physical investments. This makes most individuals entirely dependent upon limited family resources. As a result many people will find even relatively inexpensive, highly productive human investments impossible to undertake. Inadequate funds will have most impact upon supply adjustments for skills requiring lengthy education paths. It will thus affect higher skills in particular, slowing down adjustments and producing excess demand and high wages. The model also assumes that there are no non-financial constraints on people's educational choices. However, many people suffer from extra-education disadvantages which effectively prevent them from making full use of the available educational opportunities. They lack the family and social contacts that ease entry to the market. They lack informed, experienced parental support and encouragement. In short they lack the social capital for success in the market place. The result will be underinvestment in education and impaired supply responses to signals in many occupational labour markets.

The preference model not only emphasises the importance of limited resources in labour supply decisions. It also recognises the importance of domestic activities. The fact that a family has strong tastes for such activities will influence the human capital investment decisions of family members. The knowledge that they will spend some time out of the labour market in domestic work induces them to invest in educational programmes that improve their efficiency in such activities rather than in market work. This will be particularly important for women given the strong pressure of existing sex roles and labour market discrimination.

The analysis of skill adjustments using human capital theory is an analysis of supply responses. The adjustments that actually take place also depend on producers' decisons; in relation to both the provision of educational programmes and the demand for labour. It is assumed in human capital theory that people can always get places on the educational programme of their choice. In practice this is not the case. If the number of suitable applicants for a particular educational programme exceeds current capacity, it will take some time to increase the number of places by training additional teachers and constructing new facilities. As a result the supply of skills will often lag behind price signals, and the longer the educational programme the longer the lag. This could result in occupational labour markets being subject to severe cobweb patterns, as supply adjustments cause successive periods of excess demand and supply. To avoid this, individual investors would have to anticipate both the state of demand after their training and the actions of other investors. Otherwise rates of return will not be equalised and the speed with which supply adjusts will vary across occupations not only with the length of educational programmes but also with the degree of flexibility in educational provision and the degree to which providers of programmes can and do anticipate market requirements.

To the extent that educational programmes are financed or provided by the government, the number of places available will be influenced by the constraints of macro-economic policies and by political initiatives which are likely to be felt in the form of administrative leverage rather than direction by prices. This will result in the continued existence of queues for some courses, vacancies on others and non-price rationing. Individual choice will be severely circumscribed. To a large extent skill adjustments will reflect government education policies rather than individual supply decisions. The government might attempt to control applications through the provision of grants. It might attempt to anticipate skill requirements through some form of manpower planning. In practice, however, grants cannot easily be varied through time nor used to discriminate in favour of certain skills, and labour requirements are difficult to foresee using a technique that eschews prices and assumes fixed technology.

The demand for any particular skill by firms is heavily influenced by current technology and demand conditions. Technological change in the form of mechanisation and computerisation deskills certain tasks and makes others redundant. It changes the nature of some skills, raises the level of others and creates new ones. Changes in the pattern of demand alter the composition of skills required within the market. Firms in a dynamic environment are therefore, in principle at least, continually changing their demand for skills, supporting different educational programmes and recruiting different kinds of people. In this text we have little to say directly on the question of the demand for skills. However, the following points seem most pertinent to the present discussion of labour market entrants. First, whatever technological or demand conditions may require, radically altering the skill structure of a firm would involve significant adjustment costs and is therefore unlikely to take place over any short period. Successive market entrants are therefore unlikely to face very different demand conditions. Second, in practice most skill adjustment will involve the upgrading of the current workforce, including new entrants, or some part of it. Third, the possibility of technical change will lead the firm to prefer new workers who have the capacity to adjust to change. Fourth, because the structure of education could act as an expensive constraint upon technical advance by firms, there is every incentive for them to establish links with educational establishments through which they can communicate their skill requirements.

Government demand policy may alter the level of job openings in total but it cannot influence the flow of school leavers into the labour market and into all skills together, except in so far as contractions may delay entry. Demand expansion will increase the level of entry to particular skills at the expense of others if the distribution of demand is uneven across products and skills. So, if demand expansion affects higher skills more than lower skills, skill adjustments by market entrants will be greater for the higher skills; demand expansion will favour greater human capital outlays, more schooling and more highly qualified graduates.

OCCUPATIONAL MOBILITY

The second process through which skill supply adjustments take place involves workers already in the labour market changing occupations. Each instance of occupational mobility represents, on the supply side, an investment decision by a worker in which future benefits are set against costs. The size of the flow into any occupation will vary primarily with the level of its rewards relative to other occupations and the training and transactions costs of movement.

Upward occupational mobility almost always requires some form of training. It follows therefore, first, that skill supply adjustments will be greater, *ceteris paribus*, where training is readily available and training costs are lowest, in particular therefore where internal training is available so that foregone earnings are small. Short distance moves to related skills will be favoured. So too will any move involving training which is financed partially by the firm or the state. Second, mobility will be more attractive to a worker if the training provides general skills which offer her the prospect of future profitable mobility and insurance against demand changes. It will be especially attractive if it holds promise of further training and promotion. Third, mobility will be easier the more general skills a worker already possesses and the less idiosyncratic the skills required for the new occupation. Occupational specificity in current skills, on the other hand, will be a strong factor restricting mobility. On this argument therefore one might expect the amount of mobility to increase but the distance of mobility to decline as workers acquire more skills. Fourth, skill supply adjustments will depend upon the length of the expected payback period to the investment. Flows into a particular occupation will therefore increase with the stability of its demand and technology.

Occupational mobility may involve a change of firm. In a world of limited information this will involve the worker in the expense of screening and expose her to uncertainty. The higher are screening costs the less attractive will occupational mobility be. Workers will tend to limit their moves to within the same geographical location and the same industry. Whether search for an occupational move is undertaken will depend upon the perceived level of job openings in higher, but related, occupations and the wage distribution across firms associated with those occupations. Screening costs will be higher for occupational than for job mobility. The worker is likely to have a much clearer picture of the nature of a new job because the skills are the same even if the location is different. A change of occupation requires that the worker elicit information about not only her new employer but also the practice of her new skills. Since much of this information requires more than casual observation it will be expensive to acquire and thus represents a disincentive to occupational mobility.

It seems clear from this discussion that the availability of on-the-job training will be an important determinant of occupational mobility. We note here the following points. First, many training programmes raise no technological or financial arguments against provision and even finance by firms, because they are of short duration and limited sophistication and involve a combination of learning by doing, 'sitting next to Nellie', group co-operation and continuous informal instruction. Second, firms have little incentive to finance general training so they will expect some contribution from workers towards certain lumpy, high grade, formal programmes. Such costs will inevitably be some disincentive to workers, especially if they take a short-term view of their investment. This will seriously restrict the provision of such training, unless some means can be found of sharing the costs and the risks, which in practice might be possible if general and occupation-specific training can be combined.

It is also clear from the above discussion that workers will favour occupational mobility within their existing workplace or firm. It will be less costly because it obviates the need for screening and imposes no relocation costs. The worker focuses her attention upon higher skills only within her present location, which reduces the problems of acquiring information about higher skills since in this case screening by observation will often be sufficient. Moreover, existing firm- and industry-specific skills will to some degree be safeguarded. Workers can remain under the same union umbrella and they avoid exposing themselves to the possibility of further discrimination. Applications for such mobility will thus provide each firm with a significant list of potential promotions.

Our approach so far implicitly assumes that a worker periodically assesses whether a change of status, either by job or by occupational mobility, can improve her rewards. She calculates the net benefits to each investment opportunity open to her (taking into account training and search variables) and chooses the option with the highest net return. If either job or occupational mobility seems likely to be beneficial she searches and, if her search is successful, quits. If she quits, a flow through the labour market takes place. Many of the factors described in the previous section on job mobility will therefore also apply to quit decisions that preface occupational mobility involving a change of location. Occupational mobility will be assisted by family resources, constrained by family expenditure commitments and reduced by discrimination. The protection afforded by trade unions and internal labour markets will discourage occupational mobility involving a change of location. However, we note here three important points about the occupational mobility decision: successive decisions regarding occupational mobility will not be independent of one another nor indeed of the worker's original schooling decision; occupational mobility may involve a move to a lower skill level not a higher one as assumed so far; and not all occupational mobility will involve a quit. Let us consider these points in turn.

First, a certain amount of prescribed, therefore planned, occupational mobility is an integral part of each career profile. The individual therefore determines her mobility when she chooses between alternative educational paths. Certain specific occupational adjustments then take place, subject to ability, through promotion, learning by doing and on-the-job training, as laid down by the worker's chosen career path and therefore, in turn, by technology. Clearly certain career profiles involve more occupational movement than others. The higher the chosen skills the more mobility will generally be involved. The distance involved in each move will no doubt vary between career paths; this will be an important point to remember in empirical analysis and when discussing the amount of mobility in the economy and its implications for efficiency and welfare.

Any subject at a given educational level may facilitate entry into a number of different occupations. Moreover the occupational structure may encompass clusters of occupations of similar educational content rather than an evenly distributed, continuous hierarchy. Both facts reflect the existing technology of skills. To the extent that clustering of occupations of similar educational content characterises the bottom of the skill hierarchy rather than the top, less educated workers will find occupational mobility less costly and make more skill supply adjustments.

Second, some skill adjustments will arise from workers moving down the occupational hierarchy in response to wage signals. Downward mobility will generally be easier than upward mobility because training costs will be lower if skilled labour can to some degree perform less skilled tasks but not vice versa. Downward moves can therefore be of longer distance than upward moves. The decision to move down will often result from declining prospects in the worker's current occupation. It is thus more likely to be associated with push rather than pull forces operating upon labour supply decisions. Investment calculations will nevertheless be made as the worker chooses the best move. There will be a number of constraints on her decision. A general decline in demand for an occupation is likely to spill over into related skills, so alternative opportunities may in practice be limited. Retraining costs and initial loss of income may be incurred and some loss of status and pride may be involved. Workers may well be very reluctant to give up hard won skills, even if that would be the rational thing to do. All of this suggests that such downward adjustments will be sluggish as workers remain too long in their existing occupations, perhaps resorting instead to marginally beneficial job mobility.

Third, occupational mobility for some workers will not be the result of an unconstrained investment calculation and a quit. For those who have suffered or are currently threatened by discharge, the supply adjustment decision behind occupational mobility may take a very different form to that described above. Many redundant workers will be forced to consider downward occupational mobility and, in fact, to calculate the least loss move. The previous paragraph implies that a high proportion of those mobile downwards will be in this category. Redundancy payments may ease the transition. But the disadvantages of downward occupational mobility will push many discharges into inactivity, especially where a demand contraction is widespread. It may then require a period of inactivity and declining resources to initiate search.

The amount of occupational mobility will depend upon demand as well as supply forces. Variations in total demand only affect occupational mobility if they change the distribution of demand across skills.

Variations in firms' demand for skills will come primarily from changes in technology. As noted previously a crucial determinant of the level of occupational mobility is the degree to which firms make training available. To the extent that training is under-provided, there is a case for government intervention. In Chapter 8 we shall have cause to look at this in more detail.

## 7.5 The empirical study of labour supply adjustments

There is now a good deal of research, largely of a statistical kind, into certain labour supply adjustments. All such research faces a classic problem in market analysis: that of identification. How should observed behaviour be attributed between supply and demand forces? How can we be sure that behaviour outwardly consistent with the theory of workers' rational labour supply decision making is not in fact due to firms? Researchers are of course well aware of the problem and take steps to meet it but it is an ever-present cautionary note to empirical results.

HOURS

The responsiveness of the individual worker's supply of hours to changes in the wage rate depends, *ceteris paribus*, on the signs and magnitudes of the income and substitution effects. Estimates of these have been derived from statistical analysis of the equation:

$$H = a_0 + a_1 W + a_2 B + \sum_{i=3}^{n} a_i X_i \qquad (7.10)$$

using individual or aggregate data with hours of work, $H$, the wage rate, $W$, and non-labour income, $B$, measured appropriately. $X$ is a vector of variables included to standardise across the sample for differences in preferences between income and leisure and market circumstances. By regression analysis, we derive estimates of the wage and income effects, $\hat{a}_1$ and $\hat{a}_2$, respectively. Typically for men both are negative. The negative own wage effect, $\hat{a}_1$, implies that the negative income effect dominates the positive substitution effect and consequently that the supply of hours curve is backward bending. In contrast, for females $\hat{a}_1$ is positive: the substitution effect is larger than the income effect and the supply curve is upward sloping. For both men and women, however, the supply of hours is inelastic with respect to the own wage.

Despite a general consensus as to the qualitative impact of wage and income changes, there is considerable variation in the size of the estimated coefficients across different studies. This inconsistency appears to arise, first, because different studies include different variables in the vector **X** and the statistical results appear very sensitive to such differences. Important variables must often be omitted from inter-industry or inter-occupation studies due to data deficiencies. A second cause of the inconsistency is differences in the data used for the variables of equation (7.10), notably for $H$ and $B$. The supply of hours has several dimensions; an individual can adjust annual hours by varying the number of hours per day, or per week, or by adjusting the number of weeks worked per year, or indeed by some combination of the three. Whilst annual hours are theoretically most appropriate, in practice we do not have entirely reliable data on this. The most common statistic for $H$ is 'hours of work in the week before survey'. Non-labour income takes many forms. The available data are patchy and the source used varies between studies. As commonly measured, $B$ includes income from employment of other family members, which is perfectly reasonable if the supply decisions of family members are independent. If they are not, then in equation (7.10) not only does $H$ depend upon $B$, but $B$ depends, in part, upon $H$. $B$ is not exogenous in (7.10), which will give biased results were this to be ignored.

Equation (7.1) assumes a linear budget constraint. Let us examine the implications of non-linear constraints for the estimation of hours supply equations. Consider first the impact of taxes. In Figure 1.2(a) of Chapter 1, the worker faces a non-linear budget constraint due to a simple proportional tax system under which earnings above OA are taxed at the rate $t$. The budget constraint is thus given by $Y = W(1 - t)H + B$, where $t = 0$ when $Y \leqslant$ OA. This creates two problems for empirical work: how to specify the hours function with a non-linear constraint; and how to estimate it efficiently when the *net* marginal wage is endogenously determined. Workers who operate along the XY segment in Figure 1.2(a) receive wage $W$. For those who lie along the YZ segment the full-income constraint is ZK, or $Y = W(1 - t)H + $ XK, where XK is non-labour income plus a notional benefit given by $t$.OA. This suggests the supply of hours equation:

$$H = a_0 + a_1 W(1 - t) + a_2(B + t.\text{OA}) + \sum_{i=3}^{n} a_i X_i \qquad (7.11)$$

with $t = 0$ where $Y \leqslant$ OA and $t > 0$ where $Y >$ OA. For workers along YZ a change in the tax rate affects the net wage rate and the notional benefit $t \times$ OA. The former generates both income and substitution effects, the latter only an income effect.

With taxes the net wage is no longer exogenous, as simple statistical procedures require. A worker can supply hours at either $W$ or $W(1 - t)$ according to the numbers of hours he works, which is endogenous. Equation (7.11) can thus be estimated as part of a simultaneous equation model in which the complete set of constraints faced by workers is specified. For example, we might estimate (7.11) alongside the tax function:

$$t = b_0 + b_1(W.H + B) + \sum_{j=2}^{m} b_j Z_j \qquad (7.12)$$

where $Z$ are exogenous variables that determine the tax rate. The resulting estimates of the men's own wage effect, $\hat{a}_1$, are not very different from those from equation (7.10), i.e. the bias does not appear to be large, presumably because most adult male workers pay standard rates of tax. Interestingly, the results suggest that for high income workers the net impact of a cut in the tax rate is to *increase* the supply of hours even though the own wage effect is negative. Equation (7.11) gives a significantly higher estimate of the own wage effect for women than does (7.10).

A more serious source of bias for men arises from overtime. In Figure 1.2(b) individuals whose equilibrium position is along ZY are assumed to act as if they face the full income constraint ZK, that is $Y = W(1 + p)H - XK$, where $XK = p \times OZ$. From this we derive a counterpart to equation (7.11) for overtime which is estimated alongside an overtime premium function. The results suggest that estimates of the wage effect from (7.10) are biased upwards and of the income effect are biased downwards. Bias is much less a problem with female equations, presumably because women seldom work overtime.

State transfers to the low paid reduce the incentive to work and therefore the supply of hours if such payments fall as earnings increase. To assess the extent of such adverse effects one of the few major controlled experiments in the social sciences has been undertaken: the New Jersey, and Seattle and Denver Negative Income Tax project. A negative income tax was introduced for a sample group whereby the government guaranteed every family a minimum income depending on such things as the number of children. If a family received income from work it lost some part of its payment from the government. The sample of families (1500 in New Jersey between 1968 and 1971) were divided into a control group and several experimental groups each facing a different guaranteed level of income and marginal tax rate. Supply responses were then recorded. Unfortunately the disincentive effects across the sample were extremely variable, but on average produced only modest reductions in hours.

The inelastic supply of hours with respect to the own wage suggested by many studies may result from the fact that in reality most workers are not free to choose their hours. Rather, the number of hours worked is likely to be defined in part by the firm. Workers will attempt to achieve their desired supply of hours by moving to jobs or industries which offer such hours. But some leisure preferers will not be able to do this and will either drop out of the labour force or, where possible, limit their hours through absenteeism or part-time work. Some income preferers will take second jobs. There is evidence that both double job holding and part-time work are important in practice: that workers are constrained in their choice of hours and that an analysis of the supply of hours relationship alone must therefore be problematic.

Much of the empirical analysis of the supply of hours recognises the interdependence between the labour supply decisions of members of the same household. The most common approach is to estimate multiple equation models where each hours supply equation is for a particular member of the household and includes the wage rates of other family members. In the case of a two-person household we have:

$$H_W = a_0 + a_1 W_W + a_2 B + a_3 W_H + \sum_{i=4}^{n} a_i X_i$$

$$H_H = b_0 + b_1 W_H + b_2 B + b_3 W_W + \sum_{i=4}^{n} b_i X_i$$

(7.13)

where the subscripts $W$ = wife, $H$ = husband. For both men and women estimates of the response of hours to the spouse's wage, $\hat{a}_3$ and $\hat{b}_3$, are negative but small in magnitude. The supply of hours of married women is, however, more elastic with respect to husband's wage than vice versa.

Let us turn our attention now to workers' tastes and circumstances, $X$, that determine the supply of hours. First, theory suggests that preferences across various uses of time are important. This can be investigated by including in the vector $X$ variables which are correlated with individual preferences between different uses of time: for example, the presence of children. So:

$$H = a_0 + a_1 W_o + a_2 B + a_3 W_s + a_4 CH + \sum_{i=5}^{n} a_i X_i$$

(7.14)

where $W_o$ = own wage, $W_s$ = spouse's wage. Various aspects of the presence of children have been included in individual data studies. The results indicate that the presence of children of pre-secondary school age (with $CH$ a dummy variable) has a negative impact on the supply of hours of married women which is particularly strong in the case of pre-school age children. As children get older $\hat{a}_4$ declines and may become positive. A second approach is to introduce $CH$ to record the number of children. The results here indicate that the supply of hours increases with family size. The effect of children on the hours supply of married women is strongly related to the participation decision to be discussed later. It is worth noting here, however, that once the decision to participate in the labour market has been taken the presence of young children can have a positive impact on the supply of hours. For the males, having children tends to increase the supply of hours, i.e. $\hat{a}_4$ is positive, though it is small in magnitude. It thus appears that the financial responsibilities of having a family are an incentive to work longer hours.

Second, theory suggests the importance of trade unions for the supply of hours. Because data on union coverage is generally only available at an aggregate level, the effect of trade unions on hours has been considered using inter-industry and inter-occupation data. The coefficient on the unionisation variable for male workers is usually negative, confirming the predictions of our theory.

We have so far ignored the fact that many women are secondary workers who do not regularly participate but engage in household production. This suggests that the value they attach to time spent in domestic activities is above the market wage. Concentrating only upon those who supply a positive number of hours introduces bias into the coefficient estimates of equations such as (7.14). One solution to this problem is to estimate a supply function of the form:

$$H = a_0 + a_1 \hat{W} + a_2 B + \sum_{i=3}^{n} a_i X_i$$

where                                                                                    (7.15)

$$\hat{W} = \hat{c} + \sum_{l=1}^{m} \hat{d}_l Z_l$$

for all married women, where $H = 0$ for non-participants. $\hat{W}$ is calculated from a wage equation containing education, experience and personal characteristics and estimated across participants. However, this method is not easy to execute. First, the vector $\mathbf{Z}$ must be fully specified. In practice the limited number of variables used explains little of the total variation in wages. This reduces the variability of the wage variable $\hat{W}$, biasing the coefficient $\hat{a}_1$ towards zero. For example, using only education variables assigns the same wage to people in very different market circumstances (e.g. different industries or occupations). Second, secondary workers often alter their total labour supply by varying both hours and participation. Ideally, then, the two decisions should be considered together. It is to the participation decision that we now turn.

## PARTICIPATION

Labour market participants are unemployed job seekers, those in full-time and part-time employment (including the self-employed), and those temporarily absent from work due to sickness. Nonparticipants include those in full-time education, discouraged workers, those engaged in domestic activities, and retired persons. Participation is a dichotomous decision, an individual either participates or does not participate. Theory suggests that both the potential wage rate and income will be important determinants of people's participation decisions. But participation is also conditioned by social *mores.* In most families the husband is treated as the main breadwinner so that most prime age men (between 25 and 45) participate continuously regardless of wage and income levels. Variations in the participation of workers whose commitment to the labour market is less rigid are of more interest to researchers.

Theory suggests the participation model:

$$P = a_0 + a_1 W_o + a_2 B + \sum_{i=3}^{n} a_i X_i \qquad (7.16)$$

With individual cross-section data $P$ is a binary variable with value 1 if the individual participates and 0 if she does not. Where aggregate data are used the dependent variable is the participation rate. So, in inter-regional studies $P$ is (employed + unemployed) divided by population for each region. $P$ can be defined over all workers or for some subset, say for married women aged between 35 and 45. $W_o$, $B$ and $\mathbf{X}$ are as previously defined.

As in the hours analysis our initial interest is in the responsiveness of $P$ to changes in $W_o$ and $B$. Estimates of $a_1$ are positive for both men and women, so the likelihood of participation increases with the own wage. As we would expect if non-work time is a normal good, estimates of $a_2$ are negative. The small but positive own wage elasticity for men contrasts with the negative own-wage elasticity in the supply of hours equation (7.10), but any observed variation in male activity rates reflects the behaviour of young men or those in the older age groups so the results must be interpreted accordingly. The small negative income elasticity of participation for men is of similar magnitude to their own wage elasticity. On the other hand the own wage elasticity of participation estimated for women is considerably larger, though there is little consistency between the various estimates of its magnitude. It seems that studies using aggregate data produce larger elasticities than those using individual data. One reason for this might be that in the latter studies the wage is understated because it is a predicted wage $(\hat{W})$ derived as noted previously from a limited regression of wages on education, experience, etc.

Rewriting equation (7.16) to recognise that participation decisions are made in a household context we have:

$$P = a_0 + a_1 W_o + a_2 B + a_3 W_s + \sum_{i=4}^{n} a_i X_i \qquad (7.17)$$

Of particular interest here is the effect of the spouse's wage, $W_s$, on $P$. Typically $\hat{a}_3$ is found to be negative for both men and women, but is considerably larger for women.

Let us now consider the case of married women in more detail. Theory suggests that our understanding of their participation decision can be considerably improved by taking into account their status as secondary workers and their importance in producing domestic activities. Certain of the independent variables in X will be much more important for women than for men. We restrict our consideration to the presence of children. We have:

$$P_W = a_0 + a_1 W_W + a_2 B + a_3 W_H + a_4 CH + \sum_{i=5}^{n} a_i X_i \qquad (7.18)$$

where with individual data $CH$ is a dummy variable measuring age and number of children as in the hours equation (7.14). With aggregate cross-section data $CH$ measures the percentage of families with children of particular ages, or the percentage of families with different numbers of children. The effect of children on participation is similar to that on the supply of hours. Having a child represents a major deterrent to participation which declines as the child gets older. The more children there are, however, the more likely are married women, *ceteris paribus*, to enter the labour market to supplement family income. Children are clearly important in explaining the participation of married women over the life cycle. Most women work in their early twenties after which the proportion falls rapidly. It rises again for those in their early thirties though it never reaches its previous level.

The level of female participation since 1950 has increased markedly. To find out why requires quite detailed data on market conditions and family circumstances. The increase has been most marked for married women in the 45–54 year age range. It has been accompanied by a small decline in participation by men, and by single and divorced women in the younger age groups. The latter suggests that the explanation will be peculiar to married women. Thus it is unlikely that increases in the female wage rate provide the principal explanation. A number of possibilities suggest themselves. First, since children restrict participation, a decline in fertility would increase participation. But the average number of children per family has changed only slightly since the 1950s, and the evidence is that participation has increased for married women with children as well as for those with no children. A second explanation arising out of the analysis of household production in Chapter 2 is that the availability of cheaper or time-saving household technology provides an incentive for the wife to enter the labour market. Perhaps the most likely explanation, however, is the expansion of those jobs and industries which employ large amounts of female labour, particularly on a part-time basis.

This leads us on to consider the empirical analysis of the added worker and discouraged worker hypotheses: what happens to family labour supply if labour market opportunities deteriorate? In the case of a two-adult household a worsening of labour market conditions could result in the wife, and indeed the husband, dropping out of the labour market into household production where the expected return is higher: the discouraged worker effect. Alternatively, deteriorating conditions could induce the wife to enter the labour market to maintain household income: the added worker effect. To investigate this we could estimate equation (7.17) for married women for transitory wage changes. Unfortunately identifying the transitory wage variables is problematic. Consequently most researchers have investigated the relationship between participation and unemployment as an indicator of cyclical transitory changes in market conditions. If an increase in unemployment leads to an increase in participation, the added worker effect dominates the discouraged worker effect, and vice versa. Studies using aggregate cross-section data suggest that the added worker effect dominates. It is doubtful, however, whether such a data base is appropriate to measure the relationships in question. In inter-regional studies unemployment differences are more likely to reflect long-term structural imbalances than transitory fluctuations in economic activity. Time-series data suggest that the discouraged worker effect dominates. The size of the effect may, however, have been exaggerated. This is because the measure of $P$ used refers only to those people in employment $E$ or *registered* as unemployed $U_R$: it excludes those people who are looking for work but do not register , $U_U$. Consequently $(E + U_R)$ increases more than $(E + U)$ because $E$ can rise as $U_U$ falls. The approach also fails to distinguish wage-induced from jobs-induced changes. To the degree that the latter are dominant, the previous argument concerning the increasing participation of married women is supported.

So far we have considered hours and participation decisions separately. This is the usual approach but it provides only a partial insight into labour supply decisions if interdependencies exist. One approach to this problem would be to estimate both hours and participation equations (7.15) and (7.17), using data for a sample of households through time. Unfortunately such data is not readily available. The empirical analysis of hours and participation, despite obvious gaps, is fairly well advanced. On the other hand, the empirical analysis of skill supply adjustments to which we now turn is not at all well developed.

## JOB MOBILITY

As with participation, an individual's decision to quit one job for another is dichotomous: he either quits or he does not. In principle there are several different ways of conducting empirical research. Preferably one could investigate the job histories of a group of workers in order to relate the number and nature of voluntary job moves they make to their personal, occupational and industrial characteristics and to market conditions at the occasion of each move. Alternatively one might compare individual work units or industries to correlate the rate of voluntary job mobility to their market circumstances and the characteristics of their labour forces. Again, one might relate job mobility for a unit, an industry or all industry to market conditions through time. One might also use surveys of workers to compare the characteristics of movers and non-movers. Questionnaires might be used to identify the reasons for quitting and the outcome of any move. Largely for data reasons there have been relatively few explicit tests of the theories of job mobility. The information we have derives primarily from case studies of certain work units, questionnaires, and cross-section and time-series econometric studies of quit rates by industry. Few longitudinal cohort studies exist.

Sample surveys have indicated that there is a considerable amount of job stability in the labour force. Approximately 60 per cent of men were found in one UK study of a 10 year period to have remained in the same job and 80 per cent had had no more than two jobs. Quits dominate total separations. The majority of quitters change jobs without any intervening period of unemployment. A significant proportion of quits involve job mobility. One survey estimated that approximately 50 per cent of job changes resulted in no change of occupational status, though it should be acknowledged that this survey employed a very broad occupational grouping. This leads us to observe that whilst the theory in Section 7.3 relates to job moves only within an occupation, those doing empirical work have the difficult task of defining what constitutes an occupation. According to our theoretical approach two jobs should be classified as belonging to the same occupation if no additional education is required to move between them. In practice every move involves some educational input, however small, so the problem is to decide the cut-off level. The difficulty inherent in doing this is one of the reasons for the lack of separate information on job mobility. Surveys indicate the importance of quits into inactivity for women. On the other hand women appear less likely than men to quit to change jobs, *ceteris paribus*. The majority of moves appear to result in higher wages, to an extent which increases with occupational level. This is consistent with the theory of investment behind job moves. Informal information-gathering methods are by far the most important basis for search.

There are severe practical problems associated with aggregate econometric analysis of quits. First, official quits data relate to moves from industries not firms, and give no indication of the destination of the flow. It is therefore impossible to separate out job mobility from flows into inactivity or from occupational mobility. Second, UK data are available only for total separations and do not distinguish voluntary from involuntary flows. Third, there is no way with aggregate data of confidently identifying the other jobs, and therefore the wages and job openings that represent the attractions to potential quitters. Fourth, we are forced to correlate the quit rate, the number of quits per 100 workers, with the characteristics of the labour force as a whole rather than with those of workers who quit; the two may be very different. Fifth, search costs in practice are very difficult to quantify. Resort to intuitively plausible proxy variables invariably leaves us with results that are consistent with alternative explanations of quit behaviour. Sixth, the identification problem is particularly difficult in this case because of the lack of data on the fixed costs of labour which crucially determine firms' wage strategy towards quits.

The available statistics for industry quit rates suggest that voluntary job mobility is strongly pro-cyclical as theory predicts. Time series regressions reveal a positive relationship, *ceteris paribus*, between quits and vacancies, with a very short lag, and between quits and relative wages. Cross-section regression analysis also indicates that quits are sensitive to wage signals. There is some evidence that quits are negatively related to the size of the firm and to the presence of trade unions. There is some evidence in support of the screening approach, though it is as yet rather limited: quit rates have been found to be correlated with the number of job openings, the distribution of external wages and certain proxies for search costs, such as the regional distribution of economic activity.

Aggregate statistics in the UK do not permit the investigation of discharges separately from quits. However, there have been several case studies following the experiences of groups of redundant workers. These have shown that redundant workers must search longer than other unemployed workers for any new job and that they have a higher propensity to become inactive.

## OCCUPATIONAL CHOICE

The fundamental tenet of the human capital theory of occupational choice is that individuals or households make systematic assessments of the likely future income benefits from different occupations when they make their decisions between different education paths. The most direct prediction of the model is thus that the number of applications to a particular schooling programme will vary with the net return to the programme. In fact very few studies of the demand for particular educational programmes have been undertaken. Such an analysis would require information upon income profiles and net returns for specific education courses rather than for broadly defined education levels. In practice this is too severe a data requirement. Such an analysis would also require information on the number of applicants rather than on the number of entrants in order to avoid the identification problem. In practice we usually have data only on entrants. Where the government fixes the numbers undertaking education, through its control of educational establishments perhaps, it is impossible to calculate demand relationships for there is only one observation: the government target. The available studies have indicated that demand does follow prospective returns, but these studies have invariably been subject to the most severe statistical reservations.

The second major human capital prediction concerning the flow between schooling and occupations is that private net returns to different educational paths, and thus to different levels and subjects, will converge. All private internal rates of return will in the long run equal the interest rate. Empirical work to test this must unfortunately be based upon very broadly defined education levels rather than upon subjects but many calculations of rates of return have been made. In theory individuals take decisions on how far to carry their education on the basis of incremental rates of returns calculated from their own alternative expected lifetime earnings profiles. Such profiles are not directly observable. In practice therefore an average net returns figure must be calculated from income data relating to a cross section of individuals as follows. Imagine we have earnings data for a group of individuals who have all completed education programmes to reach level $i$. The group covers a broad spectrum of age–experience levels. Similar data for individuals who have attained the higher education level $j$ are also available. We use the earnings for the individuals of different ages who have reached the $i$th level to indicate the earnings any school leaver who has attained education level $i$ would receive over her lifetime. A similar profile is constructed from the data for individuals at the $j$th level. Every point on either profile actually represents current income for a different individual but we employ them to indicate the alternative expected lifetime income streams of an individual. Together with data on education costs these profiles are then used to derive an estimate of the incremental private net return to individuals undertaking education to move from level $i$ to level $j$ as described formally in Chapter 3. Such net return estimates can of course be derived for many different education steps.

The broad finding of such studies is that lifetime income profiles are higher for higher education groups. Private internal rates of return to educational investments are high, often much higher in real terms than the market interest rate or the rate of return on capital. There is little evidence that these high rates are merely transitory. Broadly speaking, post-compulsory schooling offers rates of return around 10 per cent. Acquiring a first degree appears to offer a return in the USA between 10 and 15 per cent, and significantly higher in the UK. Masters' degrees offer a higher rate of return, approximately 15–20 per cent. The results for PhDs are of the same order of magnitude as for voluntary schooling. Though less numerous, the studies of non-university formal tertiary education reveal higher returns than to a first degree.

The method of determining net returns outlined above suffers from a number of defects. First, calculations using a cross-section of individuals ignore differences in ability levels. The samples of individuals with education $i$ and $j$ each contains individuals of very different abilities. It may be that those in the $j$ group are more able. There could be able individuals, presumably on the left of the profiles, who will move on beyond $i$ and $j$. Cross-section income profiles are likely to overstate incremental returns and thus the prospects for any given individual. Second, lifetime earnings profiles derived from cross-section data cannot take into account future changes in demand and productivity, and therefore future changes in relative wages. This deficiency is only very partially met by adjusting the cross-section data for projected productivity mark-ups. Third, net returns to each educational level will be an average over a considerable number of different subjects and occupations, which makes it difficult to derive a clear picture either of the true opportunities facing any individual or of the decision-making process. Fourth, only a part of the income received by individuals in the two samples is due to education *per se*. Ability adjustments, where only two-thirds of an individual's increase in income are attributed to education, have been used but this is an arbitrary device. Fifth, earnings profiles have been found to slope up. This is partly due to learning by doing but also to additional investment. To calculate rates of return to schooling the effects of training have to be removed. Sixth, the estimated rates of return are averages across individuals who took their investment decision in perhaps very different circumstances. Finally, net returns may vary considerably across different educational establishments.

Human capital theory predicts that, because flows into occupations are sensitive to net returns, skill adjustments will tend to equalise the returns to entering different occupations. Moreover, to the extent that occupations in practice can be divided into different grades, net returns will also be equalised across grades. Because of data problems there are few empirical studies bearing upon these predictions. The available evidence is that net returns to education across grades *within* given occupational classifications are reasonably similar. But net returns are sometimes very different *between* occupations. Rates of return to different schooling disciplines are similar for arts, sciences and technology but consistently higher for law and other vocational social sciences. Significant differences in net returns have also been observed even between occupations with seemingly significant elements of transferable skills – different medical specialisations for example.

Theory predicts that resources are optimally allocated when *social* net returns are equalised. Private net returns in this case might exceed market rates of return on capital by a significant amount. The high estimated private net returns might therefore simply result from controls imposed by government and private bodies upon finance and the supply of education facilities in pursuit of the socially optimal allocation of resources. This is an argument which clearly hinges upon the level of the social net returns to education. A methodology similar to that used for private returns, but including all resource costs to society, can be used to calculate social returns. In countries where the government or private bodies are heavily involved in subsidising formal post-compulsory schooling, social rates of return are significantly below private rates of return. For example, social rates of return to a first degree are less than 10 per cent and for post-compulsory schooling up to 18 closer to 5 per cent. Whilst much depends on what precisely we take as the rate of return to capital, it would seem that the social returns to education exceed returns to many alternative uses of funds. For non-university tertiary education social rates of return are almost 20 per cent.

Evidence in support of the human capital approach to occupational choice is patchy. The limited evidence seems to suggest under-investment in education, particularly at the lower levels of the skill hierarchy. Little research has to date been undertaken to test the predictions of the theory of credentialism introduced in Chapter 4. Since credentialism and human capital produce similar predictions from very different starting points, empirical labour market analysis cannot distinguish between them. Both suggest a strong relationship between educational choice and earnings but for different reasons.

## OCCUPATIONAL MOBILITY

Skill supply adjustments through occupational mobility, like those through market entry, are difficult to study because in practice we observe actual mobility not the nature and extent of workers' attempts at mobility. We therefore have little way of knowing how far workers' investment decisions are frustrated or impaired by forces on the demand side. Systematic analysis would require continuous observation and assessment of individual workers' occupational choice decisions over their working lifetimes. As already noted such longitudinal studies are rare.

Perforce the principal methodology employed in studies of occupational mobility involves questioning a group of workers on their recent market activities. Such studies face certain problems. First, there are limits to the number of individuals that can be covered in such surveys, which is critical because sufficient examples of each kind of market decision are needed if valid inferences are to be drawn. Second, there are limits to the number of questions respondents can reasonably be expected to answer. Third, such a data source may be good in that it often provides information on attitudes but may at the same time be deficient if it relies too heavily upon accounts of past events rather than on what actually happened. Fourth, as noted earlier, there are very large problems in defining and thus in distinguishing occupations, specifying the direction and distance of moves, identifying training requirements and so on. Much of what is analysed as occupational mobility may be job mobility. Levels of aggregation and classification systems vary considerably between studies. Fifth, the success of any move is often difficult to assess, as is the existence of an intertemporal relationship between moves. In consequence the empirical work so far has tended to be more descriptive than rigorously analytical. The following general observations are offered from these studies. First, over quite long periods of time a large majority of people have been found *not* to change their occupational classification. Second, short distance moves (occupationally) occur much more frequently than long distance moves. Third, moves become more likely the higher the occupation level. Fourth, at any occupation level those with qualifications are much more likely to move up and more likely to recover from a fall than others of the same age. Fifth, questionnaires suggest that upward mobility tends to dominate downward mobility, presumably because of the increased demand for higher skills in a growing economy. Mobility downwards is relatively rare for those in the top occupational group. More than one study has found that approximately one-third of all workers in the lowest occupation group move upwards over a 10 year period. Sixth, analysis of occupational mobility within the firm indicates that very few moves between broad occupational groups take place, presumably because in this case on-the-job training is not enough. Case studies of individual firms, however, have revealed significant short distance upward internal mobility within the lowest skill grades in particular. Nevertheless, it appears that moves between firms still constitute the most common avenue for upward occupational mobility. The same case studies have indicated how at the lower skill levels voluntary downward mobility can be an important phenomenon where declining relative wages are significant. From surveys of firms there seems to be no shortage of perfectly able workers willing to undertake training and occupational mobility. Many firms are able to train people continuously simply as a reserve for the time when openings appear.

We have little direct evidence on demand for training or the net returns to different training investments. Much of this training is on-the-job and internal to the firm. The number of applications is unknown and the costs involved are unrecorded. Empirical analysis to derive net returns by the cross-section method would require us to identify a group of people who have considered a certain training programme, some of whom did not take it up and some who did. The latter subgroup would have to include people who did not go beyond this training programme otherwise we would face the problem of separating out the effects of subsequent investments. Two cross-sections by age and experience would be required. In practice these are prohibitive requirements. First, training programmes, especially on the job, are extraordinarily heterogeneous even if 'programme' has some meaning in this context. Second, identifying and approaching a sample of workers would be costly. Third, firms may not have the necessary amount or quality of cost data. Fourth, it would almost certainly be impossible to find a large enough cross-section of workers undertaking the same training. In the absence of such studies, empirical work has concentrated upon case studies of particular firms. These by and large do not provide very much insight into the supply side.

The only explicit calculations of net returns available relate to state-supported training programmes, through either government training facilities or employer organisations. The private net returns are high and the demand for places is in general strong. This indicates an under-investment which in this case appears to be largely due to restrictions on the supply of places. Studies of employer group training programmes again suggest no scarcity of good applicants, high private returns and yet there is often evidence of skill shortages in areas to which the training programmes relate.

## 7.6 The characteristics of labour suppliers

So far our analysis has been concerned with developing and testing explanations of the decision making behind labour supply adjustments. In this section we move on to consider the consequences for efficiency, but primarily for income distribution, of labour supply behaviour.

HOURS AND PARTICIPATION

Labour is a scarce factor the total quantity of which is not expanding very fast. The question whether observed adjustments of hours and participation are consistent with an efficient use of labour's productive capacity is therefore an important one. The thrust of the theory in Sections 7.1 and 7.2 was that an efficient allocation of resources can be achieved if workers make rational decisions that take full account of all market signals. In practice individuals optimise subject to constraints so for efficiency one important issue is whether the gains arising from those constraints, for example normal hours and tax structures, outweigh the losses arising from the distortions they produce. Our theory provides some basis upon which to assess such questions and upon which, therefore, to evaluate alternative policies. What advantages and disadvantages would there be, for example, in providing more part-time jobs, increasing state transfers, restricting overtime or allocating more resources to state employment services? But, because any adjustment to hours or participation is likely to have considerable impact upon individual or household income and therefore welfare, the question inevitably arises: which workers are the principal suppliers of labour time?

One would expect that older workers will supply fewer annual hours than younger people. Though they may have accumulated market skills these will no doubt have deteriorated with time. Older workers have fewer consumption demands, fewer family responsibilities, greater access to accumulated savings, and may suffer lower productivity in market activities due to impaired health. If older workers become inactive or unemployed there is less chance that they will choose to resume employment than younger workers: search and training investments will be unprofitable given their limited remaining active years; they benefit more from redundancy payments and entitlement to early retirement. One would thus expect less participation and fewer hours from older workers. Prime age workers in particular will supply more annual hours.

The available evidence is broadly consistent with these expectations. Official statistics show that for men the hours distribution with age is bell-shaped with the peak at the age group 30–39. For full-time women in manual occupations the same is true though the variation is much smaller. Women's hours increase when they switch from part-time to full-time work as they move beyond the family rearing stage. Participation for men after the years of optional schooling is high and varies little with age until 55 when the participation rate falls from approximately 98 to 83 per cent. The participation rate for women falls from over 80 per cent to around 50 per cent for the 25–34 age group then rises to 65 per cent for the 46–54 age group before falling again to 50 per cent for those in the 55–60 age category. Cross-section industry studies have found no significant effect of age upon the supply of hours for men but a positive effect of prime age upon demand for hours. Entering an age variable in equivalent regression equations for women reveals a strong negative effect on hours supplied, *ceteris paribus*, for age groups above 45. Regressions using individual male data reveal a small positive own wage effect and large negative income effect upon the hours of older workers other things taken into account: older people are particularly sensitive to reductions in their earning ability as their productivity falls.

Participation by older people has declined through time. This could be because better pensions have encouraged early retirement. Alternatively it could be because job opportunities for older people have declined; with rigid wages their falling productivity prices them out of the market. Participation rates for young people have been falling because of the growth of the education sector. Regressions for participation by age across individuals indicate that the positive own wage effect is largest for younger male workers. For women the effect is largest between the ages of 30 and 49.

In Sections 7.1 and 7.2 it was argued that the annual labour supply of workers discriminated against in the labour market will, *ceteris paribus*, be lower than that of other workers. As noted previously, official statistics are consistent with this prediction for women, though the precise role of labour market discrimination is unclear. Let us here focus upon the labour supply of black workers. Statistics indicate that black people work the same, if not slightly more, hours than whites. They are much more likely to work shifts, however, presumably to increase their take-home pay. The proportion of black workers who are completely unskilled and therefore low paid is not significantly greater than for whites but there is a significantly smaller proportion of blacks in the highest manual and all non-manual occupations. Black women tend to be much more heavily concentrated in low skilled manual occupations than white women. They work more hours than white women. Entering a colour variable into cross-section studies of hours indicates a negative effect for West Indians but a positive effect for other black groups, *ceteris paribus*. In studies using individual data the differences between black and white equations are small at most income levels, but for low income groups the negative income effect for blacks is smaller, *ceteris paribus*, than for whites whilst the own wage effect is larger. For black women the income effect is again smaller than that for white women but the own wage effect is much larger at high incomes and smaller at low incomes.

Participation statistics show little difference for black and white men. The participation rate for black women is higher than for white women. In regressions using cross-section aggregate data a colour variable has a negative coefficient when other factors are taken into account for the age groups up to 34 but positive for the rest. In individual data regressions the own wage elasticity for black men is small but larger than for white men. For black women the own wage elasticity is much larger than for white women.

Some of this evidence is inconsistent with the predicted negative effect of discrimination on annual hours. Black workers tend to earn a smaller basic wage than white (12 per cent less on average for West Indian male manual workers in one study) and they also have low family incomes. The observed similar hours and participation rates of blacks and whites are consistent with the finding that blacks have a larger negative own wage effect. For black women higher overall hours and participation rate are inconsistent with the larger positive own wage effects. But individual studies show that the elasticity of wives' labour supply to husbands' wage is much more strongly negative for black than for white women. It may be that the direct effects of discrimination are overwhelmed in practice and in statistical studies by the requirement for low income B workers to raise family income. Alternatively discrimination may be reduced by the concentration of black workers in certain areas. (The proportion of black workers in large firms, for example, is much higher than for whites.)

Consistent with the prediction in Section 7.2 skilled workers are observed to participate more than unskilled workers (92 per cent compared with 88 per cent for men using occupation groups). Econometric studies of participation have not sought to identify differences by skill but those using individual data have included educational qualifications. These have been found to have a positive impact upon participation, *ceteris paribus*. The evidence on hours is that, contrary to the predictions of Section 7.1, the least skilled workers work more hours. Of non-manual workers in one study 81 per cent worked less than 40 hours per week; 61 per cent of manual workers worked more than 40 hours. Entering a skill variable in cross-section aggregate studies of hours supply produces a positive coefficient for unskilled manual workers. Entering educational qualifications into regressions with individual data produces very strong negative effects for higher qualifications, *ceteris paribus*. One interpretation of these results is that higher skills and education are associated not only with more job satisfaction but also with increased utility from non-market activities. Alternatively it may be that the education variable is picking up an income effect. Lower income/education/skill groups supply more hours simply because their expenditure commitments leave them little choice. But the difficulty of getting a job reduces their participation because they may become discouraged.

## MOBILITY

Mobility is essential if an economy is to achieve an efficient allocation of resources. Wage movements may provide scarcity signals but mobility produces the redeployment of labour across different outputs and skills that minimises costs and maximises consumer satisfaction. Job mobility brings wages into line within single markets. Occupational mobility brings wages across skills into line with training costs. Theory suggests that if workers take rational investment decisions on the basis of market signals, bearing in mind adjustment costs, labour markets will be efficient. One task of empirical work therefore is to assess the efficiency of labour markets. But of course theory also provides a basis upon which to evaluate policy options. What, for example, are the efficiency gains and losses to be derived from legislation to protect employment or to assist employers' training programmes? Whilst mobility improves efficiency it generates both benefits and costs for individuals. In some cases, in particular where redundancies are involved, the personal losses may outweigh the gains. But, whatever happens, supply adjustments through mobility will have consequences for distribution. Since most theories of stratification regard social levels as closely related to occupations, occupational and social mobility are much the same thing. Individual differences in occupational mobility are therefore important not just for income and consumption differences but also for the distribution of status and power. Who therefore are the mobile workers?

Both regression analysis of industry data and case studies of firms show clearly that job mobility decreases with skills. However, surveys indicate that the profitability of movement increases with skills. In other words there is some indication that lower skill workers are likely to move between jobs without increasing efficiency or their rewards and suffer the costs associated with mobility. The less skilled suffer redundancy more than other groups and are thus more likely to be pressured into taking less well paid jobs.

The available evidence indicates, as noted in Section 7.4, that occupational stability is greatest for those with the lowest skills. In one survey two-thirds of those in the lowest occupations (by earnings) were still there after 10 years. Education qualifications have been found to be critically important to mobility. Of those in professional grades 50 per cent in one survey had degrees. Approximately 90 per cent of semi-skilled and unskilled workers had no qualifications at all. Though social mobility is limited for the individual there is evidence that inter-generational occupational mobility is somewhat less restricted.

The theoretical analysis of mobility emphasises human capital and search variables. That analysis suggests that job mobility will be considerably more common amongst young people. First, young people will not have had sufficient time to acquire significant specific skills. Second, young people have accumulated less labour market information. Third, their search costs will be lower. Surveys and case studies of individual firms have shown the significance of quits for young people, and indeed for all those with short tenure. Econometric work with industry data has shown that this result holds even when wages and other factors are taken into account. Case studies and surveys have also indicated that discharges include a disproportionate number of young people, presumably because they impose lower severance costs.

Our theoretical analysis would also lead us to expect that older workers will be inclined to make less occupational moves than other workers. The attractiveness of a quit is reduced by their limited working lifetime over which to recoup training outlays, lesser effectiveness in training, and strong attachment to existing skills. Older discharged workers will be more attracted to non-market activities and less attracted to search. Surveys have shown that occupational mobility declines rapidly with age. It is very low indeed for older workers in the lowest occupational groups.

In the discussion of Section 7.3 it was predicted that, *ceteris paribus*, workers who are members of groups discriminated against in the labour market will be less mobile voluntarily across jobs than other workers. There is in fact a considerable concentration of such groups in certain low skilled, low paid areas of the labour market which simultaneously reduces exposure to discrimination and effectively restricts occupational choice. The total quit rate for women exceeds that for men, but the inference from surveys is that this is due solely to the importance for women of quits into inactivity for domestic reasons. There are several factors which inhibit mobility for women. Married women are secondary workers and the investment in search required to improve their position may be regarded as prohibitive by the household. Many jobs are closed to women which will inhibit voluntary mobility. The evidence from cross-section aggregate quits studies is that *ceteris paribus* women have a lower level of job mobility than men. There is some evidence in these studies, however, that black male workers experience more voluntary job mobility than white workers, *ceteris paribus*.

There is evidence from surveys and case studies that B workers are over-represented in discharges because they are concentrated in industries subject to demand contractions, and, particularly in the case of women, because they have part-time jobs. One survey showed that 31 per cent of West Indians leaving their jobs were dismissed from their jobs as against 19 per cent for whites though the proportions made redundant were not dissimilar. The proportion of black and white women discharged were similar. The study found that blacks' disadvantage increases with occupational level which suggests that education does not protect blacks against dismissal as it does whites.

The evidence on occupational mobility for black workers is sparse. They might be expected to have less voluntary mobility than whites since they often lack the skills or education required to cross occupational boundaries and the finances to cover the necessary training. One survey indicated that 48 per cent of economically active whites had no qualifications at all as against 65 per cent for West Indians. Blacks are concentrated in the lowest skill groups where occupational stability is highest. One study revealed that occupational differences between blacks and whites in their current jobs are greater than in their initial job which is consistent with discrimination in promotion and training.

So far in this section we have found that in practice labour supply adjustments for most workers, particularly those in the lowest occupational groups, may be rather limited. Participation is not a decision variable for most men. Limits to hours worked are set by firms. Job mobility may bring only limited financial rewards and upward occupational mobility is restricted to a minority. As far as any single worker's lifetime welfare is concerned, therefore, the decision about which occupation to follow becomes absolutely crucial.

OCCUPATIONAL CHOICE

The analysis in Section 7.4 suggests that the labour market will work efficiently if educational choices broadly follow rational investment criteria. The analysis provides a means of evaluating the decisions made by individual investors, the providers of education programmes and the state. It therefore offers a framework for assessing, for example, the impact of student grants, the range of educational programmes offered, the case for state direction. But who are the principal investors in education?

In Section 7.5 we noted that net returns to education are higher than returns to physical capital indicating under-investment in human capital. One explanation is that there is both under-provision of programmes by the state and private bodies and myopia on the part of individuals. An alternative explanation is that extra-market forces produce systematic under-investment by specific groups of individuals. Let us consider these two explanations.

In Figure 7.2 the demand curve, $D$, represents the internal rate of return to each additional unit of expenditure on education for a given individual. It is downward sloping because, as noted in Chapter 3, there are diminishing returns to fixed abilities and because more education means both a shorter working life and greater foregone earnings. The supply curve represents the marginal opportunity cost of financing increments to education. If there were no capital market imperfections, the supply curve would be horizontal at the market rate of interest, $r$. At the margin incremental rates of return would be the same for every individual and education investments would vary only with the demand for education; with abilities, tastes, attitudes to risk and so on.

The first explanation for high rates of return to education is set out in Figure 7.3(a). The supply of educational facilities is exogenously restricted. Places are allocated so that each individual has an allocation of $\bar{E}$. The rate of return to education will in general be above the interest rate and different individuals will reach different education levels according to their allocation of educational facilities. If places are allocated by ability then those with demand curves furthest to the right will have higher $\bar{E}$ levels as in the figure. In principle, though higher ability people will undertake more education, there is no

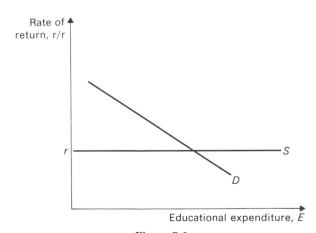

**Figure 7.2**

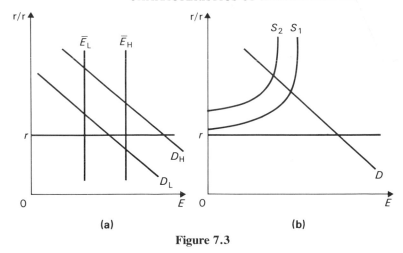

**Figure 7.3**

reason why they should earn a lower rate of return than lower ability people. It depends upon the supply of places at each level.

If insufficient numbers of people choose to undertake education at the lower levels because of myopia the rate of return will be higher than in the figure and there could even be places available at these low levels.

Consider now the alternative scenario in Figure 7.3(b) where we assume that there are severe capital market imperfections. Borrowing for education becomes increasingly difficult and expensive the more finance is required. The supply curve for any individual is thus upward sloping. As borrowing opportunities are exhausted, each family depletes its accumulated resources, and foregoes current consumption at increasing opportunity cost. In the end no further finance is available. The supply curve therefore becomes vertical. Since households have different levels of credit worthiness and accumulated resources, the location of the supply curves varies considerably. Therefore, incremental rates of return will always be above the interest rate and, for given tastes and abilities, those with the least family resources will undertake the least education and will have the highest incremental returns. No doubt low income individuals will invest not only in less education but also in lower quality education. If previous academic record is used to determine access to higher education levels the cumulative effect will be seriously to limit their progress. Furthermore, low income individuals will also underinvest in education: if low income is associated with lower social capital and thus reduced educational achievement; if the criteria for access to higher levels are signals correlated with income, e.g. recreational interests; if low income is associated with discrimination in the educational sector. Because of the lack of competition from lower income individuals, who would bring down the incremental rates of return at the margin, some individuals in the higher income groups will pursue their education further than would otherwise be the case. In a world of ability differences some higher resource individuals will invest further than low income higher ability individuals.

The evidence from the analysis of social stratification is that working class children do lack the family financial resources to overcome capital market imperfections. The implication of the model above therefore is that working class children will receive significantly smaller quantities and lower qualities of schooling than other children and they will have higher net returns to initial educational investments. The same prediction will apply with additional force to members of minority groups and to working class girls if there is discrimination within the educational sector or within the family against these groups. To the extent that discrimination inside the labour market reduces job satisfaction and to the extent that B workers specialise in domestic activities, their rate of return to compulsory education will be smaller, inactivity more likely and returns to the first optional educational investment smaller. On the other hand if discrimination decreases with educational level the incremental rate of return could actually increase with additional increments to education. This could therefore lead to a polarisation in the investment outlays of B people, some investing little compared to their A equivalents, others much more. The model indicates that under-investment in education is peculiar to certain groups. Their disadvantage in occupational choice will not be a matter of innate ability or luck but systematically related to background. Introducing restrictions on educational facilities merely strengthens this prediction.

There is statistical evidence that children from lower class families are strongly under-represented in post-compulsory schooling. The following figures merely indicate the general picture. Less than 25 per cent of university students in Britain are of working class origin (socio-economic classes (SEC) IV, V, VI; skilled, semi-skilled and unskilled manual). For most of the rest of Western Europe the figure is less than 20 per cent. (Children of working-class origin form 60 per cent of their age group.) For Britain the proportion of students in advanced further education who come from working class families is 35 per cent. Despite the growth of higher education these figures have not changed much in three decades; the growth has mainly benefited middle class families. The proportion of children in select schools (grammar, etc.) in Great Britain (before comprehensivisation) who were from working class backgrounds was around 50 per cent whereas in Europe it is again lower at approximately 20 per cent. Attrition levels are, however, higher for working class children during schooling so that only 20 per cent of those completing the course were working class. Approximately 75 per cent of children aged 16–19 in Britain from professional families receive post-compulsory schooling. The figure for children from semi-skilled and unskilled manual families is 25 per cent. Of working class children 75 per cent leave school with no qualifications at all compared with 34 per cent from SEC I and II. Of children under 5 from professional and managerial classes 50 per cent attend playgroups or a day nursery against 30 per cent of those from semi- and unskilled classes.

The percentage of women in British universities is 33 per cent; the percentage in all further education is 36 per cent. Less than 18 per cent of women in universities come from working class backgrounds. There is little difference between the proportions of boys and girls leaving school with various qualifications, but the qualifications tend to be in different subjects.

As noted previously the proportion of economically active blacks with no educational qualifications is higher than for whites, significantly so for West Indians.

Results from cross-section estimates of rates of return indicate that net returns for various levels of education are significantly higher than average for women, blacks and non-native individuals. Net returns to education are higher at the lower educational levels, where disadvantaged groups are concentrated.

## Further Reading

CHAPTER 7: LABOUR SUPPLY ADJUSTMENTS

G. Becker and B. Chiswick, 'Education and the distribution of earnings', *American Economic Review*, Vol. 56 (December 1966).
G. Cain and C. Watts, *Income Maintenance and Labour Supply* (Chicago: Rand McNally, 1973).
B. Chiswick, *Income Inequalities – Regional Analyses within a Human Capital Framework* (New York: National Bureau of Economic Research, 1974).
C. Greenhalgh and K. Mayhew, 'Labour supply in Britain: theory and evidence', in Z. Hornstein, J. Grice and A. Webb (eds), *The Economics of Labour Market* (London: HMSO, 1981).
R. Layard, M. Barton and A. Zabalza, 'Married women's participation and hours', *Economica*, Vol 47 (February 1980).
D. Metcalf and S. Nickell, 'Occupational mobility in Britain', in R. Ehrenburg (ed.) *Research in Labor Economics*, Vol. 5 (Greenwich, Conn.: Jai Press, 1982).
D. Parsons, 'Models of labour market turnover: a theoretical and empirical survey', in R. Ehrenburg (ed.), *Research in Labor Economics*, Vol. 1 (Greenwich, Conn.: Jai Press, 1977).
A. Ziderman. 'Does it pay to take a degree?', *Oxford Economic Papers*, Vol. 25 (July 1973).

# 8
# Employment adjustments

The basic model of the labour market is founded upon competition between profit-maximising firms operating subject to given production technologies, labour supply constraints and product demand conditions. There are predetermined quantities of homogeneous labour in each skill category and wages are the sole cost of employing labour. Out of this approach comes the neoclassical theory of labour demand, the central prediction of which is that worker-hours will be hired until the wage is equal to labour's marginal revenue product. All firms react to changes in product demand or wages instantaneously, adjusting hours and hiring or firing labour, so that each firm operates at the static equilibrium input solution defined by current input prices and the production function.

In this chapter we reconsider the theory of labour demand in the light of the theoretical developments discussed in Section I. We recognise that the number of hours per worker is institutionally regulated and we thus introduce overtime. We dispense with the assumption of homogeneous labour and we thus introduce uncertainty and screening. We discard the assumption of fixed quantities of labour in each skill category and we thus allow for human capital investments by the firm and by workers. The screening and training costs incurred by the firm make labour *a quasi-fixed factor* and drive a wedge between the wage and the marginal revenue product. Significant adjustment costs mean that, following any change in input or product prices, the firm does not move instantly to a new equilibrium but moves gradually using a variety of adjustment devices. We shall have cause in this chapter to consider, *inter alia*, hiring and overtime, discharges and labour hoarding, quits, and the internal labour market.

## 8.1  A model of employment adjustments by the firm

Consider the behaviour of a profit-maximising competitive firm operating in the short run with fixed technology and capital stock. Whenever the firm hires it will find it profitable, as suggested in Chapter 4, to engage in screening activities because labour is heterogeneous within each skill. It will also provide additional training. Every hire thus imposes both screening and training costs upon the firm. We begin to see that one implication of the theoretical developments discussed in Section I is that labour imposes costs upon the firm far beyond the hourly wage rate. The latter represents a variable cost to the firm, varying directly with the quantity of the labour input, worker-hours. Search and training costs are fixed costs in the sense that, though they vary with the number of workers hired and thus employed, they do not vary with labour utilisation. In fact there are fixed costs associated with employing and discharging, as well as hiring, workers. A summary of the costs associated with each worker might be as follows:

(a)  recruitment costs (RC)   from advertising, screening and selection procedures, initial training and supervision

(b)  employment costs (EC)   from state *per capita* labour taxes, insurance payments, mandatory sickness and pension contributions

(c)  severance costs (SC)   from obligatory redundancy/lay off payments, penalty clauses in contracts, dislocation to production.

Together these costs justify treating labour as a quasi-fixed rather than variable factor of production. Their existence has considerable impact upon the adjustment procedures followed by firms and therefore upon the demand for labour.

Consider the following simple model. Imagine a firm operating in the short run, initially in static equilibrium i.e. at the optimal input combination and output level defined by current input and product prices *with no fixed labour costs*. The labour input is made up of workers $(E)$ and hours, the latter being composed of normal hours $(NH)$ and overtime $(OH)$. The firm is subject to a certain number of quits, $q$, per period. We assume that it is impossible to hold stocks so that all current sales must come from current output. For a given production period, $t - 1$, we can therefore define the following relationships governing output, $X$, and employment:

$$X = f(E, NH, OH) \qquad (8.1)$$

$$E = \bar{E} - Q - R + Hi \qquad (8.2)$$

where $\bar{E}$ is labour retained from the previous period, $R$ are redundancies or permanent lay-offs and $Hi$ are hires. Since equilibrium can be maintained without incurring adjustment costs it follows that in

$t - 1$ with a constant demand

$$R = 0, \qquad Hi = Q, \qquad OH = 0 \qquad (8.3)$$

Let us now introduce fixed labour costs in period $t$. The firm's total labour costs $(C)$ will be given by

$$C = E \times NH \times W + E \times EC + Hi \times RC$$
$$+ R \times SC + E \times OH \times (W + p) \quad (8.4)$$

where $W$ is the hourly wage rate and $p$ the overtime premium.

Let us first consider how the firm deals with quits. Imagine that a single quit occurs at the beginning of $t$. The firm anticipates that hiring an identical replacement will involve *recruitment costs*. It will therefore weigh up the costs and benefits of three options. Let us assume that, because of the quit, revenue will be $RV_1$ rather than $RV_0$. The first option is to hire, the net benefit of which is $(RV_0 - RV_1) - W - RC$. The net benefit of the second option, leaving the post open, is zero. Finally the firm could adjust by using overtime. Depending upon the amount of overtime used, revenue will rise to some level $RV_2$. The net benefit of this option will thus be $(RV_2(OH) - RV_1)$. The third option will then be to use $OH^*$ overtime hours where $OH^*$ maximises this net benefit expression. Depending upon the size of the different costs involved, particularly RC, the firm might find it optimal not to hire.

If several quits occur at the beginning of period $t$, $(RV_0 - RV_1)$ will increase with the number of posts vacated. At the same time RC per hire may rise with the number of hires per period. Under such conditions we can envisage the firm replacing most quitters but not immediately. At the end of the adjustment, if fixed costs are important, the firm might not attain its previous employment level. The issues involved here are pursued in Section 8.2 where we recognise that with heterogeneous labour there is no guarantee that the firm will find an identical replacement as assumed above and also that recruitment costs are once and for all outlays whereas the overtime premium is a continuous cost.

Consider now how the firm reacts to a permanent contraction in the demand for its product alongside the imposition of *severance costs*. We assume that quits are zero. Because of fixed costs the firm will not adjust immediately to the new equilibrium and that equilibrium will differ from that defined in a world without fixed costs. The firm considers the net benefits of each course open to it. If we assume that the fall in demand is equivalent to the output of one worker, then the first option is to discharge one of its current employees. Let us assume that if this happens the fall in revenue and in wage costs will be identical. However, the firm suffers a net loss equal to $SC$. A second course open to the firm is to retain the surplus worker, in which case the net loss is W. *Hoarded labour*, as it is called, may, however, make a positive contribution by reducing costs, in which case the net loss is less than W. Finally the firm could adopt short-time working and/or make a temporary lay-off. The firm will choose the least cost option.

In practice, a demand contraction will lead the firm to consider its position with regard to several workers. It also seems likely that the marginal contribution made by hoarded labour will fall with the amount of hoarding and SC will rise with the number of discharged workers. Optimal adjustment will require the shedding of labour, but over a period of time. These issues are considered more fully in Section 8.3.

We can now see that fixed labour costs drive a wedge between the wage and marginal revenue product. Even if the firm could hire identical workers to those who quit, $E_1 E_0$ in Figure 8.1(a), because of screening and training costs the firm will hire only $E_1 E_2$ workers. $rc$ represents the cost per period of the firm's time horizon of $n$ periods arising from the once and for all payment $RC$. Across subsequent periods, the wage, W, must be less than the MRP. Formally we can write where $T$ is the length of the training period:

$$\sum_{t=1}^{t=n} \frac{W_t}{(1 + r)^t} = \sum_{t=1}^{t=T} \frac{MRP_t}{(1 + r)^t} + \sum_{t=T+1}^{t=n} \frac{MRP_t}{(1 + r)^t} + RC \qquad (8.5)$$

Similarly a firm that is contracting must pay a wage less than the MRP as a consequence of severance costs. In Figure 8.1(b) when demand

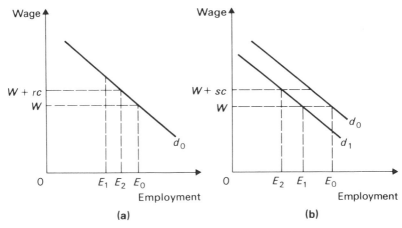

Figure 8.1

shifts from $d_0$ to $d_1$ the firm sheds labour to $E_2$ not to $E_1$ because the period severance costs *sc* must be recouped. We therefore have

$$\sum_{t=1}^{t=n} \frac{W_t}{(1+r)^t} = \sum_{t=1}^{t=n} \frac{MRP}{(1+t)^t} + SC \tag{8.6}$$

Initial training of an identical replacement creates specific skills. As noted in Chapter 3, for the firm to recoup its outlay, wages will be lower than marginal product over some part of the post-training period. Since screening and severance costs will be recouped over time they represent investments. If fixed costs vary across firms, workers will face a distribution of market wages.

In the cases analysed above of quits and demand contractions we have assumed that the firm simply responds to events. In practice the firm will attempt, as far as it is profitable, to exert some control over events. So, faced with a fall in demand, the firm might try to induce quits (if sufficient are not already forthcoming) and so obviate the need to make other labour adjustments. It could do this by reducing the wage it pays. Faced by a rise in demand or by quits, the firm might alternatively attempt to structure its internal labour market so as to minimise adjustment costs. These possibilities are considered in Sections 8.2 and 8.4 respectively.

In our analysis so far we have also assumed that the firm hires within the same skill category and thus only incurs costs of training recruits in specific skills. However, the firm might also incur costs for training recruits in general skills if it opts to adjust by hiring from a lower skill category. Whilst this imposes higher recruitment costs it may avoid a higher (scarcity) hiring wage or simply zero applications. The issues raised by such employment adjustments are discussed in Section 8.3.

We have also assumed that all labour of the same skill and quality is treated in an identical way by the firm. To the extent that firms practise discrimination and in particular employment discrimination this will affect hiring, hoarding, discharging, and training. We shall consider this in Section 8.6 when we look at the characteristics of the labour typically involved in employment adjustments.

## 8.2 The hiring decision

At the beginning of any period the firm anticipates that a certain number of workers will quit. Assuming that it expects no change in product demand, the firm faces five principal options: (a) to hire equally skilled replacements from the market; (b) to hire and train less skilled replacements from the market; (c) to promote from within and hire lower down; (d) to influence the level of quits; (e) to leave the posts vacant and adjust as efficiently as possible with its existing resources. After weighing up the relative merits of these strategies, the firm may well employ some combination of all of them. Let us for the moment, however, consider only options (a) and (e), leaving (b) and (d) until later in this section and (c) until Section 8.4.

## HIRING AND OVERTIME

The hiring of replacement labour takes place, as described in Chapter 4, in a world of heterogeneous labour even within a given skill category. In calculating the benefits of replacing a single quit by a hire the firm must therefore calculate the present value of its reservation quality, $PV(q^*)$, from knowledge of the distribution of qualities, the price of its output and its prospecting costs. If this, less the wage, $W$, and training costs, $TC$, is greater than zero (the net benefit of leaving the post empty) the firm will initiate prospecting. Recruitment costs are a once-for-all outlay whilst $PV(q^*)$ is calculated over several periods, which suggests that in practice the firm will usually attempt to find a replacement worker. Only if the firm were to calculate $PV(q^*)$ over a short time horizon with a high discount rate and if RC were large would the post simply disappear with the quit. Once prospecting has begun, with limited recall the reservation quality will fall as prospecting continues. The firm will continue to call in applicants for interview until an acceptable replacement is found. The post will disappear if, when $PV(q^* - W - TC)$ has fallen to zero, no acceptable applicant has been found so that prospecting is terminated.

If the firm faces several quits it may find that the reservation quality for each additional hire declines with the number of hires it attempts to make in any period. At the same time the cost per hire may rise with the number of hires per period. Therefore, even if the firm does eventually replace all quitters it will not try to do so immediately. The firm will spread out its hiring, for by so doing it increases the expected quality of its recruits and reduces total hiring costs. When it comes to defining its optimal adjustment path the firm must set this against the expected foregone revenue of delaying hiring.

We can set up the following propositions from this analysis. First, with a number of quits taking place at the beginning of $t$, the greater the increase in RC with hires, *ceteris paribus*, the stronger the incentive for the firm to spread its hiring beyond $t$ and into future periods. Second, the higher are prospecting costs and initial specific training costs the more likely it is that the firm will not replace all quitters. Third, the longer the firm expects to retain workers or jobs to last, the longer the discounted stream of returns to hiring and thus the stronger the likelihood of hiring. Similarly, the lower the discount rate used the stronger is that likelihood. Fourth, any expectation on the firm's part that hiring will be more profitable in the future (perhaps because more high quality people will become available or because prospecting costs will be smaller) will tend to delay adjustment. Fifth, adjustment will be more rapid if and to the degree that the firm expects revenue to fall permanently because unfulfilled orders reduce customer goodwill. Sixth, if demand is expected to rise in some future period, the discounted benefit to replacing quitters is higher. Whether the firm does in fact hire to avoid compounding its problems later will depend crucially upon its expectations as to future as compared with current hiring costs. Seventh, new employees could be more or less productive than those who quit. Profits could thus be higher after adjustment than previously, despite the incurring of recruitment costs.

In practice the alternative to hiring a replacement worker is not to do nothing but to use overtime. In principle the firm could use enough overtime to maintain its output at the $t - 1$ level, but only at a cost. The net benefit to overtime for any amount of overtime employed, $OH$, will be $[P_o.OH - OH.(W + p)]$, where $P_o$ is the average revenue product of overtime hours. If when considering a single hire the firm calculated over an infinite time horizon, it would never use overtime which involves a continuous cost whereas hiring does not. It would prospect and hire. Over a shortened horizon with high discount rates and high RC it might, however, be the case that the firm chooses to use overtime. It would use $OH^*$ hours, which maximises the net benefit expression above, as long as the net benefit is greater than zero. When faced with several quits and increasing marginal hiring costs, the availability of overtime makes it more likely that the firm will spread out its adjustment. Overtime makes it possible for the firm to spread out its hiring without forsaking all the quitters' output. Whether overtime is undertaken, how much and for how long thus depends upon the costs of hiring and the size of the elements in the net benefit calculation for overtime.

We can formulate the following predictions. First, the lower the productivity of overtime hours and the higher the premium the less likely it is, *ceteris paribus*, that overtime will be used and the shorter the period over which hiring takes place. Second, if overtime is used, the more $P_o$ falls and/or $p$ rises with the amount of overtime the less overtime will be employed, and generally the more hiring will take place in each period. Third, the higher recruitment costs and the faster they rise with the number of hires the more likely it is that overtime will be worked, the more of it will be used and for a longer period. Fourth, given that the firm recoups RC over several periods and that RC falls as fewer and fewer hires take place, overtime will decline through time. It is better than nothing when there are large numbers of unfilled posts but it becomes increasingly expensive in relative terms. Fifth, because overtime premiums in practice are significant, at the margin hiring is preferable to any amount of overtime so that in the final equilibrium no overtime is worked even when the labour input fails to attain its former level.

In practice we are likely to observe an initial response to quits made up of hires, unfilled posts, overtime and reduced output. During each successive period the amount of overtime falls. (The number of hires per period might fall too if the productivity of overtime rises and the premium falls as less overtime is worked.) The number of unfilled posts falls and output rises. The amount of overtime falls to zero as equilibrium is approached. Overtime is thus a feature of the transition between equilibria. However, since quits take place in every period, equilibrium may never be reached. This is true even if firms attempt to anticipate quits. Hiring before the event imposes a cost; a period of over-employment. Furthermore, since quit levels vary through time they cannot be precisely predicted and expensive mistakes (unnecessary hires) could be made. This implies that even forward-looking firms may never reach their equilibrium input levels so that vacancies and overtime will always be present.

The nature and size of screening costs are clearly crucial to the model above, so let us consider the hiring process in more detail. First, in Chapter 4 it was argued that employers' prospecting is made difficult by the impossibility of observing certain quality characteristics in workers by interviews alone. Hiring is always an uncertain activity: mistakes will be made. If wages could be adjusted to fit the worker there would be no problem. But if wages are fixed, clearly $\bar{W} > MRP$ for any worker hired is possible. Consequently, the firm will often use probationary periods to assess workers' quality. Clearly the costs of such periods have to be taken into account in the adjustment decision. The expected benefit of replacing a single quit will therefore take account of not only the probability of hiring a probationary worker with $MRP > \bar{W}$ and the value of the expected MRP, but also the probability of hiring someone with a productivity less than $\bar{W}$, the cost of discharging that person, and the costs of a second hire. The more costly it is to discharge people the more reluctant the firm will be to hire in $t$, choosing to put more time and effort into initial selection and screening; the more it will attempt to find reliable signals; the slower it will be to select from probationers and thus to adjust. Moreover, any adjustment undertaken need not be permanent. The firm could adjust, then discharge, then adjust again until it makes a satisfactory hire. The more costly it is to discharge people the more likely it is that the firm will insist on a probationary period, the longer it will be, and the fewer the obligations on both sides during the probationary period. It is quite possible that, with significant discharge costs, any firm in doubt about a probationer will simply discharge him if an extended probationary period is not mutually acceptable. High discharge costs and restrictions on probation, as with high recruitment costs, increase the probability that the firm will end up with a smaller workforce. The faster the increase in these costs with discharges the slower the adjustment following quits. The general point is that, once we allow for the possibility of mistakes in hiring, hiring decisions will, in part, reflect the fixed labour costs of discharges.

The second implication of introducing screening costs concerns the MRP curve. With heterogeneous labour the MRP curve becomes very slippery indeed. Imagine a firm operating in Figure 8.2 in the hypothetical world of the basic model with a fixed wage $\bar{W}$ and using labour $E$. The firm knows exactly the productivity of workers inside and outside the firm; given its technology it thus knows exactly the shape of the MRP curve. At $F_0$ the firm is operating efficiently, being on its MRP curve. We now allow a quit to take place and assume that labour is heterogeneous. If the quitter is the marginal worker, a firm adopting efficient screening techniques might hire a more efficient replacement. If a non-marginal worker were to leave, the firm might employ a more or less efficient replacement. In neither case would the firm return to $F_0$. It follows that the MRP curve is of little relevance to the firm's decision making.

Let us develop this argument further. Consider the firm located at $F_1$ after a quit by the marginal worker. The firm knows the pro-

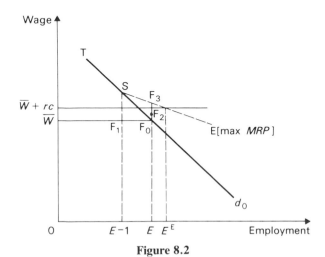

**Figure 8.2**

ductivity of the remaining workforce so a MRP curve, TS, is identifiable. But *ex ante* there is no clear optimal employment level as seen from $F_1$. There is just the possibility in an uncertain world of hiring additional labour with a MRP that covers the wage and recruitment costs. The important variable is not the MRP of the quitter but the present value of the reservation quality, $PV(q^*)$. Given the distribution of qualities in the market the firm calculates $E[\max q]$ and $E[\max MRP]$. If the latter is $F_2$ in Figure 8.2 no prospecting takes place and $E$-1 is the optimum employment level. If it is $F_3$ then $F_3$ is a point on an expected curve $E[\max MRP]$ starting at S. Prospecting begins and the firm might hire at an MRP value greater or less than that at $F_3$ but greater than $\bar{W} + rc$. Alternatively, according to its fortunes in sampling across applicants, it might hire no-one. *Ex post* therefore the optimum employment level after screening could be either $E - 1$ or $E$. Furthermore, given the quality distribution, the firm may anticipate being able to hire *more* than one worker with a MRP value of $W + rc$, in which case there is some expected employment level $E^E$ and further points on the $E[\max MRP]$ curve above $\bar{W} + rc$. Prospecting may yield recruits that take employment above or below $E^E$. This analysis illustrates two things. First, firms' decisions to prospect are not based upon a certain MRP curve but upon RC and an $E[\max MRP]$ curve. Decisions are therefore determined by the external quality distribution firms perceive and the screening strategies they employ. Different firms will make different decisions according to their RC. Second, firms will usually reach their optimum employment level at a point off their $E[\max MRP]$ curve.

## QUITS AND TRAINING

Given the costs of hiring labour to replace quits, as well as dismissals and retirements, the firm will consider the possibility of reducing the anticipated level of voluntary separations. In Sections 7.2 and 7.3 we discussed the quit decision from the workers' point of view. We can treat the quits function derived from that analysis as one of the labour supply constraints facing the firm. The supply of quits facing any firm will be a function of, *inter alia*, the net advantages workers derive from their employment in that firm compared to those obtainable elsewhere. Realised quit levels are thus not exogenously given to the firm because by raising its rewards, particularly of course wages, the firm can reduce quits. In principle, therefore, the firm will calculate the cost of reducing quits by 1 unit from knowledge of the financial costs of increasing various job rewards and their effects upon quits. If this cost (given that similar benefits may have to be given to all existing employees) is smaller than the cost of the best alternative adjustment strategy, the firm will seek to reduce quits. If the marginal cost of reducing quits rises, there will be some optimal level of quits which the firm will accept.

It follows that the higher the fixed costs of recruitment and the productivity of likely quitters the further the firm will go in reducing quits. Those firms with the highest recruitment costs will tend to have the highest wage levels and the lowest quit rates, *ceteris paribus*. There will be a permanent distribution of wages across firms reflecting the pattern of recruitment costs. There might also be a distribution of non-pecuniary rewards: pension rights, canteen facilities, recreation provisions, etc.

Consider now the possibility that the firm replaces a quit by recruiting a lower grade worker and training that recruit to the required skill level. In appointing a lower grade worker from outside the firm faces the recruitment costs described above. In addition it has to undertake general training. To recoup its outlay, as indicated in equation (8.5), wages and marginal product must diverge but in this case, as noted in Chapter 3, the outlay on general training must be recouped over the training period. Wages, however, continue to diverge from marginal product after training because of recruitment costs so a distribution of wages across the market will still be observed. It follows, first, that if firms are discouraged from undertaking investments in general training by restrictions upon wage differentials between trainees and qualified workers, adjustment to quits through hiring from lower grades will be inhibited. Second, the higher are general training costs for the firm, *ceteris paribus*, the less the firm will rely on such recruitment. Third, the greater the costs of recruiting higher grade labour and the lower the expected quality of applicants from the higher grade the more use will be made of the external hiring and training option. Finally, the greater the dropout rate of trainees the less use will be made of this option.

In this section we have so far considered the firm's demand for labour only in response to quits. Clearly the general principles governing the adjustment process apply equally well to a firm experiencing a single permanent increase in the demand for its output. It will adjust to a higher employment level over several periods, in the meantime using significant amounts of overtime, attempting to dissuade quitters and making greater demands for effort from its workforce, some of which might be paid for (say by piece rates) and some not. The particular adjustment process the firm follows will depend upon the size of its recruitment costs, the size of the demand increase, its future expectations of demand, the overtime premium and so on.

Our discussion of the hiring decision has, so far, concentrated solely upon the effects of recruitment costs. Let us now bring in fixed costs of employment, EC. The resort to overtime following a demand expansion noted above arises because recruitment costs make workers currently employed different in the eyes of the firm to workers outside. In the same way employment costs make hours of existing workers different to those of identical potential recruits. *Ceteris paribus*, higher employment costs reduce the benefits of hiring as opposed to using more hours of existing employees and thus slow down the process of adjustment. They also impinge upon the determination of the equilibrium labour input. Figure 8.3 shows a demand expansion as the shift of $MRP_1$ to $MRP_2$. Labour costs are $W + EC$, the important point being of course that EC are not once-for-all payments. It is much more likely therefore that the imposition of EC will lead the firm to a smaller labour input at $F_2$ that would the imposition of RC. Furthermore, if EC is large it could exceed the overtime premium at the margin, in which case at the new equilibrium overtime would be preferable to hiring. Overtime will not then be a transitory phenomenon, a characteristic of disequilibrium, but a characteristic of equilibrium and a permanent feature of any firm.

In practice a demand increase will lead the firm to adjust not only its labour input but also its capital input. We have ignored this possibility so far by concentrating upon short-run adjustment paths. In the immediate aftermath of the demand increase capital is likely to be unalterable so that certain labour adjustments will be attempted to compensate for the inability to increase capital utilisation, and in particular capital stocks, to the desired level. In the longer term labour inputs will be reduced as additional capital is introduced. The precise level of the demand for labour at any time will depend upon the speed and thus upon the cost of capital adjustments. We might therefore imagine an adjustment process in which firms initially use overtime extensively and raise capital utilisation. In time the

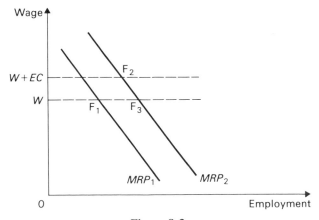

**Figure 8.3**

employment level will be adjusted upwards. Still later the capital stock is increased and hours, utilisation, and perhaps employment fall. We have noted that the higher are recruitment costs, *ceteris paribus*, the greater is the incentive for the firm to use overtime when demand initially expands. The firm also has a greater incentive to reduce quits, to increase capital utilisation and to speed up the introduction of additional capital. In final equilibrium the firm facing fixed labour costs may thus end up with more capital and fewer workers than would otherwise have been the case.

## 8.3 The discharge decision

At the beginning of period *t* imagine that a firm, initially in static equilibrium, faces an unanticipated, permanent reduction in the demand for its product and the imposition of severance costs. The firm has three principal options: (a) to discharge workers; (b) to hoard labour; (c) to influence the level of quits. The criteria governing the third option have already been discussed in the previous section. Assuming the required reduction in employment exceeds the level of anticipated quits, the higher are severance costs the more likely the firm is, *ceteris paribus*, to lower its wage (and/or other non-pecuniary benefits) to try to induce further separations. The greater the elasticities of quits to different rewards the more likely this strategy is. The less discretion the firm has over wages the less likely it is. Let us therefore consider only options (a) and (b).

Assume initially that the reduced demand is equivalent to the output of one worker. To discharge a worker the firm must inevitably incur financial penalties. It might also suffer a deterioration in its reputation in the local labour market and thus face less favourable treatment by local government, reduced levels of applications and more quits. The alternative is to reduce its output but maintain the current labour force. The excess worker contributes nothing so that the cost of this strategy is the worker's wage. The firm will weigh up these two strategies and choose the most profitable.

In Figure 8.4 the firm is initially located at $F_1$ in static equilibrium. We now introduce the contraction of demand and severance costs. If the firm chooses to discharge the single worker, the cost is $SC$. It will operate at $F_2$ below its average costs, for $W + sc$ accounts for both the wage and the unit severance cost per period of the firm's time horizon. This implies that the firm will reduce employment by more than one worker. However, if the firm decides to hoard labour it will produce at $F_1$, which is above its new MRP curve, but sells at $F_2$. The cost of hoarding is the workers wage or the unrealisable revenue $abF_1F_2$. To the extent that output can be stored for sale later when

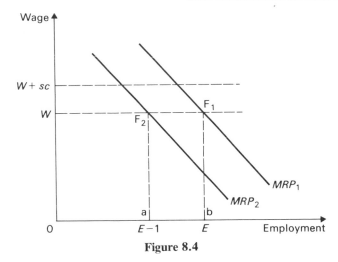

**Figure 8.4**

demand expands, (something we have ruled out by assumption), or hoarded labour can be used to reduce other costs (by capital maintenance for example) the costs of hoarding will be lower. However, given that SC represents a once-for-all cost for one worker, in this particular case hoarding is very unlikely.

With several workers in excess of the number required, with marginal severance costs and hoarding costs increasing with the numbers involved and a finite time horizon the firm will find some optimal combination of discharging and hoarding as its initial response to the demand contraction. Since hoarding costs are continuous whilst severance costs are once-for-all, we can expect the firm to adjust towards the new optimum over a number of periods, with the amount of labour hoarding falling in each period. The firm will finally reach a new equilibrium which will involve no labour hoarding but which might involve a smaller labour force than would be the case without severance costs. The larger the level and the increase in severance costs with the number of discharges, the more hoarding there will be in each adjustment period and the slower the adjustment to the new equilibrium.

We can further predict, first, that in a world where demand contractions are not permanent, the longer the firm's time horizon and the longer the firm anticipates demand to remain at the lower level, *ceteris paribus*, the less hoarding there is in each period and the faster the adjustment. If the firm feels that demand may rise again in the not too distant future, depending upon its discount rate, it may well want to hold on to the labour. If it discharged labour the firm would face recruitment costs, as well as uncertainty about the nature of new recruits when it comes to hire later. The larger the recruitment costs the more reluctant the firm will be to discharge. Second, the greater the scope for using hoarded labour profitably, the smaller the costs of hoarding and the slower the adjustment. Thirdly, severance costs arise from redundancy payments imposed upon the firm by the government, employment contracts or collective bargaining. Their value depends upon the institutional rules governing the firm's choice of who to discharge. Clearly the firm would prefer to discharge its lowest quality workers, workers in areas of the firm where excess capacity is largest or workers for whom severance costs are lowest. The more scope the firm has to choose who to discharge the more attractive the discharge option. Fourth, a significant increase in severance costs, *ceteris paribus*, will induce firms suffering declining demand to opt for a higher level of labour hoarding initially, and to adjust more slowly to the new cost-minimising input combination. This will reduce the flow of labour into unemployment following the demand contraction. Fifth, the imposition of employment fixed costs as well as severance costs makes the new equilibrium employment level smaller than it otherwise would be because such payments are continuous rather than once-for-all. It also makes hoarding more expensive and will therefore speed up the adjustment to the new equilibrium and thus increase the immediate flow into unemployment during a contraction.

Labour hoarding, like overtime, is essentially a transitory phenomenon. It exists only during the firm's adjustment from one equilibrium to another. It has important implications, however, for economic analysis. First, since hoarding means that labour is not being used efficiently it is one element, at the level of the firm, of under-employment and of disguised unemployment at the national level. Our analysis indicates, however, that such behaviour is profit maximising. Hoarding is part of the efficient adjustment to a new equilibrium, and ar͜ɔes directly as a result of fixed labour costs.

Second, the existence of labour hoarding has important implications for the measurement of excess demand in the economy. Excess demand has conventionally been measured by the difference between unemployment and vacancies $(U - V)$. The existence of hoarding means that when product demand falls unemployment will not rise as quickly as it would without fixed costs. Excess demand should consequently be measured as the difference between unemployment plus hoarding and vacancies. If the relationship between unemployment and hoarding remains constant through time, then *changes* in $(U - V)$ give a consistent indication of changes in excess demand if not of its precise level. If, however, the relationship between unemployment and hoarding is variable, say because fixed costs change through time, then changes in $(U - V)$ are an unreliable indicator of changes in excess demand. The same level of $(U - V)$ in two periods may be associated with very different demand conditions.

Third, labour hoarding has obvious implications for the measurement and analysis of productivity trends within the economy. Because of increased labour hoarding, productivity per head will fall significantly as total demand falls. It will then rise rapidly as labour hoarding is reduced with the upturn of demand. Any calculation of the underlying rate of growth of labour productivity needs, therefore, to be based upon the complete cycle in business activity, allowing for any changes in fixed labour costs.

To conclude our analysis of the firm's adjustments to a demand contraction let us introduce temporary lay-offs and short-time working as alternative options to hoarding where the firm anticipates some future revival of demand. Temporary lay-offs involve under-utilising available labour, whilst short-time working involves under-utilising available hours. In one sense both are less expensive than hoarding because the firm does not pay in full for this labour or these hours. It incurs only a holding payment. On the other hand, if either method results in the firm eventually losing labour it could be more costly than hoarding. Since both involve continuous payments either could be more expensive than discharges. The prevalence of temporary lay-offs and short-time working will therefore depend crucially upon the length of time before the firm expects demand to recover, its discount rate, the size of the financial obligations involved and the increase in separations induced. Such adjustment mechanisms may be resisted by unions if they deprive the worker of the opportunity of earning a full wage elsewhere or of entitlement to full state financial assistance. The firm derives a benefit from temporary lay-offs and short time, which will be greater if the government makes a contribution, in that an immediate labour input is available to it without recruitment costs. Workers benefit from paid leisure time, a future job promise, no search costs and a wage rate which includes compensation for the possibility of such breaks in employment.

## 8.4 Demand variations, fixed costs and internal labour markets

Let us now consider a world in which the firm faces a regular cyclical variation in the demand for its product, quits take place continuously and there are significant fixed labour costs. Even without a formal model we can anticipate the following features of the firm's adjustment process following the discussion of the two preceding sections.

Starting at point $S_1$ in Figure 8.5, a fall in demand will initially be met by natural wastage or quits. At some point, say $S_2$, however, the

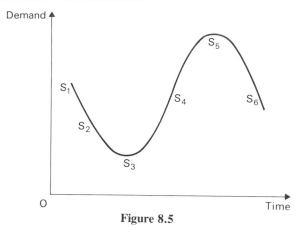

**Figure 8.5**

firm will begin to hoard labour, deliberately induce quits and discharge workers. The knowledge that demand will eventually rise is a strong inducement to hoarding. The less the anticipated length of the cycles and the severity of the downturns the stronger is that inducement. Product demand expectations, how they are formed, adjusted and implemented, will be crucial to the precise form of the firm's labour adjustment here. Once the bottom of the cycle is reached at $S_3$ and demand begins to rise the firm will begin to reduce labour hoarding (i.e. rearrange tasks to increase its efficiency). At some point in the upturn, say $S_4$, it will begin to discourage quits, to hire and to use overtime. Again the mix will depend crucially upon the product demand expectations as well as the relative size of the different labour fixed costs. It will also begin at say, $S_5$, to *dishoard*; to use organisational changes for a short period to push the productivity of labour beyond conventional limits. When demand eventually begins to contract, it reduces dishoarding and overtime to begin the next cycle at $S_6$. In this analysis hiring and discharging, overtime and hoarding, temporary layoffs and dishoarding, never overlap. But if the firm produces several products, with different demand cycles, employs imperfectly substitutable groups (departments) of labour, and faces different quit behaviour and different fixed costs across its labour force, it will be observed to hire and discharge, for example, at the same time.

Though highly simplified, the above scenario generates the following predictions. First, the level of employment will fluctuate less than the level of output, principally because of hoarding and the use of overtime. Second, at the bottom of the cycle there will be hoarding and at the top overtime. In a world where demand contractions and expansions are not once-for-all, the firm never attains equilibrium. It is always in the process of adjusting to the past and to the future. The firm always has an employment level above or below the target level associated with current demand; it moves around the marginal revenue product curve never along it. Third, since the firm cannot continually adjust its wage, the relationships between the wage and the marginal revenue product will not be constant; sometimes $W > MRP$ and sometimes $W < MRP$. Fourth, a rise in severance costs, *ceteris paribus*, will increase hoarding during the downturn. It will reduce hiring during the upturn because there is more hoarded labour available and also because it becomes more costly to hire only subsequently to fire. The result of less hiring and firing is that the firm will resort less to the market place to meet its labour requirements, so unemployment will fluctuate less. If the rise in SC were to take place in the expansion stage of the cycle, unemployment would show a smaller fall than previously. Greater hoarding will put back hiring and overtime adjustments. Because higher severance costs reduce hiring in the boom period the firm will use more overtime and dis-hoarding at the top than previously. Fifth, if recruitment costs rise, *ceteris paribus*, the direct effect is to reduce hiring in the expansion and induce the firm to use more overtime/dishoarding. This implies that firing will be delayed during the downturn. When discharging and hoarding take place the former is less profitable given the costs of rehiring. The increased scope for dishoarding delays hiring and over-time in the next upturn. So again the firm becomes less involved in the external market place for labour. The outcome for overtime is indeterminate because, though the price of overtime relative to hiring has fallen, which induces more of the former, the falling price of hoarding relative to discharging increases hoarding and thus overtime in the next expansion. Sixth, a rise in employment costs, *ceteris paribus*, makes hoarding relatively more expensive and thus in the downturn induces more discharges. A significant rise in employment costs during the downturn would lead to an immediate sharp increase in discharges, a *shakeout* of labour, and a sharp rise in un-employment. During the upturn, because hiring has become rela-tively more expensive compared to overtime, the firm will rely more on the latter to meet its labour requirements. In this case therefore the underlying level of unemployment will rise as fixed costs increase. Overtime will rise as fixed costs increase. Overtime will become a much more important adjustment mechanism than previously was the case.

In the face of a permanent once-for-all increase in demand, *ceteris paribus*, part-time labour would never be used in the firm's adjust-ment process. Recruitment costs per worker are the same for full-time and part-time appointments. Total recruitment outlays would nevertheless be higher, for the firm must recruit more part-time labour to meet the demand expansion than it would full-time labour. However, if severance costs and/or employment costs for part-time labour are lower than for full-time labour, in a world of demand cycles the firm will find it advantageous to use part-timers to negotiate its adjustment path. The amount used will depend upon the increase in recruitment and severance costs with the numbers involved, but *ceteris paribus* the lower are the severance costs the more part-timers will be employed, the greater the hiring and firing of labour, the greater the dependence upon the labour market and the faster the adjustment to the desired employment level. The analysis of leisure preferers in Chapter 1 suggested that in a world of hours restrictions there will be individuals willing to work less than normal hours at a lower rate of pay than that for normal hours. We can thus predict that adjustments on the basis of part-time employment will be more important the more flexibility there is in setting part-time hours and wages, the more leisure preferers at each skill level there are, and the lower the transactions costs for firms producing with significant numbers of part timers.

## INTERNAL LABOUR MARKETS

In a world of significant fixed labour costs, where firms hoard labour, use overtime extensively and attempt to manipulate quit levels, the firm's relationship with the external labour market will differ radically from that described by the basic model of the labour market. In that model the internal labour market of any single firm is simply a microcosm of the market as a whole. Wages and wage structures are everywhere identical. Entry to the firm is possible at every level, and mobility within and across firms is unrestricted and competitively determined. The introduction of fixed costs can produce highly structured, largely self-contained internal labour markets.

We argued earlier that firms will attempt to reduce the level of quits in response to labour turnover. Clearly firms with the highest costs of turnover will find it most profitable, *ceteris paribus*, to deter quits. Certain firms will display high wages and few quits whilst others, perhaps in the same labour market and even the same product market, will display low wages and high quit rates. Both will be equally profitable strategies reflecting differences in the size of the firm's fixed costs. Obviously the inducement not to quit need not necessarily be in monetary terms but could include fringe benefits and job conditions. More interestingly it could include promotion guarantees, assurances of job security and access to training. The firm could find it profitable, therefore, because of fixed labour costs, to create an internal labour market which shields its incumbents from external market forces. Internal workers get preference for all vacancies, and new appointments are made only at the bottom of the job hierarchy. Firms adhere to specified promotion ladders up which workers move after specific training paid for by the firm. The level of fixed costs determines how structured the internal market becomes. Large firms with a technology that necessitates high market place search costs and significant specific training will be most anxious to deter quits and thus most likely to develop structured internal markets. The cost involved in operating a structured internal labour market will be lowest for firms whose demand is not subject to extreme variations.

Firms with the highest fixed labour costs will adjust to demand changes primarily by overtime, hoarding, dishoarding and vacancies. Hiring and discharging will be used infrequently. The firm's contacts with each external labour market will thus be limited. Assuming it has some degree of leverage in product markets the firm's internal wage structure will not be constrained by external forces. Although wages are above market levels, internal adjustments may still be the most efficient. The very stability of the workforce will be a strong factor working towards the institutionalisation of wage structures, work practices and internal relationships.

There are other reasons for thinking that fixed labour costs will lead certain firms to develop structured internal labour markets. We referred earlier to the possibility that the firm may adjust to vacancies by making internal promotions. Where fixed labour costs are high this will often be the most efficient adjustment mechanism because of the uncertainty associated with hiring. The firm knows very little *ex ante* about the quality of workers drawn from the marketplace but it already has a good deal of accurate information about members of its current workforce. Screening costs are thus negligible and mistakes rare. Large firms, in particular, will have a wide choice of promotion candidates and will rarely have reason to go outside. The 'certain' net returns to an internal promotion (even if some general training is required) will invariably exceed the 'expected' net returns to appointing a suitable outsider.

Our analysis also suggests that the need for training will be an important factor leading to the development of a structured internal labour market. If the firm hires from outside it will have to finance the specific training required. It can save on these costs by appointing internal applicants who already have considerable amounts of specific human capital. The internal candidate will require general training that an outsider might not need, but since internal training facilities are available to provide specific training these may easily be adapted to offer internal workers cheap and therefore readily acceptable general training. Internal promotion will also be beneficial because the more specific training the firm provides for workers the more closely they are tied to the firm and the greater the stability of the workforce. Using internal recruits enables the firm to anticipate its requirements; to operate always with a short list of trained, screened candidates ready to fill immediately any post which falls vacant. Established, continuous, internal training and recruitment may be additionally beneficial if the firm anticipates that severe shortages in the market will sometimes preclude hiring in the future, or if training generates externalities, for example from improved production techniques. There can also be little doubt that the prospect of training and promotion acts as an incentive to the existing workforce, especially in large units where competition amongst workers for jobs is strong. Training and promotion often lead to supervisory positions of one form or another. Again specific skills will be crucial, including perhaps internal candidates' knowledge of the personality of the workforce.

Specific skills are central to the development of structured internal labour markets, but not simply because of the recruitment costs they imply. Let us consider these skills in more detail. Specific human capital requirements make certain otherwise technically similar jobs (and therefore the workers that perform them) different from one another. The specific skills associated with a job arise in part from the nature of the technology a firm adopts. Often the same machinery will be developed differently by different firms according to their circumstances. But the specific skills required also depend upon the way in which production is organised. Specific skills also arise because jobs are performed by teams of workers who acquire the technical and social expertise of working together effectively. Finally they arise because jobs are located within peculiar information and communication structures which existing workers learn to operate efficiently. The implication is that specific human capital is important across a very wide range of jobs and workers; that most jobs can be treated as peculiar to themselves; and that most workers inside firms are significantly different in the firms' eyes to those outside. Furthermore, such skills cannot be taught adequately outside the firm since it is involvement in the particular job that generates the human capital. So the firm both pays for and provides specific training internally and thus acquires the facilities and organisation to do so.

The existence of specific human capital makes individual wage contracts difficult to design for three reasons. First, by its very nature specific human capital changes through time. Firms want workers to develop and employ their skills as fully as possible and are willing to pay accordingly. But the dynamic nature of the skills creates uncertainty about what the firm should contract for in return for its wage offer. Second, workers need not reveal the true nature of their skills to the firm or to new workers. Third, possession of specific skills gives each worker a certain amount of personal bargaining power which induces unilateral action and imposes significant bargaining costs upon the firm. The development of a structured internal labour market may well offer the firm a more efficient device for allocating resources internally than an open market. A formal unified job and wage hierarchy encourages collective action by workers and reduces opportunism and bargaining costs. Workers will not under-reveal their skills, since performance of tasks is the criterion determining promotion and access to additional training. Similarly workers have every reason to acquire more skills. The stable, continuous and flexible system of negotiation on job specification and rewards in structured internal labour markets reduces uncertainty by providing the firm with a mechanism for meeting each change as it comes. Collective bargaining is an essential part of this system.

Substantial fixed costs induce the firm as part of its profit-maximising strategy to isolate itself from the external market. For some firms wages will be significantly higher than outside at all skill levels – both because of the extensive training but also as an inducement to workers to stay. Wage structures will be fairly rigid as part of the promotions schedule. There will be significant amounts of internal upward mobility, but little voluntary mobility out or new hirings. Individual workers in such internal markets stay in their jobs much longer, have steeper lifetime earnings profiles, have greater job security, earnings stability and fringe benefits: they have good jobs in virtually every sense.

Those workers lucky enough to be in highly structured labour markets earn economic rents. In time, however, given that such firms will receive large numbers of applicants for any job, they will be able steadily to raise the quality of their labour force. In the final analysis high paying, high fixed cost firms will employ the best workers. Whether workers then earn rents depends upon the availability of good quality people and the costs of identifying quality workers.

## 8.5   The empirical study of employment adjustments

If the preceding sections have brought out some of the important factors shaping firms' employment adjustments they have also illustrated something of their complexity. Any study aimed at testing these ideas obviously faces a very difficult task. Ideally such a study would concentrate upon a number of firms following through time their labour demand adjustments, both qualitatively and quantitatively, to changing circumstances taking into account technology, product demand and labour market conditions. One would like to know the quality of labour, the skill content and nature of the jobs, and the cost structures of each firm. Unfortunately such a study is not feasible. Only a few firms could be covered, so how representative would they be? Quite reasonably, there would be time limits to how long any firm would be prepared to be observed. The day to day affairs of a firm are dynamic, complex, sometimes messy; how far then could one reasonably attribute certain events to specific causes? How easy would it be to detach oneself from the minutiae of everyday events? Firms would only rarely have the statistical information (in a form) suitable for academic research, how does one get at the bank of knowledge and the expertise embodied in management? Not surprisingly, therefore, our store of empirical knowledge on labour demand is both limited and fragmented. Research has taken two lines: on the one hand investigating labour demand at a highly aggregated level using official data and employing statistical techniques; on the other hand investigating specific issues in labour demand theory within a small number of firms using a case-study approach.

Perhaps the principal device for investigating labour demand at the aggregate level has been the employment function. This is a relationship between employment and output which on certain assumptions can be derived directly from the classical theory of the firm and cost-minimising (or profit-maximising) criteria. So, for a given firm $i$ we could define for period $t$

$$DE_t^i = f(K_i, X_i, W_i, r_i)_t \tag{8.7}$$

as the static solution. $DE$ is the desired employment level defined at the beginning of $t$. $K$ is capital and $X$ is the output or demand expected for period $t$. $W$ and $r$ are the prices of labour and capital respectively. Since the firm faces fixed labour costs it will not attempt to achieve the desired employment level immediately but will adjust towards the desired employment level over a number of periods. We can thus write

$$E_t^i - E_{t-1}^i = \lambda(DE_t^i - E_{t-1}^i) \tag{8.8}$$

where $E_{t-1}^i$ is the employment level at the end of period $t-1$ and $\lambda$ is a proportional adjustment factor with a constant but unknown value between 0 and 1. Typically it has been assumed that the production function has a Cobb–Douglas form

$$X = AE^\alpha K^\beta \tag{8.9}$$

This allows us to reformulate equation (8.7) using equation (8.8) as an employment function:

$$\log E_t^i = \log a + b \log X_i + c \log(W/r)_{it}$$
$$+ d \log K_{it} + e \log E_{it-1} \tag{8.10}$$

where $e$ equals $(1 - \lambda)$ and $\alpha$ and $\beta$ can be derived by manipulating the estimates of $a$, $b$ and $c$. Statistical analysis of (8.10) would provide an estimate of $\lambda$ and thus of the speed of adjustment. In practice empirical work has used industry data. The results are statistically robust and indicate employment adjustments of the order of 20–30 per cent per quarter to output changes for manual workers.

The employment function is a useful part of the economist's rather restricted empirical armoury but it clearly has its limitations. First, whilst $\lambda$ depends upon fixed labour costs it is a catch-all term, the estimation of which does not allow us to identify the impact of any individual fixed cost nor to isolate the impact of fixed costs from other factors. Second, because of data deficiencies most empirical studies face considerable problems with the capital input variable. Third, equation (8.10) describes only the labour demand adjustment in terms only of numbers of workers. Adjustments also take place simultaneously through hours. Furthermore, adjustments towards full equilibrium always involve some change in capital stocks and utilisation. $K$ will thus be endogenous and should not appear on the right-hand side of equation (8.10). The adjustment of any one input will, in part, be a response to disequilibrium in other input levels. Equation (8.10) should be estimated alongside input demand functions for hours, capital stocks and utilisation and each equation should include all input prices and some partial response to the deviation from desired levels of the other inputs. Fourth, labour is treated as completely homogeneous. Important differences may, however, exist in the way the firm treats different labour inputs if their fixed costs vary. In this case employment functions should be disaggregated across the labour inputs. Industry data also raise a problem if adjustment processes vary significantly within what is defined in official sources as an industry. Fifth, the assumption that production functions can be described as Cobb–Douglas is very restrictive. Such functions embody excessively rigid constraints upon the elasticity of substitution between inputs. These restrictions have created practical problems because empirical results have consistently implied increasing returns to the labour input. Sixth, the analysis of employment functions assumes that no supply restrictions exist – labour supply curves are horizontal so that all variations in employment can be causally related to demand side factors. Finally, the use of optimisation techniques to derive the employment function assumes that the firm in making its adjustments always operates on the production function, i.e. always operates most efficiently in the static framework sense at each stage. This rules out labour hoarding or dishoarding. These caveats may perhaps sound rather daunting but they indicate ways in which both the quantity and quality of the information to be culled from the employment function technique need to be improved.

Indeed much recent empirical work has been undertaken along these lines. The analysis of employment functions rules out labour hoarding but attempts have been made, again using aggregate data, to investigate this particular adjustment mechanism. The principal problem is to find a way of measuring labour hoarding at any moment in time. This has been done indirectly as follows. Hoarding involves a fall in output proportionately greater than the fall in employment. It thus constitutes a difference between actual and optimal labour productivity. The difference increases with the amount of hoarding. Therefore, suppose we measure actual labour productivity per person hour for any industry $i$, $m_t^a$, through time, and thus through the demand cycle. We assume that the level of productivity at each peak in activity measures the optimal utilisation of labour at that time. Extrapolating between peaks thus gives the optimal productivity $m_t^*$ at every point in time. The ratio $(m^a/m^*)_t$ provides an index of hoarding through time. Since $m_t^* = (X_t/L_t)^*$, output in $t$ could be produced by $X_t/m_t^* = L_t^*$ labour so that hoarding is $(L_t - L_t^*)$ person-hours. Given that we know $m_t^*$, we can convert this to an output figure for each point in time.

Such measures of hoarding have been calculated at various levels of aggregation. Studies of the relationship between the business cycle and hoarding measures have identified the negative correlation suggested by theory. It appears that labour hoarding and unemployment are not strongly correlated, which suggests that neither alone can be a good indicator of demand pressure. The turning point in labour hoarding leads that in unemployment at the top and bottom of the cycle as one would expect but the size of the lag suggests that unemployment will be a poor indicator of excess demand. Finally, hoarding variables have been found to perform satisfactorily in equations to explain wage changes where unemployment as the sole measure of excess demand has proved inadequate.

Such measures of labour hoarding have obvious limitations. First, the assumption that optimal resource use is achieved at each peak is extreme. Every turning point does not necessarily represent equal strength. During some expansions demand may turn down before full capacity use is reached and the optimal use of resources achieved. It assumes no hoarding or dishoarding at the peaks. Second, it is assumed that the firm is able to reach its most efficient input combination at each peak with overtime assumed to have the same productivity as normal hours. Third, constant returns to the labour input are assumed so that a given decline in labour productivity can be converted into hoarding units at each output level by the same output to labour ratio.

Overtime is central to the labour adjustment procedure. Studies of the demand for hours, $H_t$, at the aggregate level can be conducted, as noted earlier, through the same technique used for employment functions, i.e. to examine statistically with industry data equations of the form

$$H_t = \log a + \sum_j b_j \log FPR_{jt} + c \log X_t$$

$$+ d \log H_{t-1} + e \log(E_t - E_{t-1}) \quad (8.11)$$

where $d$ measures the adjustment factor for hours to its desired level and $e$ measures the adjustment factor for hours as a response to disequilibrium in the employment level. Each $b$ measures the hours response to changes in a particular factor price ratio, $FPR_j$. Empirical work has indicated that hours variations are important to the firm and that hours are rapidly adjusted.

The demand for hours has also been analysed statistically within the framework of inter-industry wage structures. A model can be set up which contains both demand and supply equations for hours,

$$D^i_H = f(W_i, Z_i, FC_i, A_i) \quad (8.12)$$

$$S^i_H = f(W_i, Y_i) \quad (8.13)$$

to explain variations in average wages levels across manufacturing industries. $Y$ and $Z$ are vectors of variables introduced to standardise the labour input and measure the differences in market conditions across industries. $FC$ measures fixed costs by industry and $A$ measures the extent of recent employment adjustments made by the industry. So $D^i_H$ is expected to vary positively with $FC$ and negatively with $A$. The system is estimated simultaneously. In practice, unfortunately, rather dubious proxies have to be used for $FC$ and $A$, permitting interpretations of the results that have nothing to do with fixed costs. Such studies also use highly aggregated data which brings together units with very different fixed costs characteristics.

All aggregate statistical studies suffer from inadequate data on fixed labour costs, but are these costs significant enough to warrant the close attention of theorists and researchers? Various restricted surveys and calculations of the importance of fixed costs have been made. These tentatively suggest that employment costs can add 40 per cent to wages and hiring costs can amount to 10 per cent of the average hired workers annual wage. These are clearly not insignificant figures. As yet, however, we know very little about the size of specific fixed cost elements, their variation across the market and through time and the effects upon them of various changes in market institutions.

The significance of overtime to firms can be seen directly from surveys of its prevalence and distribution. Such surveys indicate that overtime is widespread, but that certain industries rely much more heavily upon it than others. The total amount of overtime appears to vary more closely with the number of workers doing overtime than with the length of overtime taken on. The data indicate, however, that a small group of workers undertake very considerable amounts of overtime. These facts are consistent with the proposition from Chapter 1 that by moving jobs workers can reduce the effects of normal hours restrictions. They also seem to indicate the existence of a group of workers who are strong income preferers. The fact that institutionally determined normal hours have fallen much more than total hours is consistent with the proposition that income preferers have in the past been frustrated by limits to the amount of overtime working available. Surveys also reveal that firms very rarely have difficulty getting workers to do overtime, which suggests that the *level* of hours is primarily determined by demand side forces.

However, there is evidence that non-competitive forces, as well as fixed costs, may play some part in explaining observed patterns in overtime. Where wages are particularly low unions exert pressure upon firms to provide permanent opportunities for overtime and to use overtime rather than hire new labour. This is to enable workers (presumably income preferers) to raise their weekly wages to a satisfactory level. It is this, so it is argued, rather than the need to carry out maintenance and repairs and to synchronise shiftwork, which explains why substantial amounts of overtime are worked at the bottom of the business cycle. It is worth making the point here that firms operate in a world in which cost-minimising adjustments are sometimes in sympathy with non-competitive forces, for example in the case of labour hoarding, and sometimes in conflict, for example in the case of selecting discharges and promotions. In certain circumstances very different models of the labour market will generate similar predictions and cannot, therefore, be refuted by casual empiricism. Empirical work is complex and research into the internal labour market provides an illustration of this.

The emergence of closed, structured internal labour markets as described earlier arises out of and is perfectly consistent with competitive cost-minimising behaviour on the part of firms. The degree to which an internal market is structured will vary from industry to industry along a continuous scale reflecting the level of fixed labour costs, the degree of heterogeneity of labour and thus the uncertainty in recruitment, the level of search costs and specific training requirements. The form of the internal labour market may even vary from firm to firm within a given industry if fixed costs vary across firms. However, in Chapter 5 structured internal labour markets are predicted by a totally different analysis of the firm: in which both unions and employers practice non-competitive and perhaps non-maximising behaviour and labour markets are unlikely to allocate resources efficiently. Empirical analysis in this area has two primary objectives: first to establish whether closed structured internal markets do exist and just how widespread they are; second, if they do exist, to establish the nature of these markets and the circumstances in which they exist. The latter would give a clue as to whether competitive forces are at work.

Such empirical analysis uses a case-study approach which requires considerable information on the firms involved and inevitably faces many of the problems described at the opening of this section. We can identify the main issues. First, investigators need to look at the firm's recruitment procedures and recruitment history. At how many levels does it recruit? How much internal mobility takes place and what form does it take? What criteria govern job advertising and selection procedures? Second, they need to study the nature of the internal wage structure. How far does it replicate that of other firms with similar labour requirements? How stable has it been over time? Do wage differentials reflect scarcity or training costs? Third, they need to study the function of training inside the firm. How much training accompanies internal mobility? How much can be said to be in specific skills? How much skill mobility inside the firm is there? Fourth, they need to study the system of rewards, job security, promotion channels and job hierarchies. How much do these match the wage structure? To what extent are these competitively determined, technologically determined, or the outcome of institutional forces? Finally they need to study mobility out of the firm. How much is in response to market signals? Are quits markedly lower in certain firms? Does this reflect the existence of structured internal labour markets? Do firms consciously set wages and other rewards to deter quits?

One interesting point is how far internal labour markets differ between firms operating in consistently tight external labour markets and those operating in slack labour markets. Competitive theory, which emphasises the firm's decision making, would predict the growth of structured labour markets to be less likely in the latter. Slack markets contain no shortage of possible external recruits of the appropriate skills and of a high quality. Market wages and recruitment costs will be low so quits will not be expensive. Non-competitive theory, which emphasises workers' decision making, would predict the growth of structured internal labour markets even in slack areas as workers seek to protect their positions by institutionalised wage structures, protected promotion, limited entry, job protection rules and so on.

The available evidence from case studies of the internal labour market is limited but valuable. The results suggest that internal wage structures often differ quite markedly between firms in the same labour market (defined by labour input, output and geographical location). Internal wage structures are extremely complex. High payers for one grade of worker, however, tend to be high payers for all labour and increases in wages tend to move the whole structure upwards through time. The structure is not sensitive to external competitive market forces. There also appears to be significant recourse by firms to internal mobility. However, there is also evidence in favour of the competitive approach in the form of significant interfirm mobility. The amount of internal mobility varies with market conditions, the length of intra-firm promotion ladders is limited, and entry is not restricted to the lowest rungs of the job hierarchy.

The overall impression seems to be that internal labour markets are worth further study but that they are unlikely to yield easily to analysis based upon simple structured or open market models. Nevertheless, firms appear to be conscious of the costs of recruitment and training in their attitudes to hiring, quits and redundancies.

## 8.6  The characteristics of hires and discharges

So far we have examined how fixed labour costs affect firms' employment adjustments on the assumption that these costs are the same for all workers. We have also assumed that firms treat productively identical workers in exactly the same way and that both the internal and external labour markets are competitive. In this section we relax these assumptions to consider which workers are most affected by employment adjustments. To simplify the discussion we direct our comments primarily towards differences between workers in terms of their skill classification.

If fixed labour costs were to vary systematically between different categories of labour within a firm, labour adjustments would affect each category differently. Recruitment and severance costs are in fact likely to be higher for skilled workers than for unskilled workers. Recruitment costs are higher because the firm must undertake more prospecting. The skilled labour force is more heterogeneous than the unskilled, and hiring mistakes are more expensive. The firm will also have to undertake more initial specific training given that there is likely to be a positive relationship between skill level and the importance of the specific element. Severance costs also increase with skills because discharging skilled people causes most dislocation to production and because severance payments increase with earnings and status. For similar reasons recruitment and severance costs will be lower for young, short tenure and trainee workers. The incidence of fixed employment costs is less clear *a priori*; any flat-rate elements will bear relatively more heavily on the employment of unskilled labour because of their lower pay but higher grade employees are more likely to be covered by occupational pensions and by comprehensive sick pay schemes.

Given that variations in fixed costs across the labour force do exist, consider the implications for the hiring decision of a firm operating in a world of changing demand conditions. First, the firm will be quicker to hire unskilled than skilled workers when demand increases, since the former are cheaper to hire and to dismiss later if the hire turns out to be a mistake or if demand turns down. Second, the firm will adjust its skilled input by making more intensive use of existing workers. Both arguments suggest that firms will adjust their skilled labour input upwards with less and slower hiring than its unskilled input and make greater use of overtime and dishoarding by skilled workers.

Given the significant costs of recruitment the firm will also go to greater lengths to deter quits by skilled people; structured internal labour markets will develop further in skilled areas. Long-term rewards to skilled labour deter quits into unskilled jobs when the latter's wage rises relatively. Adjustments for skilled labour will thus principally involve internal mechanisms – training, promotion, regrading – rather than hiring from outside and competitive bidding for labour.

The firm will generally derive most benefit from hiring workers who stay with the firm longer which suggests that it will differentiate between groups of applicants according to their expected quit rates. The preference for low quitters will be stronger in skilled jobs. Prospecting will take time for skilled labour, probation periods will be more common and longer, and will impose fewer obligations on both sides. In hiring a skilled worker the firm will attach considerable importance to the worker's job history. It will employ various informal as well as formal channels to elicit information on previous job stability. The firm will not devote anything like the same cost or time to unskilled labour. It will to some extent rely upon a high quit rate to negotiate demand variations.

In response to a fall in product demand the firm will be most willing to discharge unskilled and any other workers who impose low severance costs. Employment adjustments for the unskilled will mean more and quicker discharges than for the skilled. If the reduction in demand is not seen as permanent, severance costs will include costs of subsequent recruitment, which again favour discharging unskilled employees.

*Ceteris paribus*, the costs of hoarding skilled labour are higher than for unskilled labour. However, skilled labour is more versatile;

hoarded skilled labour can do the work of discharged unskilled workers, but not vice versa; it can also do many cost-saving jobs within the plant. The resulting differential between hoarding costs is likely to be smaller than the differential between severance costs, so that skilled labour is more likely to be hoarded when demand falls. This suggests that during contractions redundancies will contain a disproportionate number of unskilled workers.

Temporary lay-offs and short-time working are less expensive than discharging or hoarding because they involve an element of unpaid-for labour hoarding. Their value to the firm depends upon the payments that must be made and on the number and cost of separations they induce (which depend on the length of time they are operated). Given their limited specific skills significant numbers of unskilled workers might be lost by such schemes. This might lead the firm to discharge unskilled labour which is less expensive to recruit and to rely on temporary lay-offs and short-time working only for those workers within skilled groups with the lowest recruitment costs.

The final method of adjusting employment downwards is to encourage quits. This will be an attractive adjustment where severance costs are significant but recruitment costs are low, especially where workers have high elasticities of quits to rewards so that a small reduction in rewards is enough to induce the desired quits. To the extent that different groups of workers respond to different components of job rewards and have different recruitment costs, quits could be encouraged selectively. Quits by married women could be induced by limiting flexibility in hours, or reducing creche facilities. Quits by younger people and by the unskilled might be induced by restricting training and promotion opportunities.

The firm will hire and use overtime, hoard and discharge at different stages of the business cycle. The firm's adjustments will differ for different groups of workers: because fixed costs vary with skills there is an asymmetry in the experience of skilled and unskilled workers in terms of both wages and employment. Employment of unskilled workers will fluctuate more than that of skilled workers, who will be hoarded in the downturn and brought back into productive employment during the upturn. This leads to a higher recurrence of spells of unemployment for an unskilled worker and a higher unemployment rate for the unskilled group as a whole. Wages of unskilled workers will fluctuate more than those for skilled workers, causing the skill differential to widen during recessions and narrow during upturns. The firm will adjust unskilled wages as necessary to lose workers in the downturn. For skilled workers, however, because of specific skills, such turnover would be costly. Therefore their wages are maintained during the downturn to discourage quits. During the upturn the firm will make use of hoarded skilled labour rather than hire skilled labour only to face high severance costs later. Therefore it will not need to bid the skilled wage upwards to attract labour. Demand variations and fixed labour costs can create a significant demand for part-time workers. Part-time will be preferred to full-time workers if they have a higher average hourly productivity, if they can be paid a lower hourly wage and, particularly, if they have lower employment and/or severance costs. Part-time employment will fluctuate strongly with the business cycle, generating employment instability and proneness to unemployment for the workers involved. In practice hourly rates of pay are significantly lower for part-timers than equivalent full-timers and some fixed costs of employment and severance can be avoided altogether for workers who earn below a specified level or work fewer than a specified number of hours per week. The UK has greater legal and institutional differences between full- and part-time workers than most other countries, and an exceptionally high level of part-time working. Approximately one in five members of the workforce ($4\frac{1}{2}$ million people, of whom 84 per cent are female) work part-time, and the number increased considerably during the 1970s. In practice it is unskilled people who work part-time. It is not possible to pay a significantly lower wage to part-time skilled labour, the fixed costs cannot be so easily reduced, and the adjustment costs of operating many skilled part-time workers would be large for technological and specific human capital reasons. Many workers therefore suffer the wage and employment disadvantages of unskilled labour in employment adjustment processes plus the disadvantages associated with part-time work.

These arguments suggest that the interaction between demand variations and fixed labour costs creates significant differences between the welfare levels of skilled and unskilled workers. Skilled workers can expect to remain in a job and earn a fairly steady wage; the unskilled, although they may have brief periods of high earnings, face repeated periods of low earnings and/or unemployment. It is also skilled workers who are most likely to be found within structured internal labour markets while the unskilled are recruited from and returned to the external market as demand dictates. Skilled workers therefore benefit from good conditions of work, organised promotion structures, training facilities and union organisation. The gap between a skilled and an unskilled worker is likely to increase over time as the skilled worker progresses up the internal job hierarchy. The initial hiring of workers at the bottom of the internal wage structure is therefore crucially important. So too is the initial labour market experience of the worker. Once employed in firms using open internal labour markets, workers will have little opportunity of moving up the skill ladder and will also suffer employment instability as a result of the adjustment processes adopted by their employers. If job stability becomes an important criterion for selection into structured internal labour markets unskilled labour will find it difficult to work the transition later in their careers.

The impact of employment fixed costs upon firms' adjustment procedures is likely to have similar disadvantageous effects for unskilled labour as recruitment and severance costs if the flat-rate element in employment costs is significant. If the flat-rate element increases, this will raise the relative price of unskilled labour against other inputs including skilled labour. This will generate a more sustained shakeout of unskilled labour and a more important long-term unemployment problem for the unskilled.

If there are significant differences in the labour market experiences of skilled and unskilled workers the question arises as to the characteristics of these two groups. In Chapter 7 we argued that individuals from lower class backgrounds are at a disadvantage in access to education and are constrained in their ability to be economically mobile. The available data suggests a very strong systematic relationship between class of origin and achieved class so that the chance of being an unskilled worker is very high for children born into unskilled workers' families. This suggests that lower class individuals not only have lower earnings potential but are also continually most liable to the welfare disadvantages associated with technically efficient adjustment behaviour by firms.

So far we have assumed that firms do not practice discrimination. If employers do discriminate against certain groups of workers, these groups will be at a disadvantage in the adjustment process. First, the discriminating firm will in general choose to hire, train and promote A workers, *ceteris paribus*, in preference to B workers (the group discriminated against). Second, it will prefer to use A labour for overtime working, full-time as opposed to part-time employment and to hoard A labour. Third, it will prefer to discharge and to induce quits from B rather than A labour.

Discrimination in hiring need not arise because of adverse preferences by employers. Within a given skill level the firm's decision whether to hire or not depends on its *perceived* distribution of quality across applicants and its prospecting costs. If the firm perceives workers of different age, sex or racial groups as having different quality, or as imposing different prospecting costs, then different hiring decisions may be reached for different groups. If the real differences between groups are either non-existent or less than those perceived by the firm, the firm's actions will amount to employment discrimination. Suppose that a quit takes place from a job requiring a minimum quality level $\bar{q}$. The firm perceives the distribution of qualities over one group of workers, say male applicants, as being at a higher level than but otherwise the same as the distribution of qualities across female applicants. If prospecting costs are the same for both groups the firm will calculate a higher reservation quality for men than for women. If the female reservation quality is below $\bar{q}$, the firm will only interview men for the job. If both reservation qualities are above $\bar{q}$, the firm will prospect across male applicants first, and will only consider women if prospecting among men is unsuccessful and the male reservation quality falls to the female level. Inadequate information about B labour may arise because historically they have not been a significant segment of the labour market. Of course, if the firm ever does interview and hire women it will discover the true distribution of qualities and thus discrimination will disappear. Discrimination will persist if firms always appoint A workers, because they perceive the B labour quality distribution to be markedly inferior and never prospect in that market or because they can always fill the limited number of posts from the A group or because though the reservation quality falls for A workers as the firm makes unsuccessful prospects it falls simultaneously for B workers. Even if a few B workers are hired, the fact that their average quality exceeds the perceived level may not be seen as significant but as the result of luck or of efficient prospecting to identify the exceptional cases.

Discrimination in hiring can also come about if the firm considers workers to be of equal quality, but faces higher prospecting costs for some categories. This could happen, for example, if the firm has evolved cheap, effective and reliable methods of attracting male applicants and assessing their quality which do not work for women. The result will again be different reservation qualities for men and for women. Women will either not be interviewed at all, or only if lack of suitable male applicants causes the firm to switch markets. If the relative level of recruitment costs for different groups of workers varies across firms then this may give rise to segregated labour forces where the same job may be done, for example, by women or black workers in one firm but by white men in another.

The analysis of labour market discrimination thus predicts that the groups most disadvantaged by employment adjustments will be women, minority racial and ethnic groups, perhaps the young and the old, and perhaps also those with sickness or unemployment histories. However, since such groups are also unskilled, whether their observed disadvantage can be explained in terms of labour market discrimination or lower fixed costs is an empirical issue. The analysis required to distinguish the two factors is complex, and so far few definitive points have emerged except that both play some significant part. Discrimination and differentials in fixed costs are not independent but have a cumulative effect on the disadvantaged position of B workers in the firm's labour adjustment process. Extra-market discrimination and social structures assign women and minority ethnic and racial groups to the unskilled category on entry to the labour market. Labour market discrimination then assigns them to firms with open internal labour markets. The dynamics of fixed costs, even without further discrimination, contain them in low pay, high turnover, low security employment. The initial assignment of market entrants to jobs again appears critical to the workers' lifetime welfare. For some this is a matter of luck, for others it is their sex or colour that counts. Empirical evidence on discrimination in hiring is limited to case studies and is often difficult to interpret, partly because hiring standards and job requirements are rarely made explicit. The evidence available suggests that firms do habitually prefer certain categories of workers for specified jobs. They appear particularly concerned to appoint married men between 25 and 40 to skilled jobs. Firms behave as if they perceive differences between groups of workers, but how real those differences are is difficult to determine, as is whether they originate inside or outside the labour market. Even if such behaviour has some efficiency rationale it will result in discrimination against, say, individual high quality women who have a low propensity to quit but are treated as 'average' female applicants.

Labour adjustments take place in a world of non-competitive behaviour by workers and their representatives. The analysis of trade unions suggests that their activities will be important to the adjustment process. First, the union will exert some influence upon the mix of hiring and overtime, discharges and hoarding in order to stabilise employment at a level consistent with its wage target. Second, the union will seek to impose rules about which workers should be hired or discharged, to ensure, for example, that hires come from union members and that discharges comply with last-in first-out (LIFO) rules. It will then be the long-standing rather than the most productive employees who are retained. The union may insist that compulsory early retirement be offered to older workers who, *ceteris paribus*, are likely to have been with the firm longer and thus have high redundancy payments. This will conflict with the firm's interests and with efficiency. Third, the union will be an important force for the creation of a structured internal labour market and for internal rather than external adjustment procedures. Fourth, unions will promote discrimination in adjustment procedures if workers have tastes for discrimination or if such restrictions on labour supply serve a useful purpose in realising wage objectives.

How far the union influences the firm's adjustment processes will depend *inter alia* upon the union representation, the competitive base of the firm and product demand variability, but the following arguments suggest that union pressure is likely to benefit skilled workers more than unskilled workers. First, for historical and economic reasons skilled labour tends to be more strongly unionised. Second, skilled unions have the most bargaining power. Third, skilled workers are more likely to be found in the technologically based industries that enjoy monopoly power, sustained demand growth and less cyclical variability. Fourth, women and other groups discriminated against not only suffer from male-dominated unions; they themselves are not strongly organised. As predominantly unskilled labour they thus suffer doubly. Fifth, union policies will be determined by those with most impact in the union. Since skilled workers have most voice by dint of status, seniority and age, their interests will dominate union decisions. Sixth, to the extent that skilled workers represent a higher social stratum they will be treated more favourably by employers and administrators. Both on ideological and practical grounds social organisation requires the support and involvement of skilled groups.

Empirical evidence suggests a consistent tendency for the nature of employment adjustments to be related to trade union representation. The hiring of unionised labour varies less than that of non-unionised labour; the quit rate and discharge rate are lower and internal labour market structures are more important. However the level of union representation is highest where fixed costs are most significant, and therefore disentangling their respective influences is extremely difficult.

Throughout this section we have, for purely illustrative purposes, concentrated upon the distinction between skilled and unskilled labour. Fixed costs are likely to be highest for professional workers. Fixed costs for skilled manual and non-manual labour will exceed those for unskilled labour. Within each of these categories substantial differences will exist. Our analysis demonstrates how these differences might be analysed; how they interact with discrimination and non-competitive forces; and their importance for the welfare of individual workers.

## Further Reading

CHAPTER 8: EMPLOYMENT ADJUSTMENTS

R. A. Hart and T. Sharot, 'The short-run demand for workers and hours', *Review of Economic Studies*, Vol. 45 (June 1978).

T. Hazledine, 'Employment functions and the demand for labour in the short run', in Z. Hornstein, J. Grice and A. Webb (eds), *The Economics of the Labour Market* (London: HMSO, 1981).

D. I. MacKay, D. Boddy, J. Brack, J. A. Diack and N. Jones, *Labour Markets under Different Employment Conditions* (London: George Allen & Unwin, 1971).

W. Y. Oi, 'Labour as a quasi-fixed factor', *Journal of Political Economy*, Vol. 70 (October 1962).

J. Taylor, *Unemployment and Wage Inflation* (London: Longman, 1974).

M. L. Wachter, 'Primary and secondary markets: a critique of the dual approach', *Brookings Papers on Economic Activity* Vol. 3 (December 1974).

O. E. Williamson, *Markets and Hierarchies: Analysis and Antitrust Implications* (New York: The Free Press, 1977).

# 9
# Wages

The analysis of wages is central to the study of labour economics. In competitive theory wage movements provide the signals by which resources are allocated and the mechanism by which efficiency is achieved. Wages are also the largest element in most people's incomes and thus the principal determinant of their economic welfare.

In the basic model of the labour market wages are determined by the relationship between the market marginal revenue product curve for each category of homogeneous labour and the supply of that labour based upon workers' goods/leisure choices and their consumption preferences across different educational programmes. In this chapter we seek to extend the analysis of wages on the basis of the theoretical developments discussed in Section I. In particular, we look to human capital theory to provide insights into both the nature of the wage determination process and the structure of wages across the labour market. Within that framework we then consider the impact of trade unions and discrimination.

## 9.1 The analysis of wages

Wages in the basic model are determined by the interaction in each skill market of the combined demand for labour of profit-maximising firms and the supply of labour from utility-maximising workers. No agent, firm or worker, can alone influence wages. Competitive processes, arising from a great number of individual decisions working through the hidden hand, form the basis of the wage determination process. Scarcity is everywhere the over-riding criterion governing the wage level and differences in scarcity levels determine the structure of wages across the economy.

We have already seen in Chapter 4 how that analysis can be modified to allow for uncertainty. Within each labour market different firms set different wages according to the quality of their information, the screening strategy they adopt and, in particular, according to the level of their screening costs. Contrary to the basic model, wage differentials will thus emerge and indeed persist as long as workers incur screening costs. Significant wage dispersions within individual labour markets have indeed been widely recorded.

We have also seen in Chapters 5 and 8 how the basic model can be modified to embrace complex, unique and protected wage structures within individual firms. In Chapter 8 we noted the role of specific human capital in producing structured internal labour markets. In wage setting, great importance is attached by firms with high fixed labour costs to preventing quits and thus avoiding recruitment and training costs. The internal wage structure therefore comes to reflect the particular structure of fixed labour costs across the skills within each firm. We also noted in Chapter 5 how non-maximising behaviour by firms, along with reference bargaining by workers, can affect the wage determination process and lead the internal wage structure to deviate from that predicted by considerations of scarcity. Case studies of individual work units have shown that the internal wage structure varies considerably between units. Established relativities appear to be important and are not the same in any two units. Wage structures only rarely appear to respond to scarcity.

In this chapter, we are not concerned either with wages across firms within individual occupations or with wage structures within firms, but with wage structures across occupations. Whilst, in practice, these three wage dimensions interact and complement one another, we assume hereon that intra-market wage differences do not exist and that wage structures within similarly composed firms are the same.

In the basic model the competitive process governing wages recognizes only the education/consumption choices of individuals in determining labour supply. The total labour supply curve to each market is inelastic. The supply curve to each firm is horizontal at the market wage. Of course, this reflects the use of a wide definition of each skill or occupation. The wider we define each skill the less technically feasible it is for workers to switch across markets and so the less elastic is the supply curve.

The basic model also ignores the positive and negative utility workers derive directly from their work activities. In fact, the level of supply to any occupation will depend upon the characteristics of the work associated with that occupation and the nature and distribution of tastes for those characteristics across workers. The characteristics that seem important here relate to the following: the physical conditions of the work, for example, the danger, dirtiness and exertion; the security of employment and income; the opportunities for independent action and creativity; the responsibility falling upon the worker; the uncertainty of successful performance. In this chapter, we shall not pursue the analysis of wage structures in terms of compensating differentials. We merely note that labour economists have gained some insight pursuing this theme. For example, an investigation of wage differentials as a reflection of differences in the probability of unemployment across the market place helps us to understand the position in the wage structure of skills susceptible to strong demand variations and to short-time working or temporary lay-offs. The investigation of wage differentials as a reflection of the impact of different technologies through unit size helps to explain the position in the wage structure of certain skills in manufacturing industry.

Whilst we do not pursue further the implications of differences in utility from work, the analysis in this chapter is a development of the idea of compensating differentials. One source of such differentials, not so far mentioned, will be differences in the costs to workers of acquiring their skills, i.e. differences in training costs. Whilst this is an important insight, further analysis of it within the basic model would be severely restricted. The process of wage determination is unsatisfactory in that it fails to provide a coherent model of occupational choice. In providing just this, human capital theory generates an analysis of wage determination and wage structures that raises the link between wages and training expenditures to a central position.

Let us try to identify the features of the human capital approach which distinguish it from the basic model, and at the same time relate it to the analysis of supply and demand adjustments of Chapters 7 and 8, which attach some importance to adjustment costs. The basic model assumes that the supply of labour to any skill is insensitive to changes in relative wages. Education decisions are consumption decisions. In Figure 9.1(a) the supply curve to market $i$ is vertical, and fixed if tastes for education and work characteristics are stable. As a result, the wage paid in market $i$, and thus to any individual in the market, varies with demand. The model therefore attaches little importance to education decisions and assumes that the adjustment costs of occupational mobility are prohibitive. Demand changes affecting some of the firms using labour $i$ will induce sufficient job mobility to maintain wage parity across firms because the model assumes zero costs of adjustments for workers and firms. The effect of supply changes upon wage levels and wage differences between individuals depends critically upon the elasticity of demand for labour, and in turn on the demand for the goods produced by that labour and the substitutability of factors.

In Figure 9.1(b) the supply curve is not vertical because wage movements change educational decisions and bring about occupational mobility. After a demand increase, wages increase and educational inputs increase. The relative wage always reflects the level of training costs at the margin, so with no difference in abilities the curve will be horizontal in the long run. Any given change in demand brings about the same change in educational inputs. The model therefore relates changes in individual wages directly to changes in educa-

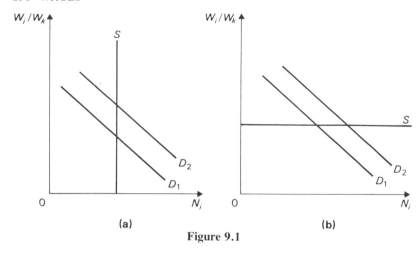

**Figure 9.1**

tion. Supply always adjusts, there are no education restrictions, no adjustment costs for firms and zero transactions costs of occupational and job mobility. The costs and amount of education are the key variables in the analysis.

## 9.2 The human capital model of wage determination

In Chapter 3 the human capital model was used to analyse individuals' decisions about investment in education. Since the benefits from such investment take the form of increased wage earnings, human capital theory provides a theory of wage determination across individuals. The basis of this theory can be stated as follows: in a competitive labour market individuals will be paid according to their marginal productivity; they increase their productivity by undertaking human capital investments; therefore wages depend on the amount of investment undertaken.

Let us initially consider an extremely simple human capital model of wage determination. This assumes that jobs are identical in all respects other than in the amount of human capital they require and pay wages which are constant over time and known with certainty. All human capital investments are undertaken prior to entry into the labour market, i.e. through schooling, there are no supply restrictions on education and no consumption benefits from education; individuals are all of equal ability and face no financial or other constraints on their choices about education, and all workers stay in the job they first enter for $N$ years, before retiring. In this case the only reason why people earn different amounts is that they do jobs requiring different amounts of education. Human capital theory suggests that, since individuals who undergo education start to work later, they will have to earn more once they do start. So

$$W_j = f(E_j), \qquad f_1 > 0 \qquad (9.1)$$

where $E_j$ is the amount of education undertaken by individual $j$. Equation (9.1) expresses the fundamental hypothesis of the human capital theory of wage determination: that wage differentials between individuals reflect their differing amounts of education. Since in developed countries people are compelled to undertake a minimum length of education, wage differentials arise from differences in workers' post-compulsory schooling. The next stage is to derive a specific form for the relationship in equation (9.1). Suppose that each educational programme lasts one year. We would expect someone with one year of post-compulsory education to earn more than someone with none at all, but how much more? And will this differential be the same as that between two people with 9 and 10 years of education respectively?

In the human capital model each year's education brings an incremental rate of return $r_S$. We assume that this is constant for each additional year of education. Let us define $W_0$ as the annual earnings of someone with no optional education. If for simplicity we ignore direct costs, this represents the investment of someone staying on for one year of education. The relationship between $W_0$, wages after one year's education, $W_1$, and wages for further amounts of education can be shown as follows:

| Year of optional education, S | Amount invested | Return on investment | Wages at end of year |
|---|---|---|---|
| 1 | $W_0$ | $r_S W_0$ | $W_1 = W_0 + r_S W_0 = W_0(1 + r_S)$ |
| 2 | $W_1$ | $r_S W_1$ | $W_2 = W_1 + r_S W_1 = W_0(1 + r_S)^2$ |
| 3 | $W_2$ | $r_S W_2$ | $W_3 = W_2 + r_S W_2 = W_0(1 + r_S)^3$ |

The last column of this table indicates a simple relationship between the wage our individual receives and the length of time she spends in education, $S$:

$$W = W_0(1 + r_S)^S \qquad (9.2)$$

If we express this relationship in continuous terms and take logs, it becomes

$$\log W = \log W_0 + r_S S \qquad (9.3)$$

The human capital model relates wages to one variable, $S$, by means of one parameter, $r_S$, and a simple exponential function. Let us consider the predictions of the model.

First, because in the model the logarithm of an individual's earnings is positively and linearly related to her years of schooling, each successive year brings in the same proportional increase in wage, $r_S$ per cent. Therefore each additional year of schooling brings about a larger absolute addition to earnings. Second, individuals with different amounts of education all have the same present value of lifetime earnings discounted to minimum school-leaving age: the extent to which people with more education get higher wages exactly balances the cost of their deferred entry into the labour market. Third, anything which reduces the foregone earnings cost of higher levels of education, e.g. paying wages to university students, or youth unemployment, will reduce the wage differential associated with higher education. Fourth, this will also happen to the extent that higher education has consumption benefits. Fifth, the same thing will happen if the jobs filled by more highly educated people are cleaner, safer, more secure and more prestigious than jobs requiring little education. Sixth, if everyone retires at the same age, rather than having the same number of working years as assumed above, the wage differential for each year of education will have to be larger. Seventh, age–earnings profiles are horizontal, at a level which depends only on $S$. Eighth, the higher is $r_S$ the bigger the wage differential associated with each year of education.

The schooling model therefore generates testable predictions about the determination of an individual's wages. But what does it predict about the distribution of wages across individuals? First, since $W_0$ and $r_S$ are treated as constant, the wage dispersion arises from the distribution of years of education $S$. Since $S$ has a geometric rather than an arithmetic relationship with $W$, a normal (i.e. symmetrical) distribution of $S$ will give rise to a positively skewed distribution of wages. Second, the difference between the wages of someone with 10 years and someone with 9 years of education is greater than that between the wages of someone with 1 year and someone with 0 years of education. Third, the model predicts that a rise in the mean level of $S$ will increase the spread of wages. This is a pessimistic conclusion since it suggests that increased education will not reduce inequalities in income, as is often supposed. Fourth, any policy which increases the variability of $S$ in the labour force, such as the introduction of new types of educational programme, or repeated changes in the minimum school leaving age, will increase the dispersion and skewness of wages. Sixth, the higher is $r_S$ the greater will be the dispersion and skewness of wages.

The schooling model, in relating wages simply to years of education, ignores the multitude of other factors which affect wages. But, even if the model is correct in identifying educational investments as the principal determinant of wages, it could be argued that it is not simply the quantity of schooling, $S$, that matters but also its quality and the amount of subsequent education. Undoubtedly, quality does vary enormously between educational establishments: people who reach minimum school leaving age in the best schools have already had more human capital investment and therefore have a higher earnings potential than people who have received worse education. In principal, this problem can be dealt with by relating wages to quality as well as quantity of education. The schooling model includes only human capital investments made before entering the labour market, and therefore ignores the possibility of on-the-job training (OJT). In practice, training is likely to have profound effects on the distribution of wages across individuals.

Let us consider therefore a model in which a worker enters the labour market after $S$ years of optional education so that she could earn £$W_S$ a year. She takes a job which involves OJT for the first $T$ years. Some fraction, $k_j$, of her working time in the $j$th year of work experience is devoted to investment. We assume that $k_j$ falls from a maximum value when $j = 0$ to become zero when $j = T$. The time invested adds to earning power as in the schooling model, but detracts from current earnings. Earnings are derived only from that fraction of time, $(1 - k_j)$, which is not invested. Therefore in this model, unlike the schooling model, there is a gap between human capital earnings power and actual market earnings. We call the former $Y$ and the latter $W$. The gap represents OJT investment.

In the post-schooling investment model, then, the worker makes an annual investment which we assume is a declining fraction $(k_j)$ of her accumulating earning power $Y_j$. To be worthwhile this investment must increase earnings by more than the costs of the investment. We assume that each unit of training brings a constant rate of return $r_T$. The earning power over time of an individual who enters the labour market with earning power $Y_S$ $(= W_S)$ can be derived as follows:

| Year of experience, j | Amount invested | Return on investment | Earning power accumulated at end of year j |
|---|---|---|---|
| 1 | $k_1 Y_S$ | $r_T k_1 Y_S$ | $Y_1 = Y_S + r_T k_1 Y_S = Y_2(1 + r_T k_1)$ |
| 2 | $k_2 Y_1$ | $r_T k_2 Y_1$ | $Y_2 = Y_1 + r_T k_2 Y_1$ |
| | | | $= Y_S(1 + r_T k_1)(1 + r_T k_2)$ |
| T | $k_1 Y_{T-1}$ | $r_T k_T Y_{T-1}$ | $Y_T = Y_S(1 + r_T k_1) \ldots (1 + r_T k_T)$ |

The last column of this table shows that earning power after $j$ years' work experience depends on the amount of time invested in training in each year:

$$Y_j = Y_S(1 + r_T k_1)(1 + r_T k_2) \dots (1 + r_T k_j) \tag{9.4}$$

In order to simplify this relationship it is necessary to make some assumption about how $k_j$ behaves over time. The simplest possible assumption is that it declines linearly over the training period:

$$k_t = k_0 - k_{0t}/T \tag{9.5}$$

In this case, the total amount of time spent in training, $\chi$, in $j$ years of work experience is given by

$$\chi = \int_{t=0}^{j} k_t \, dt \tag{9.6}$$

and this is the investment on which the rate of return $r_T$ is earned, so (9.4) becomes

$$Y_j = Y_S(1 + r_T)^\chi \tag{9.7}$$

If we express this relationship in continuous terms and take logs, it becomes

$$\log Y_j = \log Y_S + r_T \chi \tag{9.8}$$

$$= \log Y_S + r_T \left[ k_0 j - \frac{k_0 j^2}{2T} \right] \tag{9.9}$$

Equation (9.9) explains earning power, which, when OJT is taking place, exceeds current earnings $W_j$:

$$W_j = (1 - k_j)Y_j \tag{9.10}$$

thus

$$\log W_j = \log Y_j + \log (1 - k_j) \tag{9.11}$$

$$= \log Y_S + r_T k_0 j - \frac{r_T k_0 j^2}{2T} + \log (1 - k_j) \tag{9.12}$$

which, after substituting in from (9.3), becomes

$$\log W_j = \log W_0 + r_S S + r_T k_0 j - \frac{r_T k_0 j^2}{2T} + \log (1 - k_j) \tag{9.13}$$

Equation (9.13) is therefore one version (different assumptions about the behaviour of $k_j$ give slightly different equations) of the post-schooling human capital investment model of wage determination. Although more complex than the schooling model of (9.3), it is still a remarkably simple model containing only two variables – years of schooling $S$ and years of experience $j$. The model explains wages after $j$ years' experience; it therefore yields predictions about individuals' age–earnings profiles.

First, the model predicts that the log of earnings is related linearly to years of schooling but non-linearly to years of experience. Earnings continue to rise with experience, as in Figure 9.2, as long as training is taking place, i.e. for $T$ years. They will then be constant unless human capital deteriorates. The shape of an individual's profile, i.e. the relationship between wages and experience, depends critically on three different parameters: $r_T$, $k_0$ and $T$, all of which vary across individuals. These parameters determine between them both the upward slope of the profile and, given $W$, its peak value. Second, people with the same values of $r_T$, $k_0$ and $T$ but different levels of $S$ will have age–earnings profiles which are parallel, but that of the person with less education will be lower throughout. Third, the higher is $k_0$, given $T$ and $r_T$, the steeper is the age–earnings profile and the higher its peak value. More investment is undertaken in any year of work experience and therefore earning power rises faster and further, but at the expense of market earnings during the training period. The

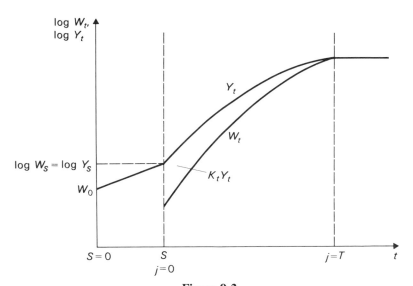

**Figure 9.2**

investment gap between $Y_t$ and $W_t$ in Figure 9.2 is wider. Therefore, if two people with the same level of $S$ have different values of $k_0$ their age–earnings profiles will diverge with increasing $j$. Fourth, given $k_0$ and $T$, the higher is $r_T$ the higher and steeper the age–earnings profile will be, because the greater the addition to earning power from any amount of investment. In this model $r_T$, like $r_S$, has been assumed constant across successive units of training. If $r_T$ declines, the age–earnings profile will become flatter. Fifth, the longer is the training period $T$, the more training is undertaken, the higher is peak earnings and the later in the individual's working life is the peak reached. In the limit, if the individual receives training throughout her working life her age–earnings profile will rise continuously.

This model therefore generates predictions, which are in principle empirically testable, about the determination of individuals' earnings over their whole working lifetimes. But what does it predict about the distribution of wages across individuals? All the predictions for the distribution of wages derived from the schooling model can be derived from the extended model. Further predictions can now be made, however, because earnings will vary across individuals with the same level of $S$ if they undertake different amounts of post-school investment. First, the model suggests that, treating $r_S$ and $r_T$ as constant, the wage dispersion arises from the distribution across individuals of years of schooling and amounts of training. The latter depends on $j$ but also on $k_0$ and $T$. Second, the addition to wages from each year's experience depends primarily on the behaviour of $k_j$; if $k_j$ declines fast enough then the absolute as well as proportionate increase in wages will decline with $j$ so that the difference in wages between someone with 10 years and someone with 9 years of experience is smaller than that between someone with 1 year and someone with 0 years of experience. Third, any increase in the mean level of training involved in work experience will increase the dispersion of wages. Fourth, the more variation exists in amounts of post-schooling investment at each level of $S$, the greater the dispersion and skewness of wages. Fifth, if the amount of training involved in jobs which already have a high investment content increases, the distribution of wages will become more dispersed and more skewed. Sixth, the higher $r_T$ the greater the dispersion and skewness of wages. Seventh, if there is a positive correlation between schooling and training so that people with a high level of $S$ also undertake a lot of post-schooling investment, then the dispersion and skewness of wages will be greater. Eighth, in this case the average age–earnings profiles for workers with different levels of $S$ will diverge as $j$ increases so that the dispersion of wages increases with age. Ninth, since age–earnings profiles are concave from below, demographic factors contribute to the dispersion of wages; one reason for the dispersion is that workers are at different points on their age–earnings profiles. Therefore, any demographic change, such as a rising proportion of very young workers, which increases the percentage of workers at the extremes of the distribution will increase the dispersion of wages.

The human capital models identify education differences as the critical determinant of wage differences across individuals. But they offer no explanation as to why some individuals invest in more education than others. However, we have considered this question in Section 7.6. Educational qualifications are not randomly distributed across the population. Even if all individuals invest sufficiently for both the rates of return, $r_S$ and $r_T$, to be equalised at the margin across individuals, levels of educational investment will be different due to a combination of differences in ability, educational restrictions and income constraints. This implies that equation (9.13) can be only a starting point for making comparisons across individuals. In fact, Section 7.6 suggested that because of income constraints, it is very unlikely that either rates of return or education levels will be equalised across individuals. So, two people with the same education could earn very different wages. Because $r_S$ and $r_T$ vary across individuals and social groups, the underlying relationships between wages and time spent in education and work experience behind equation (9.13) are complex. We return to consider the effects of stratification upon wage determination in Section 9.6. Returns to education will also differ, however, according to whether individuals are in highly union organised jobs and according to sex and colour. In the next section we consider the impact of trade unions on wage determination. In Section 9.4 we consider discrimination.

The human capital approach in this section is a starting point to the analysis of wage determination, the real value of which can only be assessed by empirical tests of its predictions. Despite, or perhaps because of, its simplicity, does human capital theory help us to begin to understand the process of wage determination? In Section 9.5 we look at some of the empirical work that has been done in this area.

Finally, we note that the human capital approach to wage determination provides predictions about the wage structure across occupations and industries. Applied to the occupational wage structure the model predicts, first, that the difference in wages between any two occupations will reflect the difference in the amounts of schooling and training necessary to achieve the skills required for those occupations. The ranking of occupations by wages and the differential at each stage will reflect the education costs associated with occupations. Second, whilst occupational differentials change in the short run with product demand changes, productivity and so on, in the long run the wage structure alters only because of changes in educational costs between occupations. As noted in Chapter 3, occupations differ in the extent of the general skills required. This is one reason why investment in human capital will not reach its optimum level. In the case of the most general types of OJT, where it is up to the individual worker to act as entrepreneur for her own investment, problems will arise because of lack of funds. In the case of specific training, there is an incentive for firms to provide and finance the investment. Most OJT contains both specific and general elements, and therefore promises risks and rewards to both worker and employer. Since there are no institutions designed to share out the costs and benefits, there is little likelihood that investment in training will be carried out to the optimal level. In particular, training containing a high degree of general skills will be deficient, with consistently high rates of return at the margin, *ceteris paribus*. Individuals in those occupations with training requirements that are general across firms will earn high wages. Those occupations will have higher places in the wage structure than would otherwise be the case.

Wages theory develops from individual wage determination into occupational wage structure. Despite the theoretical problems associated with inter-industry wage differentials, which arise largely because industries do not fit readily into economic models based upon single markets, labour economists have nevertheless been interested in analysing them. This partly reflects the practical, everyday importance of the industry classification, partly the availability of industry data. To the extent that the industry wage is basically a complex weighted average of occupational wages, human capital analysis predicts, first, that the industry wage structure will reflect the numerical importance of occupations that have significant educational requirements. Second, the industry wage structure will change in the long term primarily because of either technological changes which alter the relative importance of education-intensive occupations, and/or changes in the technology of occupations or in the education programmes that they require, which alter their educational costs. Wages will be higher in industries with significant amounts of skills general across firms in the industry because of the likely under-investment in them. Some empirical studies of wage structures across occupations and industries are considered in Section 9.5.

## 9.3 Trade unions and wages

The analysis of trade unions in Chapter 5 suggested that the presence of a union in a particular sector will increase the wage paid above the competitive level. The exact size of the increase will depend, *inter alia*, upon the marginal rate of substitution between wages and employment in the union's utility function, the union's ability to control supply, the elasticity of demand for the product of the firms in the controlled sector, the workers' willingness to undertake and sustain industrial action and the monopoly power possessed by the firm.

Consider an individual worker in a fully unionised labour market or occupation $i$. Let us assume that the union is able to achieve an adjustment to the wage of $m$ equal to $W/W^c$ where $W$ is the final wage and $W^c$ the wage if no union were present and competition prevailed. Let us assume that the union's mark-up is related to $W^c$ geometrically, so

$$W = W^c e^m \qquad (9.14)$$

$$\log W = \log W^c + m \qquad (9.15)$$

Using equation (9.3), we know that $W^c$ will be determined by the human capital input required for occupation $i$:

$$\log W^c = \log W_0 + r_s S \qquad (9.16)$$

so

$$\log W = \log W_0 + r_s S + m \qquad (9.17)$$

Let us propose that the union mark-up varies by occupations according to the level of human capital required, so

$$m = m_0 + bS, \qquad b > 0 \qquad (9.18)$$

A number of the arguments set out in Chapter 5 support this proposition: the elasticity of demand for educated labour is lower than for other workers (it is a complement to rather than a substitute for capital and it represents a smaller percentage of total costs); unions have more control over labour supply in educated sectors (through control of educational qualifications); and the costs of industrial action are higher for employers of educated labour (given their association with high capital costs). Using equation (9.18), (9.17) becomes

$$\log W = \log W_0 + m_0 + r_s S + bS \qquad (9.19)$$

Equation (9.17) implies, first, that the lifetime earnings profiles of two people, one unionised, one not, will be parallel, *ceteris paribus*, but that of the unionised individual will always be higher. Second, the lifetime income profile of those individuals in occupations where $m$ is largest will be higher than for other workers. Third, from equation

(9.19) the difference in wages between two individuals, one with 10 years of education, the other with 9 years, will be greater than the difference for another two individuals, one with 1 year, the other with 0 years of education, because of the effects of education outlays noted previously, but also because of a higher union mark-up. This implies that education programmes, as investments, represent not merely a path to occupations that are more productive but an entrance to occupations where unions have more leverage. The rate of return to schooling becomes $r_s + b$. Fourth, all the arguments noted previously about the effects of the distribution of schooling and training upon the distribution of wages apply with additional force now. For example, if the distribution of $S$ is skewed, the distribution of $W$ will be more skewed with than without unions. Fifth, for given values of $m_0$ and $b$, initially the more people there are in union-covered areas the greater the dispersion of wages. After the majority of the working population are in covered areas further increases will generally reduce the dispersion. Sixth, any tendency for highly educated individuals to be more likely to be covered by unions will make the distribution of wages across individuals more skewed.

In equation (9.18) the union mark-up is assumed to be the same for all workers with education level $S$. Theory would predict, however, that the returns to union membership, $m$, will vary within and across occupations according to their technological and demand conditions. Non-competitive forces, here resulting from union restrictions on entry, make it even more difficult for workers to move between jobs to equalise returns to union membership than it is for them to invest up to the level where returns to education are equalised. The union mark-up for an individual worker will therefore vary with his industrial and geographical location. Any correlation between years of schooling and access to locations where union leverage is greatest will increase the dispersion and skewness of wages.

The analysis makes no distinction between the types of union agreement individuals are subject to. In practice there will be workers who are subject only to agreements negotiated nationally which cannot take into account the specific circumstances of individual work units. There may indeed be little workplace organization associated with such agreements, which tend to be infrequent and restricted to a limited number of issues. Other workers will be subject to agreements which are negotiated entirely within the work unit by local union representatives. Bargaining takes place on a continuous basis over a very wide range of issues and is always sensitive to local conditions. The very nature of such arrangements suggests that workers subject to them will benefit most from union activities. The size of the wage adjustment $m$ will thus depend upon the form of union representation.

In the above model, the individual receives the union wage adjustment because he is in a unionised sector. In practice the analysis holds if all workers in the sector $i$ are covered by collective agreements, even if they are not all union members. This raises the question, of course, why workers should join unions at all. Without going into this very far, it is clear that union membership has some of the characteristics of a public good. Wage gains are common to all covered workers, whether they belong to the union or not. In practice, exclusion is impossible. Given the cost of joining a union, if unions were there merely to get the union wage adjustment, the classic free-rider problem would arise and union membership would be very low. This helps to explain why unions prefer closed shops but also establishes that membership must have other benefits (even if these satisfy only an option demand); for example, collective support to guarantee job security, satisfactory working conditions and fringe benefits. Membership also provides welfare facilities for the worker in the form of legal assistance, health and insurance services and so on.

Our analysis ignores the heterogeneity of labour within each education level. Amongst the members of any education category, higher quality people will attract higher wages since quality is a significant dimension of productivity. If higher quality people are more likely to be in unions, the wage distribution will be more skewed. We must be careful in using equation (9.19). Unless a quality variable is included, the effect of quality (as with schooling if it was inadequately included) would be attributed to unions.

Having introduced labour heterogeneity at each education level we must recognize that firms faced by a trade union will alter their hiring strategy. Since labour is more costly the firm will attempt to raise the quality of its hires by increasing its prospecting. The firm might be so successful that, in time, the wage increase due to the union will be largely paid for in higher output. In these circumstances, if equation (9.19) includes a quality variable, the welfare implications of union activities must be derived from the wage mark up net of the change in quality. For any individual worker access to the union wage will depend upon his quality because it is this which determines his acceptability to those firms where unions are effective.

We recall from the analysis of specific human capital that certain firms will develop structured internal labour markets. In practice, such markets will be characterised, simultaneously, by monopoly power in product markets, superior rewards offered in the labour market and extensive unionisation. On this argument any wage adjustment, $m$, above the competitive level is in part the result of production technology. Union membership is the worker's means of access to the benefits of that technology. But it will be difficult to separate out the effects of unions from those of technology and monopoly, even if they are included in equation (9.18), because they are highly correlated.

Finally, we have noted in our discussion that the union mark-up varies with $S$ and with the worker's location. But there is no explicit statement in equation (9.18) of the factors that determine the size of the mark-up. Also, though the model leaves us with the impression that being a union member is valuable, there is no indication as to who might belong to unions and, therefore, as to who might benefit from them.

To measure the effects of trade unions upon wages across individuals using the above analysis we might proceed as follows. Let us define $W^u$, the wage for an individual covered by a trade union agreement, as simply the competitive wage, $W^c$, for his labour market, subject to a proportional union mark-up.

$$W^u = W^c \, e^m \tag{9.20}$$

where $m = W^u/W^c$ is assumed to be constant for all workers in the economy. For individuals not unionised the wage $W^{nu}$ will be the competitive wage,

$$W^{nu} = W^c$$

Thus for any individual $j$ we have

$$W_j = W^{nu} \, e^{md_j} \tag{9.21}$$

Where $d_j$ is 1 if the individual is covered, zero if he is not.
Thus

$$\log W_j = \log W_j^{nu} + md_j \tag{9.22}$$

Since the non-union wage arises from competitive market forces, we can define $\log W^{nu}$ in terms of a vector of variables, $\mathbf{X}$, that capture the individual's quality and market location. The essence of the argument in the previous section is that of this vector, human capital endowments, $S_j$, will be the most important and should be singled out. So we have

$$\log W_j = md_j + r_s S_j + g(\mathbf{X}_j) \tag{9.23}$$

If we have data for a sample of individuals on $W$, $d$, $S$ and $\mathbf{X}$, we can use the equation

$$\log W_j = a_1 d_j + a_2 S_j + \sum_{i=3}^{n} a_i X_{ij} \tag{9.24}$$

to derive an estimate of $a_1$, the union differential.

One crucial assumption here of course is that $W^{nu} = W^c$: the wages of individuals in non-unionised areas are not affected by the advent of unions in the covered areas, either through the market (by spillovers of labour) or through institutional forces (by parallel wage negotiations). This is a strong assumption if unions are active in parts of an industry so that union labour can easily switch between the unionised and non-unionised areas of the same industry.

The impact of unions upon the industry (or occupational) wage structure can be analysed as follows: imagine that some workers in a particular industry (occupation) $i$ are covered by collective agreements. The average wage across these workers is $W^u$. The average wage across the non-unionised workers is $W^{nu}$. The average wage for the market, $\bar{W}_i$, will thus be some weighted average of the union and non-union wages. If we specify $\bar{W}_i$ as a geometrically weighted average of the two sub-sector wage rates we can write

$$\log \bar{W}_i \equiv \lambda_i \log W_i^u + (1 - \lambda_i) \log W_i^{nu} \qquad (9.25)$$

where $\lambda_i$ is the proportion of the labour force in market $i$ unionised. From (9.25) we derive

$$\log \bar{W}_i \equiv \lambda_i (\log W_i^u - \log W_i^{nu}) + \log W_i^{nu} \qquad (9.26)$$

If we define $W_i^c$ as the competitive wage and specify the relative union wage effect $(r_i)$ and the non-union effect $(k_i)$ as

$$r_i = \frac{W_i^u - W_i^{nu}}{W_i^{nu}} \quad \text{and} \quad k_i = \frac{W_i^{nu} - W_i^c}{W_i^c}$$

then

$$r_i = (W_i^u / W_i^{nu}) - 1 \quad \text{and} \quad k_i = (W_i^{nu} / W_i^c) - 1$$

or

$$r_i + 1 = W_i^u / W_i^{nu} \quad \text{and} \quad k_i + 1 = W_i^{nu} / W_i^c$$

or

$$\log(r_i + 1) = \log W_i^u - \log W_i^{nu} \quad \text{and} \quad \log(k_i + 1) = \log W_i^{nu} - \log W_i^c$$

Thus equation (9.26) becomes

$$\log \bar{W}_i = \lambda_i \log(r_i + 1) + \log W_i^{nu} \qquad (9.27)$$

$$\log \bar{W}_i = \lambda_i \log(r_i + 1) + \log(k_i + 1) + \log W_i^c \qquad (9.28)$$

From the previous section we can specify the competitive wage $W_i^c$ for an occupation in terms of the educational requirements **S** of that occupation, and for an industry in terms of the occupational composition of the industry **δ** and the educational requirements, **S**, of those occupations. Equation (9.28) becomes

$$\log \bar{W}_i = \lambda_i \theta_i + \Omega_i + f(\delta, S)_i \qquad (9.29)$$

where

$$\theta_i = \log (r_i + 1) \quad \text{and} \quad \Omega_i = \log (k_i + 1)$$

If we have data for various industries on $\bar{W}$, $\lambda$, the educational variables **S** and worker/industry characteristics $X_i$, and the union effect is constant across industries, we can derive an estimate of the union/non-union wage differential, $r$, by regression analysis of a relationship:

$$\log \bar{W}_i = a_0 + a_1 \lambda_i + a_2 S_i + \sum_{k=3}^{n} a_k X_{ki} \qquad (9.30)$$

where $\hat{a}_0 = \hat{\Omega}$, $\hat{a}_1 = \hat{\theta} = \overline{\log (r + 1)}$ and $S_i$ is the educational level of workers in $i$.

The two methods set out above for estimating the union differential are based upon the manipulation of identities for wages across unionised and non-unionised individuals or groups. They are not based upon any theoretical model of union activities. Consequently in estimating equations (9.24) and (9.30) $d_j$ and $\lambda_i$ are exogenous variables. To the extent that theory suggests that $d_j$ and $\lambda_i$ are determined, *inter alia*, by variables in the **X** vector, we cannot estimate the union effect without specifying fully the determination of $d_j$ or $\lambda_i$.

The quality of estimates of the union effect from equations (9.24) and (9.30) depends upon our ability to specify the human capital variables effectively. As noted in Section 9.2, a single variable measuring years of schooling is a very limited index of education requirements. Furthermore, the human capital wage equation must be correctly specified; in particular $r_S$ must be constant across individuals.

Equations (9.24) and (9.30) estimate the union effect on the assumption that it is constant across the sample of individuals or industries. There is good reason to expect on theoretical grounds that unions have more scope to affect wages in some parts of the economy than in others. Technology and demand conditions vary considerably both within and between industries. It is therefore difficult to assume that, even if $\hat{a}_1$ were a reliable estimate of the average union effect, such an average would be at all useful.

Neither method described above for estimating $m$ allows for variations in $m$ across the labour market. Therefore neither provides a test of specific hypotheses about the nature as opposed to the existence and size of the union effect. How might our theory of union activities be developed within the present framework? We must specify the causal relationship behind $m$, introducing variables $Z$ suggested by theory. So, in the industry/occupation data method we might write

$$\theta_i = a_1 + \sum_{k=n+1}^{p} a_k Z_{ki} \qquad (9.31)$$

Using this we can rewrite equation (9.30) as

$$\log \bar{W}_i = a_0 + a_2 S_i + \sum_{k=3}^{n} a_k X_{ki} + \left( a_1 + \sum_{k=n+1}^{p} a_k Z_{ki} \right) \lambda_i \qquad (9.32)$$

The test of our theory on unions therefore lies in the performance of each of the variables in $Z$. As noted at the beginning of this section, theory suggests the importance of the union's trade-off between wages and employment, the elasticity of the demand for labour and so on. Theory also suggests that the union effect will vary with the level of union coverage because this will determine both the union's ability to control supply and the elasticity of supply of substitutes for unionised labour. On this basis we might set up the model

$$\theta_i = a_1 + a_2 \lambda_i + a_3 D_i \qquad (9.33)$$

where $D_i$ is a measure of demand conditions included on the grounds that firms are more amenable to union demands in industries where demand is strong. So

$$\log \bar{W}_i = a_0 + a_1 \lambda_i + a_2 \lambda_i^2 + a_3 D_i \lambda_i + a_4 S_i + a_5 A_i \qquad (9.34)$$

where $A_i$ captures the age of the labour force.

For individual data we must specify

$$m_j = a_1 + \sum_{k=n+1}^{p} a_k Z_{kj} \qquad (9.35)$$

where $Z$ are the variables suggested above which determine wage leverage in individual $j$'s labour market. We could then derive the equivalent to equation (9.34) as

$$\log W_j = a_1 d_j + a_2 \lambda_j d_j + a_3 D_j d_j + a_4 S_j + a_5 A_j \qquad (9.36)$$

where $\lambda_j$ and $D_j$ are the level of union coverage and the state of demand in $j$'s labour market and $A_j$ is his age. From the industry data method we get an estimate of the wage differential between workers in fully covered and fully uncovered industries. The individual data method gives the differential between covered and uncovered workers. The industry method gives no indication of the size of the union effect in relation to the competitive wage.

Union membership provides access to the union wage differential, but all workers do not have the same access to trade unions. Discrimination, to which we now turn, acts directly upon individual wages but also works through union membership.

## 9.4 Discrimination and wages

Chapter 6 showed how tastes for discrimination can generate wage differentials between equally productive workers. In this section we extend our analysis of labour market discrimination and wage determination using the human capital approach. We continue to refer to A and B labour, where the latter is the group discriminated against.

The human capital model predicts that, if there is no labour market discrimination, the wage determination processes for A and B workers will be identical. Individual wages are related to individual productivity characteristics, **X**, of which the models of Sections 9.2 and 9.3 single out years of schooling and training as the critical components. So for any two representative individuals, one from the A group and one from the B group, we have

$$\left. \begin{array}{l} \log W^{\mathrm{A}} = \log W_0 + r_S S^{\mathrm{A}} + \displaystyle\sum_{i=1}^{n} a_i X_i^{\mathrm{A}} \\[4mm] \log W^{\mathrm{B}} = \log W_0 + r_S S^{\mathrm{B}} + \displaystyle\sum_{i=1}^{n} a_i X_i^{\mathrm{B}} \end{array} \right\} \qquad (9.37)$$

where we have assumed an optimal allocation of resources that equates all rates of return to schooling $r_s$. Any difference between A and B workers' wages $(W^{\mathrm{A}} - W^{\mathrm{B}})$ must arise from differences in schooling. Difference in tastes and abilities exist across individuals, but not across groups. Therefore any difference in schooling $(S^{\mathrm{A}} - S^{\mathrm{B}})$ must be due to discrimination in the schooling sector, or differential treatment in the family, or social *mores* restricting education that impinge on B workers more than upon A workers. Differences in personal qualities will also exist between individuals but not across groups, so $(X_i^A - X_i^B) = 0$.

Labour market discrimination might occur in the form of restricted access for B people to training programmes, in which case in equation (9.13) $k_0^B$ will be less than $k_0^A$ even if $r_T^B$ equals $r_T^A$. Labour market discrimination occurs if B workers get paid less than equally productive A workers: this implies that the wage determination process works differently for A and B workers. We assume no difference in income constraints across A and B groups in order to focus upon labour market discrimination. In terms of the schooling model, discrimination means that log $W_0$ will be lower for B people than for A people.

But discrimination can also produce differences in people's education investment decisions. Wage discrimination will reduce the incremental rate of return to schooling for B workers, $r_S^B$, below that for A workers, $r_S^A$, if the wage difference between A and B workers increases with successive increments of education. If, more likely, there is employment discrimination in the promotion structure or restriction on entry to certain industries or firms, so that B workers, despite identical skills, always have a lower chance than A workers of being offered higher posts, $r_S^B$ will be below $r_S^A$ for all educational increments. This will be the case, for example, if B workers are

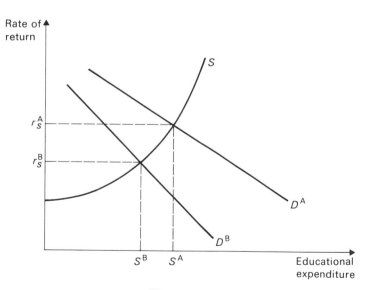

**Figure 9.3**

excluded from structured internal labour markets. As a result, when B workers have invested to the point where schooling returns at the margin equal the costs of alternative uses of funds, $r_S^A$ will exceed $r_S^B$ and $S^A$ will exceed $S^B$. In terms of the analysis in Section 7.6, the demand curve for education for B workers, $D^B$, is everywhere below that for A workers, $D^A$. The supply curve may be upward sloping but, by assumption, the same for A and B people. Discrimination will also affect wages if personal quality is less well rewarded by firms in the case of B people. To the extent that these characteristics are controllable, B workers will choose to supply less of them. So we have

$$
\left.
\begin{aligned}
\log W^A &= \log W_0^A + r_S^A S^A + \sum_{i=1}^{p} a_i X_i^A + \sum_{i=p+1}^{n} a_i^A X_i^A \\
\log W^B &= \log W_0^B + r_S^B S^B + \sum_{i=1}^{p} a_i X_i^A + \sum_{i=p+1}^{n} a_i^B X_i^B
\end{aligned}
\right\} \quad (9.38)
$$

where we have assumed that A and B workers adjust $p$ of their personal characteristics (timekeeping, reliability, etc.) to equalise returns at the margin. The remaining characteristics (age, dexterity, etc.) cannot be adjusted. We continue to assume that $r_S^A$, $r_S^B$, $a_S^A$, $a_S^B$, are the same for all individuals within each group. In this model labour market discrimination is indicated, assuming rational behaviour, by the differences between the parameters $r_S^A$ and $r_S^B$, $a_i^A$ and $a_i^B$ (for $i = p$ to $n$) and by the difference between $X_i^A$ and $X_i^B$ (for $i = 1$ to $p$). The difference $(S^A - S^B)$ could be due to either labour market or extra-market discrimination, or both.

It follows from (9.38), first, that $W^B$ will be below $W^A$ both because B workers are paid less than A workers at each grade and also because B workers undertake less education. Second, the absolute difference $(W^A - W^B)$ increases with $S$. The wage difference between an A worker with 10 years of schooling and a B worker with 9 years will be greater than the difference between an A worker with 1 year and a B worker with 0 years education. Third, the dispersion and skew of the A wage distribution will be greater than that for B workers. *Ceteris paribus* there will be considerably fewer B workers at the top of the overall distribution and more at the bottom. Fourth, an increase in the general level of schooling will increase the differences between the wages of the A and B groups. Fifth, any tendency on the part of those with higher education to acquire more schooling will widen the gap between A and B groups. Sixth, any increase in labour market discrimination will have a compound effect upon wage differentials because of its long-term implications for schooling. Seventh, any decrease in extra-market discrimination, or a favourable change in social *mores*, will have a favourable compound effect upon wage differentials.

The fact that tastes do not appear in equation (9.39) makes it impossible to attribute discrimination, if it exists, to tastes. Tastes for discrimination cannot be directly measured and finding appropriate proxy variables is problematic. Any proxy for tastes entered into the equation (9.38) would be correlated with $S$ and $X_i$ anyway, since tastes together with rewards to quality determine $S$ and $X_i$. But some form of standardisation for quality is essential.

We noted in Chapter 6 several reservations about the tastes approach to discrimination: the persistence of discrimination requires non-competitive markets; the concept of a taste for discrimination itself; the lack of contact between A employers and B workers. But adverse tastes are not the only possible source of discrimination in the labour market and, since other approaches have rather different policy implications, it is worth considering whether they generate predictions for wage structures which are both unique and testable.

We saw in Chapter 5 that a monopsonistic firm faces a marginal cost of labour curve which lies above the labour supply surve, and will employ less labour than a competitive firm at a lower wage. The monopsony model produces discrimination if there is a significant difference between the supply elasticities of A and B labour. The monopsonist then has greater monopsony power over the group with

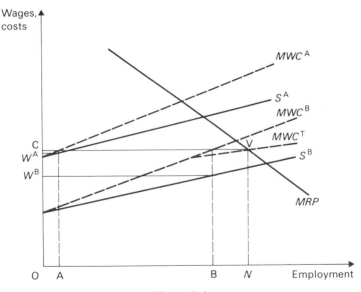

**Figure 9.4**

the less elastic supply, and can increase its profits by paying members of this group lower wages than the other group.

The monopsonist's demand for labour is given by the marginal revenue product curve, and profit-maximising employment is at the point V in Figure 9.4 where *MRP* equals total marginal wage cost, $MWC^T$. Total employment of N is divided among A and B workers so as to equalise the marginal cost of each kind of labour at the level C. This results in employment of A and B respectively and, because A and B workers have different supply curves, they get different wages. B labour has the lower elasticity of supply and therefore receives lower wages. The monopsony model emphasises supply-side differences between A and B workers as the cause of discrimination. B workers could have a lower elasticity of supply to the firm than equally productive A workers because both the financial and psychic transactions costs of labour mobility may be higher for B than for A workers, or because B workers have a narrower range of alternative job openings and have less access to transport and to labour market information. The monopsony model gives

$$\left. \begin{aligned} \log W^A = \log W_0^A + r_S S^A + \sum_{i=1}^{n} a_i X_i^A \\ \log W^B = \log W_0^B + r_S S^B + \sum_{i=1}^{n} a_i X_i^B \end{aligned} \right\} \qquad (9.39)$$

As stated the monopsony model generates wage discrimination. The returns to education will not differ between A and B people, unless the elasticity of supply of B people falls relative to that of A workers as the occupation level rises. So equations (9.39) look like (9.37) except for the intercept term. However, there is no reason why monopsony should not produce employment discrimination, in which case the monopsony and tastes wages models would be indistinguishable. No measure of monopsony appears in (9.39) and the measurement of supply elasticities is not easy anyway.

Non-competitive behaviour by trade unions can also lead to wage differentials between equally productive A and B workers. This is the crowding hypothesis: unions exclude B workers from many jobs, particularly skilled jobs, which crowds B workers into a small number of jobs and lowers workers' wages there. For wage discrimination to persist in the long run no firm must be able to hire B workers into restricted jobs otherwise they could achieve significantly lower costs and competition would erode discrimination. Crowding might arise as A-dominated trade unions, using closed shops, exclude B workers from membership and thus exclude them from jobs. This reflects a deliberate attempt by unions to ration the supply of labour to certain jobs and thus maintain members' wage levels. B workers provide an identifiable group of workers who can be the instrument of this rationing policy. Employers faced with strong unions will have little choice but to accede to union policy, even if they themselves are non-discriminatory. The effect of crowding on wage differentials depends on the sizes of the A and B workforces, the distribution of skills in each and the number of jobs in the sectors B workers are excluded from and crowded into. Trade union behaviour of this kind will exclude B workers from the benefits of structured internal labour markets: from training, promotion, job protection and so on.

Finally, we recall that the existence of uncertainty in labour markets could lead to wage differentials between A and B labour. If either employers have inadequate (perhaps incorrect) information on the quality of B people or prospecting is more costly for B people, firms will limit their screening for higher quality posts to A labour. Although such discrimination will be eroded by increased information, it will take a substantial number of B workers performing well in skilled jobs to provide such information. They may simply never get the opportunity. The wage differential will be associated with bad habits for B people which then produce the inadequate information and higher prospecting costs to perpetuate it. Since wage differentials in the crowding and uncertainty models arise from employment discrimination they will affect returns to education and thus produce predictions not dissimilar to those contained in equation (9.38). No measure of prospecting costs or of information structures is available to us. Again, the discrimination models are indistinguishable.

The central idea to emerge from the previous analysis is that discrimination has indirect as well as direct effects upon wages. If, through any of these discriminatory mechanisms, B workers are effectively excluded from skilled jobs for any length of time, productivity differences between A and B workers will emerge and will be continuously reinforced, a process which paradoxically reduces the measured effect of discrimination. If B workers are confined to unskilled jobs they also develop the working habits associated with such jobs, such as rapid turnover. Thus the average characteristics of the two groups diverge, no doubt reinforcing expectations. In principle, labour market discrimination can produce wage differentials between equally productive A and B workers that, in time, produce productivity differences where none existed before. This indicates the inherent difficulty of separating the contributions of productivity differences and discrimination to wage differentials: some part of the former may be due to the latter. In the next section we look at empirical studies of the impact of discrimination on wages which attempt to separate these two components.

## 9.5 The empirical study of wages

WAGES AND EDUCATION

In Section 9.2 we looked at two models in which individuals' wages depend on their human capital investments: the first includes only schooling, the second includes both schooling and post-schooling investments. In this section we consider how each model might be empirically tested and the kind of results that have been obtained.

Evidence from surveys on the earnings of groups of workers classified by educational level shows that age–earnings profiles are higher throughout for more highly educated workers. For instance, men with first degrees earn more than men with HNC qualifications from their first entry into the labour market, and the gap widens with age. The same information can be presented in the form of the present values of earnings associated with different educational levels. Using a discount rate of 4 per cent, workers with a first degree had a discounted present value of lifetime earnings roughly twice as high as that for workers with no qualifications. This is true for men and women. Increasing the discount rate narrows the gap between the present values of earnings for different educational groups until at 12 per cent the difference virtually disappears. Survey evidence therefore suggests that it is worth investigating human capital models more rigorously.

Let us first consider the schooling model, which relates differences in wages simply to differences in amount of education received:

$$\log W_S = \log W_0 + r_S S \tag{9.3}$$

This model can be estimated through a regression of the logarithm of earnings on years of schooling ($S$): the intercept gives an estimate of $\log W_0$, and the slope gives an estimate of the rate of return to schooling $r_S$. This exercise usually yields a sensible value for $r_S$ (i.e. of the same order of magnitude as estimates from the cross-section method of calculating rates of return discussed in Chapter 7). But the equation explains only a small part of the variation in earnings, and there are in fact a number of problems of data and of specification which render this exercise of only limited value.

First, the theoretical model relates to the determination of individual wages, and should therefore be tested using individual data. Good data of this kind is difficult to get hold of. Second, the theoretically appropriate dependent variable is earning power with $S$ years of schooling; the available data measure market earnings which for some people will be affected by post-school investments. Third, earnings can be measured per week or per year, with significantly different results because more highly educated people work more weeks per year. Fourth, the theoretically appropriate independent variable is schooling outlays, for which $S$ – years of schooling – is no more than a proxy. It takes no account of quality of education, though this could be crudely allowed for by including a dummy variable which takes the value 1 for high quality educational establishments. In the UK, in particular, the educational system is split into sectors and many workers leave school at the minimum school-leaving age and then study part-time to acquire qualifications. In this case years of full-time education is not a good proxy for schooling investments and highest qualification achieved might be a better variable to use.

Even with better data, however, equation (9.3) will produce a biased estimate of the relationship between earnings and education because it omits variables which affect earnings and which are correlated with education. The direction of bias is unclear because some omitted variables (e.g. ability, family background) are positively and others (e.g. experience) are negatively related to education.

One omitted variable is expenditure on training and so now we move on to consider the post-schooling investment model:

$$\log W_j = \log W_0 + r_S S + r_T k_0 j - \frac{r_T k_0 j^2}{2T} + \log (1 - k_j) \quad (9.13)$$

Results using annual male earnings for the UK and USA suggest that schooling and training explain about 30 per cent of the variance of earnings. The coefficients on $S$, $j$ and $j^2$ are all significant and of the anticipated sign. The estimated rate of return to education, $r_S$, is about 10 per cent. Neither the rate of return to training, $r_T$, nor the value of $k_0$ can be identified from (9.13) unless the value of the training period $T$ is known. US results suggest that if $T = 20$ years then $k_0 = 0.58$, indicating that at the beginning of a working life more than half the worker's time is devoted to investment, and $r_T$ is lower than $r_S$ ($r_T = 6.3$ per cent).

Many of the data problems which arise when estimating equation (9.3) apply to equation (9.13). In addition there is the problem of measuring $j$ – years of work experience. Data on actual work experience are hard to come by and 'potential work experience' (age – years of schooling – 5) is often used. This proxy is obviously of limited use for groups of workers with discontinuous labour force experience, which is one reason why this model has almost invariably been applied only to male earnings. Like the schooling model, equation (9.13) omits variables such as ability which, if correlated with human capital variables, will cause coefficients on these variables to be biased. An additional problem is the possibility of a relationship between education and training. It is only possible to obtain reliable estimates of their separate effects on earnings if they are independent, so that the age–earnings profiles for people with different levels of education are parallel, and the parameters through which experience affects earnings ($r_T$, $k_0$ and $T$) are all constant across different values of $S$. In the model above, $r_T$, $k_0$ and $T$ have been assumed to be constant, but it seems *a priori* more likely that there is some relationship between the level of education, the rate of return to training, the investment ratio on beginning work, and the length of the training period. For instance, it might be that individuals who undertake a lot of education before starting work do jobs which involve more OJT. In this case, by treating these concepts as constant when they are in fact variable and related to $S$, the coefficient on $S$ becomes biased. Respecification of the model to allow for the possible relationship between $S$, $r_T$, $k_0$ and $T$ involves introducing interaction terms into equation (9.13) and leads to significantly different parameter estimates. $r_T$ increases with $S$, and is found to be above $r_S$ even for those with least education. $k_0$ and $T$ are both negatively related to $S$.

As stated above, estimation of an equation like (9.13) explains about 30 per cent of the variance in annual earnings. It can be argued that this is an underestimate of the true explanatory power of education variables because individuals with the same value of $j$ are assumed to have undertaken the same amount of training. If we drop this assumption individuals with the same level of schooling who undertake different amounts of OJT will have different age–earnings profiles. But these profiles must intersect since the heavy investors in training earn less at the beginning of their working lives in order to earn more later. Therefore it has been suggested that the effects of training and education on earnings can be separated by using data for the single year in which age–earnings profiles cross.

In Figure 9.5, individuals A and B both have $S$ years of education, both go into jobs involving OJT and therefore initially earn less than $W_S$. B does more investment and earns less than A until year of experience $j_c$ – the cross-over year. Therefore in year $j_c$ individual differences in post-schooling investments do not affect earnings, and we can estimate $r_S$ from

$$\log W_{ijc} = \log W_0 + r_S S \qquad (9.40)$$

This approach raises the problem of identifying $j_c$ in any data set. The value of $r_S$ estimated from equation (9.40) is lower than that derived from equation (9.13) but doubts remain about the reliability of the estimate because equation (9.40) omits other independent variables. However, using this model as much as 50 per cent (UK) or 66 per cent (USA) of the variance in annual earnings can be explained.

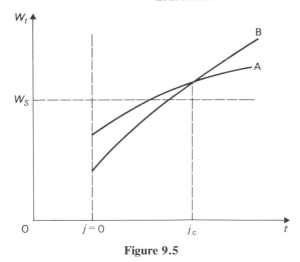

**Figure 9.5**

Education variables, therefore, seem to be able to explain a significant amount of the variation in individual wages. While these results provide support for the human capital theory of wage determination, they can be interpreted in a fundamentally different way. In human capital theory wage increases are earned by incurring costs of education or training. Therefore the whole difference between earnings at different educational levels, or the whole increase in earnings with experience is interpreted as due to investments. An alternative interpretation of the positive relationships between earnings, education and experience stresses the importance of ability as a determinant of both earnings and educational level, and the possibility of costless learning.

## WAGES AND UNIONS

So far empirical research into the impact of unions upon wages has concentrated upon identifying whether, and to what extent, the union wage differential exists. Furthermore, most such studies have· used aggregate data.

Industry studies suggest that the average wage in a labour market whose labour force is completely covered will be approximately 25 per cent higher than the average wage for a completely uncovered labour market. (More relevantly, the wage in a sector with 80 per cent coverage will be 12 per cent higher than in one with 30 per cent coverage). The union wage differential estimated from individual data is notably smaller than this, 8–12 per cent. The union differential is higher for workers in manufacturing industry and for workers subject to local agreements than for those subject to national agreements only. In fact in the latter case the differential is very small. Estimates from cross-section studies, at different points in time, show that the union differential rose from the mid 1960s through the 1970s. In general the union/non-union differential varies countercyclically with the relative effectiveness of strike and quit threats.

Some observations on the research procedures behind these results are in order. First, there are two data problems. The wage variable should be hourly earnings given that it is this variable that enters models of labour supply and utility-maximising union behaviour. The unionisation variable should be a measure of the number of workers affected directly by the union wage strategy. Where coverage significantly exceeds membership, the former would appear to be the appropriate variable.

Second, the estimated industry equation will be mis-specified if $\Omega_i$ ($= \log (k_i + 1)$), representing the effect of unionisation upon the non-union wage, is a non-random variable across the sample and is omitted from equation (9.30). Data for $\Omega_i$ are not available. To the extent that $\Omega_i$ is correlated with $\lambda_i$, estimates of the union effect will be biased. If, as one might anticipate, the non-unionised sector effect is positively related to $\lambda_i$, the union effect will be overestimated.

Third, the range of estimated values for the union mark-up is wide. In part this reflects the use of different data bases, industry, occupation or individual, as well as different samples. In part it reflects the use of different measures for the wage and unionisation variables. In part in reflects the fact that the estimates come from different countries and the use of different independent variables in **X**. Even so the range is considerable. Consequently, though the union effect appears to be significant, its precise value remains in some doubt.

Fourth, parallel data on individual earnings and unionisation are sometimes not available. This problem has been overcome, with some loss of efficiency, by using a measure of the unionisation level of individual $j$'s industry instead of the dummy variable $d_j$.

Fifth, and crucially, the value of any estimate of the union wage effect depends upon our ability to specify the human capital variables and the vectors ($\mathbf{X}_i$ and $\mathbf{X}_j$) fully and accurately. Omitting important variables, if they are correlated with $\lambda_i$ or $d_j$, will bias our estimates. In practice in industry studies, particularly for the UK, human capital variables have been problematic. Using the proportion of workers classified as skilled or otherwise, and other less obvious proxy variables, has marred attempts to identify the union wage effect. Other proxy variables introduced to standardise for differences in personal characteristics and market circumstances have been many and varied but have not always been entirely satisfactory. Failure to capture differences in labour quality and in market characteristics will tend to bias our estimates upwards.

There have been few attempts to test specific hypotheses about the determinants of the union mark-up. There are significant problems in identifying operational variables to measure the theoretical constructs of union models. Hypotheses relating to elasticities or bargaining power, for example, have not been tested specifically. It does appear from industry studies, however, that the differential will be higher in markets where demand conditions are tight and where unionisation is high, as suggested in equation (9.34).

Using individual data poses special problems. Individual data on many of the personal characteristics and market structures that foster unionisation are not available. Therefore we have to use dummy variables to capture the effects of these factors. For example we might have

$$\log W_j = a_1 d_{1j} + a_2 d_{1j} d_{2j} + a_3 d_{1j} d_{3j} + \ldots + g(\mathbf{X})_j \quad (9.41)$$

where $d_1$, as before, is 1 if $j$ belongs to a union, $d_2$ is 1 if the elasticity of demand for labour is high, $d_3$ is 1 if the worker has considerable specific human capital and thus low substitutability, and so on. Obviously, this is not entirely satisfactory. However, a simple operational form for this approach given the limited data available might be

$$\log W_j = a_1 d_{1j} + a_2 d_{1j} d_{4j} + a_3 d_{1j} d_{5j} + \ldots + a_n d_{1j} d_{4j} d_{5j} + g(\mathbf{X})_j \quad (9.42)$$

where $d_4$ is 1 if the worker is in a concentrated industry and $d_5$ is 1 if the worker has skill qualifications. Results using this format produce statistically satisfactory estimates and indicate that the union mark-up varies significantly between industries and between regions. It increases, but not significantly, with unit size and declines with concentration. There is a strong indication that in the UK the mark-up is greater for the skilled than for the unskilled.

## WAGES AND DISCRIMINATION

Most statistical research into discrimination has attempted simply to measure the effect of discrimination on wages. Human capital earnings functions are used, containing a vector of education and quality variables $\mathbf{X}$, to standardise for productivity differences between A and B workers

$$\left. \begin{array}{l} \log W^{\mathrm{A}} = \alpha^{\mathrm{A}} + \beta^{\mathrm{A}} \mathbf{X}^{\mathrm{A}} \\ \log W^{\mathrm{B}} = \alpha^{\mathrm{B}} + \beta^{\mathrm{B}} \mathbf{X}^{\mathrm{B}} \end{array} \right\} \quad (9.43)$$

These earnings functions pass through and define the average wage levels:

$$\left. \begin{array}{l} \bar{W}_A = \alpha^A + \beta^A \bar{\mathbf{X}}^A \\[6pt] \bar{W}_B = \alpha^B + \beta^B \bar{\mathbf{X}}^B \end{array} \right\} \tag{9.44}$$

The overall wage differential $\bar{W}^A - \bar{W}^B$ is then decomposed into a non-discriminatory component and a discriminatory component: the former arises from differences in the average levels of the $X$ variables between A and B workers; the latter arises from differences between the coefficients in the two functions.

This technique is explained below using a diagram (Fig. 9.6) in which all the $X$ variables are represented by a single productivity characteristic $S$. The higher line represents the estimated earnings function for A people, with A people on average at point V, B people at Y. On the assumption that in the absence of discrimination, both A and B workers would be paid according to the A earnings function, the non-discriminatory wage for B people $\hat{W}^B$ is at point Z in the figure and is shown by

$$\hat{W}^B = \hat{\alpha}^A + \hat{\beta}^A \bar{S}^B$$

Since

$$\bar{W}^A - \bar{W}^B = (\bar{W}^A - \hat{W}^B) + (\hat{W}^B - \bar{W}^B)$$

$$= [(\hat{\alpha}^A + \hat{\beta}^A \bar{S}^A) - (\hat{\alpha}^A + \hat{\beta}^A \bar{S}^B)]$$

$$+ [(\hat{\alpha}^A + \hat{\beta}^A \bar{S}^B) - (\hat{\alpha}^B + \hat{\beta}^B \bar{S}^B)]$$

$$= [\hat{\beta}^A(\bar{S}^A - \bar{S}^B)] + [(\hat{\alpha}^A - \hat{\alpha}^B) + (\hat{\beta}^A - \hat{\beta}^B)\bar{S}^B]$$

$$\qquad\quad (1) \qquad + \qquad\qquad (2)$$

(1) represents the non-discriminatory and (2) the discriminatory component; (2) divided by the overall wage differential therefore measures the proportion of the total wage differential which can be attributed to discrimination.

Let us first look at the results obtained using this methodology, and then consider its problems. First, when applied to either black/white or male/female wages, the coefficients on the two earnings functions have been found to be significantly different. Second, the relative importance of the two components varies between studies depending

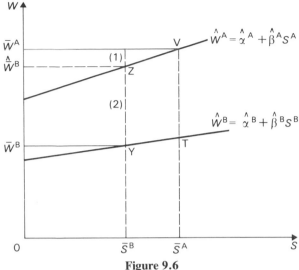

**Figure 9.6**

on the kind of data used and on the variables included in **X**. Data can be collected from general surveys or from individual occupations or firms. The less aggregate the data and the more variables included in **X**, the more of $\bar{W}^A - \bar{W}^B$ can be explained and the less is left for the discriminatory component (2). This is an important point. If earnings of A and B workers are related to a number of variables including one which standardizes for occupation/job, then the narrower the occupation/job classification used the more important this variable becomes and the more significant employment discrimination appears to be relative to wage discrimination. In the limit, if earnings of A and B workers within a single occupation are compared and the functions include variables to measure job level or grade virtually the whole of the wage differential is 'explained'. Wage discrimination disappears and we are left with employment discrimination and the question why B workers are in lower grade, lower paid jobs than equally productive A workers.

The empirical work on the impact of discrimination on wages therefore suggests that, first, labour market discrimination exists, i.e. B workers do on average earn less than equally productive (to the limits of our measuring ability) A workers. Second, differences in productivity characteristics also play a significant part in explaining wage differentials. Third, wage differentials arise more because B workers are concentrated in lower grade jobs than because they earn lower wages than A workers on the same job.

Let us now consider the problems associated with this method of measuring discrimination. First, the fact that the coefficients on the earnings functions (9.42) are different is not in itself proof of discrimination. There are two arguments to suggest that even in the absence of labour market discrimination A and B workers might receive different rewards to quality. First, we have already argued in Section 7.6 that if on average B workers have less financial and social capital than A workers they will face a higher cost of funds for financing investments in human capital (see Fig. 7.3b). But this argument suggests that B people should earn a higher return than A people, $r_S^B > r_S^A$, while the empirical results for equations like (9.43) show the opposite. Therefore, as in Figure 9.7, although different income constraints between A and B groups are relevant, the lower return to B workers indicates that discrimination, represented by the lower demand curve for B workers in Figure 9.7, is dominant. Second, it can be argued that even in the absence of labour market discrimination men and women would face different earnings functions, and different rewards to productive capacity, because of their specialisation in market and non-market work respectively. Therefore discrimination is overestimated by the earnings function method because the difference in coefficients is partly due to the household division of labour. For instance, if married women choose to invest less time in OJT because of their expectations of intermittent labour force participation, then even if they receive the same rate of return to training as men the coefficient on experience in the female

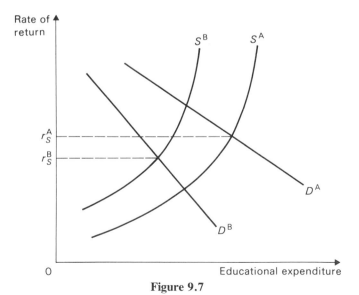

**Figure 9.7**

earnings function will be lower than in the male function. A check on this can be made by running separate regressions for single and married men and women: the difference between the single men's and women's coefficients gives an estimate of discrimination uncontaminated by the effects of the division of labour within the household. Studies which have done this have found that the total difference between male and female coefficients is made up of three smaller differences between the coefficients for married and single men, single men and single women, and single women and married women respectively. These three are of approximately equal size so, since only the middle difference measures the effects of labour market discrimination, studies which include single and married men or women in the same earnings function overestimate the effects of discrimination on wages.

Second, in this method of measuring discrimination differences in productivity variables are considered not to arise from discrimination. However, the analysis of Section 9.4 has shown that labour market discrimination will have a feedback effect on workers' decisions about how much human capital to acquire, and therefore this method underestimates the effects of discrimination on wages. Third, even if we accept the theoretical possibility of dividing the overall A/B wage differential into a discriminatory and a non-discriminatory component, there is more than one way of making the division. The problem is that we have no measure of the competitive wage for either A or B people. Above we used the A earnings function to derive the competitive wage for B people, $\tilde{W}^B$. The alternative would be to assume that in the absence of discrimination A workers would be paid a competitive wage given by the B earnings function; $\tilde{W}^A = \hat{\alpha}^B + \hat{\beta}^B \bar{S}^A$. This involves using point T rather than point Z in Figure 9.6. The choice of how to decompose the wage differential poses an index number problem. If discrimination affects both A and B earnings then neither method is correct since without discrimination the common earnings function would contain a third set of coefficients. In practice the weights involved are usually quite different and so the measured impact of discrimination on wages can vary substantially according to which set is chosen.

Even if this method can be taken to yield a reliable estimate of the proportionate contribution of discrimination to wage differentials, it is not clear how to interpret the resulting number because the analysis provides no indication of where the discrimination is coming from, who is doing it and why, and therefore yields no policy conclusions. Some of the empirical studies have been rather loosely linked to the employer's tastes for discrimination model via the suggestion in Chapter 6 that when A and B workers are not equally productive the wage differential does not simply measure the strength of tastes for discrimination but contains a component due to the difference in marginal productivities:

$$(9.44) \qquad W^A - W^B = P^*(Q'^A - Q'^B) + D_B \qquad (9.44)$$

where $D_B$ is the market discrimination coefficient. However, we have seen in Section 9.4 that it is difficult to distinguish between models using the earnings function approach, and really the empirical work described above cannot be said to fit the employers' taste for discrimination model more than other models since they all suggest that wage differentials can be split into two parts with discrimination as that part not due to productivity differences.

To go beyond mere estimates of the effects of discrimination we might look beyond the earnings function approach to test secondary predictions from the various models in Section 9.4 about wage differentials either over time or in different areas/markets. We would expect differentials to be greater where B workers are concentrated into a narrow range of jobs, relatively unorganized and have few alternative employers (monopsony model). We would expect differentials to be greater when unemployment is high (information model). We would expect differentials to be greater in more concentrated industries; or when the relative supply of B workers increases (employer tastes model).

Unfortunately, the problem with such simple statistical tests of different models, apart from that of approximating the theoretical concepts with observable data, is still to devise tests which will actually distinguish between the models. For instance, suppose we found that wage differentials between A and B workers had increased during a period of rising B employment. This is consistent with both the employers' taste model and the crowding hypothesis, which have quite different explanations of discrimination and policy implications. The problems are particularly acute for empirical work on models involving a taste for discrimination. Suppose we find that in two regions where the proportion of B workers in the labour force is the same the wage differential is quite different. An explanation in terms of the neoclassical theory would be that in the region with the higher differential tastes for discrimination are stronger. With no measure of tastes and no way of knowing what factors influence tastes for discrimination this hypothesis is untestable. One answer to this problem is to move away from statistical studies of overall wage differentials to a disaggregated approach to the study of discrimination. We shall consider this further in the next section.

# OCCUPATIONAL AND INDUSTRIAL WAGE STRUCTURES

Further empirical analysis of the relationship between humai. investments and earnings has been undertaken focusing upo. occupational wage structure. According to the competitive modc. workers in occupations that require significant training will receive higher earnings than those employed in other occupations to compensate them for the costs incurred in acquiring skills. One could thus estimate the counterpart of equation (9.13) for occupations instead of individuals where the data are now average values for each occupation. Results suggest that over two-thirds of the variation in occupational earnings can be explained by schooling and on-the-job training. In contrast to results using individual data schooling is the principal determinant of earnings, explaining as much as 40 per cent of occupational wage variation.

Whilst these results suggest a strong statistical relationship between education and average earnings across occupations, they must be interpreted with caution. In the first place there is considerable variation within occupations in both earnings and education. Second, within many occupations, covering the majority of workers and including those with considerable variation in schooling, no relationship has been found across individuals between education and earnings. Finally, no account is taken of institutional and non-competitive factors. There is, in fact, evidence to suggest that the firm a person is employed in, and in particular its internal wage structure, is more important in determining individual earnings than his occupational group. If non-competitive variables are correlated with education their omission will bias the estimated education parameters upwards.

It has proved difficult to assess the impact of firms' non-competitive behaviour upon wages by occupation. What evidence there is suggests that monopsony is not widespread across occupational labour markets. However, in one occupation where the degree of employer concentration is large there is considerable monopsonistic exploitation with an estimated differential between marginal revenue product and earnings of between 50 and 80 per cent.

Most evidence on occupational wages has, however, been concerned with changes over time in the wage structure. These changes have usually been measured by the ratio of skilled to unskilled manual wages. Studies in a variety of countries have found a narrowing of the skill differential during the period 1900–1950 from around 2.0 to between 1.5 and 1.2 depending on the particular country concerned and groups of workers covered. Associated with this long-run trend has been a reduction in the overall dispersion of the occupational wage distribution.

A number of explanations have been proposed for the decline in the skill differential involving both the supply and demand for skilled and unskilled workers. The development of mass production technology and a decline in the skill content of many jobs has meant a shift in demand away from skilled to semi- and unskilled labour. Major sources of semi- and unskilled labour, such as immigration and agriculture, have dried up. Moreover, the increased provision of state education and the extension of compulsory schooling have reduced the cost of acquiring additional schooling and thus increased the supply of workers capable of undertaking skilled work. The narrowing in the skill differential has not been a smooth process. The most significant reductions occurred during the two world wars which generated excess demand in unskilled markets: the less skilled were more likely to undertake military service, whilst the increased wartime demand for all grades of labour meant that skilled jobs had to be filled by semi- and unskilled workers and in particular by women entering the labour market.

Since 1950 the ratio of skilled to unskilled wages has stabilised. The most significant factor behind this is the increased labour force participation of women providing an additional supply of labour mainly to semi- and unskilled jobs and thus acting as a counterbalancing force to those considered above that narrow the skill differential.

So far we have considered long-run trends in the occupational wage structure. We concluded in Chapter 8, however, that the fixed costs associated with skilled labour will mean that fluctuations in demand over the business cycle are concentrated upon low skilled occupations. One would anticipate, therefore, that the skill differential will move inversely with the business cycle. This has indeed been the case historically. More recently, however, the cyclical relationship has been much less prominent, the most likely reason being the increased effects of non-competitive forces such as trade unions and custom upon wage determination.

In Section 9.2 we noted that in the long run competitive forces should ensure that wage differences between industries will arise only from differences in their occupational mix. Since we have already seen that wage differences between skilled and unskilled workers have declined over time one would expect, according to the competitive thesis, the dispersion of the industrial wage structure also to have declined over time. Evidence from a variety of studies suggests, however, that such a compression has not taken place: rather there has been considerable stability in the industrial wage structure. For a number of reasons purely descriptive comparisons of the industrial wage structure at different points in time are of limited value for testing the importance of competitive forces. In the first place it is necessary to assume that the observed wage structure is in equilibrium. Second, the comparison is useful only if the skill mix of industries is not changing over time. Empirical analysis has therefore moved to investigate the industrial wage structure econometrically: the most common approach is to estimate an equation of the form

$$W_j = a_0 + \sum_{i=1}^{n} a_{ij} X_{ij} \qquad (9.45)$$

where $X_i$ are variables included to test either the competitive hypothesis or other explanations for inter-industry difference in wages. Studies differ considerably in the list of variables used though typically they include the following: skill mix; age structure; female intensity; monopoly power; average plant size; productivity; capital intensity; method of payment; trade union power; and the regional distribution of the industry. Results suggest that the occupational skill mix of an industry is an important determinant of its average earnings: those industries that employ more skilled workers have higher average earnings. However, differences across industries in skill structure explain only a small proportion (less than 25 per cent) of the total variation in industry average earnings. Of course, the skill variable (percentage defined as unskilled, say) is a very limited measure of the industry skill structure. Variables included to measure non-competitive behaviour are usually found to explain about as much of the total variation in industry earnings as skill structure, though studies disagree as to which variables contribute most. This presumably reflects the fact that measures of plant size, concentration, etc., are all highly correlated making it impossible to identify their individual contributions.

## 9.6 The characteristics of wage earners

In previous sections of this chapter we developed and tested various explanations of the wage determination process. In this section we employ these models to ask who does well and who does badly in the wage determination process and to identify the characteristics of workers at different points of the wage structure. The importance of this question for equity is obvious: since 80 per cent of total personal income comes from employment and self-employment, most people's standard of living is dependent on what the members of their household earn. We then consider the importance of wages to income inequalities: their contribution to poverty at one extreme and to top incomes at the other.

## EDUCATION

The human capital model of wage determination suggests that individuals' wages are mainly determined by their educational investments, and the empirical evidence supports this. We therefore want to know who does and who does not acquire a lot of education. Section 7.6 suggests that people of high ability will undertake more education than people of lower ability. Also, for a given ability level, individuals from low income backgrounds acquire less education than children from higher classes. Therefore, if earnings depend on education and education depends on class origins, it follows that earnings will depend on class origins. Survey evidence supports this deduction: average earnings are about 10 per cent higher for male workers whose fathers were in white collar jobs than for those whose fathers were in semi- or unskilled occupations. Closer analysis shows that home background affects earnings both directly and, via education, indirectly. The direct effect means that for a given level of education higher class people earn more than lower class people, i.e. they get a higher return to their education. In terms of the analysis of Section 7.6 this can be explained by class discrimination in job openings: higher class individuals are more likely to get the highest paying jobs at any educational level. The direct effect is, however, somewhat less important than the indirect effect.

Section 7.6 also shows that women and black workers undertake less education than white men, although the gap between men and women is marked only at the top of the educational range. The human capital model predicts therefore that women and black workers will be over-represented in low-paid jobs, which is indeed the case. There is also a direct effect of sex or race on earnings: women or blacks earn less on average than white men with the same amount of education. We return to this point later.

## UNIONS

The analysis of trade unions in Chapter 5 suggests that union members earn significantly more than non-members and empirical work appears to confirm this prediction, although there is considerable doubt about the exact size of the mark-up. So, if union membership moves individuals up the wage structure it is important to know who belongs to unions, particularly to unions where the mark-up is highest. The distributive impact of unions will be quite different if it is low earners who are most likely to belong to unions, and to unions with higher mark-ups, than if it is high earners who do best out of union membership. The analysis of union behaviour in Sections 9.3 and 9.5 indicated that the union mark-up does vary, so that different workers stand to gain different wage increases from joining a union, or more correctly from being covered by a union. *Ceteris paribus* the union mark-up will be higher for skilled than for unskilled labour, higher in tight labour markets, higher in larger capital-intensive firms and so on. The union mark-up will vary across occupations, industries and regions, in part according to the incidence of these variables.

Empirical analysis of the effects of unions on wage differentials can be summarised as follows. In the USA black male workers are more likely than other workers to belong to unions, and also receive the highest mark-up. Therefore the effect of unions is to narrow the black/white wage differential. In both the UK and USA women are less likely to be unionised than men. In the USA they receive a lower mark-up, therefore the effect of unions is to widen the male/female wage differential; in the UK there is some evidence that women receive a higher mark-up so the total effect is ambiguous.

In both the UK and USA skilled manual workers are more likely to belong to unions than unskilled workers. There is conflicting evidence as to whether the mark-up increases with skill level, so that the overall effect of unions on wages between skills is unclear. However, there is clear evidence that the greatest effect of unions is on manual workers' wages; non-manual workers have much lower levels of unionisation and small or even negative estimated mark-ups. There is also evidence that the union mark-up is highest in high wage industries. Unionisation is particularly low in the service sector which has both low earnings and a low mark-up. On the whole, therefore, these results suggest that low earners are less likely to belong to unions and will receive a lower mark up if they do belong; *ceteris paribus* unions widen the earnings distribution. Two observations are worth making on this conclusion, however. First, levels of unionisation amongst the unskilled have been increasing, unions have amalgamated and skilled unions have opened their membership to the unskilled. Each has the effect of narrowing the earnings distribution. Second, union activities have led to a reduction in the dispersion of wages for the same skill across regions of the country and across firms within each industry. To the extent that there has been more scope for such activity amongst the unskilled, unions will narrow the earnings distribution.

## DISCRIMINATION

In the previous section we looked at statistical studies of the impact of labour market discrimination on wages and concluded that, as yet, these neither produce an entirely reliable estimate of the significance of discrimination nor help us to decide how and why discrimination takes place. In this section we therefore look at two other sorts of evidence: first, circumstantial evidence on the location of B workers in the wage structure and, second, evidence from case studies.

A good deal of evidence on the labour market position of B workers is presented in Chapters 7 and 12, so here we look only at the earnings of female workers. The gap between male and female average earnings (full-time women earn on average about two-thirds as much as men) does not demonstrate the full extent of the divergence between their earnings distributions. Female median earnings are equal to the bottom decile of male earnings, while male median earnings represent the top decile for women. Therefore the very bottom of the overall earnings distribution is almost entirely composed of women: three-quarters of low-paid, full-time workers are female. And at the top end of the distribution there are very few women; one inquiry found that only 2 per cent of workers earning higher incomes were women. Both within occupations and overall the dispersion of earnings for full-time women is less than for men, although the inclusion of part-time workers reverses this finding. The concentration of women in the lower range of earnings plus the very few in higher levels makes women's earnings more skewed than men's. Age–earnings profiles for women are both lower and flatter than for men, so that the wage differential widens with age. A human capital explanation would be that women undertake less educational investment than men, which we have seen to be true. However, women earn much less than men with the same amount of education: the earnings distribution for women with degrees coincides well with that for men with no qualifications at all. The industrial and occupational distributions of male and female employees are quite different and the degree of segregation has been increasing over time. Women are twice as likely as men to be in non-manual jobs and are far more concentrated into a small number of occupations. Over a half of non-manual female workers come under one broadly defined occupation, (clerical work), and the same is true for manual female workers, (catering, cleaning, ـic).

None of the above can be said to prove the existence of labour market discrimination; although the fact that B workers earn less than A workers with the same qualifications is a strong indication. To go any further we need to know why B workers are concentrated into unskilled low-paid jobs and why they earn less than A workers in the same occupation. We should thus look at the process by which A and B workers get their first job and at any subsequent mobility. The analysis of this text suggests that occupational and job mobility, particularly for B workers, is limited and therefore that the initial selection process is extremely important. We have some evidence on this from experiments and case studies.

Tests have been carried out in which pairs of workers, with identical experience and qualifications but of different race or sex, apply for the same job either in person or in writing. These show that the pair rarely face the same probability of being offered any given job: employers have fixed ideas about what kinds of workers are suitable for which jobs, possibly based on lack of information about worker quality. A firm is therefore likely to suggest that a black applicant should try for a different lower grade job, or that a male applicant would be bored to death by an assembly line job. Such experiments are necessarily limited in scope, but provide direct evidence of discrimination, as do some of the cases brought under the race and sex discrimination legislation.

There exist numerous case studies of individual firms, occupations or industries, which consistently reveal a tendency for the proportion of B workers to decline rapidly with skill level, both within and between occupations. B workers are concentrated in jobs with very limited promotion prospects and, where they are in integrated jobs, tend to get much less training and promotion than A workers. It is not clear whether this shows discrimination because of the identification problem: women are often secondary workers and do not want to acquire work responsibilities incompatible with their households' demands for domestic activities. However, black workers, for whom the supply-side pressures to work are if anything stronger than for white male workers, also have difficulty in getting promotion.

Let us now move on to consider the contribution of earnings to overall income inequality. The distribution of income is an extremely complex issue, and no single data source can answer all the interesting questions one might ask. Figure 9.8 illustrates the distribution of annual pre-tax income between tax units in 1978/9 by a histogram. This shows clearly the skewness of the distribution: modal income

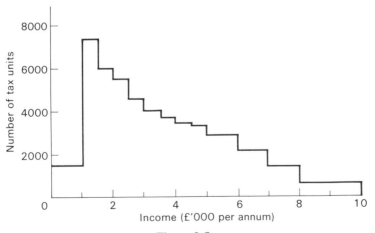

**Figure 9.8**

was in the £1000–£1500 range while mean income was £4110. However, the histogram is truncated at an income level of £10 000 and therefore cannot show the length of the upper tail of the distribution. The level of inequality is in practice substantially higher than it appears from the diagram because, although not many people had incomes above this level, some had incomes far above it. The top 1 per cent of tax units (300 000 units) had incomes above £14 630 but the range within this group is such that the top tax units get hundreds of thousands of pounds, which means that they lie way beyond the right-hand side of the histogram.

Much the most important source of income is employment, which provides 72 per cent of all income. A further 6 per cent comes from self-employment. The importance of different sources of income varies with income level as shown in Figure 9.9.

Let us look first at the bottom end of the income distribution. Figure 9.9 shows that the bottom 25 per cent of income units do not get much of their income from employment. One might conclude from this that the overlap between low pay and poverty is limited, but this would be incorrect for two reasons. First, although only 20 per cent of all families with incomes below the poverty (supplementary benefit) level have the head of the family in full-time work, these families account for about a third of all the individuals in poverty. Second, many of those receiving transfer payments would be low paid if or when they were in employment. The largest single group in poverty is retired people: almost two-thirds of all elderly people live

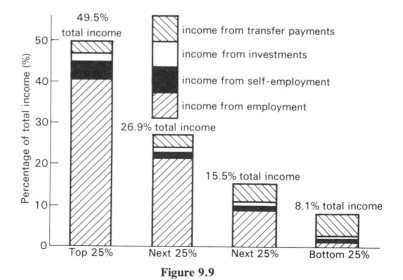

**Figure 9.9**

in or on the margins of poverty. The minority of old people who are not poor achieve this by virtue of having had good jobs when they were working, jobs whose level of pay enabled them to accumulate assets and which provide occupational pensions. Another group whose poverty is clearly linked to the labour market is the unemployed: Chapter 10 shows that there is a strong relationship between low pay and unemployment. Workers who have badly paid unskilled jobs are both the most likely to become unemployed and the most likely to suffer financial hardship while unemployed because they stay unemployed longest and have low levels of family resources. The poverty of sick individuals also has some relationship with their labour market status: people from the lowest socio-economic group have the highest morbidity rates, partly due to the kinds of work they do but more due to their environmental conditions and financial constraints. Also, unskilled manual workers are less likely than others to be covered by private sick pay schemes and therefore more likely to suffer financial hardship through sickness. Finally, many of those inactive and living in poverty will have become discouraged by low wages and lack of job openings: this applies particularly to single-parent families. This discussion suggests a strong relationship between an individual's wage when employed and his chance of being in poverty, not just while he's working, but throughout his life. The effects of low wages extend into retirement and may well be transferred to the next generation. There is a strong chance that children who grow up in poverty due to the low earnings of their parents will grow up to be badly paid themselves and spend their adult lives also in or on the margins of poverty.

Although low pay does not lead inexorably to poverty, it does make a substantial direct and also an indirect contribution to poverty. The extent and composition of low pay is therefore worth examining to find out who ends up right at the bottom of the wage structure. There are several possible ways of defining low pay. Using the definition of two-thirds of the median earnings of adult full-time men, some 4.5 million full-time workers, 20 per cent of the adult male workforce and 57 per cent of the adult female workforce, are low paid. Although no broadly defined industry or occupation is completely free of low-paid workers, the incidence of low pay varies systematically across these classifications and also across regions. The highest proportions of low-paid workers are found in agriculture, clothing and footwear, distribution and other service industries; in farming, selling, catering and cleaning; in East Anglia and the South-West. The chance of any individual worker being low paid depends on his personal characteristics. As already made clear, women are far more likely to be low paid than men; manual than non-manual workers and, within manual workers, unskilled than skilled. The incidence of low pay also varies with age, being lowest for prime age workers, and with union status; union members are less likely than non-members to be low paid. The central variable here is skill level, and the association between low pay and other variables such as age or occupation reflects to a considerable extent the relationship between the latter variables and skill level. However, other factors do exert an independent influence: a male worker of a given skill level is less likely to be low paid in some industries and areas than in others.

Now let us move up the income distribution: how important are earnings at the top of the distribution, and what kind of workers end up at this level? Figure 9.9 shows that the top 25 per cent of tax units get a higher proportion of their income from employment than any other group, but this is not true of the very highest incomes within the group. The top 1 per cent of tax units receive 5.3 per cent of total income, only half of which is derived from employment. At this level both investment income (19 per cent) and self-employment (28 per cent) make a sizeable contribution.

There are considerable difficulties in comparing the incomes of employees with those of the self-employed which include returns on physical capital and to risk-bearing as well as payments for labour services. The available evidence shows that the distribution of income from self-employment is more unequal than that of employment income and that average income is much higher for the self-employed. Self-employed tax units are concentrated at the top of the overall income distribution: about 9 per cent of all tax units but 25 per cent of the top decile and 75 per cent of the top percentile are self-employed. This is reflected in the average income levels at equivalent points in the distribution of employment and self-employment incomes: the average income of the top 1 per cent of self-employed tax units is about 3.5 times the equivalent for employed tax units. For reasons of technology, the industrial distribution of the self employed is quite different from that of employees: self-employment is concentrated in agriculture, construction, distribution and services and is relatively uncommon in manufacturing. The highest earning group of the self-employed is close company proprietors, whose pay would seem to have something in common with that of other executives, although they have more discretion over what to pay themselves. The next highest paid group consists of the professions. The scope for self-employment varies across the professions, but it is usually the highest paid who make the move from employment to self-employment. Professional jobs require long training periods after which human capital theory would suggest that earnings will be high. However, professional salaries are higher, and often much higher, than required to compensate for educational costs, largely because professional associations exercise tight control over entry. The amount of investment required to obtain these qualifications may effectively exclude able people from low income households who face a high cost of funds. The tendency for men in the higher grade professional, administrative and managerial class to have fathers from the same class is strong, and increases with income. Apart from the self-employed, who else gets right to the top of the income distribution? It is not easy to answer this question because the number of employees at this level is too small to show up in the main data sources for earnings, and because at this level earnings are supplemented considerably by income from investments and fringe benefits. One inquiry into higher earnings chose a cut-off level which included 0.3 per cent of the employed workforce. About 70 per cent of this select group were in management, and 93 per cent were in the private sector. A slightly lower definition of 'high pay' would include considerably more public sector workers, who it could be argued get more non-pecuniary benefits. It is difficult to identify the wage determination mechanisms at the very top of the earnings distribution, because such is the skewness of the distribution that even within this tiny group the range of earnings is enormous: from £10 000 to over £50 000 when the inquiry was conducted in 1975. Managerial jobs, which are apparently similar in terms of level and job content, pay widely different salaries in different industries, in different firms within an industry and even in the same company. There is little in the personal characteristics of the very highly paid to explain this variation because, although they are clearly distinguishable from the majority of the labour force by being much more likely to hold degree-level qualifications, and to come from the top socio-economic groups, they are not distinguishable from one another in these respects. The wide range of earnings suggests a lack of competition consistent with the idea that managerial jobs are at the top of structured internal labour markets and therefore protected to a considerable extent from external competition. Within firms salaries can be determined hierarchically so that each grade maintains its customary differential over the one below. Therefore managers' pay will depend on the number of grades below them and on the level of pay in their firm. The evidence suggests that managers of larger firms get higher salaries and that managers' pay varies with the general level of pay in an industry.

## Further reading

CHAPTER 9: WAGES

A. B. Atkinson, *The Economics of Inequality* (Oxford: Oxford University Press, 1975).

M. Blaug, 'The empirical status of human capital theory: a slightly jaundiced view', *Journal of Economic Literature*, Vol. 4 (September 1976).

B. Chiplin and P. Sloane, *Sex Discrimination in the Labour Market* (London: Macmillan, 1976).

R. Layard, D. Metcalf and S. Nickell, 'The effect of collective bargaining on relative and absolute wages', *British Journal of Industrial Relations*, Vol. 16 (November, 1978).

R. Layard, D. Piachaud and M. Stewart, *The Causes of Poverty*, Background Paper No. 5 for the Royal Commission on the Distribution of Income and Wealth (London: HMSO, 1978).

B. Malkiel and J. Malkiel, 'Male–female pay differentials in professional employment', *American Economic Review*, Vol. 63 (September 1973).

D. Metcalf, 'Unions, incomes policy, and relative wages in Britain', *British Journal of Industrial Relations*, Vol. 15 (July 1977).

J. Mincer, *Schooling, Experience and Earnings* (New York: National Bureau of Economic Research, 1974).

R. Perlman, *Labor Theory* (New York: John Wiley, 1969).

G. Psacharopoulos and R. Layard, 'Human capital and earnings: British evidence and a critique', *Review of Economics and Statistics*, Vol. 46 (1979).

M. Stewart, 'Relative earnings and individual union membership in the UK', *Economica*, Vol. 50 (in press).

# 10

# Unemployment

A person is unemployed if he is currently without a job, but is actively looking for one, and would accept a job offered at the going market wage rate for his skills without placing unduly restrictive conditions upon the nature of his future employment. In this chapter we employ theoretical apparatus from Section I to consider the causes of unemployment and its part in the workings of the labour market.

During any single period workers enter and leave the state of unemployment whilst at each point in time there is a certain number of workers unemployed. The theoretical analysis of unemployment can thus be developed, in terms of flows, in a dynamic setting or, in terms of stocks, in a static setting. We base our analysis in Sections 10.1–10.3 for the most part upon a static equilibrium model of the labour market. In Section 10.4, however, we introduce some dynamic analysis.

Unemployment is important to economists because it indicates under-utilisation of labour and therefore, perhaps, a failure of the economic system to use its scarce resources efficiently. Furthermore the level of unemployment, and its distribution across the workforce, will be key factors in determining individual and social welfare. For these reasons we shall have cause to look closely at the nature of unemployment and the characteristics of the unemployed.

## 10.1 Unemployment in a simple static macroeconomic model

Consider an economy which has one frictionless market for homogeneous labour. The only quantity variable is the number of workers, $N$. The demand for labour, $DL$, responds to the real wage $(W/P)$ but, because workers suffer money illusion, the supply of labour responds to the money wage $(W)$. In Figure 10.1(a), therefore, there is a different curve $DL$ for each price level $(P)$, a higher price inducing a higher demand. We assume complete money illusion, so there is only one supply curve $SL$. Our model of the economy also contains goods, money and bond markets but for simplicity we concentrate upon the goods market. In Figure 10.1(b) total expenditure or effective demand, which is made up of consumption, investment and government expenditure is indicated by the line $EE$. The level of consump-

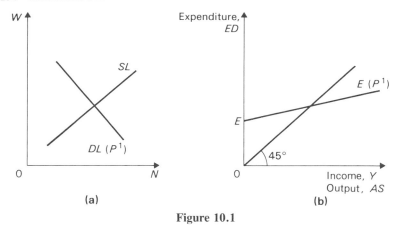

**Figure 10.1**

tion is determined by the level of income ($Y$), the level of investment by the interest rate ($r$) plus an exogenous element. There is a different EE curve for each price level. The higher is $P$, the higher the transactions demand for money in nominal terms. With a given money supply equilibrium can only be achieved with a higher $r$ in order to release money from speculative balances. An increase in $P$ therefore produces a lower level of investment and effective demand and a downward shift of EE.

A competitive economy with wage, price and interest rate flexibility will generate an equilibrium solution. In Figure 10.2 prices will adjust to equate effective demand ($ED^1$ at price $P^1$) with aggregate supply ($AS^1$ at price $P^1$), the latter derived from the demand for labour function $DL(P^1)$, employment $N^1$ and the short-run production function PF. There is clearly no unemployment at this equilibrium. $WP - N^1$ members of the working population are inactive rather than unemployed where $WP$ is the size of the working population. In real wage/employment space labour demand and supply intersect at $W^1/P^1$.

Suppose now that $W^1$ becomes the minimum wage for labour so that, effectively, the labour supply curve becomes AGB in Figure 10.3(a). An equilibrium solution involving unemployment is now possible. Assume a fall in exogenous investment, reducing effective demand to $EE^2(P^1)$ and creating excess supply in the goods market of $AS^1 - Y^2$. The resulting price reduction, say to $P^2$, will do two things. First, it shifts the labour demand function to the left, reducing employment and the level of output. Second, it reduces the transactions demand for money, inducing a fall in the interest rate. The resulting increase in investment will partially offset the initial fall in exogenous investment. The expenditure function shifts up. If there is

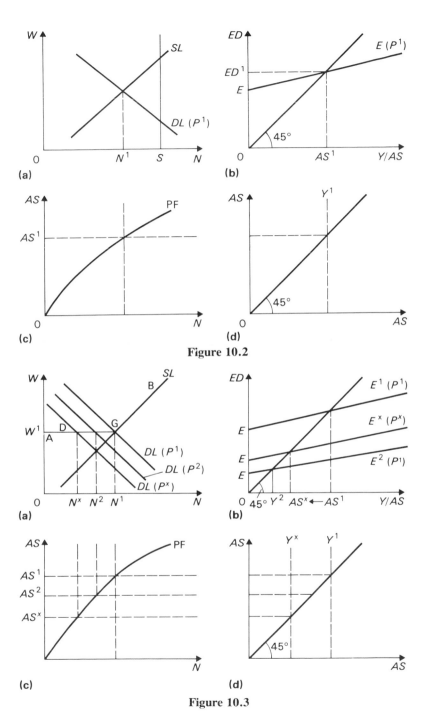

**Figure 10.2**

**Figure 10.3**

still excess supply in the goods market further price reductions take place until, at price $P^x$, $Y^x = AS^x$. Since wages have not altered from $W^1$, labour supply is unchanged whilst demand has shifted to $DL(P^x)$ so there is unemployment equal to $N^xN^1$ workers.

In the event of an increase in the minimum wage from $W^1$ to $W^2$ the labour supply curve becomes FHB in Figure 10.4(a). Equilibrium will again involve unemployment. The higher minimum wage with prices $P^1$ induces a fall in the demand for labour to $N^2$ and a rise in labour supply to $N^3$ along $SL$. The fall in demand means a lower supply of goods, $AS^2$. With excess demand $Y^1 - AS^2$, product prices rise. This shifts $DL$ to the right and increases output, thus partially offsetting the initial supply reduction. It also raises the interest rate and reduces investment and effective demand. The price increases until, at $P^x$, $Y^x = AS^x$. Output will be lower than it was to begin with, and there will be unemployment equal to $N^xN^3$ workers.

The economy is in equilibrium once price level $P^x$ has been reached. There is no automatic mechanism in the model to eradicate unemployment. If, however, the government were to increase effective demand, by either fiscal or monetary policy, it could reduce

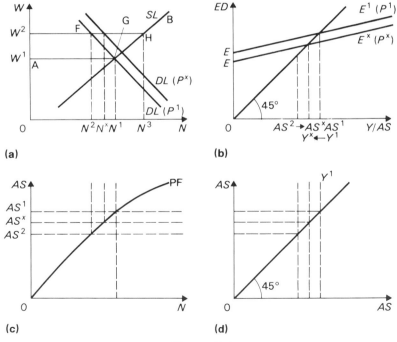

Figure 10.4

unemployment. An increase in government spending would initially induce excess demand for goods as the *EE* schedule moved upwards in Figure 10.3(b). The resulting price increase would, on the one hand, shift the *DL* function to the right and increase employment and the supply of goods, and on the other hand raise *r* and therefore offset the initial policy-induced increase in demand for goods. *P* will rise until the excess demand is removed. Employment, output, the interest rate and prices will be higher and unemployment lower. By choosing the appropriate increase in spending the government can achieve zero unemployment at G. Alternatively, an increase in the money supply would cause excess supply in the money market and so reduce the interest rate. This would increase investment and induce excess demand for goods. The rise in *P* will increase the demand for labour and the supply of goods. The interest rate will increase towards its original level, checking the expansion of demand. Given the appropriate increase in the money supply, prices can be driven up till unemployment is removed. In equilibrium employment, output and prices will be higher, the interest rate and unemployment lower. If the minimum wage rises continuously then, *ceteris paribus*, the government must continuously increase its fiscal or monetary expansion to prevent unemployment.

The above model of unemployment suggests the following. First, since at any given rigid wage, say $W^1$, inactive workers also suffer from money illusion, changes in ED, exogenous or policy-determined, will not change the level of inactivity. However, raising the minimum wage will.

Second, though the model assumes total money illusion this is not essential to the results. If workers respond to price changes, the SL function will shift to the left with any price increase thus reducing the multiplier effect of exogenous or policy demand changes. However, as long as the SL function responds less than the DL function all the qualitative results above hold.

Third, because of workers' money illusion the government faces an upward sloping aggregate supply curve relating prices and output, as in Figure 10.5. This means that by appropriate monetary or fiscal policy it can always increase employment and reduce unemployment at the expense of some increase in prices. Money illusion permits the government to reduce real wages to the equilibrium level through price adjustments. The slope of the curve in Figure 10.5 depends in part therefore upon the degree of workers' money illusion.

Fourth, unemployment in the above analysis is involuntary in the following specific sense. Each of the $N^xN^1$ workers unemployed in Figure 10.3(a) would be prepared to work at the going money wage, even if the real wage fell. They are 'denied' work because effective demand and prices are not high enough to generate sufficient jobs.

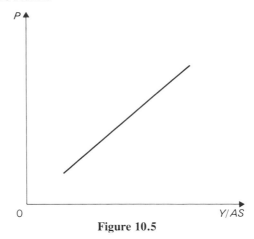

**Figure 10.5**

Unemployment is thus involuntary in that it is sensitive to government-induced changes in effective demand.

Fifth, the central policy implication of our analysis is that the appropriate corrective measure for unemployment, given rigid money wage levels, lies in government expansionary policies. There is little an individual unemployed worker can do to terminate his unemployment since the jobs are simply not there at wage $W^1$ over which he has no influence.

Sixth, the model predicts that in equilibrium at D in Figure 10.3(a) unemployment will exceed vacancies, indeed in this frictionless market vacancies will be zero. An expansionary policy to reach G will bring about both zero vacancies and zero unemployment.

## 10.2 Unemployment in a multimarket static macroeconomic model

The last prediction is obviously at odds with the real world. Let us therefore respecify our model so that the economy is made up of a large number of labour markets, delineated by skills and geographical areas. We continue to assume, for the moment, that each market is internally frictionless but we recognise the existence of significant friction *between* markets. Consider now the economy in Figure 10.3(a) which has moved from zero unemployment equilibrium G to equilibrium at D as a result of the fall in exogenous investment. The average wage level remains at $W^1$ and wages in all sub-markets are unchanged, because we assume that wages are everywhere rigid downwards. At the new level of aggregate demand $Y^x$ there will be some distribution of labour demand across the various sub-markets.

That distribution of labour demand is very unlikely to match the distribution of labour supply at the prevailing wage structure. We will therefore observe excess labour demand (vacancies) in some markets and excess labour supply (unemployment) in others. Unemployment will be greater than $N^x N^1$ workers because of and to the extent of the unfilled vacancies. Without friction vacancies would eventually disappear with labour mobility. But, since there are significant training and transactions costs, ability variations and so on, as long as effective demand remains at $Y^x$ we observe both permanent vacancies and unemployment.

If the government increases effective demand the distribution of the additional demand will be critical. We assume that with total effective demand restored to the level $Y^1$, few sub-markets reach equilibrium. Total unemployment will be lower and total vacancies higher at G than D, but vacancies and unemployment coexist at G despite government intervention.

Let us consider the relationship between unemployment ($U$) and vacancies ($V$) further. Suppose the average wage rate is rigid at $W^1$ and prices are zero. There are $N^1$ workers offering their labour, zero jobs, and thus unemployment equals $N^1$. As prices rise following an increase in effective demand, the demand for labour rises. In a perfectly frictionless world as jobs are created they are immediately filled. The rise in jobs and the fall in unemployment are perfectly synchronised. Vacancies never exist until the demand for labour is $N^1$, after which point unemployment is zero. The relationship between $U$ and $V$ is L-shaped as in Figure 10.6(a). Unemployment and vacancies never coexist. Suppose, however, that inter-market friction exists. As jobs are created friction does not initially impede appointments since unemployment greatly exceeds vacancies. But at some point a job is created in a sub-market which is not filled immediately and a vacancy arises. Further injections of demand generate further

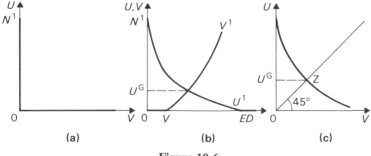

**Figure 10.6**

jobs, only some of which are filled. The result is that vacancies arise, as in Figure 10.6(b), before unemployment falls to zero. The more extensive is friction the sooner vacancies appear and the more rapid their rate of increase with the expansion of demand. The relationship between unemployment and vacancies at different demand levels will be a convex curve, as that shown in Figure 10.6(c). At point G in Figure 10.3(a) demand and supply of labour are equal. *Ex post*, demand is identical to the number of employed people, $E$, plus the number of vacancies, $V$. Supply is $E + U$. At G therefore $U = V$. The intersection of $N^1U^1$ and $VV^1$ in Figure 10.6(b) and the point of intersection, Z, of the UV curve in Figure 10.6(c) with a 45° line correspond to G, and thus $U^G$ records the level of unemployment at G.

Our model so far assumes that all firms in some sub-markets experience vacancies whilst all firms in others face unemployed workers. Let us now introduce friction *within* sub-markets. Imagine that the structure of wages inside each market at G persists at D in Figure 10.3(a) and that the fall in effective demand from $Y^1$ to $Y^x$ involves a change in the share of each firm (industry) in total demand, some firms actually obtaining increased absolute and relative demand. If there is any friction within labour markets workers freed from one firm could not immediately gravitate to more successful firms. As a result vacancies and unemployment will coexist inside each labour market. Unemployment at D will thus be higher than previously predicted to the extent that, in addition to the vacancies in excess demand markets, there are also vacancies in excess supply markets. As demand expands following government intervention the structure of the demand increase across firms within each sub-market will be important. We would normally expect to find more excess demand firms in each and every market at G with the result that unemployment induced by intra-market friction falls between D and G. $U^G$ in Figure 10.6(c) therefore now measures the unemployment at G in Figure 10.3(a) arising from both intra- and inter-market friction.

The following implications follow from the above multimarket static model. First, at G, the market clearing point, there are both unemployment and vacancies. Given effective demand $Y^1$, the level of unemployment at G depends upon the distribution of labour demand between and within labour sub-markets. Expanding demand from D reduces unemployment until it equals vacancies at G. A further expansion of demand will reduce unemployment below $U^G$ as the number of firms with excess demand for labour is increased. As in Figure 10.6(b) this could continue until unemployment is reduced to zero. Since the levels of unemployment and vacancies at each point of the demand expansion from D depend upon the structure of demand

and the severity of friction in the labour market, the government has two kinds of instrument with which to combat unemployment: aggregate demand management and policies aimed at individual labour markets.

Second, if the structure of demand and market frictions are constant or always in a given relationship to the level of demand, then, as demand expands and contracts, the economy moves along a single UV curve. The level of unemployment (and vacancies) at the market clearing point G will thus be constant through time. We may then define two forms of unemployment, demand deficient (DDU) and non-demand deficient (NDDU). The former measures unemployment in excess of the level at the market clearing point G. The latter is the level of unemployment at G, $U^G$. With knowledge of the UV relationship it would be possible to identify these quantities at each point in time. With the UV curve shown in Figure 10.7, a current unemployment level of $U^1$ and market clearing unemployment of $U^2$, $DDU = U^1U^2$ and $NDDU = U^2$. Assuming the government aims to achieve the market clearing position, it now knows the specific amount of aggregate demand expansion required, i.e. sufficient, given policy multipliers, to reduce unemployment by $U^1U^2$. Any further reduction in unemployment could come from policies aimed at specific labour markets. The former represents a movement along the UV curve, the latter a policy-induced shift of the curve inwards.

Third, though the analysis above indicates that the government can reduce unemployment below $U^G$ by increasing effective demand, there are costs to such action. An increase in demand beyond $Y^1$ will raise the average wage level. This implies that along the segment XU of the UV curve in Figure 10.7 $W$ is rising; we are moving up the

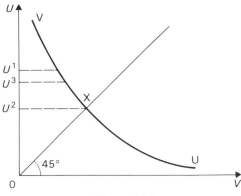

**Figure 10.7**

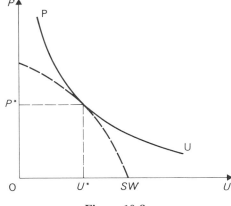

**Figure 10.8**

labour supply curve and the labour force is growing. If the UV relationship is to be stable we must introduce additional assumptions about the nature of and interaction between demand structures, friction, sub-market wages movements and the level and distribution of labour force activity. Furthermore, reducing unemployment below $U^G$ will require sufficient demand expansion and price increases to employ the additions to the labour force.

Fourth, since government targets relate to prices as well as to unemployment, the above analysis implies that the government has a welfare choice to make. In Figure 10.8 the range of options for unemployment and prices are shown as PU. To specify the target level of unemployment requires a social welfare function. With the function $SW$ in Figure 10.8 the government will attempt to maintain aggregate demand at a level consistent with unemployment $U^*$ and price level $P^*$. This might of course involve a target average wage level $W^*$ above $W^1$. It should be apparent from this analysis that there is nothing special about the point G (where $U = V$) in Figure 10.3(a) as far as economic efficiency, welfare and thus government policy are concerned. Similarly the notion of full employment as a target has little meaning except when derived from some welfare optimisation process. In a world encompassing many labour sub-markets, all in disequilibrium, there is no justification for defining the market clearing outcome as optimal. Given the consequences for prices zero unemployment would also be an inappropriate target. Assuming the government can specify $U^*$, and that unemployment is a clear measure of excess demand in the labour market, $(U - U^*)$ is an unambiguous measure by which the government can steer the economy. Having identified the UV curve in Figure 10.7, if the government's target is $U^3$, $U^1U^3$ represents demand deficient unemployment and thus the guide for demand expansion.

Fifth, the analysis above suggests that unemployment can be reduced by specific labour market policies to shift the whole UV relationship inwards. In practice this may be difficult for governments to do if their policy instruments are directed towards the macroeconomy. Thus although in theory a target unemployment level can be achieved by changing either the level of demand or the structure of demand and the severity of friction, in practice demand management may be the most common policy. Furthermore, whether governments choose to introduce specific labour market policies will depend upon their costs as well as benefits.

We can in principal divide unemployment at any point in time into two types – structural and frictional (SU and FU). The former arises out of an imbalance of demand and supply and friction *between* markets; the latter arises out of an imbalance of demand and supply and friction *within* markets. This distinction is useful if the exact values of SU and FU at any point in time can be determined and if different policies are appropriate. Given that the UV relationship is stable disaggregation is in fact possible. Imagine an economy with $U > V$ in aggregate and with $L$ out of $K$ sub-markets in excess supply. Therefore $U_i > V_i$ for $i = 1 - L$. Clearly all vacancies in these $L$ markets result from internal friction.

$$FU = \sum_{i=1}^{i=L} V_i$$

because for this number of unemployed a job in the same market is available. In excess demand sub-markets ($i = L + 1$ to $K$), in each of which $U_i < V_i$, all unemployment,

$$\sum_{i=L+1}^{i=K} U_i$$

is frictional since all the unemployed could obtain jobs in that market. Thus for the whole economy we have:

$$FU = \sum_{i=1}^{i=L} V_i + \sum_{i=L+1}^{i=K} U_i \qquad (10.1)$$

The unemployed in the $L$ excess supply markets for whom no internal vacancy exists, i.e.

$$\sum_{i=1}^{i=L} (U_i - V_i)$$

require jobs from the

$$\sum_{i=L+1}^{i=K} (V_i - U_i)$$

available in the $(K - L)$ excess demand markets. Since we have assumed

$$\sum_{i=1}^{i=L} (U_i - V_i) > \sum_{i=L+1}^{i=K} (V_i - U_i)$$

SU is measured by the vacancies in $(K - L)$ excess demand markets which cannot be filled internally:

$$SU = \sum_{i=L+1}^{i=K} (V_i - U_i) \qquad (10.2)$$

Alternatively, if for the whole economy $V > U$, then equation (10.1) will again give FU but, since

$$\sum_{i=1}^{i=L} (U_i - V_i) < \sum_{i=L+1}^{i=K} (V_i - U_i)$$

all the workers looking to the $(K - L)$ excess demand sub-markets for jobs could be employed, so:

$$SU = \sum_{i-1}^{i=L} (U_i - V_i) \qquad (10.3)$$

In our model structural and frictional unemployment exist at every level of demand, but both will be smaller the higher the level of demand. The critical piece of information for government policy is the breakdown of NDDU, $U^*$, into its structural and frictional components, $FU^*$ and $SU^*$. These provide targets for policies to shift the pattern of demand and reduce frictions. Intra-market frictions and thus frictional unemployment arise from information deficiencies, transactions costs, entry barriers, inertia, and so on. The government can counter these with public employment services, a free or low cost communication system, counselling and introduction services, initial screening and financial assistance. Structural unemployment arises from an imbalance of demand across industries or geographical areas and from the difficulties workers face in moving between skills and locations. The government can counter demand imbalances by public investment, and incentives to investment in given industries and regions. It can counter frictions by financing retraining and by grants to workers who move. The cost of these measures must be set against their efficiency and welfare benefits; there is therefore some optimum level $U^{**}$ below $U^*$ to which the government will wish to reduce NDDU.

Sixth, any exogenously determined or government inspired once-for-all change in the structure of demand or in the severity of frictions within labour markets will shift the UV relationship. The effect this has upon unemployment will appear alongside that of any demand change. If unemployment falls from $U^2$ to $U^1$, UV analysis indicates that $U^2U^3$ in Figure 10.9 is due to demand policy, $U^2U^1$ to the shift factor.

Let us now consider some of the limitations of the approach to unemployment set out in the static models above. First, there are obvious practical difficulties in specifying policy targets given the problems of identifying society's welfare function, the price effects and unemployment multipliers of demand policies and the costs and effectiveness of state intervention in labour markets.

Second, generating policy targets via the UV relationship depends critically upon the stability of that relationship. So too does any attempt to attribute shifts in UV curves *ex post* to specific policy or exogenous changes. In a complex, dynamic labour market stability is difficult to presume. The assumption that unemployment and vacancies are not directly causally related is also problematic. For example people may enter the labour force and unemployment to search for jobs, attracted by the number of vacancies.

Third, starting from equilibrium at D, an expansion of demand

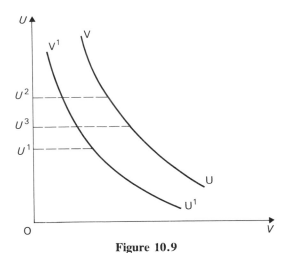

**Figure 10.9**

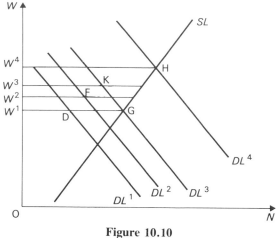

**Figure 10.10**

reduces unemployment and increases vacancies. Figure 10.3(a) implies that wages will not arise until point G is reached, but in a multi-market economy this is very likely to be wrong. As demand expands from $Y^x$ some markets and firms will change from excess supply to excess demand long before $Y^1$ is reached. Wages will be bid up and thus the average wage will rise. Wage increases reduce the demand and increase the supply of labour and therefore widen the unemployment gap. In Figure 10.10 the demand expansion shifts market equilibrium from D to F to K. The larger the demand increase the larger will be the average wage increase. In fact, therefore, the government must expand demand sufficiently to clear the market at H rather than K since the supply of labour is higher at H than K. We have no way of knowing *a priori* whether unemployment is higher at H than at G, but it is lower than at D. This implies that the relationship between $P$ and $U$ will be steeper than in Figure 10.8: the trade-off between unemployment and prices is less favourable. Any inflexibility or lag in wage increases will temper that effect.

Fourth, the assumption of money illusion is critical. Surely at some stage employees will realise that by fixing their labour supply in terms of money wages they allow the government to reduce their welfare by demand management. If on the other hand we allow them to bargain in real terms, how much they are aware of and responsive to price movements becomes critical. Suppose it were the case that workers respond fully to price changes, but not immediately. This means that the government can only maintain its unemployment target by injecting *repeated* equal increases in demand so as always to keep the actual price level above that expected by workers. Each unemployment

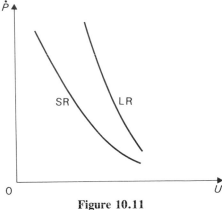

**Figure 10.11**

level would thus be associated with a price increase, $\dot{P}$, as in Figure 10.11, rather than a price level. The slope of $\dot{P}U$ depends upon the time lag in workers' responses. The social choice involves trading off inflation against unemployment.

But surely workers will come to anticipate the government's actions and determine their labour supply in the expectation of price increases? If we allow for this the important question is how accurately do workers anticipate price movements and how fully are they able to build them into their labour supply responses? If the wage increase in response to a price change is less than 100 per cent of that price change, then the government retains its power to determine the unemployment level. By keeping prices moving upwards ahead of workers' expectations of inflation $(\dot{P}^e)$, it can maintain the real wage necessary for its employment target. Of course the higher is $\lambda$ $(= \dot{P}^e/\dot{P})$, the higher the rate of inflation necessary to achieve a given target. The nature and causes of unemployment and the policy options open to the government thus depend crucially upon the size of the wage response. If the government sticks to a single unemployment target, and thus expands demand and prices at a constant rate, wage changes will come closer to price changes. The $\dot{P}U$ trade-off becomes steeper. One question for policy is thus the proximity of $\lambda$ to one in the long run.

## 10.3  Voluntary unemployment

The model developed in the previous two sections assumes that workers suffer money illusion or fail fully to anticipate inflation. Since it focuses entirely upon unemployment as a stock it fails to identify the underlying behavioural relationships that generate labour flows and thus provides few insights into how economic agents respond to market frictions. In this section we reconsider the assumption of money illusion and introduce labour market flows into the analysis.

Let us assume that workers always determine their labour supply on the basis of real wages and that the minimum wage is fixed in real terms. Any change in prices shifts the SL function defined against money wages to the left to exactly the same degree it shifts DL to the right. In a single labour market economy the minimum real wage is, say, $w^1 = (W^1/P^1)$ in Figure 10.12(a). If private investment falls, effective demand falls and prices fall. The demand for labour falls but the supply of labour increases to the same extent so the economy remains at $E^1$ in Figure 10.12(a) and moves to $E^2$ in Figure 10.12(b). What happens in the rest of the economy is that the fall in prices continues until the reduced demand for money so lowers the interest rate that private investment rises to its former level. Flexible prices, the interest rate in particular, maintain equilibrium permanently; so no unemployment arises from exogenous events.

Now assume that the minimum real wage rises from $W^1/P^1$ to $w^2 = W^2/P^1$. In Figure 10.12(a) unemployment equals the number of workers represented by the distance AB. The excess demand for goods raises prices but since wages rise similarly the market remains at A. Prices will rise until the increased demand for money pushes the interest rate up sufficiently to reduce investment and effective demand to a level consistent with the output produced by the smaller

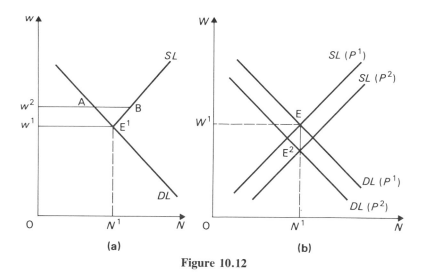

**Figure 10.12**

employment at A. Any fall in investment at the new real wage level will induce demand changes that maintain the economy at equilibrium A. At A any increase in government spending merely pushes wages and prices up together so the real wage remains at $w^2$. The interest rate rises causing the substitution of public for private effective demand. Unemployment cannot be reduced by government macro-economic policies. By fixing their labour supply according to real wages workers render such policies ineffective. Unemployment must be voluntary according to our earlier definition.

In an economy with many labour sub-markets there will be some where minimum real wage levels are permanently either above or below the market clearing level. If $w^2$ is the average real wage across sub-markets, excess demand areas must be less important than excess supply areas. Vacancies exist to the extent that there are frictions in moving between and within markets so unemployment at A will exceed the number of workers represented by AB. The government cannot reduce unemployment simply by expanding demand to reduce real wages and thereby inducing employers to create more jobs *in all markets*. As demand expands wages and prices go up together so that the levels of unemployment and vacancies are unchanged. The government faces a vertical relationship between prices and unemployment, not the upward sloping relationship of Figure 10.8. The amount of unemployment at A depends upon the distribution of demand across markets, the distribution of rigid real wage levels, and the severity of market frictions. It also depends upon the nature of the supply adjustment decisions taken by workers and to analyse these we must introduce labour market flows.

Assume the economy is at A and a fall in exogenous investment occurs. This creates an excess supply of goods at price level $P^1$. Firms react by dismissing workers as prices fall. A flow into unemployment takes place. Later, as investment rises again due to lower interest rates and the real wage returns to $w^2$, there is a flow of workers from unemployment back into jobs. In the present model inadequate information is assumed to be the critical friction limiting that return flow. Search theory suggests that the flow back into employment, and thus the level of unemployment at the market equilibrium point A, will depend upon the costs of acquiring information, state unemployment payments, and the characteristics of the wage distribution. The level of unemployment at any moment is thus a function of union wage policy, the institutional factors governing information flows and search variables. Since most of these are outside the government's control and assumed constant through time, unemployment at A will be constant and can be referred to as the natural unemployment level $U^N$ (or natural rate assuming a constant labour supply at the equilibrium real wage). If search is concerned with real wages, demand changes cannot alter either $U^N$ or the employment level at A. Unemployment is voluntary in two senses: it cannot be corrected by demand management and it arises out of the optimal search behaviour of utility-maximising workers. The model predicts that unemployment will not deviate from the natural level in the long run but that deviations are possible in the short run. Suppose the government increases effective demand at A in Figure 10.12(a). Prices and money wages rise but the real wage remains the same. Suppose, however, that those currently unemployed do not realise that price and wage increases are general. They determine their reservation wage, $r^*$, from the distribution of market money wages observed at A prior to the government's intervention. The effect of that intervention is to shift the whole wage distribution to the right, as in Figure 10.13. Some unemployed workers will come across acceptable wage offers much more quickly than they otherwise would have and so terminate their search and take a job. Employers will be misled into increasing their demand for labour in the belief that the price increase is peculiar to their product and fail to anticipate that the labour supply response to a general price increase will increase wages. There is a flow out of unemployment and thus, *ceteris paribus*, the level of unemployment at A falls. By selection of the appropriate demand injection, and therefore of money wage and price increases, the government can achieve unemployment levels below the natural level.

In time employers will realise that all wages and prices have risen to the same degree. They will then discard workers and resume their original employment targets. Workers will also come to realise that

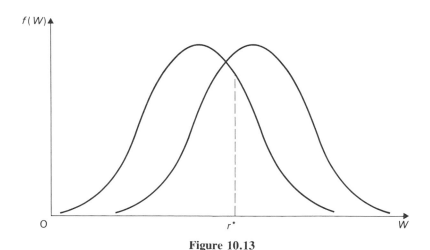

**Figure 10.13**

they have misread events, re-enter unemployment and recalculate $r^*$ from the new wage and price levels. Unemployment will return to the natural level. To maintain its unemployment target the government must inject a further similar expansion of demand. Assuming that they are again unaware of this manipulation, employers will continue at the higher employment level and workers, receiving further unexpected wage increases, will not resume unemployment. The larger the deviation from the natural level the government aims at, the larger must be each period's demand expansion and thus price increase. This gives us a relationship, SR, between unemployment and inflation shown in Figure 10.14.

Unemployed workers will in time come to anticipate fully price and wage changes, especially if the rate of inflation is held constant. In the long run the value of the coefficient $\lambda$, as defined earlier, will be unity. Unemployment can be induced below its natural level only with unanticipated inflation. The latter exists in the short run but persists into the long run only if the government follows a policy of *continually* increasing the *rate* of price increases. In long-run equilibrium with fully anticipated inflation and constant $\dot{P}$ the government faces an inflation unemployment trade-off which is a vertical line at $U^N$ as in Figure 10.14. The implication is that the government should not attempt to reduce unemployment below $U^N$ by demand management both because it will fail and because in the process, having pushed inflation up to $\dot{P}^1$ to achieve $U^*$, equilibrium will be restored at $U^N$ but with an inflation rate $\dot{P}^1$. If the government subsequently wishes to lower the rate of inflation, it must bring down price expectations. It does this by systematically reducing demand so that actual price and

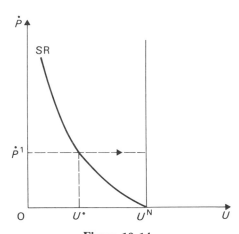

**Figure 10.14**

wage changes are less than expected. Unemployment will temporarily exceed $U^N$ perhaps with high, if eventually falling, rates of inflation. There is only one stable equilibrium level of employment and unemployment in this model, at which anticipated and actual rates of change of prices are the same. In the long run the distinction between NDDU and DDU is invalid. There is no such thing as a UV relationship. Any short-run relationship will collapse as market forces drive the economy towards $U^N$, which is not, by and large, sensitive to government policy.

The model above has certain key features. First, it relies heavily upon the assumption that in formulating their labour supply decisions workers *fully* anticipate price changes and wage changes.

Second, the model introduces labour market flows into the analysis, though it does so at a rudimentary level. There are so far only two flows, involuntary flows from jobs to unemployment following demand changes and flows the other way. One could incorporate voluntary flows into unemployment into the model. Assume the government increases demand, generating price and wage increases. This may well lead workers who are searching for better jobs *whilst employed* to believe that the wage increase they receive is peculiar to them, which reduces the likelihood of a quit into search unemployment. This increases the scope for forcing unemployment below $U^N$ – at least in the short run. Once workers realise, however, that all wages have risen, the unemployment level will gradually return to a level consistent with optimal search behaviour, i.e. to $U^N$.

Third, the voluntary unemployment (VU) model, like the involuntary unemployment (IU) model earlier, assumes rigid wages in certain sectors of the labour market; the former assumes rigid real wages whilst the latter assumes rigid money wages. If, however, there were sub-markets which did not have rigid wages, then in principle over time movements of labour towards these areas should bid wages down sufficiently to absorb the unemployed workforce. Why then might this not happen? Part of the explanation may be that the non-rigid wage sectors are simply not large enough to absorb the workforce displaced elsewhere. Second, there may be technological limits to the substitution of labour for capital as wages fall in the non-rigid areas. There may also be limits to the expansion in demand for the products produced in those areas as their relative costs and prices fall. Third, non-rigid wage sectors may be linked to rigid wage areas. For example, firms in the former may not allow their wages to diverge too far from others in order to ward off unionisation. Fourth, there may be social forces limiting wage variations for similar workers across industrial and geographical markets. Fifth, many of the areas in which flexible wages might exist have either come under state control or become subject to state regulation such as minimum wage legislation.

Finally, the process of adjustment through mobility may simply be too slow to bring low levels of unemployment in a changing economic environment. Throughout the analysis of the IU and VU models so far we have built wage rigidities and price expectations into a model of competitive product and labour markets. The VU model denies money illusion and argues that rigidities are neither widespread nor strict enough to generate heavy unemployment on their own. Rigidities arise primarily from adjustment costs, lags and government intervention. The economy is seen to be potentially flexible and self-regulating and therefore the competitive approach is broadly appropriate. But the IU model attaches considerable importance to wage rigidities as well as to disequilibrium in product markets. It is both necessary and valuable therefore to consider, if briefly, the IU model in which non-competitive firms set prices according to some fixed mark-up on costs, and wages are determined through collective bargaining. Wage rigidities arise from institutional pressures within internal labour markets and from trade union activities.

At each employment level wages respond to price changes but the exact degree of response depends upon the bargaining power of the union, as well as the extent to which workers' price expectations are correct. At the same time unions can achieve real wage improvements to the extent that their bargaining power leads to money wage increases above price increases. Demand expansions do not bring immediate price responses from oligopolistic firms who operate with stable prices, predetermined profit margins, and planned slack. Increased demand generates output and employment responses which at least in the short run require limited price increases. Cost increases bring immediate price and output adjustments.

Either a fall in effective demand or a union-induced wage increase can therefore generate increased unemployment, the former with constant prices but reduced output, the latter with higher costs and prices, reduced productivity, competitiveness and lower output. Increased government spending will reduce unemployment for, though higher demand improves the union's bargaining position and therefore raises wages and prices, output will rise to the extent that countervailing power in bargaining restricts wage increases. This in turn increases productivity and competitiveness.

To conclude this section let us survey the IU and VU models to distinguish their analyses of the causes of unemployment. In the IU model the immediate cause of rising unemployment is the failure of the government to stabilise effective demand at a sufficiently high level. The underlying cause is either falling investment and rigid money wages or a rising minimum wage level due to union bargaining and consequent declining competitiveness. Though neither prevents the achievement of employment targets, government policy can produce continuously rising unemployment. In the VU model rising unemployment is temporary and the immediate cause is a reduction in government expenditures and thus effective demand. The underlying cause is a previous attempt by the government to reduce unemployment below the natural level. As a result inflation increased to undesirable levels. The reduction in spending and increase in unemployment result from a desire to reduce the level of inflation.

In the VU model the level of long-run unemployment will not be insignificant. This is because there are severe frictions within labour markets primarily resulting from government intervention. The VU model emphasises optimal search behaviour, particularly by job changers, and thus the frictions within markets produced by state policies: for example, housing policy as it increases the costs of mobility; state payments to the jobless as they increase search; government-induced fixed costs as they impede employment adjustments; trade unions and government policies to establish wages in many areas above competitive levels. The high level of unemployment will be voluntary; optimal for the individuals involved though not for society if the interventions do not arise from rigorous social welfare calculations. If the friction could be reduced the long-term level of unemployment, $U^N$, could be reduced. On the other hand, further state intervention could increase the natural rate significantly. The VU model thus underlines the importance of information and uncertainty in the labour market, search behaviour and its parameters, and state interventionist policies. It argues that workers and consumers are invariably better judges of their own interests than the state, are better informed, and are more flexible and sensitive to market signals. State intervention, however well intentioned, is thus often inappropriate and indeed can seriously exacerbate the effects of unavoidable friction. Governments would be better advised to reduce intervention, act against non-competitive behaviour where appropriate and promote market forces.

In the IU model the long-run level of unemployment depends critically upon the adjustment coefficient $\lambda$ and society's tastes across inflation and unemployment. It will also depend upon price expectations, trade unions' ability to exact full compensation in wages for actual price changes and their persistence in trying to increase their money wage level. Labour market friction is not seen to pose the severe problems anticipated in the VU model. The IU model emphasises demand imbalances, redundancies, inter-market friction, occupational and locational immobility and thus structural unemployment. It attaches great importance to the availability of job openings and imperfections in the provision of and investment in training. It places great stress upon demand imbalances between regions and industries rather than within industries. In the long run unemployment can be maintained at low levels by demand management, despite friction, because the government does have the means to focus demand expansion upon certain regions and industries. This, plus the fact that slack exists, prices are rigid, productivity improves and wage adjustments are restricted by employers, means that unemployment targets do not involve high inflation. The IU model does not attach great significance to government intervention in the labour market as a cause of unemployment. Intervention is seen as necessary to counter market failure, is therefore generally socially justifiable and indeed often beneficial to employment. The IU model instead directs attention to market failure, long-term disequilibrium, the prevalence of declining industries and their regional concentration, and underinvestment in training.

## 10.4  A dynamic view of unemployment

The IU model above is constructed entirely in static terms. The VU model introduced labour market flows but only in a limited form. In this section we set up a theoretical framework which is based entirely upon flows and thus generates a dynamic view, albeit a simplified one, of unemployment. The framework is general enough to encompass both involuntary and voluntary unemployment. It assists our inquiry into the nature and causes of unemployment because it introduces and relates many of the behavioural relationships underlying labour market adjustments formulated in Chapters 7 and 8, but mainly ignored so far in this chapter.

During each period of time $t$, as Figure 7.1 shows, there are many types of flow within the economy. A single firm $i$ will experience a change in its employment level ($\dot{E}_{it}$), the nature of which we simplify to the following identity:

$$\dot{E}_{it} \equiv Hi_{it} - (K_{it} + Q_{it} + R_{it} + D_{it}) \qquad (10.4)$$

where $Hi$ are hires, $K$ are involuntary separations due to retirement, death, sickness, etc., $Q$ are quits, $R$ are redundancies or lay-offs, and $D$ are dismissals due to misconduct, failed probation, etc. Quits may be moves into inactivity, $Q^I$, into unemployment, $Q^U$, or into other jobs, $Q^j$. For the whole economy we have:

$$\dot{E}_t \equiv (Hi_t - Q_t^j) - (K_t + Q_t^I + Q_t^U + R_t + D_t) \qquad (10.5)$$

We assume that only involuntary separations, $K$ (*all* of whom leave the labour force when they leave their jobs), quits into inactivity, $Q^I$, and moves between inactivity and unemployment, $N^{IU}$, change the size of the labour force, $S$. Therefore:

$$\dot{S}_t \equiv N_t^{IU} - K_t - Q_t^I, \qquad \dot{S}_t, N_t^{IU} \gtreqless 0 \qquad (10.6)$$

We assume that hires come only from the unemployed or directly from other jobs and that all redundancies and dismissals go into unemployment. Unemployment is given by

$$U_t \equiv S_t - E_t \qquad (10.7)$$

so unemployment changes as:

$$\dot{U}_t \equiv \underbrace{N_{t2}^{IU} + (Q_t^U + R_t + D_t)}_{\text{inflow}} - \underbrace{(Hi_t - Q_t^j)}_{\text{outflow}} \qquad (10.8)$$

The IU model emphasises the effects of changes in demand in changing unemployment through $Hi_t$ and $R_t$ in both the short and the long run. The VU model emphasises the role of unanticipated price and wage changes in altering $Hi_t$ and $Q_t^U$ and thus unemployment in the short run. We can do little to extend the theoretical analysis of demand deficient unemployment here because no wage and price variables appear in the present framework. But we can extend the analysis of non-demand deficient unemployment or the natural level of unemployment.

The outflow from unemployment can be expressed as:

$$(Hi_t - Q_t^j) \equiv \frac{U_t}{DU_t} \equiv U_t \times PLU_t \qquad (10.9)$$

where $DU$ is the expected duration of an unemployment spell and $PLU$ is the probability of leaving unemployment. The VU model and search theory suggest that PLU for any worker depends crucially upon the extent of endemic market friction, government interventions, particularly in the form of state payments to the unemployed, and workers' search and training costs ($SC$). The IU model suggests that PLU will depend crucially upon the level of vacancies, the industrial and regional distribution of demand, $DD$, and firms' recruitment and training costs, $RC$. So

$$(Hi_t - Q_t^j) \equiv U_t \times PLU(RR_t, SC_t, V_t, DD_t, RC_t) \qquad (10.10)$$

where $RR$ is the replacement ratio.

If initially we treat vacancies and redundancies as exogenous, assume that movements in and out of the labour force vary according to equation (7.5) and that quits into unemployment are given by equation (7.8),

$$N_t^{UI} = N^{UI}(V_t, U_t, RR_t, SC_t, RC, DD_t)$$

$$Q_t^U = Q^U(V_t, U_t, RR_t, SC_t, RC, DD_t)$$

then equation (10.8) becomes:

$$\dot{U}_t = G(U_t, V_t, R_t, D_t, RR_t, SC_t, RC, DD_t) \qquad (10.11)$$

or

$$u_t = u(u_{t-1}, v_t, r_t, d_t, RR_t, SC_t, RC_t, DD_t) \qquad (10.12)$$

where small letters stand for rates, e.g. $u$ is the unemployment rate. This is a dynamic form for the UV relationship, the term $u_{t-1}$ introducing the dynamic element. Only if $U_t = U_{t-1}$ will the economy be in equilibrium. Otherwise unemployment will change continuously as the economy adjusts towards equilibrium. The nature of the adjustment process and the final equilibrium position depend upon the exact form of the behavioural relationships and adjustment costs in the model.

In Figure 10.15 we draw equation (10.12) downward sloping in $u/v$ space. There will be a different curve for each value of $u_{t-1}$. The curve drawn is derived from (10.12) when $u_t = u_{t-1}$ for given values of $r$, $d$, $RR$, $SC$, $RC$ and $DD$.

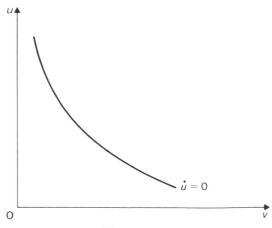

Figure 10.15

Vacancies and redundancies are not, however, exogenous to equation (10.12). They arise from a difference between desired employment ($E^d$) and actual employment ($E^a$). Suppose there are $n$ firms with $E^d > E^a$. Their desired hiring is

$$\sum_{i=1}^{n} (E_{it}^{d} - E_{it-1}^{a})$$

To the extent that desired hiring is not accomplished, vacancies occur equal to

$$V_t = \sum_{i=1}^{n} (E_{it}^{d} - E_{it-1}^{a}) \tag{10.13}$$

so

$$\dot{V}_t = \sum_{i=1}^{n} (\dot{E}_{it}^{d} - \dot{E}_{it}^{a}) \tag{10.14}$$

which, from equation (10.4), where $Hi > 0$ and $R = 0$, gives:

$$\dot{V}_t = \sum_{i=1}^{n} [\dot{E}_{it}^{d} - (K_{it} + Q_{it} + D_{it} - Hi_{it})] \tag{10.15}$$

Given that hiring varies with recruitment costs, unemployment and the replacement ratio, and that $E^d$ increases with current effective demand ($ED$), we have for the hiring sector:

$$\dot{V}_t = V(u_t, k_t, q_t, d_t, RR_t, RC_t, DD_t, ED_t) \tag{10.16}$$

where $DD$ measures the matching of separations and demand across the $n$ firms in the hiring sector.

Suppose that these are $m$ firms with $E^a > E^d$. Total excess labour in these firms is

$$\sum_{i=1}^{m} (E_{it-1}^{a} - E_{it}^{d})$$

To the extent that employment cannot be reduced to the desired level, the firms will have hoarded labour, $Ho$.

$$Ho_t = \sum_{i=1}^{m} (E_{it-1}^{a} - \dot{E}_{it}^{a} - E_{it}^{d}) \tag{10.17}$$

which, from equation (10.4), where $H = 0$ and $R > 0$, gives:

$$Ho_t = \sum_{i=1}^{m} [E_{it-1}^a - (K_{it} + Q_{it} + R_{it} + D_{it}) - E_{it}^d] \quad (10.18)$$

Given that redundancies vary with severance costs, $VC$, we have for the redundancy sector:

$$r_t = r(k_t, q_t, d_t, VC_t, DD_t, ED_t) \quad (10.19)$$

Using (10.19) we can substitute $r_t$ out of (10.12); using equations (7.7) and (7.8) we can substitute $q^U$ and $q^i$ out of (10.16) and (10.19). Thus we can derive simultaneous equations for $u$ and $v$ for the whole economy:

$$\left.\begin{aligned} u_t &= u(u_{t-1}, v_t, k_t, q_t^1, d_t, RR_t, SC_t, RC_t, VC_t, DD_t, ED_t) \\ v_t &= v(v_{t-1}, u_t, k_t, q_t^1, d_t, RR_t, SC_t, RC_t, VC_t, DD_t, ED_t) \end{aligned}\right\} \quad (10.20)$$

or

$$\left.\begin{aligned} u_t &= u(u_{t-1}, v_t, S_t, D_t, AC_t, ED_t) \\ v_t &= v(v_{t-1}, u_t, S_t, D_t, AC_t, ED_t) \end{aligned}\right\} \quad (10.21)$$

where $S$ are structural elements $(k, q^1, d, RR)$, $D$ demand elements $(DD)$ and $AC$ adjustment costs $(SC, RC, VC)$. During any period $t$, neither $\dot{v}$ nor $\dot{u}$ will be zero. But the equilibrium for the economy can be identified by setting $\dot{v} = \dot{u} = 0$. In Figure 10.16 we draw equations

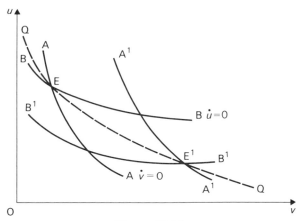

**Figure 10.16**

(10.21) as AA and BB for $\dot{v}$ and $\dot{u} = 0$ respectively, for given levels of $S$, $D$, $AC$ and $ED$. If the economy is anywhere off the two curves the levels of $u$ and $v$ will change until point E is reached. For different values of $ED$ there will be different AA, BB curves and alternative equilibrium points. The locus of equilibrium points is described by QQ, the dynamic uv relationship.

Starting at E, if $ED$ rises the economy would no longer be on QQ or indeed upon AA or BB. Adjustments occur until the economy reaches the intersection of the two curves $A^1A^1$ and $B^1B^1$ at $E^1$. For each value of $S$, $DD$ and $AC$ there will be a different curve QQ. As long as $S$, $DD$ and $AC$ remain the same the economy will opeate around the single uv relationship QQ as demand varies.

What are the implications of this model for understanding the nature and causes of unemployment? Any change in ED will set in motion changes in unemployment and vacancies which define a new equilibrium, but it may take the economy some time to achieve it. A cyclical demand pattern, *ceteris paribus*, might therefore produce continuous loops around QQ and it will not be possible to observe the equilibrium relationship. It will thus be difficult to use a simple empirical uv relationship either to set policy targets or to assess the significance for unemployment of specific changes in market conditions. Recorded unemployment and vacancies will not give a clear indication of the state of excess demand in the economy, even without measurement errors. Recorded $u_t$ and $v_t$ are taken after adjustments have occurred and reflect in part past changes in demand conditions to which firms are still adjusting. Because of adjustment costs each firm will try to anticipate employment adjustments. For the whole economy there could be a serious overstatement of vacancies as firms anticipate quits which simply involve job to job moves.

Unemployment at any point in time must be seen as part of a system that is in disequilibrium and non-stationary. It must be analysed not merely in terms of the forces making for disequilibrium but also in terms of those governing the path towards equilibrium: the costs and institutional factors governing the speed with which workers adjust their labour supply and firms can adjust actual to desired employment levels. We would also have to take into account not only the costs of adjusting employment but those of adjusting hours, capital stocks and capital utilisation. The discussion of both Chapters 7 and 8 is therefore clearly very pertinent to unemployment analysis.

Equations (10.8) and (10.9) indicate that it is useful to analyse unemployment in terms of the determinants of the flows in and the flows out. Outflows are determined simultaneously with duration by the factors determining the probability of leaving unemployment for each unemployed worker. Let us look first at the inflows. First, the model suggests that unemployment depends upon the rate of growth of the labour force, $\dot{S}_t$. It will thus be sensitive to the age structure of the population and in particular the numbers of people of school leaving age. If bulges do occur in birth rates they will, *ceteris paribus*, generate unemployment, and youth unemployment in particular, at some later date. The age structure of the population will also be a major determinant of quits into inactivity, which are often due to increased demand by households for domestic activities, and which reduce the labour force. Through time the level of unemployment will depend upon workers' decisions regarding participation, so it will be particularly sensitive to the number of married women entering the labour market. The discussion of Chapter 7, particularly that on household labour supply decisions and the movement of relative wages for women, has considerable bearing upon unemployment. So too do search variables and aggregate demand through their effect upon job openings and the discouraged worker effect. Any growth of female-intensive industries will have a significant effect upon the long-run levels of female employment and unemployment. So too will changes in the conditions governing women's access to state benefits, and information and training systems.

Second, the model identifies the role of redundancies in determining unemployment. We have assumed that all redundancies enter unemployment. This is, of course, an important empirical issue as is their overall prevalence. The discussion of Chapter 7 suggested that in practice much will depend upon whether redundancy is anticipated or forewarned, upon the level of redundancy payments, and upon the extent of market opportunities and therefore the returns to on-the-job search. The IU model emphasises redundancies, as a central part of firms' adjustment processes and as a key determinant of unemployment.

Third, involuntary separations, $K$, in our model all leave the labour force. Again this is an empirical issue but one would anticipate that such an assumption may be inappropriate for workers forced to leave their jobs for health reasons. These workers may well experience a period of temporary inactivity but then they begin a period of unemployment prior to returning to employment. For the economy as a whole over some period of time $K_t$ may therefore make a significant contribution to unemployment.

Fourth, the VU model attaches some importance to flows into unemployment through quits, $Q^u$. Such flows have been discussed in Chapter 7, so here we need only restate the role played by the replacement ratio and by workers' perceptions of job opportunities.

Turning to the probability of leaving unemployment for employment and therefore to *duration*, two important aspects of equation (10.10) are worth noting and investigating. First, PLU will not be constant for any worker over the period of his unemployment. Second,

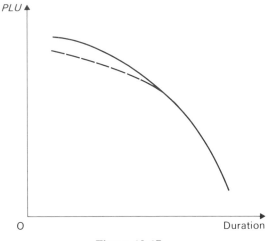

**Figure 10.17**

PLU will depend upon the previous location of the worker in the labour market. In Figure 10.17 we have drawn *PLU* for a particular worker as a downward sloping curve with respect to duration, i.e. the longer a person is unemployed the less likely he is to leave unemployment for employment. The other side of this is that the longer a person is unemployed the more likely he is to become inactive (which is reflected in $N_t^{IU}$ in equation (10.8)). Search theory argues that the longer a person is unemployed the lower is his reservation wage, the less choosy he becomes and the more likely he is to find an acceptable offer. Figure 10.17 implies that stronger counteracting forces exist, particularly on the demand side. First, the longer a worker is unemployed the more accustomed to unemployment he becomes, the less effective his search and the less productive his skills. Second, the longer a person is unemployed the less attractive he becomes to employers. They may use his duration as a screening device to indicate quality. They may anticipate a fall in the worker's productivity as skills become obsolete or at least decline with under-utilisation. Third, the longer a person is unemployed the more difficult it becomes for state employment services to place him. The result is that they steadily commit less and less resources to placing him. On these arguments PLU falls because unemployed workers receive fewer and fewer offers as unemployment continues. The question of their choosiness does not arise.

PLU for the individual may depend upon whether he had previously quit from employment or been dismissed or been made redundant. The VU model does not emphasise this distinction and considers search behaviour by quitters and redundancies similar and thus focuses upon the market variables bearing upon optimal duration calculations. The IU model on the other hand singles out redundancies for attention. Workers made redundant are likely to have long unemployment durations. First, they will find suitable vacancies harder to find given the demand/skill imbalances that underlie their experiences. Second, they may be handicapped in their applications by the fact that they were singled out for redundancy. Third, they may suffer psychologically from being dismissed. Fourth, they may have been identified by the firm as least valuable whereas quitters may select themselves on the basis of their superior marketability.

The probability of leaving unemployment will depend upon the replacement ratio. The precise nature of this effect will depend upon the form and level of state assistance. In general state assistance will shift the whole *PLU* curve in Figure 10.17 inwards. Because the IU model emphasises the market experiences of workers who enter unemployment involuntarily it attaches less significance to the disincentive effect. The VU model emphasises the importance of variations in inflows to variations in unemployment: workers decisions, market imperfections and thus the supply side. The IU model stresses the importance of variations in duration, market imbalances, vacancies and thus the demand side.

## 10.5 The empirical study of unemployment

Numerous statistical studies have been made of the UV relationship to assess its stability, to disaggregate total unemployment, and to assess the effects of specific policy measures upon the labour market. In principle the approach is very simple, requiring only data on $U$ and $V$ and the use of regression techniques to estimate a non-linear UV relationship. In general the empirical work for the UK indicates a stable UV relationship into the 1960s and market clearing unemployment levels of 2–3 per cent, the largest component of which was frictional. It appears the UV relationship shifted at the end of the 1960s and through the 1970s. The exact cause of the shifts (changes in fixed labour costs or changes in distribution on the demand side or changes in RR on the supply side) is disputed and difficult to resolve by this technique. Disaggregating total unemployment through the 1960s and 1970s indicates significant demand-deficient unemployment even in peak years. UV analysis for individual regions indicates the importance of demand deficiency to depressed regions when the economy as a whole is tight.

UV studies have their limitations. First, use of registered unemployment data means that many non-searchers are included and many searchers are excluded, especially amongst women workers. Data collection relies on voluntary declarations and is related to state payment systems for which there is restricted eligibility. Even with survey data our definition of unemployment may well be difficult to apply given the problems in deciding whether a person is actively searching for a job. Vacancy data is likely to be biased downwards because of under-reporting by firms who rely on their own recruitment systems. This must be set against the upward bias due to their anticipating quits. Evidence points to an understatement by as much as two-thirds. Results are thus difficult to interpret using theoretical constructs. Second, it appears that the relationship has been liable to shift further outwards in recent times and some researchers would claim that a stable relationship no longer exists, if it ever did.

The results reported above for UV studies are consistent with the IU model, particularly the existence and stability of the UV curve, the continuing importance of structural unemployment and of demand deficiency in depressed regions at low national unemployment levels. Direct tests of complex if stylised models like the IU and VU models are, however, very difficult. Much of the empirical work has concentrated upon the existence of a trade-off between $\dot{P}$ and $U$, which we shall consider in the next chapter.

There is evidence that labour market rigidities are widespread enough to prevent unemployed workers from moving out of falling demand, rising minimum wage areas. Union-enforced wage parity across regions within industries does much to explain this. The observed prevalence of cost-plus pricing, however, does not in itself indicate non-competitive behaviour until the forces bearing upon the mark-up are identified.

The evidence is that in the UK normal demand variations do not have a great impact upon inflows to unemployment, contrary to both the IU and VU models. In the USA they do have an effect, but primarily on the involuntary flow, as in the IU model. In the UK demand variations do have a consistent and significant impact upon duration, particularly through their effects upon job offers, in line with the IU model.

Because of its central position in the VU model the relationship between $U$ and RR has received much attention. Statistical analysis is, however, hampered by data problems: state payments are complex and the level of take up well below 100 per cent; data for the duration of unemployment relate to uncompleted spells of the unemployed rather than to completed spells. Time-series studies have been conducted with the unemployment level as the dependent variable. Regression estimates are obtained from an equation of the form:

$$U_t = a_0 + a_1 \, \text{RR}_t + \sum_{i=2}^{n} a_i X_{it} \qquad (10.22)$$

where **X** is a vector of variables capturing structural and cyclical determinants of unemployment changes. Such studies have produced evidence of significant disincentive effects. Unfortunately this method suffers from many defects. First, the choice of variables for **X** alters the findings. No rigorous theory or modelling of the labour market is used to derive equation (10.22). Therefore its results cannot support one model against another. Second, estimates of $a_1$ obtained from a reduced form equation of labour market mechanisms are difficult to interpret without knowledge of the structural relationships. Third, precise specifications of the appropriate RR is complicated. It would appear, for example, that RR should relate to the average unemployed or marginal employed worker rather than the average employed worker.

It would seem therefore that cross-section studies of individual data offer more promise of efficient estimates. Since most state benefit systems are not rigorously search related, the theoretical case for an effect upon duration must rely upon their role in extending household resources through the search period. The impact of RR is derived from regressing the conditional probability of re-employment against duration, personal characteristics, demand variables and RR. The data relate to individuals and are collected by sample surveys. Broadly, the results suggest that increasing RR does shift the PLU curve downwards (the elasticity of duration with respect to RR is between 0.6 and 1), but only at short durations (the dashed curve in Figure 10.17). The disincentive effect declines rapidly after 4–5 months and by the 10th month is negligible. Such results are fairly robust but obvious problems still exist. First, the data on RR are often hypothetical rather than based on actual receipts: RR has to be calculated as the amount each unemployed individual should receive given existing regulations but allowing for a take-up factor. Second, it would seem appropriate to use marginal rather than average RR because it is the workers' receipts in the next period, rather than over some past period, that matter. Third, the results relate to the early 1970s when total unemployment was relatively low compared to recent times. The results are, however, consistent with the argument that, with few offers being made to long duration unemployed, RR simply cannot be important since they have little chance to refuse jobs. The evidence from surveys is that significant numbers remain unemployed involuntarily because of a lack of sufficient and/or suitable openings.

If we turn from durations to flows, the available evidence points against any very strong impact of RR upon $U$. First, most unemployed workers are found to have become unemployed involuntarily. The length of forewarning is often so short as to allow the worker little scope for systematic search. A high proportion of voluntary moves are young people who have low RR values. Second, the inflows into unemployment in the UK have varied little through time despite changes in the RR. It is interesting to note in this respect that flow variations in general appear to be much more important to unemployment in the USA than in the UK, and vice versa for duration. But US state assistance is regarded as even less generous than the UK's. The lack of a systematic relationship between $U$ and RR in the UK is not altogether surprising. First, replacement ratios, contrary to popular myth, approach unity only for a very small number of the unemployed. They decline rapidly with duration. State assistance, as in most countries, is not generous given the low definitions of poverty to which assistance is related. Second, in practice few individuals are eligible for benefits above the basic level. Take-up rates for means-tested assistance are far below 100 per cent. Third, high replacement ratios are usually associated with low incomes in work rather than massive state assistance. It is the low earnings and the poor opportunities that determine inflows to unemployment and delay re-entry to jobs.

The evidence from cross-section studies on PLU is that, as in Figure 10.17, it falls with duration, very rapidly after 6 months, so that the probability of leaving unemployment for someone with 12 months duration is very low indeed. This appears to arise because PLU declines with duration for each individual unemployed worker. But it also appears to arise because PLU is lower for some individuals than others, so that successively less employable people are left in the higher duration categories. We consider this in the next section.

## 10.6   The characteristics of the unemployed

So far we have attempted to explain why unemployment occurs and the form it takes. What our theorising has not done is to explain why certain workers experience unemployment and not others. Unemployment may well be an unavoidable aspect of a dynamic and efficient economy, but it is not in practice randomly distributed across the labour force. Since it involves a welfare loss for those experiencing it, identifying the principal characteristics of the unemployed is both a valid and important exercise, which at the same time throws light upon the question of causation. The distribution of unemployment can be analysed in two stages: first looking at how inflows are distributed across the labour force, and second looking at how different durations of unemployment are distributed across the unemployed.

## THE FREQUENCY OF UNEMPLOYMENT

If the economy generated four million or so new unemployment spells each year from a labour force of twenty-four million, and if every spell were to be experienced by a different worker, everyone would have a spell of unemployment once every 6 years. In a working life of 42 years this would mean that every worker would experience approximately seven spells (of unspecified duration). The precise number of spells and the size of the labour force would vary from country to country but the final prediction is unlikely to vary much. From casual inspection, it is evident that large numbers of workers never experience unemployment. This implies that the incidence of unemployment falls heavily upon a minority of the labour force, some of whom experience several spells of unemployment in any year. How can theory help to identify why and how this unequal distribution occurs?

Search theory generates several relevant predictions concerning the flow from jobs to unemployment. The first concerns the phenomenon of individuals moving between several jobs over relatively short periods with intervening periods of unemployment. Job hopping arises in part because jobs cannot be assessed by inspection alone, particularly if the worker lacks basic information on the nature of the labour market. Acquiring information requires the worker to take up the job offered. If the worker is then dissatisfied with what she has learnt she will quit and try somewhere else, possibly with a period of unemployment in between. Such job sampling is likely to be practised by young workers. They start with little labour market knowledge or search technique, their costs of search are lower and their potential earnings streams are longer. We would thus expect to find that young workers constitute a disproportionately large number of the unemployment spells recorded in any one year. Voluntary moves into unemployment may be a small proportion of all separations but a large proportion of them involve young people job shopping. It is essential if such behaviour is to be cost effective, privately and socially, that the spells of unemployment should not be long. This is generally the case. Young people's total experience of unemployment in any one year is not extraordinary.

Second, search theory predicts that some workers enter unemployment voluntarily as part of a rational search procedure. We would expect that the individuals most likely to choose voluntary unemployment will be those who receive compensation for foregone earnings and transactions costs. The people most likely to fit this description will be those with high replacement ratios because of large families and so on. However, as previously noted, quits into unemployment except by young people are relatively rare. Many of them are unpremeditated (due to rows with colleagues for example) where the size of RR is of little significance. It is difficult to identify any specific characteristics of such quitters. One other important group for whom separations from jobs into unemployment may be important is the chronically sick. Generally such workers leave jobs to go initially into inactivity. But they may subsequently move frequently between inactivity, unemployment and jobs, depending on their physical condition, the state of the job market and the regulations governing state assistance. Their total annual experience of unemployment may therefore be significant, even if the duration of single spells is not.

Human capital theory provides a number of predictions on the distribution of flows into unemployment. First, one would expect the highest proportion of spells to be incurred by workers possessing the least specific skills. Most workers enter unemployment involuntarily, having been discharged because of falling demand. Chapter 8 would lead us to expect that the workers to be dismissed will be those least expensive to replace when demand recovers, while those with significant specific human capital will be hoarded. Skilled labour imposes greater recruitment costs. This implies that unskilled and part-time labour will suffer most, as will short tenured workers who, *ceteris paribus*, will have had little time to acquire specific human capital. This provides an additional reason for anticipating that a disproportionate number of unemployment spells will involve young people, though in this case involuntarily.

Because many of those becoming unemployed possess little human capital they have low wages and high replacement ratios. It follows that a correlation will be observed between high RR levels and the incidence of flows into unemployment, but this reflects association rather than causation.

Our earlier theorising predicts that certain groups in society will suffer labour market discrimination. *Ceteris paribus*, they will be the most likely sections of the workforce to suffer when firms shed labour. To the extent that they are also crowded into industries and occupations in decline or subject to extreme demand variability, they will experience even more problems in holding on to employment. We would thus expect female and minority group workers to constitute relatively more of the annual spells of unemployment than native male workers, for example.

An analysis of non-competitive forces in the labour market would predict the following about the distribution of unemployment. First, to the extent that the productivity of workers declines with age, it will sometimes decline below the union agreed wage and older workers will thus be the first to be discharged. Redundancy payments legislation may reinforce this. Second, unstructured labour markets offer few avenues for internal promotion, and are subject to the greatest variability of demand. We would anticipate therefore that workers in sectors where internal labour markets are unstructured will experience a disproportionate number of unemployment spells in any specified period.

The evidence from surveys is that a totally disproportionate number of spells of unemployment involve the young, the old, the unskilled, the sick and B group workers, as predicted. There is little evidence for such groups that unemployment ultimately improves their financial status, or that unemployment helps in the transition between jobs. Particularly in respect of the unskilled involuntarily unemployed, it appears therefore that inflows could usefully be reduced by expanding demand to reduce redundancies and generating sufficient alternative jobs to ease job search. At any employment level policies to rectify demand imbalances and increase skills, and policies of special assistance to the disadvantaged groups, will be valuable and effective.

If certain groups of workers experience more spells of unemployment than others in any one period, the question arises whether particular workers experience *recurrent unemployment* throughout their working lives. The existence of such a group would be of significance: first, because they and society at large could not be gaining much in the way of better information, job advancement and thus productivity from such severe job instability; second, because they must be suffering financially given that their total experience of unemployment must be significant even if each spell is short, and also given that they have little chance of fulfilling the qualifications for continued full entitlement to state assistance; third, because of the implications of recurrent unemployment for future labour market success. It is a worrying possibility that unemployment begets unemployment and that recurrent unemployment goes hand in hand with recurrent periods of inactivity leading to progressively worsening market experiences. The evidence suggests that such a group does exist and that most of them are young and/or unskilled and/or sick.

## UNEMPLOYMENT DURATION

Completed spells of unemployment vary considerably in length; some last only a day whereas others last for years. The frequency distribution of spells across durations is positively skewed, but there are considerable numbers of spells, and thus people, in the right hand tail. One way to investigate the distribution of duration is to look at the characteristics of people whose spells have lasted more than 12 months. There are several reasons for anticipating that these people will not be a representative cross-section of the working population or even, indeed, of the unemployed: the probability of leaving unemployment depends upon particular characteristics of the unemployed worker.

Search theory would predict the following. First, in geographical areas where economic activity is concentrated, like conurbations, workers will be prepared to search longer but their probable underestimation of demand will produce higher probabilities of leaving unemployment. One would thus expect rural workers to be overrepresented in the long duration group. Second, the probability of leaving unemployment will be lower for those workers with higher replacement ratios; generally workers with large families and/or low incomes in work. Third, unemployed workers from households containing other working members have lower costs of inactivity and search than those with inactive dependents and expenditure commitments. One would anticipate on this argument, therefore, that unmarried men will be more strongly represented amongst the long duration unemployed than married men, and men with working wives more than men with inactive wives. Fourth, the probability of leaving will be lower for those with few qualifications since firms use qualifications as signals in recruitment. Fifth, workers with previous experience of unemployment will have lower current probabilities of leaving unemployment as firms use employment stability as a signal. Sixth, workers living in areas where the predominant industries are declining may have lower reservation wages but the lack of job openings and the strong competition for them means longer duration.

The first prediction from human capital theory is that at any skill level workers with more specific human capital will have lower probabilities of leaving unemployment than others. Such workers will set a higher reservation wage than the market justifies. Workers with general skills have shorter durations because their skills are readily marketable. Unskilled workers are also more attractive to firms since they impose lower recruitment, severance and training costs. Both arguments suggest duration increases with skills. But on the other hand, the probability of leaving unemployment for skilled workers will be higher to the extent that they can if necessary do unskilled jobs. Furthermore, the unskilled are less geographically mobile, and have less wealth out of which to finance search and training. They are relatively easily replaced by capital, whereas skilled labour and capital are complements.

Older workers will have low probabilities of leaving unemployment. Neither firms nor the workers themselves are able to recoup the costs of search and training required to match such workers to the available jobs. Skills will have deteriorated or become obsolete and retraining will be expensive. Yet the length of time over which the costs can be recouped is short. It is often impossible to accommodate lower productivity by paying a lower wage (even if the workers themselves would accept this) because of union or technological constraints. Any record of sickness or disability jeopardises the worker's chances of leaving unemployment because it reduces expected returns to the firm, as it shortens the expected benefits stream or reduces the benefit levels. For the same reason women of child-bearing age will be less likely to leave unemployment than other women workers.

Duration will also be affected by labour market discrimination and non-competitive behaviour. Any B group worker will find getting offers more difficult than the average unemployed worker. Trade union or state activities to raise wages in certain sectors of the labour market might extend duration for the appropriate categories of labour as workers queue for entry.

The available evidence shows that those employed for more than 12 months duration are a large group and amongst them at any point in time there will be a disproportionate number of older, unskilled, sick people. Since they appear to get almost no job offers their duration is largely involuntary and without obvious benefit to the economy. The cost to the individuals themselves, however, is large. State payments in general decline with duration. Their savings have been exhausted and their confidence damaged.

Demand variations do appear to affect the size of the group. At low levels of unemployment, specific policies to help the long-term unemployed would be efficient as well as equitable. It is unlikely, given their inferior position in employment, that their assisted re-entry would have marked displacement effects or induce wage inflation.

Empirical evidence indicates that single men are more likely to enter unemployment than married men with no children and have longer durations. Both the frequency and the duration of unemployment increase for married men with number of children, even when the replacement ratio is taken into account. The explanation for increased duration may be that having more children makes men more immobile, but increased immobility cannot account for the higher frequency of unemployment for this group.

Long-term and recurrent unemployment are types of structural unemployment, but they appear in a form not recognised explicitly in the IU model: as particular individuals whose personal characteristics do not equip them to fill the available jobs. A disturbing ramification of this is that there may be a group of workers who suffer both recurrent and long-term unemployment through their working lives, each experience of unemployment leading inexorably to the next and worse experience. Do many of the young people job sampling on entering the labour market later become the recurrent or long-term unemployed? How important are early labour market experiences? Even more important, how many of those experiencing severe unemployment now come from families with a history of unemployment? Whilst these questions are not empirically resolved, it is clear that, given the strong association between unemployment and low skills and wages, unemployment is primarily a working class experience. Both the frequency and duration of unemployment are observed to be vastly higher for the lowest social groups. Given that class is strongly hereditary it would be very surprising if unemployment were not. The long-term and recurrent unemployed will be the most disadvantaged of the working class. The unemployment rate in one study for a given year increased from 1–3 per cent for the upper and middle classes to 14–19 per cent for workers in the lowest class. The incidence and duration of unemployment for the latter group are also very sensitive to movements in business activity.

## Further Reading

CHAPTER 10: UNEMPLOYMENT

A. B. Atkinson and J. S. Flemming, 'Unemployment, social security and incentives', *Midland Bank Review* (Autumn 1978).
D. Benjamin and L. Kochin, 'Searching for an explanation of unemployment in interwar Britain', *Journal of Political Economy*, Vol. 87, (June 1979).
J. Creedy, *The Economics of Unemployment in Great Britain* (London: Butterworth, 1981).
B. Hansen, 'Excess demand, unemployment vacancies and wages', *Quarterly Journal of Economics*, Vol. 84 (February 1970).
C. Holt, 'Job search, Phillips wage relation and union influence: theory and evidence', in E. S. Phelps (ed.), *Microeconomic Foundations of Employment and Inflation* (New York: Norton, 1970).
D. Maki and Z. Spindler, 'The effect of unemployment compensation on the rate of unemployment in Great Britain', *Oxford Economic Papers*, Vol. 27 (November 1975).
S. Nickell, 'The effect of unemployment and related benefits on the duration of unemployment', *Economic Journal*, Vol. 89 (March 1979).
S. Nickell, 'A picture of male unemployment in Britain', *Economic Journal*, Vol. 90 (December 1980).

# 11

# Inflation and the labour market

An economy experiencing continuously, rapidly rising prices could suffer both important inefficiencies arising from market distortions and significant welfare losses. Because labour market mechanisms are central to the process of inflation, a discussion of the causes, nature and consequences of inflation is a natural part of any analysis of how the labour market functions. Such a discussion focuses, in particular, upon the relationship between price changes and demand conditions, so inevitably the discussion of this chapter will overlap with the discussion of unemployment in the previous chapter.

We examine two questions. First, and principally, what role does the labour market play in causing inflation? Second, what effects does inflation have upon welfare and upon the efficiency with which labour markets allocate resources? In Section 11.1 we analyse inflation within the involuntary unemployment model and in Section 11.2 we consider the voluntary unemployment model. In Section 11.3 we investigate a cost-push approach.

## 11.1   Inflation in the involuntary unemployment model

Consider, as in Section 10.2, an economy made up of a large number of firms and labour markets. Within each labour market workers supply labour on the basis of nominal wages, $W$, and expected prices, $P^e$. Firms demand labour on the basis of real wages, $W/P$. Money wage levels once established are rigid downwards. Figure 11.1 shows the position in a representative labour market $i$, initially in equilibrium at $Q$ with expected prices $P_1^e$ equal to prices $P_1$, zero unemployment, no price or wage changes. The money wage becomes the rigid wage $W_1$ with the labour supply curve $XQY$.

If now exogenous investment falls, product demand declines and prices will fall to $P_2$. The labour demand curve shifts to the left. The labour supply curve shifts to the right with $P_2^e$, assuming workers anticipate some price reaction. Unemployment $U_2 = JF$ arises. $P$ and $P^e$ continue to fall until the excess demand in product markets is eliminated, say at $P_3$ and $P_3^e$. Unemployment is then $U_3$. We assume the fall in demand is such that every firm in the economy experiences excess labour supply.

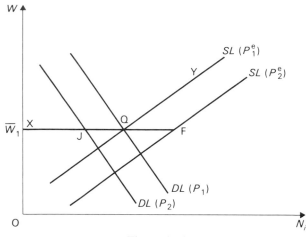

**Figure 11.1**

For sub-market $i$ we can write:

$$U_i = (DL - SL)_i = D(\bar{W}_1/P_3, q)_i - S(\bar{W}_1/P_3^e)_i + V_i \quad (11.1)$$

where $q$ is the marginal physical product of labour and $V$ records the vacancies arising out of intra- and inter-market frictions. At the new equilibrium wages are still $\bar{W}_1$. In time labour supply shifts to $SL(P_3^e)$ after which no further wage or price changes take place.

We now recognise explicitly that the principal source of the rigid wage $\bar{W}_1$ is trade union activity. Since unions react to upward price movements the minimum wage will respond to any government intervention.

Suppose the government injects additional demand into the economy so that product prices increase to $P_4$. Prices for firm $j$ in sub-market $i$ will increase according to $i$'s share in the demand expansion and $j$'s importance to market $i$. In Figure 11.2, depending on the distribution of total demand, the demand curve of firm $j$ moves to the right to $DL(P_4)$, labour supply shifts to the left to $SL(P_4^e)$. The change $P_4 - P_3 = \Delta P^G$ is less than $P_4^e - P_3^e = \Delta P^e$ so we are assuming that $\lambda = \Delta P^e/\Delta P^G$ is less than one. In excess supply firms like $j$ the average wage will rise as unions try to protect their real wage by increasing the minimum wage. They do so on the basis of imperfect price expectations, so $\Delta \bar{W}_0 = \alpha \lambda \Delta P^G$, where $\alpha$ indicates the bargaining strength of workers. In other firms the new demand curve will intersect the supply curve close to N on the left or the right of N. Wages will rise as a result as those firms experience difficulty in filling vacancies. Over all firms the average wage increase is $\Delta W = \theta \Delta P^G$. The minimum

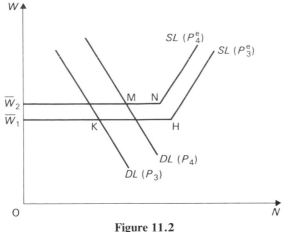

**Figure 11.2**

wage, which we can now interpret as that for the whole economy, moves up to $\bar{W}_2$. As long as $\theta < 1$ the level of total unemployment will generally fall: to $U_4 = MN$. The overall level of vacancies will rise. Thus for the whole economy we have:

$$\Delta U = (U_4 - U_3) = U(\Delta P^G, \lambda, \Delta q, \Delta W, DD) + \Delta V \quad (11.2)$$

where $DD$ captures the distribution of demand across firms.

The rise in wages will itself, by increasing costs, induce a further price increase. But then further wage reactions occur. Let us assume that L represents the position of the economy after the price and wage spiral has worked itself out; as in Figure 11.3 the spiral is assumed to converge. So let us now interpret $\Delta W$ in equation (11.2) as the sum of all wage reactions.

Once L is reached with $P_L$ and $U_L$, if demand is then held constant by the government at the new higher level, in time, because $P^e = P_L$, the labour supply curve would shift further to the left, to $SL(P_L)$, and the minimum wage would rise to re-establish the previous real wage level. Consequently unemployment would rise back towards $U_3$. Anticipating this, and to maintain unemployment at $U_L$, the government raises demand again, injecting a further price increase $\Delta P^G$ and inducing a further immediate wage response of $\theta\Delta P^G$ and a repeat of the wage–price spiral. Having achieved $U_L$, henceforth the government must expand demand at a steady rate, with a consequent steady rate of inflation.

Since in Chapter 10 we established the existence of a relationship between $U$ and $V$ (taking into account $\Delta W$) through the UV curve,

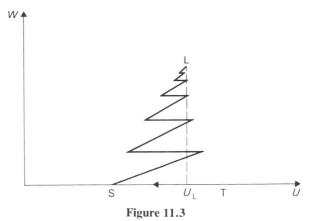

**Figure 11.3**

equation (11.2) becomes:

$$\Delta U = V(\Delta P^G, \lambda, \Delta q, DD, \Delta W) \tag{11.3}$$

so

$$U_t = V(\Delta P_t^G, \lambda, \Delta q_t, DD, \Delta W_t, U_{t-1}) \tag{11.4}$$

Equation (11.4) is a dynamic relationship for unemployment. It is in fact the same relationship as equation (10.11) in Chapter 10, though here we focus on its wage and price variables rather than upon adjustment costs. Given that the final change in prices, $\Delta P$, is the initial price increase associated with the government's intervention plus the sum total of all the consequent price effects from the induced wage increase, we have:

$$\Delta P = \Delta P^G + \Delta P(\Delta W) \tag{11.5}$$

The cumulative wage change through the spiral depends upon the minimum wage adjustments in excess supply firms and the wage adjustments in excess demand firms. The latter depends upon the number of vacancies and the relative importance of those firms in total employment:

$$\Delta W = (\Delta P^G, \alpha, \lambda, \beta, DD, V, \Delta q) \tag{11.6}$$

where $\beta$ shows the effect of a change in wages upon firm's prices. Equation (11.4) becomes:

$$U_t = Z(\Delta P_t, \alpha, \lambda, \beta, \Delta q_t, DD, U_{t-1}) \tag{11.7}$$

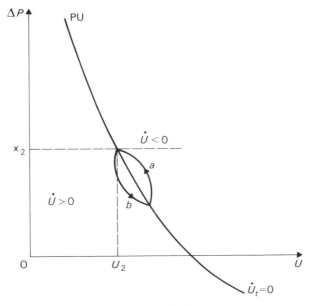

**Figure 11.4**

Figure 11.4 shows the set of curves relating $U_t$ and $\Delta P_t$ for given values of $\Delta q_t$, etc., each curve representing a different value of $U_{t-1}$. Equilibrium requires that $U_t = U_{t-1}$ or $\dot{U}_t = 0$, so $\dot{\text{P}}\text{U}$ represents the locus for equilibrium values of $U$ and $\Delta P$. The $\dot{\text{P}}\text{U}$ curve is downward sloping left to right. Its slope depends upon $\alpha$, $\beta$, and $\lambda$.

Consider the nature of this model further. First, though we have set it up with unemployment as the key variable, we can of course rewrite it as:

$$\Delta P = Z'(U_t, \alpha, \lambda, \beta, \Delta q_t, DD) \qquad (11.8)$$

This represents a reduced form of our model in which part of $\Delta P$ is exogenously determined and part the outcome of an interactive process between wages and prices in the labour market.

Second, the model describes a demand-pull inflationary process. An expansion of nominal demand by the government generates an increase in output and in prices and money wages. The government continues to expand demand as long as there is deemed to be excess supply of labour. In this model the government has decided upon an activist policy to reduce unemployment because the economic processes underlying Figure 11.1 fail to clear the labour market. Since the product market is in equilibrium there are no warranted price increases to lower the real wage, so only by relaxing the money wage minimum constraint, $\bar{W}$, can employment be increased. The government is drawn to an activist policy by public concern about the consequences of unemployment and awareness that money wage reductions are unlikely to be forthcoming.

Third, *ceteris paribus*, for any given target unemployment, $U^*$, inflation will generally be lower the higher the growth of labour productivity. Higher productivity makes for a higher demand for labour, offsetting the effects of any minimum wage increases. On the other hand, if productivity increases are concentrated in tight labour markets, higher productivity increases the pressure on wages because vacancies arise faster than they otherwise would.

Fourth, once wages begin to rise in tight markets, the higher the level of vacancies in those markets the greater the size of the wage adjustments. In any firm there is a non-linear relationship between $\Delta W$ and $V$; the more vacancies there are (and remember unemployment will simultaneously be falling) the more eager will the firm be to bid up wages in order to hold on to its existing labour force and to encourage applications. The speed of wage increases, through a whole series of negotiations with individual workers, increases as $V$ increases. The lower the overall level of unemployment the more tight markets there will be and the greater will be the upwards wage adjustments required to fill job openings. Equation (11.6) will be non-linear between $\Delta W$ and $V$ and so will equation (11.8) between $\Delta P$ and $U$. In Figure 11.4 the $\dot{P}U$ curve will be more steeply sloped the lower $U_t$; i.e. convex to the origin. Following from the above point, if for any target level of $U_t$ each period's demand injection can be shifted towards labour markets where firms are not facing severe recruitment problems, $\Delta P$ can be smaller. In general therefore, evening out the distribution of demand through the economy will reduce inflation. It follows from Chapter 10 and equation (10.11) that reduced friction and adjustment costs will, like a more even distribution of demand, shift the $\dot{P}U$ curve in towards the origin.

Fifth, the higher is $\lambda$ the steeper is the $\dot{P}U$ curve. Any government injection then brings a stronger minimum wage reaction and wage/price interaction. Each period's price change to maintain $U^*$ must be higher. The higher are $\beta$ and $\alpha$ the more effect the wage repercussions of a given government action have upon prices, and the less resistance there is to the unions efforts to maintain their real wage. The $\dot{P}U$ curve is steeper and $U^*$ is associated with a higher rate of inflation.

Sixth, a movement from a point on the $\dot{P}U$ curve to a higher point on the same curve because of a demand increase does not take place along the $\dot{P}U$ curve itself. In Figure 11.4 for any rate of inflation, say $x_2$, any value of $U$ to the right of $U_2$, the value associated with $x_2$, is 'too large' and a fall in $U$ is warranted. Conversely for points to the left of $U_2$: increases in $U$ are warranted. As long as our postulated adjustment processes are well behaved, a move from one equilibrium inflation/unemployment combination to another following a demand increase will involve an orderly progress through the $\dot{U} < 0$ disequilibrium sector: say along the path a. For a subsequent demand contraction the pattern followed might be b, so during the course of the business cycle anti-clockwise loops about the equilibrium $\dot{P}U$ curve will be observed.

Seventh, any exogenous price increase, for example a rise in import prices, would act immediately on the union wage and on labour supply, but there would be no positive effect upon labour demand. The spiral in wages and prices would then be associated with rising unemployment, as in Figure 11.5. In trying to maintain its unemployment target, therefore, the government has to increase demand sufficiently to cover the unemployment consequences of exogenous price increases. The additional element to $\Delta P^G$ will itself have an interactive effect on wages and prices. There is every reason to believe therefore that, *ceteris paribus*, higher prices from outside the economy will have a compound effect upon the inflation rate required to maintain $U^*$, as long as the higher import prices last. The $\dot{P}U$ curve shifts outwards and the government may opt for a higher $U$, higher $\dot{P}$ combination.

What role, if any, might be played by a prices and incomes policy (PIP) in this model? Price controls would make it impossible to achieve the unemployment target. Price increases are central to reaching and then maintaining the target $U^*$. Wage control will impede those firms with severe difficulty filling job openings, unless special arrangements are made to cover such circumstances. There would be some loss for their customers. However, wage controls will

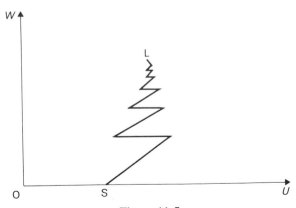

**Figure 11.5**

clearly prevent the minimum wage rising in excess supply areas when the government injects expenditures. A small rate of price increase is therefore required to maintain any unemployment target. Wage restraint has the effect of making the $\dot{P}U$ curve flatter and shifting it inwards. However, if it fails to alter any of the parameters of the model, its effects last only as long as the policy lasts. The policy must permanently reduce $\alpha$ and/or reduce $\lambda$ otherwise workers will subsequently act to restore the previous level of $\Delta W$ and thus $\Delta P$.

Though the long-term role for a PIP is limited, it may serve the important short-term function of getting the economy through a difficult period of slow growth, low demand or rising import prices. However, the central policy implication of the model is that the rate of inflation is determined entirely by the government's demand policy. By operating a flexible exchange rate the government can maintain any domestic unemployment target on the $\dot{P}U$ curve. The exchange rate offsets the effects of different inflation rates on trade balances. Rapid and rising inflation reflects deliberate government policy to keep unemployment low. To bring inflation down the government has only to reduce effective demand and face the cost of an inevitably higher level of unemployment.

Central to the approach so far is the assumption that the increase in wages induced by the demand expansion does not offset the price effects upon labour demand. It is $\Delta W < \Delta P$ that is absolutely essential to producing the trade-off between $\dot{P}$ and $U$ in Figure 11.4 and thus the menu for policy choice. But suppose the government holds on to a given level of $U$ and $\dot{P}$ for any length of time; surely workers will respond to this and expectations will adjust?

Let us imagine that both $\alpha$ and $\beta$ are unity so that the slope of the $\dot{P}U$ curve depends only upon $\lambda$. Let us assume that price expectations are formed on the basis of some distributed lag function of past price changes as:

$$\dot{P}_t^e = a + b\dot{P}_{t-1} + c\dot{P}_{t-2} + d\dot{P}_{t-3} \qquad (11.9)$$

where the weights decline as the lag increases. The sum of the weights if $\dot{P}$ remains constant through time gives

$$\dot{P}_t^e = \lambda\dot{P}_{t-1}$$

where $\lambda < 1$. So:

$$\dot{W}_t = \lambda\dot{P}_{t-1} \qquad (11.10)$$

This allows us to draw up a set of $\dot{P}U$ curves, each one relating to a different value of $\dot{P}_{t-1}$. In Figure 11.6 the economy is initially at point

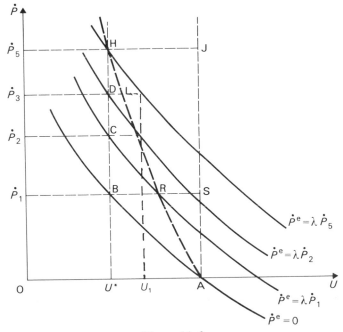

**Figure 11.6**

A (point Q in Figure 11.1). With the government's injection of demand, if the target is $U^*$, we move to B along the curve for price expectations based upon zero past inflation. After several periods of inflation $\dot{P}_1$ the economy now operates along the curve $\dot{W} = \lambda \dot{P}_1$, so to maintain $U^*$ the government has to raise its demand injections to take the economy to point C. Again after some period of inflation $\dot{P}_2$ the economy has drifted away from $U^*$ so the government must increase its demand intervention once again, taking the economy to D. The process will continue with the actual and expected rates of inflation moving steadily closer together but only at the expense of higher rates of inflation. At some point such as H expected and actual rates of inflation will be constant. $\dot{W}_t = \lambda \dot{P}_{t-1} = \lambda \dot{P}_t$ and unemployment remains at $U^*$. For different values of $U^*$ we can trace out a locus of equilibrium points like H. This locus is drawn in Figure 11.4, so we can now identify that as the long-run $\dot{P}U$ curve to distinguish it from the family of short-run $\dot{P}U$ curves in Figure 11.6.

The policy implication of this analysis is that reducing demand will reduce inflation. But to reduce inflation from $\dot{P}_5$ to $\dot{P}_3$ in Figure 11.6 unemployment must rise to $U_1$ before expectations adjust and bargaining processes take the economy to L. A PIP may have an important part to play in speeding up this transition given the rigidities in the bargaining structure under conditions of contraction. Permanent indexation of wages to prices would, in this model, make it impossible for the government to achieve $U^*$ but, used in conjunction with a PIP, it might assist the transition to a lower inflation rate.

But what happens if the economy were to come to rest at H? Surely workers, realising that they were continually underestimating the rate of inflation through the expectations formation mechanism in equation (11.9), would adjust the coefficients of their lag function or reformulate that function so that $\lambda$ approaches unity. With several periods of inflation $\dot{P}_5$ the obvious strategy would be to use $\dot{P}_5$ as the guide to future inflation. In either case the effect will be to shift the economy from H towards J with $\lambda = 1$. The government has no option then, if it wants to maintain $U^*$, but to generate accelerating inflation. No point on the vertical line above $U^*$ is stable for any length of time.

The implication of this analysis is that though $\lambda < 1$ in theory generates a sloping $\dot{P}U$ relationship, it is unlikely that faulty price expectations can in practice justify the existence of a $\dot{P}U$ policy trade-off. This is not to say that $\lambda$ will equal unity; there are good reasons for thinking it will not. First, despite the government's attempts to hold $U^*$, in practice exogenous events will cause the level of $U$ and therefore of $\dot{P}$ to vary considerably, which will make it difficult for unions to anticipate inflation correctly. Second, the government will never be able to hold the economy at a point like H because, even with no exogenous shocks and a constant increase in government expenditures, the distribution of demand across markets will be continuously changing. This means that $\dot{W}$ in excess demand markets will vary; so therefore will $\dot{W}$ overall and thereby endogenous $\dot{P}$ and $U$. So the economy operates around not at H. Third, the unemployment target will not be constant through time, given that the government is trading off more than two policy objectives and that governments change.

The economy will describe a function something like the long-run $\dot{P}U$ curve, but the policy use of the function does not depend on $\lambda$ being less than one. $\dot{W} < \dot{P}$ need not be due to faulty expectations on the part of workers. In deriving Figure 11.6 we constrained both $\alpha$ and $\beta$ to be unity. Both influence the slope of the $\dot{P}U$ curve. The closer is $\alpha$ to zero (the greater firms' resistance to wage claims), the less reason there is to expect the economy to drift away from the target unemployment level once the government has established inflation at the level defined by the long-run $\dot{P}U$ curve, whatever the value of $\lambda$. $\dot{W}$ will be less than $\dot{P}$ for several reasons. First, there are institutional factors impinging upon $\dot{W}$ that restrict adjustment to $\dot{P}$

and to excess demand: the infrequency of wage negotiations; unions' reluctance to disturb differentials; the transactions costs to firms of altering wages, especially if the change is not to be permanent. Second, the unions' success in raising money wages in markets without high vacancy levels will depend upon the level of competition faced by firms. We shall have cause to return to this important issue in Section 11.3, but as long as $\alpha < 1$ the policy choice implicit in Figure 11.4 exists.

Workers are passive agents in this scenario: they simply react to the government's actions. But the size of their response, in the form of wage claims, to inflation is extremely significant. We have noted that $\Delta W$ will be very sensitive to wage changes in excess demand areas. But suppose that wages in each market are determined in part according to established relativities, as discussed in Chapter 5. Then, as demand is raised, the wage in each excess demand area will pull up wages in certain excess supply areas and in some areas of lower excess demand.

Let us pursue this line of argument further, by dividing the change in money wages in any market $i$ into two components: a disequilibrium component, due to excess demand, and an equilibrium component, due to attempts to maintain established differentials. At almost any conceivable level of $U^*$, *even if demand is held constant*, the average wage rate across disequilibrium components will rise. This is because the distribution of constant demand is continually changing; in each period new sectors experience the vacancies, hiring difficulties and wage increases whilst wages in the sectors now experiencing excess supply are unlikely to fall. Prices in consequence rise continually. Because wages are non-linearly related to vacancies the average wage increase must be larger if demand is continually focused on a small number of (different) areas.

Each group of workers will simultaneously respond to price changes and to wage changes elsewhere through established relativities. Depending on the set of differentials that describes the wage structure, average wages will go up by an amount determined by the structure of equilibrium wage increases. In the next period wage and prices rise again. Unemployment will rise, and to prevent this the government must raise the level of money income. To preserve the ṖU trade-off we must assume therefore that at each level of unemployment there is some rate of demand expansion and of inflation that over the whole economy keep the system in balance so that the wage structure is preserved, there is no tendency for the wage–price interaction to explode or for unemployment to change, and $\dot{W}_t = \dot{W}_{t-1}$.

In this model the economy has an inherent inflationary bias at virtually any level of unemployment. We have assumed, however, that stochastic macro-equilibrium can be achieved. This is probable at high unemployment levels with few excess demand areas and relatively little excess demand. But at lower levels there are many excess demand markets each facing significant wage pressure. Given non-linearity in wage responses and the interaction between equilibrium and disequilibrium wage components the $\dot{P}U$ curve is likely to look like II rather than I in Figure 11.7. At very low levels of unemployment such are the interactions between excess demand elements and reference bargaining that the wage and price changes are never stabilised and the wage–price spiral continues indefinitely. The government is forced to enter continually higher demand injections. The $\dot{P}U$ curve becomes vertical. Whilst at some levels of unemployment the $\dot{P}U$ curve is downward sloping, we should note that stochastic equilibrium is very sensitive to alterations in the degree of demand imbalance and in productivity growth across different sectors and of course to any changes in established wage relativities.

The critical issue from this analysis is an empirical one: at what level of unemployment does the $\dot{P}U$ curve become vertical? If it is a very low level the area of choice for governments remains large. In this model the importance of wage rigidities is stressed, as are governments' desires to achieve low unemployment levels by activist policies. Price expectations are, however, ignored with unions concerned for relative wages rather than absolute real wages. A PIP has an even stronger role to play in this analysis than previously. Wage guidelines may be very useful if they influence the standards used by workers in relativity bargaining, in time 'talking them down'. Since all wage claims contain elements of imitation of wages in excess demand areas there is potential for some kind of interactive bidding up or

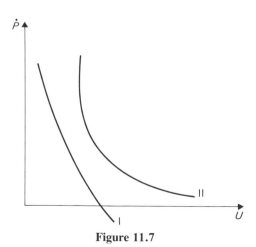

**Figure 11.7**

down. But of·course there are limits to this if the guidelines are patently inconsistent with observed wage changes in excess demand areas. The analysis also suggests the possibility of reducing inflation by making markets more responsive to excess supply, and by evening out demand.

## 11.2 Inflation in the voluntary unemployment model

In the VU model wages are set in real terms. Only in the short run is inflation unanticipated and unemployment below the natural level $U^N$. In Figure 11.8 therefore the economy initially operates at A (which corresponds to point A in Figure 10.12). A government-inspired increase in demand initially shifts the economy to B along the short-run $\dot{P}U$ curve for $\dot{P}_t^e = \dot{P}_{t-1} = 0$ to achieve the target unemployment level $U^*$. The result of this inevitably is to shift the short-run $\dot{P}U$ curve to $\dot{W} = \dot{P}_1$. (The model assumes explicitly that $\alpha = \beta = \lambda = 1$.) To maintain $U^*$ the government must increase the rate of inflation to $\dot{P}_2$ at L. But in time the short-run curve shifts to $\dot{W} = \dot{P}_2$ so a further increase in the level of inflation is required, to $\dot{P}_3$ at N. The long-run $\dot{P}U$ trade-off is thus vertical at $U^N$ for it is only at points like T, K and M that $\dot{P}$ is constant.

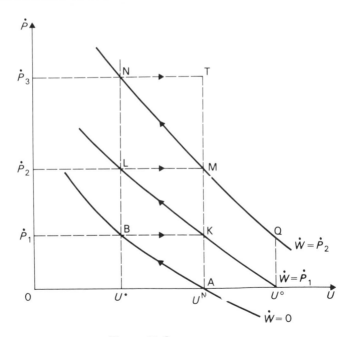

**Figure 11.8**

The movement from B to K arises because, as in Figure 10.12, the labour supply curve shifts to the same degree as the demand curve, so competitive forces on firms produce an equal money wage increase. Alternatively one might argue that unions bargain in real terms and simply maintain their current real wage by adjusting their wage demand to compensate fully for price increases, which they anticipate correctly. But wage and price changes diverge only whilst and to the extent that $\dot{P}^c < \dot{P}$. Inflation arises from government activist policies; inflation is a demand-pull phenomenon; unions are again basically passive agents in the process.

Why do governments continue to pursue such obviously unsatisfactory policies? One explanation might be that they simply do not accept this interpretation of the way the economy works. Alternatively it could be that though they recognise and accept the level of unemployment $U^N$ as necessary they have an over-optimistic view of its precise value. One might also explain government behaviour in terms of continued pressure from the population at large to increase the supply of government services and interventions in the economy which, because they require additional borrowing, have multiple effects upon total money demand.

The analysis suggests that inflation can be remedied by a policy of demand contraction. Starting at M with $\dot{P}_2$, $\dot{P}^c = \dot{P}_2$, if the government reduces the rate of increase of demand and thus prices to $\dot{P}_1$ unemployment will rise to $U^0$ but in holding the economy at Q the short run $\dot{P}U$ curve will eventually shift to $\dot{W} = \dot{P}_1$ and the economy to K. In principle, therefore, by demand management the government, at the expense of a period of unemployment, can reach point T and zero inflation. The level of unemployment required depends upon the slope of the short-run $\dot{P}U$ curves, which in this model depends in turn upon the elasticities of labour demand and supply. The duration of unemployment $U^0$ depends upon how long it takes price expectations to adjust downwards, which may be longer than they take to adjust upwards.

There is no role in this model for employers' resistance, so $\alpha = 1$. Wage settlement simply reflects workers' price expectations: competitive forces see to that. The model can thus be written as:

$$\dot{W} = \dot{P}^c - u(U - U^Z) + \dot{q} = \dot{P}^c - u(U - U^N) + \dot{q} \qquad (11.11)$$

$$\dot{P} = \dot{W} - \dot{q} \qquad (11.12)$$

$$\dot{P} = \dot{P}^c - u(U - U^N) \quad \text{or} \quad (U - U^N) = V(\dot{P} - \dot{P}^c) \qquad (11.13)$$

Money wages simply respond to actual prices and productivity in the long run. But in the short run they vary with expected prices and the deviation of the unemployment level from the zero inflation unemployment level, $U^Z$, which in this competitive model is the natural rate $U^N$. Prices vary fully with wages and productivity, the mark-up, $\beta$, is equal to 1. Unemployment deviates from the natural rate only if expected prices are different from actual prices. In the long run, because $\dot{P} = \dot{P}^e$, $U$ must equal $U^N$.

The formation of expectations by workers is critical to the inflationary process. The VU model assumes that workers have developed an expectations adjustment mechanism such as:

$$(\dot{P}_t^e - \dot{P}_{t-1}^e) = \theta(\dot{P}_{t-1} - \dot{P}_{t-1}^e) \tag{11.14}$$

which gives:

$$\dot{W}_t = a + b\dot{P}_{t-1} + c\dot{P}_{t-2} + d\dot{P}_{t-3} \ldots \tag{11.15}$$

where the parameters on past prices decline with the lag, but sum to 1. When $\dot{P}$ is constant workers are assumed to learn quickly so that the economy moves quickly from B in Figure 11.6 not to R but to S, and similarly from H to J. The time this takes depends on $\theta$: in the VU model $\theta$ is large so the economy is effectively always operating in the long run. The difference between the IU and VU models of inflation can thus be presented as a difference of opinion over adjustment times: both see $\lambda$ eventually approaching unity, but the IU model regards the adjustment period as long enough to offer policy options. Any set of events that throws the economy away from the government's target will disturb the expectations adjustment process and thus the movement towards long-run equilibrium. The $\dot{P}U$ trade-off can still be used as a policy guide if the government can quickly identify the demand injection required to steer the economy on the current short-run $\dot{P}U$ relationship; i.e. if the government continuously has better information than workers.

In the VU model any form of PIP has little or no value. It is excess demand in the market which draws wages up: firms and unions operate in real wage terms. A PIP might slow down the adjustment of wages to higher demand but not for long, and in the process it will cause distortions in resource allocation. The only conceivable role for a PIP in maintaining $U^* < U^N$ arises if the government can thereby continually convince the unions that price rises will be less than the government knows and plans that they will be. In a world of exogenous shocks to the economy this might work for some time but, given that the government aims at a certain $U^*$ and $\dot{P}$, unions will soon come to distrust the PIP guidelines as a clue to future inflation and will turn to some other expectations formation mechanism. A PIP policy along with other state interventions, could so distort market functions that unemployment increases and the $\dot{P}U$ curve temporarily becomes positively sloped.

In the $VU$ model unemployment falls only temporarily whilst price changes are unanticipated. $U^*$ can be maintained only while unions reformulate their expectations. But if workers continually find that their reformulations prevent them from warding off real wage reductions, might they not turn to some alternative and quicker method of adjusting their price expectations? Might they not look beyond past price increases and use all potential sources of relevant information? Suppose all agents share a common and accurate view of how a given increase in government intervention affects the level of economic activity. In that case it would be irrational for workers to wait until actual price increases occur before adjusting their price expectations. They can avoid any erosion of their real wage by anticipating events and using the original demand expansion itself as the basis for expectations adjustments.

Suppose, for example, all agents know that the underlying long run relationship between inflation and the rate of growth of the money supply, $\dot{M}_t$, is:

$$\dot{P}_t = \dot{M}_t + e_t \qquad (11.16)$$

when $e_t$ is a random variable with zero mean for unpredictable demand shifts. Agents know that nominal demand expansions affect prices directly, and output only indirectly through changes in actual prices relative to expected prices: money is neutral. The rational expectation for inflation is then:

$$\dot{P}_t^c = \dot{M}_t^c \qquad (11.17)$$

Suppose that the growth of money demand is altered as:

$$\dot{M}_t = a_0 + a_1(U^N - U^*) + \xi_t \qquad (11.18)$$

where $U^N$ is the known level of unemployment for zero price changes and $\xi_t$ is a random error term with zero mean representing errors in money management. Each agent uses the government's past record to obtain estimates of $a_0$ and $a_1$ and to identify $U^*$. Given sufficient information $\hat{a}_0$ and $\hat{a}_1$ will be unbiased estimates so the part of $\dot{M}_t$ not predicted $(\dot{M}_t - \dot{M}_t^c)$ will be $\xi_t$. Thus

$$\dot{P}_t - \dot{P}_t^c = \dot{M}_t - \dot{M}_t^c + e_t \qquad (11.19)$$

$$= \xi_t + e_t$$

If agents use current money statistics in this way to formulate price expectations they will arrive at or be induced to arrive at the wrong expectations only by unforeseen changes, $\xi_t$. Equation (11.13) becomes:

$$U_t - U_t^N = V(e_t + \xi_t) \tag{11.20}$$

The government cannot bring about deviations from the natural rate, even temporarily, except by manipulating $\xi_t$ in a totally unpredictable way: something which is at odds with governments' natural inclinations and with achieving and maintaining desired levels of unemployment. There is then no such thing as a short-run PU relationship, only the vertical long-run curve, in this version of the VU model, and any form of activist policy by the government is totally ineffective.

Such an approach to expectations formation can be criticised in that it assumes that labour market agents have complete statistical information and knowledge of the structural relationships within the economy and the causation underlying them. This is a considerable assumption if those relationships are complex. Such an expectations approach subsumes in workers' behaviour that they recognise that everyone will follow the same approach and reach the same conclusions. The approach assumes that there is instantaneous reliable information on $U^*$ and $\dot{M}$ otherwise workers must formulate expectations about $M$ and the government will again have some room for reducing real wages.

Whilst the menu for choice to government disappears, inflation can at least be reduced relatively painlessly. Instead of having to raise unemployment above $U^N$ to lower price expectations the government merely has to announce and maintain appropriate long-term targets for $\dot{M}_t$ in order to reduce expected and thereby actual price changes.

In principle the rational expectations approach is totally destructive of *any* government initiative to guide the economy. In the IU model the equivalent relationship to equation (11.16) is rather more complex given that fiscal policy has a role to play in altering income. But, in principle, if the unions know that relationship and know the mechanisms by which monetary and fiscal policies are governed, then they can always fully anticipate inflation and generate the vertical long-run PU curve. The point about equations (11.16) and (11.18) is that they represent a very clear cut view of the economy with consequently restricted data demands for unions. But simplicity is no substitute for accuracy. The analysis continues to assume of course that $\dot{W}$ deviates from $\dot{P}$ only because of faulty expectations.

In the VU model inflation is a wasteful product of ill-conceived government policy. The government should reduce demand and allow unemployment to rise towards $U^N$. This may cause increasing $\dot{P}$

and $U$ until expectations adjust, but monetary announcements and strict adherence to the deflation will speed the transition. The government should beware of policies which raise $U^N$ and impair market mechanisms. Indexation of wages to prices will ease the transition because it links wages to realised rather than anticipated inflation and it is the former which the government can directly affect. Indexation accelerates the fall in inflation by reducing the effects of past inflationary experience.

The principal reservations about the VU model, as noted in Chapter 10, concern, first, its strong underlying faith in the power of the competitive market economy which leads it to reject wage rigidities and the independent significance of trade unions. Second, we can now see that the model attaches little significance to bargaining as a determinant of wages: $\alpha$ and $\beta$ are assumed to be equal to unity. Bargaining simply produces the results that market forces would otherwise produce alone. Third, inflation is a demand-pull phenomenon so the VU model has some difficulty in explaining concurrent high inflation and increasing unemployment. Possible explanations are that the economy is adjusting towards $U^N$ so that inflation will fall in time, or that $U^N$ is rising because governments persist in high demand policies, but neither appears convincing. Fourth, the existence of a statistical correlation between money and prices is not inconsistent with either the IU or the cost-push model of inflation. Fifth, the cost of running the economy at unemployment levels above $U^N$ in order to reduce $\dot{P}$ may be a serious reduction in industrial performance, competitiveness, even social cohesion. The long-term costs of curing inflation by this method could outweigh the benefits. Sixth, the dismissal of incomes policies is unnecessary: a PIP could actually increase efficiency in resource allocation by loosening rigid relative prices and wages.

## 11.3   Inflation and cost-push pressures

Within the IU model there are several arguments which hint at the desirability of modelling cost-push inflation: a period of continuous price increase not instigated by an increase in the level of demand. First, in Section 10.1 we noted that an exogenously determined rise in the minimum wage $\bar{W}$ will produce both price increases and unemployment. Second, in Section 11.1 we noted the possibility of an interaction between prices and wages. Third, we recognised the importance of exogenously determined price changes. And finally we noted the effects of bargaining according to relativities. Let us now pursue the cost-push theme.

Consider the case of an economy with a single unionised labour

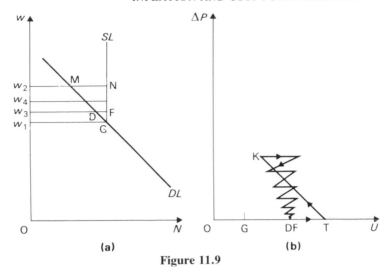

**Figure 11.9**

market wherein the minimum real wage is established as in Figure 11.9(a) at 'G. We draw the supply curve vertical, indicating that real wage increases do not increase labour supply because it is known that entry is prevented by union restrictive practices. Workers suffer neither money illusion nor incorrect price expectations. Assume now that the union deliberately attempts to increase the real wage above the equilibrium level $w_1$ at the expense of employment by way of a money wage claim $\Delta W_1$. Through the collective bargaining process the union is persuaded to accept $\alpha \Delta W_1$, where $\alpha$ is $< 1$. Unemployment of MN results with the real wage at $w_2$: we assume workers cannot or choose not to go elsewhere. Firms have some degree of monopoly power so they can pass some part of the wage increase on to consumers in the form of a price increase. Let us assume they can do this to the extent $\beta$ so that $\Delta P = \alpha \beta \Delta W_1$. The result is that the union will not have achieved the real wage increase it expected. Instead of $w_2$ it gets $w_3 = w_1 + \alpha(1-\beta)\Delta W_1$. If $\alpha > \beta$ the real wage is higher than the competitive level so that unemployment occurs; DF in Figure 11.9(a).

In the next period the union will make a money wage claim to compensate for the price increase, equal to $(\alpha\beta)\Delta W_1$. Bargaining will produce a settlement of $\alpha(\alpha\beta)\Delta W_1$ and result in a price increase of $\alpha\beta(\alpha\beta)\Delta W_1$. This process will continue through a series of rounds, the final result of which will be a real wage increase to

$$w_4 = w_1 + \frac{\alpha(1 - \beta)}{1 - \alpha\beta} \Delta W_1 = w_1 + \phi\Delta W_1$$

and consequent unemployment above DF but below MN. In Figure

11.9(b) the economy moves from G to T (where $U = MN$) to K and finally, after the period of wage and price changes is completed, to DF. Each round of bargaining allows the firm to persuade the union to temper its real wage claim a little further and the union to offset a little further the firm's ability to pass wage increases on into prices. The wage and price increases become steadily smaller at each round until at DF the economy operates with $\Delta P = 0$ and involuntary unemployment.

Consider the nature of this solution. First, if $\beta = 1$ then the union cannot make a real wage gain whereas if $\beta = 0$ it must achieve the real wage $w_2$ resulting in unemployment MN. The higher is $\alpha$ the greater the real wage gain for the union and the higher the final unemployment level. In the extreme case where $\alpha = 1$, whatever $\beta$, the union achieves its target wage change $\Delta w_1$. If $\beta$ falls with each period of bargaining the final real wage will be closer to $w_2$ than is $w_4$. In practice $\alpha$ and $\beta$ will be related since one would expect employers' resistance to union claims to stiffen the smaller is $\beta$. Second, firms may avoid the full employment consequences of the union's real wage gain by cutting profits, investment and research, thus allowing labour's share to increase and moving off their labour demand curves. Third, in practice $\Delta W_1$, the claim, and $\alpha$ will be related within the bargaining process so that it is $\alpha \Delta W_1$ which is determined. The union cannot increase $w_4$ by raising $\Delta W_1$ because $\alpha$ will fall. There is some optimal level for $\Delta W$ and $\alpha$ within the bargain. Hence we shall, for ease of exposition, model this process entirely through $\Delta W$, holding $\alpha$ constant.

One could imagine the process described here taking place as a series of separate bargains through time, in which case one would predict a period of declining rates of inflation following the union's intervention. We shall treat the process as stages of a single wage bargain, in which case there would be just one price adjustment $\Delta P_1$ equal to the sum of the changes in Figure 11.9(b).

Productivity changes can be introduced into the model as follows. Let us go back to the equilibrium at G and imagine that the union is not attempting to alter the level of unemployment. In the face of productivity change of $\Delta q$ the union submits a claim of $\Delta W_0 = \Delta q$. The result of collective bargaining is that the real wage will rise by $\phi \Delta W_0 = \Delta w_q$. If productivity continues to grow by $\Delta q$ the real wage will grow by $\Delta w_q$ per period. Such growth reflects the outcome of the basic bargain between labour and capital on the division of total product. It is a bargaining equilibrium real wage: the two sides are mutually reconciled to it. It will only change, assuming constant $\Delta q$, if one or other side succeeds in increasing its share. Otherwise both sides come to terms with the existing division, which persists through time. Unions still continue to claim $\Delta W_0$ but accept $\Delta w_q$: they do not increase the size of their money wage claim in the next period. $\Delta W_0$ is a form of protection, to which we must return later. The system is stable in that wage changes are constant in both nominal and real terms and $\Delta P = 0$, because $\Delta q$ covers $\phi \Delta W_0$. If now we reintroduce the union's attempt to raise its real wage faster than $\Delta W_q$ at the expense of employment, the money wage claim will be $\Delta W_1 + \Delta W_0$. The final real wage increase will be $\Delta w_5 = \phi[\Delta W_1 + \Delta q]$. If the union is reconciled to this in the following bargaining periods, assuming the union does not attempt to increase unemployment any further, negotiations will again take place simply around the distribution between the firm and workers of the productivity increase $\Delta q$. $w$ will again grow by $\Delta w_q$.

But suppose in some later period the union does attempt to increase its real wage further at the expense of employment: it submits a money wage claim $\Delta W_2 + \Delta W_0$. $\Delta W_2$ may be less than $\Delta W_1$ because the union has already made some real wage gain and is therefore operating with higher unemployment than previously. It also predicts a lower $\alpha$ this time round if it submitted $\Delta W_1 + \Delta q$, so it claims less than this. A similar wage–price interaction will take place as before, leading to a real wage gain of $\phi[\Delta W_2 + \Delta q]$. The rate of change of wages and prices, $\Delta P_2$, through the adjustment period will be smaller than in the first instance. Suppose in some later period still the union tries again to raise the real wage at the expense of employment. The real wage gain is smaller than in the second instance because $\Delta W_3$ is smaller than $\Delta W_2$. The cumulative adjustment of prices, $\Delta P_3$, and wages will also be smaller, as will the increase in unemployment. We can therefore set out a relationship as in Figure 11.10 between the cumulative change in prices and the final level of unemployment. The further away from the initial unemployment level $U_0$ the market is working the lower the change in prices and wages through the period of adjustment.

Suppose, however, that at some stage the government decides that it cannot allow the level of unemployment to rise any further. So when the union submits the wage claim $\Delta W_3 + \Delta q$ the government intervenes by raising the level of money demand in the economy. It does so sufficiently to enable the firm to pass wages on in prices so as to prevent any real wage gain over and above $\Delta w_q$. Prices must rise by $\Delta P_4 > \Delta P_3$. We assume that because the union has not achieved any part of its objective it will not be reconciled to $\Delta w_q$ and will resubmit its claim $\Delta W_3 + \Delta q$ in the next round. To maintain unemployment level $U_3$ the government will have to increase demand again, resulting in the same change in money wages and prices $\Delta P_4$; similarly in the next period. The government continually frustrates the union's plans to achieve its higher unemployment target, but at the expense of committing itself to continually increasing money wages and prices.

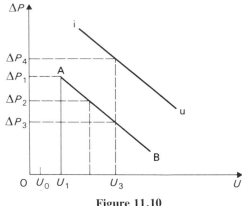

**Figure 11.10**

The lower the unemployment level the government finds intolerable, the earlier it must act against the union's intervention and the higher the level of inflation to which it becomes committed. The rate of inflation only falls if the union tempers its real wage target or the government decides to relax its unemployment target.

Our analysis implies the existence of an inflation/unemployment relationship iu, but this is a very different relationship to that in Figure 11.4. Is it a menu for policy choice? Having initially set out for a real wage increase through the claim $\Delta W_3$ the union has been 'persuaded' to accept $\Delta w_q$. The agency of this persuasion has been employers but behind them has been the government. If the union is prepared to accept the outcome the system is stable: the union is prepared to recognise the position of the firm as valid and implicitly to accept the government's commitment to $U_3$. Effectively the government and the union through the bargaining process agree to the final real wage growth and unemployment level. If the union is not reconciled to the managed solution in the next period of bargaining it will submit a money wage claim higher than $\Delta W_3 + \Delta q$, or force $\alpha$ up, and it will continue to do so whilst it finds the solution involving $U_3$ unacceptable. As a result, if the government is to maintain $U_3$ it will have to commit itself to accelerating inflation. Only certain points on the iu curve are therefore likely to be stable: those points to which the bargaining process can reconcile the union. Some increase in unemployment beyond $U_0$ in Figure 11.10 is inevitable. The higher is productivity growth $\Delta q$ the easier it will be to dissuade the union from high unemployment levels because high real wage gains are taking place. In Figure 11.11(a) therefore, with the higher change in productivity $\Delta q_1$, the stable range of outcomes occurs around $U_1$ rather than $U_2$ for $\Delta q$. In principle it is possible to imagine that there is no basis

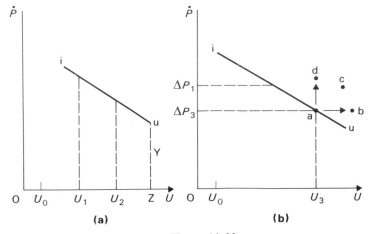

Figure 11.11

whatsoever for agreement with the union in which case the only stable solution is at Z in Figure 11.11(a) where the union chooses the final level of unemployment. It is possible of course that after a period of inflation workers will submit higher money wage claims and tolerate higher price changes to get the real wage gain $\Delta w_q$. In this case, zero inflation is never realisable. The economy settles at Y rather than Z. In general the government's target, $U^*$, is a product of its ability to persuade agents into a stable $\dot{P}U$ combination, and thus partly depends on the temper of wage bargaining.

The role of the money wage claim, $\Delta W_i$, deserves special attention in our model. Bargaining essentially produces agreement over the unemployment/real wage combination. Why then, once this is agreed, does the money wage claim not descend to the level of the real wage gain, obviating the need for price changes? Bearing in mind that we are dealing with a bargaining model there are several reasons why $\Delta W_i$ will exceed $\Delta w_q$ based upon the notion that this provides some degree of protection for the participants. First, if the union were to agree to $\Delta W_i = \Delta w_q$ there is the risk that the firm will pass that wage increase on in prices so that the real wage growth turns out to be less than $\Delta w_q$. Second, the union in any one firm might be able to agree with the employer on such an arrangement but cannot rely on the existence of such agreements elsewhere. Third, the union will want to check that the effects which firms claim price changes will have on demand do actually occur. Otherwise it would pay firms to understate the level of productivity growth and overstate market restrictions. $\Delta W_i$ is thus the union's guarantee that it will get $\Delta w_q$. In one sense $\Delta w_q$ is settled first: $\Delta W_i$ is the claim which, given the bargaining processes through $\alpha$ and $\beta$ and suitable protection, leads to $\Delta w_q$. The union will not therefore increase $\Delta w_i$ unless it wants to increase its target real wage level. $\Delta W_i$ becomes part of the formula for successful negotiations in which both sides are seen to compromise. In time, given stable conditions and under persuasion from firms and the government, $\Delta W_i$ will decline and iu will shift down. The stability of the system is sensitive to changes in the bargaining behaviour of firms. If firms come to recognise that the government is committed to some unemployment target then $\alpha$ could drift upwards. Firms will become less inclined to face up to the costs inevitably associated with negotiating the union real wage targets downwards. They know that they can pass on any wage increase in full because they know the government will validate the increase. Inflation will increase steadily above $\Delta P_4$ at $U_3$. The assumption that employers do resist wage claims, that $\alpha < 1$, is therefore crucial. In practice this is likely to be the case because of competition between firms: those who resist most have most to gain by government inspired higher prices. The firm may also fear that the government might not validate its wage settlements; that lack of resistance to wage claims might lead the union to advance even larger wage claims and indeed claims of a non-pecuniary kind. Rigidities in wage adjustment mechanisms also have a role to play here.

In this model the formation of the union's real wage aspirations and money wage claims through time are crucial. If, as suggested in Chapter 5, the real wage target has a growth path set in terms of the historical growth of real wages then, once some agreement over the bargaining outcome has been achieved, *ceteris paribus*, the rate of inflation can be maintained from period to period at a stable level. Time has a reinforcing effect. Temporary changes in demand, productivity, and the bargaining coefficients will not cause the target to vary.

If the underlying growth of productivity were to decline significantly and permanently, however, the level of profits and investment at the going rate of growth of money wages will decline and employment will begin to fall. Two things might happen. On the one hand, the level of unemployment rises, and the economy moves from point a in Figure 11.11(b) to point b. In time this causes the union to revise its target real wage downwards and money wage claims fall. The economy moves back towards a with a lower growth of real wages. Given reluctance to accept this outcome, the likely solution is at c where the real wage growth is consistent with the lower productivity growth, but some compensation is sought in a smaller real wage reduction which for stability the government has to accommodate, but which involves higher inflation and unemployment. Alternatively, the government might maintain $U_3$ by increasing demand to allow firms to pass on more of their cost increases as price increases. The level of inflation must rise and the rate of growth of real wages fall. The economy moves from a to d in Figure 11.11(b). It is likely that d will not be a stable point. The union will increase its money wage claim and a period of accelerating inflation will occur. In time tacit agreement is reached over a new stable iu combination involving both a lower rate of growth of real wages and a higher level of unemployment than the previous agreement. We assume the economy moves from d to c, but the two processes could lead to different iu outcomes which would have important policy implications.

If we extend our model to include more than one market inflationary forces become stronger. Imagine that human capital conditions and institutional forces produce between them a structure of wages across markets that is stable over time. Now suppose that the attempt to increase real wages by claim $\Delta W_3 + \Delta q$ represents the action of one particular union. We have already seen that the government frustrates the attempt by raising prices. But the union has moved up the money wage hierarchy. The result is that, if other workers wish to restore their previous relative position, another group will make a similar claim in the next round The government has to raise demand to stop the new claim altering the unemployment level. In the next period some other group will make the same claim. Inflation therefore arises from the government's attempts to prevent leapfrogging in the money wage structure from increasing unemployment. Only at some later stage will the initial instigator of the leapfrogging try again to improve its own position. This kind of process develops a momentum of its own. Indeed, the importance of reference bargaining makes it possible to envisage circumstances in which the money wage spiral begins and continues as unions persistently try to protect and improve their own position in the wage hierarchy without any intention or expectation of increasing unemployment.

Reference bargaining as described above is consistent with a stable $\dot{P}U$ combination. However, if different unions have different objectives and face different bargaining conditions the government will have to accept different unemployment targets in each market. It will also be more difficult to get all groups to agree on the stable inflation solution if their money wages are related. Periods of instability are more likely simply because any one of a number of groups of workers might decide to try and force its way up the wages league and increase its real wage. Accelerating inflation might force the government to relax its unemployment target to accommodate some real wage gains along with a higher inflation rate: say in the case where the union sector as a whole attempts to widen its differential over the non-union sector.

We do not observe the iu curve in Figure 11.10. Once a stable solution has been reached we merely observe short-term adjustments to variations in economic variables. Changes in the target growth rate will arise out of changes in past real wage movements which reflect underlying changes in productivity. But, as noted earlier, the adjustment process may take some time and involve a period of accelerating inflation or rising unemployment. We can therefore write

$$\left(\frac{\dot{W}}{P}\right)^*_t = f\left(\left(\frac{\dot{W}}{P}\right)_{t-n}, \dot{U}_{t-k}, \ddot{P}_{t-k}\right), \qquad f_2 < 0, f_3 < 0 \qquad (11.21)$$

where $(\dot{W}/P)^*_t$ is the current target real wage change, $n$ represents a long series of lags and $k$ a shorter period. Several recent periods of rising unemployment and accelerating inflation (along with bargaining and government pressure) will bring about a fall in $(\dot{W}/P)^*$, with the former variables probably more effective than the latter.

In general we observe the continual adjustment of the economy around a given target real wage growth path. For example, suppose there is an exogenously determined fall in demand. With given money wage growth rates this will induce higher changes in prices and then money wages as unions pursue their real wage target. This period of accelerating inflation leads to one of increased unemployment. If the government does not intervene the union will eventually reduce the size of its money wage claims. The rate of inflation will decline. To moderate the rise in unemployment during the contraction unions will allow the real wage and its growth rate to decline. The more unemployment the more moderate unions' claims. We observe a transitory downward sloping $\dot{P}U$ relationship. But once demand begins to rise again and unemployment falls unions revert very quickly to their former real wage target. Wage claims rise and inflation accelerates. Unions may attempt to reach the real wage level they would have attained had the demand contraction not occurred. They might even attempt to recoup some of their losses during the contraction. So, in Figure 11.12 the real wage falls from a to b during the contraction. If the union merely re-establishes its original target real wage path it follows the dashed line and if it recoups some of its losses it follows the dotted line. Either way there is rapid inflation through the adjustment period.

In an open economy a large rise in import prices will lead to a rise in wage claims and a period of accelerating inflation which will again induce higher levels of unemployment. The economy will follow the pattern of Figure 11.12. If the rise is permanent the union will have to become reconciled to a lower real wage path. To preserve stability this may involve a new $\dot{P}U$ compromise in which the government

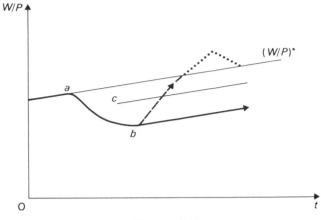

**Figure 11.12**

accepts a higher level of unemployment and a higher rate of wage and price inflation: in Figure 11.12 the economy moves from a to c and a lower growth path after a period of real wage instability.

In our model unions are concerned with real wages. Any increase in taxes will effectively reduce real income (if no account is taken of government spending). To maintain the target real wage path unions will raise their money wage claims. This will bring about a period of price and wage instability unless and until the government and unions can agree to a higher unemployment/higher inflation compromise.

Let us now consider the nature of the model described above. First, the union wage adjustment is seen to produce involuntary unemployment in the sense in which that term was defined in Chapter 10. Second, the process of inflation is cost push in a specific sense. Left to itself the initial adjustment to the union wage would in the end peter out. The process only persists because and whilst the government intervenes. Cost changes may provide the stimulus to inflation but there must be some continuous nominal demand adjustment if it is to continue: inflation is always a monetary phenomenon. In the model the labour market is crucial because it is a labour market agent, unions, that plays the central part in precipitating money wage adjustments. Any increase in union determination to achieve a higher real wage path makes it unlikely that any previous stable level of inflation will remain acceptable. Money wage claims will rise and will go on rising if the government continues to frustrate the union's intentions. In the end the likely result is that the government will have to accept a stable solution involving a higher level of both unemployment and inflation. Third, whilst in our analysis the government deliberately increases nominal demand, one can imagine circumstances in which inflation continues to accelerate without government action. If the money supply is to some extent determined by the level of economic activity rather than by government policy, then rising wages will induce the growth in money needed to finance continuing inflation. Fourth, from Figure 11.12 it is clear that a government can do little to reduce inflation by increasing the level of unemployment unless this lowers the target wage path. Otherwise its actions simply induce a period of rising unemployment, notably in the public sector, and accelerating inflation in the private sector. Eventually unemployment and inflation will fall temporarily, but then inflation will rise again and will attain stability at higher rates than initially when demand expands. Fifth, we have noted that a significant reduction in the rate of growth of productivity could, in the transition to a new agreed $\dot{P}U$ combination, involve a period of rising unemployment and accelerating inflation. If demand is falling it will be very difficult for the government to achieve stability except at very high levels of unemployment.

The model treats the government as essentially passive. The government's intervention is a response to the unions' efforts to raise its real wage path: an attempt to protect the level of unemployment. The level of inflation depends crucially upon unions' real wage aspirations and the level of money wage claims seen as necessary to achieve those aspirations. The model does, however, recognise a positive role for government intervention. First, the rate of inflation will depend upon the ability of the government outside negotiations to persuade the union to accept its unemployment target. *Ceteris paribus* the more successful it is the less chance of instability and the greater the scope for getting equilibrium with low unemployment and stable inflation. Second, the level of inflation depends upon the government's ability to persuade the union that a lower rate of growth of money wage claims would not lead to a lower rate of growth of real wages: that all that will happen will be that the demand expansion and inflation rate for a given $U^*$ can be lower.

This suggests that an incomes policy has a special function in the model. First, it can be the agency through which, at any growth of productivity, the union and the government agree to long-term real wage and unemployment targets. This complements the bargaining process. Second, an incomes policy can provide the agency through which the government can negotiate down the level of money wage claims. As part of this the government might guarantee automatic index-linking of wage settlements to subsequent price changes. Third, the policy also provides a basis for supporting firms' resistance to union wage claims. The government could for example impose a tax on any firm that settles for money wage rises above a certain level, supplemented possibly by policies to increase competitive pressures upon firms through the market place. Fourth, an incomes policy may provide a structure through which the necessary adjustments to shocks to the system and to structural changes can be achieved with minimum instability in the form of accelerating inflation and/or rising unemployment.

Other policy implications of the cost-push model of inflation differ from those of demand-pull models. First, the government should always keep the level of demand high through fiscal and monetary policy. Deflation, planned or unplanned, significantly increases the rate of inflation as well as imposing welfare costs from unemployment. Second, the government should try to maintain a high stable rate of growth of productivity. This will make low unemployment targets attainable and assist the government in its efforts to bring down money wage claims. Third, flexible are preferable to fixed exchange rates which induce periodic bouts of harmful deflation by the government. But, since rapid domestic cost-push inflation requires devaluation which feeds back strongly into wage bargaining through import prices, some form of import controls might be a better way of managing the balance of payments. Fourth, the government should try to stabilise the wage structure, letting relative unemployment rates and vacancy levels guide the allocation of labour within the economy. Fifth, high levels of demand do not generate severe pressures on wages from the supply side of the labour market because unions bargain according to their target real wage path. High demand can thus lead to increased profits and investment.

The cost-push model has many features which seem to fit the real world, but perhaps it lacks the theoretical precision of, say, the VU model. First, the model explains only inflation in one country: it cannot account for the phenomenon of world-wide inflation. Second, to explain rapid increases in inflation the model must posit a rise in unions' aspirations or exogenous price shocks, both of which are treated in an *ad hoc* manner. Third, the formation of the real wage target is not analysed rigorously. Fourth, there is a tendency in emphasising non-market forces to underestimate the impact of market conditions on bargaining outcomes. Fifth, the mechanisms by which the money supply accommodates cost-push inflation need to be fully specified. Sixth, real wage resistance makes sense but the reasons why unions persist in following money wage strategies which can be seen merely to raise prices and unemployment are not clear. Is this simply irrational behaviour or do certain groups do well out of inflation? We return to this question in Section 11.5.

## 11.4 The empirical study of inflation

Perhaps the most obvious test of the demand-pull models of inflation set out in Sections 11.1 and 11.2 would be, following equation (11.8), to look for a statistical relationship between price changes and the level of unemployment. In fact most studies have concentrated upon the underlying relationship between wages and demand embodied in equation (11.6). Such tests elevate the interaction between wages and prices emanating from those firms experiencing hiring difficulties to a central place in the explanation of inflation. Instead of using vacancies as the demand variable, however, most such studies have used unemployment. They have used official time-series aggregate data on wage rates and unemployment to estimate the following equation:

$$W_t = a + bU_t^{-c} \qquad (11.22)$$

which incorporates a non-linear specification consistent with the arguments on the $\dot{P}U$ curve in Section 11.1. Early results confirmed the existence of such a relationship, which has come to be known as the Phillips curve after its first researcher. Phillips, using UK data for the period 1881–1957, found that with a rate of unemployment of $2\frac{1}{2}$ per cent wage inflation would be about 2 per cent per annum. Given that productivity was growing at about 2 per cent, $2\frac{1}{2}$ per cent unemployment would give price stability.

The principal problems associated with such research are as follows. First, the results pertain to wage movements and do not bear directly upon price inflation. It is implicitly assumed in these studies that wage changes are always fully passed on to prices. Second, the equation ignores changes in wages in markets where finding labour is not a problem: it does not explicitly take into account therefore the initial government-induced product price effect, $\Delta P^G$, and its consequences for labour markets. Third, the equation uses unemployment as the independent variable rather than vacancies. Given the existence of a stable UV relationship there would be no problem here, and it is a fact that there is considerable uncertainty as to the reliability of official vacancy statistics. Unemployment statistics are not entirely satisfactory, however, because they often relate only to registered unemployment.

Through time the specification and estimation of the Phillips curve has been improved considerably. First, researchers have employed increasingly sophisticated methods of estimation using more and better data. Second, the rate of change of unemployment has been added, usually successfully, to capture the effects of disequilibrium and loops around the equilibrium relationship referred to in the discussion of Section 11.1. Third, various alternative measures of excess demand have been used: vacancies, vacancies minus unemployment, and measures to incorporate hidden unemployment and labour hoarding have all been tried in different functional forms. In general equation (11.22) gives the best results. Fourth, a variable recording the rate of change of prices (using various lag formulations) has also been successfully included, on the argument that workers will try to compensate for past price changes. Fifth, various measures of the range of unemployment have successfully been included, indicating that inflation at any level of unemployment increases with the regional and industrial dispersion around that level. Sixth, earnings data rather than wage rates have been used as the dependent variable. The results are very similar, because the two series usually move closely together.

Estimates of the extended Phillips curve for the UK were able to explain 80 per cent of the variation in wage changes up until the mid 1960s. The relative importance of the various independent variables in the equation changed with the period over which it was estimated, however. Unemployment was found to be easily the most important variable before the First World War. After that the price term became increasingly more important. Such Phillips curves have now been estimated for a very large number of countries. They have also been estimated for different regions. The results indicate that the reaction of wages to unemployment varies considerably, presumably reflecting the different industrial compositions of the regions and by implication therefore their different demand structures. In the process of trying to improve the specification further, various other explanatory variables have been included in the wage equation. In many cases, as with profits and productivity, there seems to be little theoretical reason for the inclusion and such variables have added little to the explanatory power of the basic equation.

We have said that most empirical work has focused upon the wage equation. Only a few of the early studies of inflation looked at price changes. What is more they were concerned not with the final reduced form relationship of our model, equation (11.8), but with the relationship that links prices and wages: the firm's reaction function in equation (11.5),

$$\dot{P} = a + b\dot{W} + \sum_{i=t-1}^{n} c_i \dot{I}_i \tag{11.23}$$

where $I_i$ are the prices of other inputs, including import prices. Whilst such relationships perform reasonably well statistically, they are based on a rather rigid adherence to cost-plus pricing rules and thus allow little scope for measuring the direct effects of demand on prices in product markets, as represented in equation (11.9), through $\Delta P^G$

and $\Delta W_i$. Nor do they readily identify the effect of demand upon the mark-up. What reliable evidence there is suggests that the mark-up is less than unity, and that it does vary with demand conditions.

It was not until the 1960s that doubts began to surface about the value of the Phillips curve. From the mid 1960s the relationship began to lose its predictive capacity. Re-estimates of the basic relationship were found to explain little of the recent variation in wages: inflation was much higher than predicted and indeed latterly inflation and unemployment were observed to rise together. A number of explanations for this were suggested, including the increased importance of institutional and non-competitive forces in the labour market and possible changes in basic labour market parameters as indicated by the shift in the UV relationship. The observed higher levels of inflation and the growing importance of the price variable to the estimated Phillips curve, however, led researchers to explore the role of expected prices in the wage equation, giving

$$\dot{W}_t = a + bU_t^{-c} + d\dot{P}_t^e \qquad (11.24)$$

This reformulation has come to be known as the expectations-augmented Phillips curve and has been widely researched. From our theorising it is apparent that the estimates of $d$ provide a clue as to the value of the bargaining parameter $\alpha$. The empirical problem of course is to find data on price expectations. In one sense research on the extended Phillips curve provided the most elementary solution to this problem $\dot{P}e_t$ was simply equated with $\dot{P}_{t-1}$. The results of those studies implied that $\alpha$ was significantly less than unity. However, equating $\dot{P}_t^e$ with $\dot{P}_{t-1}$ implies very naive behaviour on the part of workers.

Before developing equation (11.24) we should recognise the problems arising from the existence of both short-run and long-run $\dot{W}U$ relationships. What exactly is our data picking up? The usual assumption is that in long periods of time-series data we are isolating the long-run relationship. What exactly should we then expect from the IU and VU models for the coefficient on $\dot{P}^e$? The former would expect $d < 1$ and the latter $d = 1$. In the IU model we suggested earlier the possibility of modelling price expectations formation as a distributed lag structure, where the weights sum to less than one. In the VU model it was suggested that expectations are formed through an adaptive expectations structure where the weights sum to unity. The latter gives a relatively simple estimation procedure which of course makes it attractive. Given:

$$\dot{W}_t = a + bU_t^{-c} + d\dot{P}_t^e$$

we have:

$$\dot{W}_{t-1} = a + bU_{t-1}^{-c} + d\dot{P}_{t-1}^e \qquad (11.24)$$

The adaptive expectations system is

$$\dot{P}_t^e = \theta \dot{P}_{t-1} + (1 - \theta)P_{t-1}^e$$

and thus: (11.25)

$$\dot{P}_t^e = \theta \dot{P}_{t-1} + \left(\frac{1 - \theta}{d}\right)(\dot{W}_{t-1} - a - bU_{t-1}^{-c}) \qquad (11.26)$$

Substitution into equation (11.24),

$$\dot{W}_t = a + bU_t^{-c} + d\theta \dot{P}_{t-1} + (1 - \theta)(\dot{W}_{t-1} - a - bU_{t-1}^{-c}) \qquad (11.27)$$

$$= \bar{a} + bU_t^{-c} + b(1 - \theta)U_{t-1}^{-c} + d\theta \dot{P}_{t-1} + (1 - \theta)\dot{W}_{t-1} \qquad (11.28)$$

The empirical work on augmented Phillips curves like equation (11.28) has in general failed to produce a satisfactory explanation of the wage change process, although a wide variety of parameter estimates and correlation coefficients have been reported. The equation does not fit recent data particularly well. Contrary to the predictions of the VU model $d$ is significantly different from 1. The estimates of $\theta$ suggest an unreasonably long period of adjustment. There are, however, considerable problems associated with such tests. First, and most important, equation (11.28) may be read as a test, not of equation (11.24), but of the hypothesised expectations formation mechanism: it is this that is being rejected. There are strong prior reasons for doubting the value of the adaptive expectations mechanism. Why should the lag structure be geometrically weighted? Why should we impose the restriction that the weights sum to unity? More important, it seems a particularly silly rule for workers to follow. It implies that they ignore the trend of inflation: they consistently underpredict when inflation is increasing. If inflation steadied or even accelerated at an even rate surely workers would recognise this very quickly and adjust their expectations? To investigate this, quantitative and qualitative data from surveys have been used to construct a direct time-series of price expectations. These data have then been used to test the adaptive expectations mechanism in equation (11.25) and the results have supported that mechanism. Alternative lag structures have yielded results more favourable to the VU model. Second, the statistical analysis of equations like (11.28) involves important problems of identification and statistical biases in the estimates. Is it the wage equation we are observing or the price equation or some hybrid? To avoid these problems multiple equation systems have been estimated: generally to the detriment of the augmented Phillips curve model.

The results for the augmented Phillips curve are not particularly sympathetic to the IU model because the estimated coefficient on the unemployment variable has often turned out to be statistically insignificant in studies using the most recent data. The parameter estimates, for what they are worth, generally imply a fairly steep $\dot{P}U$ relationship, especially if the statistical problems are treated rigorously. One reaction of researchers has been to extend further the list of independent variables in the wage equation to test the predictions of the cost-push variant of the IU model. So, in particular, variables to measure trade union aggressiveness have been included. The problems associated with such a concept are as many as, if not more than, those associated with the concept of price expectations. Researchers have used various proxies including the rate of growth of trade union membership, the level of strike activity in different forms, the level of profits, the government in power and so on. On the whole these proxies perform badly in the estimated equations.

More recent work has been concerned with modelling the inflationary process, recognising that the economy is open to trade and that price expectations on the part of firms should be included. One version of such a model would be

$$\dot{W} = a + bU^{-c} + d(\dot{P}_m^e + \dot{e}r) + e\dot{P}_c^e + f\dot{P}_f^e \qquad (11.29)$$

where $\dot{P}_m^e$ is the expected rate of change of prices of foreign goods in foreign currency terms and $\dot{e}r$ the expected rate of change of the exchange rate. $\dot{P}_c^e$ and $\dot{P}_f^e$ are the expected price changes of consumers and firms respectively. Tests of this model using survey data for expectations have proved much more sympathetic to the VU model. The earliest prediction of $U^N$ for the UK was about 1.7 per cent, but subsequent studies have produced much higher estimates of about 5 per cent.

Not many tests of the rational expectations model have been conducted so far. Given that

$$\dot{W} = a + u(U - U^N) + \dot{P}^e \qquad (11.30)$$

since there is likely to be a relationship between unemployment and the difference between potential national output, $Yp$, and actual output, $Y$, we can write

$$\frac{Yp - Y}{Yp} = S(U - U^N) \qquad (11.31)$$

If $\dot{P}^e$ is formulated along the lines suggested by rational expectations according to current and lagged monetary growth $\dot{M}$ and government expenditures $G$, then

$$\dot{P}^e = f(\dot{M}, G) \tag{11.32}$$

and we have

$$\dot{W} = a + k\left(\frac{Yp - Y}{Yp}\right) + f(\dot{M}, G) \tag{11.33}$$

The tests of such a wage equation have shown the demand variables to be significant and the parameter on the expected inflation variable to be close to one.

The apparent failure of the augmented Phillips curve to explain recent wage behaviour has led to more research into the cost-push approach to inflation. One important prediction of that approach is that the money wage change in any period will be related to the difference between the target real wage change $(\dot{W}/P)^*$ for the period and the actual real wage change $(\dot{W}/P)$. Unemployment enters the story as a determinant of the rate at which a discrepancy between actual and target real wage changes affect the current money wage growth rate. This basic idea can be developed in various different formats, but consider the following relationship:

$$\dot{W}_t = \left(\frac{\dot{W}}{P}\right)^*_t + \lambda\left(\frac{\dot{W}^*}{P} - \frac{\dot{W}}{P}\right)_{t-1} + \gamma\dot{P}_{t-1} + \alpha U \tag{11.34}$$

Here the current money wage change is determined by the target real wage change for the period plus a catch-up term for previous failures of actual real wage growth to match target growth, plus an expected price change term measured by the change in prices in the previous period and plus the unemployment variable. In most empirical studies the target real wage change is proxied by a trend term on past real wage movements but it is possible to let the target vary with the level of unemployment, for example, or with the imposition of an incomes policy. The real wage terms on the right hand side can be specified either gross or net of tax.

The results of the limited empirical work on such relationships indicate that on the whole they perform as well if not better than the best augmented Phillips curves, especially with recent data. The unemployment variable is significant and the coefficient indicates a flatter $\dot{P}U$ curve than do augmented Phillips curves. Net wage models perform better than gross wage models. There is evidence that the target is not immutable but is affected by the state of demand conditions.

The real wage hypothesis emerges from a different model of inflation, with very different policy implications, to that of the augmented Phillips curve, yet so far empirical work has not really convincingly favoured one or the other. The problem with the tests of the target real wage hypothesis is that they do not directly test the importance of institutional forces or bargaining. To the extent that the real wage target appears to be related to unemployment this can be taken to mean that the two sets of results are very similar – unemployment and the target real wage are both simply market demand variables. The use of a trend term to proxy the target real wage is not helpful so there is a strong case for further modelling of the formation of real wage targets.

Statistical studies of prices and incomes policies have in general found their effects upon prices and wages to be small and short term. Such effects are usually isolated by entering dummy variables in different forms into time-series wage or price equations or by estimating such equations for policy on and policy off periods. Dummy variables are not a particularly efficient way of representing PIPs because PIPs vary so much in intention and method. The results also depend heavily upon having a satisfactory model of inflation to work with. Even where the effects of the policy have been found to be significant their termination has been followed by a period of restoration of real wage losses.

## 11.5   The consequences of inflation

Inflation is a monetary phenomenon which only affects the allocation of resources and economic welfare if it changes real economic variables: relative prices; relative wages and incomes; real wages; real interest rates; exchange rates or real wealth. In practice there are several reasons for thinking that inflation does affect real magnitudes.

Economists have distinguished between the consequences of inflation which is anticipated and those of inflation which is unanticipated. By anticipated inflation we mean inflation that is foreseen perfectly accurately, but is not completely incorporated into the behaviour of economic agents. So, for example, inflation would be described as anticipated if $\lambda$ in our wage equations were 1 but $\alpha$ was less than 1. Inflation is only neutral in its allocative effects when it is not only fully anticipated but fully adjusted to. In practice this is not likely to happen. Let us consider how anticipated inflation might affect efficiency and welfare.

First, even if, in any particular wage bargain, firm and workers agree about the future course of inflation, they may disagree about what this should mean for their bargain. The firm will obviously be much more interested in the rate of change of the price of its own output. If this is less than the overall rate of inflation the firm will regard a wage settlement which compensates for general price increases as excessive and will resist such a settlement. The resulting shift in the wage distribution may disturb highly sensitive wage relativities. Those workers who negotiate infrequently will suffer more than others, as will groups who rely on discretionary government settlements rather than collective bargaining. Groups with strong union organisation and most bargaining leverage will do best. Workers whose incomes are directly related to money revenues, such as professional workers, will also do well. Non-manual workers are likely to fare better than manual workers in inflationary periods because more of their total rewards comes in non-pecuniary forms. Therefore for certain groups of workers it is perfectly rational to submit wage claims which fuel inflation. One possible benefit of inflation, however, might arise if wages are rigid downwards. Changes in relative wages can then only be achieved through differential rates of wage inflation. Whether there are efficiency gains depends on how wages are determined. One significant efficiency cost of inflation will be an increase in the frequency and in the difficulty of wage negotiations and thus, on both counts, in the transactions costs of bargaining and the number of breakdowns.

Second, if personal income tax brackets are fixed in nominal terms wage inflation will move individuals up through the tax bands without any action by the government. Unions could then be pursuing wage claims which effectively make some of their members worse off. With progressive tax rates the proportion of income taken by taxes rises. Fiscal drag, as this effect is called, by and large shifts the burden of taxation from labour to capital because income from assets is often taxed on nominal values, as with capital gains tax, and company profits taxation sometimes has adjustments for inflation built in. The burden of fiscal drag falls most heavily on taxpayers at the top and bottom of the scale. The overall effect is to make the income tax system more progressive, and perhaps more progressive than the government intended it to be. However, some of the largest increases in average tax rate occur at low income levels where fiscal drag pulls people on low incomes into the tax net.

Third, in a world in which the legal tender bears no rate of interest, inflation will induce asset holders to economise on their holdings of money. The higher the expected rate of inflation the greater the incentive to switch to low-risk interest-earning assets. The cost of inflation is the additional pecuniary and non-pecuniary costs of the asset-switching transactions it induces. These costs could be eliminated if banks paid interest on current account balances, but then other costs would arise from making all payments by cheque. The failure to pay interest on the legal tender amounts to a tax on holding money. Inflation provides the government with a stream of revenue from this source: the higher is inflation, the larger the revenue. The distributive consequences of this effect of inflation depend largely on how the revenue is spent.

The fourth, and probably most significant, distributive effect of inflation also arises from the government's failure to incorporate anticipated inflation fully into its actions. Pensions and other social security benefits are the main source of income for most of the poorest members of society. These benefits are usually fixed in nominal terms with irregular and unsystematic upratings, and even when they are indexed the automatic adjustments often prove inadequate. If the real value of unemployment benefit falls, any disincentive effects will be reduced but recipients suffer because the basic level of benefit is very low. Occupational pensions have often been fixed in nominal terms on retirement, and if there is no adequate inflation-proofing mechanism the standard of living of pensioners falls drastically. Occupational schemes covering high income groups are usually superior to those for low income groups in this respect. State pensions are now inflation-proofed to an extent which represents a distributive shift towards lower income groups.

Fifth, inflation has important effects on equity through the ownership of housing. Owner-occupiers receive income in kind, in the form of a flow of housing services, which is by definition inflation-proof. At the same time, mortgages are calculated on an annuity basis. This means that the present value of the stream of annual payments, discounted at the current interest rate, equals the sum borrowed. The annual repayment is constant in money terms and therefore declines in real terms in inflationary times. This effect has generally outweighed that of the periodic increases in nominal interest rates. Borrowing from building societies and banks for housing is concentrated among higher income groups and therefore the effect of inflation here is to increase inequalities in income. High initial real payments are a penalty for first time house buyers, hit the young in particular and favour those with personal and family wealth. In principle this could be overcome by changing to a system of rising nominal annual payments which keep the real value constant. However, in practice no machinery exists to operate such a system and the need to renegotiate mortgage repayments every year would impose great transactions costs.

All fixed nominal interest payments suffer exactly the same problem; the classic example being fixed interest government debt and in particular war loan. But dividends on industrial ordinary shares and returns from building society shares and life insurance schemes have also failed to keep pace with inflation. People continue to save by these means, even though they offer negative real rates of interest, simply because there are no better alternatives available. Therefore inflation redistributes income from lenders to borrowers. The overall implications for equity are unclear. Low income people have few debts, because they cannot find lenders, and so do the very rich, who hold bonds.

Sixth, in periods of rapid inflation it pays to delay settling accounts and to speed up collection of payments. To the extent that large firms are more successful in pursuing these policies inflation will penalise smaller units.

In any period of inflation the prices of individual goods rise at different rates. The evidence suggests that in practice the prices of those goods which take a higher proportion of the expenditure of low than of high income households, i.e. necessities, have risen faster than those of other goods. Official price indices, because their weights are derived from the allocation of total expenditure, measure the effects of inflation on those who do most spending, who are, of course, higher income groups. On the above argument, therefore, the official rate of inflation underestimates price increases for poorer people, and will not provide an adequate method of indexing the wages of low-paid workers or social security benefits.

Inflation may have the psychological effect of making people worse off both because they become extremely conscious of price changes and because their real wage declines between wage settlements even if it is fully adjusted at each settlement. Families will also feel worse off if housekeeping money is not inflation adjusted, so that the quantity or quality of domestic activities deteriorates.

Both the efficiency losses and the distributional costs from unanticipated inflation will be much larger than from anticipated inflation. Economic agents' adjustments will be unsystematic and partial, so inflation will diminish real incomes and change relative prices. With variable rates of inflation, for example, workers will find it very difficult to predict price movements accurately. Unions' and firms' expectations are unlikely to coincide, which may cause conflicts in bargaining. It is difficult to generalise about the effects of unanticipated inflation on efficiency and equity without knowing who fails to anticipate inflation, when and why. One might expect, however, that low income groups are most likely to be hit. Wealthholders, particularly those without a diversified asset portfolio, will also lose out in the immediate aftermath of an increase in inflation.

Unanticipated inflation also poses problems by generating uncertainty. The problems are likely to increase with the rate of inflation because, whether or not price level variability increases with inflation, people seem to think it does, possibly because high inflation attracts more attention.

Price level uncertainty is itself a source of disutility and generates noise in market signalling. Most important, it discourages all long-term monetary contracts because the associated risks increase. If only fixed interest stocks are available, individual savers, like those planning pensions, cannot calculate what sum they should put aside to provide a given standard of living in retirement. Capital holding and savings are reduced. Firms prefer to invest in short-term projects which may be less productive, and also borrow short. They cannot calculate the real cost of long-term borrowing because there is so much uncertainty about the future rate of inflation. Index-linked bonds could resolve this problem, but few exist because of the difficulty of specifying the appropriate index: any official index will be useless if its weights are generally believed to be irrelevant or variable. Thus uncertainty reduces money holdings, penalises savings and discourages investment. The necessity to negotiate contracts more frequently also imposes costs. Inflation encourages people to move out of nominal assets into real assets. Those who respond slowest get hurt most. As people adjust a substantial change in portfolio choice is effected, which raises the inflation rate at any unemployment level. Such changes are costly and not at all instantaneous: it takes time to institute the new machinery of decision making appropriate for an inflationary world. Old habits and methods die hard.

Universal indexation, by which all wages and the interest rate are automatically adjusted for actual price changes, would remove the need to anticipate future price changes. This is particularly important in that it keeps relative price signals in line with general price movements. In principle indexation could remove all uncertainty problems, but in practice there are significant administrative costs to such a scheme. The effects of anti-inflation policies on the real economy depend on the kind of policy pursued. Tight monetary policies will affect small firms most immediately, through high interest rates. Fiscal policies are likely to be felt by public sector employees most immediately. A PIP, to the extent that it works, may squeeze wage differentials if flat-rate guidelines are used, and restrict high productivity areas. To the extent that a PIP raises the relative wage of low-paid workers there may be an offsetting cost from increased unemployment of low-paid workers.

Inflation does have efficiency and equity effects. Quantification is difficult but important. Governments seem prepared to go to some lengths and impose considerable costs to reduce inflation, when certain institutional changes, mainly involving the government's own activities, could considerably reduce the welfare costs of inflation.

# Further Reading

## CHAPTER 11: INFLATION

D. Begg, *The Rational Expectations Revolution in Macroeconomics* (Oxford: Philip Allen, 1982).

J. Fallick and R. Elliott, *Incomes Policies, Inflation and Relative Pay* (London: George Allen & Unwin, 1981).

J. Flemming, *Inflation* (Oxford: Oxford University Press, 1976).

R. Jackman and R. Layard, 'An inflation tax' *Fiscal Studies*, Vol. 3 (March 1982).

R. Jackman, C. Mulvey and J. Trevithick, *The Economics of Inflation*, 2nd edition (Oxford: Martin Robertson, 1981).

D. Laidler and D. Purdy, *Inflation and Labour Markets* (Manchester: Manchester University Press, 1974).

J. Meade, *Stagflation I: Wage-Fixing* (London, George Allen & Unwin, 1982).

D. Mitchell, *Unions, Wages and Inflation* (Washington, D.C.: Brookings Institution, 1980).

M. Parkin and M. Sumner, *Inflation in the UK* (Manchester: Manchester University Press, 1978).

# 12

# The labour market, efficiency and distribution

In this text we have described developments in labour market analysis which are essentially refinements of the basic model. Building upon the traditional approach is no doubt methodologically sound and intellectually creditable but has been seen by some as too abstract, cautious and limited in view of the inability of the traditional approach to explain many important labour market problems and to offer credible policy recommendations. The pervasive and persistent incidence of long-term unemployment, job instability, low investment in education, all concentrated on specific social groups – racial and ethnic minorities, those in inner city areas, young people and women – it has been argued, requires not merely the refinement of the traditional theoretical paradigm but a complete reformulation of our approach to labour market mechanisms. In the first section of this chapter we draw together various arguments from previous chapters to consider the ways in which developments in labour economic theory have extended our understanding of the implication of labour market mechanisms for efficiency and distribution. In Sections 12.2 and 12.3 we consider segmented labour market models as alternative scenarios to the traditional labour economic model. Finally in Section 12.4 we consider the implications of the preceding discussion for future developments in labour economics.

## 12.1 Developments in the analysis of efficiency and distribution in the labour market

In the basic model of the labour market an efficient allocation of resources requires that labour supply decisions on hours, participation and mobility are made on the basis of relative prices by rational utility-maximising individuals. Labour demand reflects the outcome of cost-minimising decisions by firms in response to relative factor prices. A central element of an efficient allocation is that wages should equal MRP and there should be no excess labour demand or supply in any single market or in the labour market as a whole.

Developments in labour market theory generate a large number of additional insights into the nature of efficiency. First, we have seen that labour supply decisions are taken under conditions of quite severe and complex constraints. Whilst efficiency requires that individuals respond to market prices, we have seen how significant non-market signals, for example from domestic activities, can be in practice. Given the amount of government intervention, the hours constraints and so on, it seems unlikely that actual labour supply decisions can be understood by a model quite as simple as the basic model. Our analysis of the most important constraints offers a basis for analysing efficiency in real labour markets, particularly in relation to hours and participation.

Second, since the basic model treats education as a consumption good it generates no theory of occupational choice. In providing such a theory the human capital approach offers important insights into the nature of schooling decisions, occupational mobility, on-the-job training and state intervention in education. It generates a number of interesting predictions about the nature of wage structures across individuals, occupations and industries. It offers a range of criteria for assessing efficiency, principally through the agency of investment analysis, rates of return and discounted net benefit streams.

Third, the principal insight provided by the analysis of uncertainty is the importance of screening costs for both workers and employers. These costs have been shown to be useful to understanding wage differentials for identical labour, signalling by market participants, credentialism and job mobility, and for indicating how an efficient allocation of resources might look very different from that predicted by the basic model.

Fourth, training and screening costs, as fixed labour costs, lead to the analysis of constrained employment adjustments by firms and, in collaboration with the concept of specific skills, of structured internal labour markets. This analysis offers much insight into the role of overtime, hiring and firing, and training and promotional hierarchies inside the firm. Hoarding in particular represents an instance of excess labour which, in direct contrast to the predictions of the basic model, is perfectly consistent with efficiency.

Fifth, non-competitive forces, through trade unions, discrimination and internal labour markets, do not appear in the basic model. Recent analysis indicates both the nature of these forces and precisely where and how the distortions they introduce appear. The analysis indicates that there are important efficiency gains from unions (in providing information, for example) and from internal labour markets (in increasing employment stability). The analysis of discrimination as a consequence of uncertainty suggests that discrimination, however undesirable, may be an endemic if not unalterable characteristic of labour markets.

Sixth, the analysis of uncertainty, state intervention and fixed labour costs as frictions in labour markets, and of union policies towards wages and employment, provides some insight into the causes and inefficiencies of unemployment. In the involuntary unemployment model, demand deficient unemployment in particular seems to represent a considerable waste of resources. Similarly, failure to introduce specific labour market policies to reduce recurrent and long-term unemployment seems to imply inefficiency. On the other hand there is evidence that unemployment in some form is an adjunct of an efficient dynamic economy. The same analysis simultaneously provides the basis for understanding the complex issues surrounding inflation and the scope for government action.

An analysis of allocative efficiency is of little value to welfare assessments of labour market mechanisms without an investigation of their consequences for income distribution. What does the analysis of this text reveal? First and foremost, it links incomes firmly to the acquisition and improvement of skills. Schooling and training provide the basis for profitable occupational choice and mobility, security during firms' employment adjustments, substantial protection against unemployment and reduced hardship if it does arise, access to structured internal labour markets and smaller losses from inflation. Lack of educational qualifications is correlated with a low position in the wage hierarchy, inferior jobs, long hours, low trade union protection, job instability and weak attachment to the labour force.

At the same time our model offers various reasons why certain groups – women, blacks, the young and the old, and the sick – may have serious labour market disadvantage within given skill levels. For certain workers at the lowest skill levels these effects interact and compound to produce the marginal worker referred to in Chapter 1.

Our analysis of the mechanisms producing low skill levels highlights low abilities, imperfect capital markets, institutional restrictions but most important of all, family income constraints. The analysis therefore relates the labour market success of individuals closely to their class origins.

The insights into efficiency and distribution within the labour market provided by recent developments in labour market analysis will no doubt be extended as the ideas here are refined and tested. But let us try finally to identify the perspective through which the operations of the labour market have been analysed. First, there is a belief that the economic system is founded upon competitive forces and all agents are essentially rational decision makers. Elements of non-competitive behaviour are grafted on to, and subject to, these competitive forces. For example, unions are seen to be influential in only certain areas and are always subject to demand and cost conditions, especially in the long term. Second, inequalities in income, and the class divisions that produce them, are marked but could be effectively offset by gradualist reforms, primarily fiscal policies, which alter the distribution of total final receipts across individuals. Third, there is strong confidence in the market mechanism as a means of allocating resources and thus a predeliction for policies which set the ground rules for market operations without restricting them. Fourth, it is accepted that because society is essentially a pluralist structure, with experts involved in every area of decision making, research, rational debate and collective interest will lead to continuous and legitimate reform.

## 12.2 A segmented labour market approach

In recent years dissatisfaction with the traditional approach to labour market analysis has led to the development of alternative explanations of the way the labour market operates. One such alternative paradigm is based on the proposition that over time the labour market has become divided into self-contained segments composed of non-competing groups of workers. Segmented labour market (SLM) models were initially developed in response to what was seen as the failure of traditional economic analysis adequately to explain urban poverty and the labour market disadvantage of minority groups and, in particular, its failure to recognise how far social and institutional constraints restrict the options of many workers.

To support their claim that labour market mechanisms are far from accurately portrayed by conventional analysis, SLM economists document a number of empirical findings. First, there is evidence that widespread and substantial discrimination against women and racial and ethnic minorities persists over time, in direct contradiction to neoclassical tastes theories of discrimination. Second, contrary to human capital theory, despite the fact that there has been a narrowing in the distribution of educational attainment, the distribution of income has remained stable and considerably more unequal than that of education. Third, policies aimed at redistributing earnings by increasing skills, such as vocational training and increased expenditure on schooling, have had little impact on the employment and earnings prospects of disadvantaged workers and on the incidence of poverty. Finally, SLM economists point out that in their own empirical studies human capital theorists are unable to explain more than 50 per cent of the total variation in individual earnings. The emphasis conventional economics places on individual characteristics that are conventionally associated with productivity is thus unwarranted. SLM economists argue strongly that, by and large, those at the lower end of the labour market are not there because they lack the skills and motivation necessary to operate in better paid employment. They argue that theoretical and empirical attention should be focused on the nature of the job structure and the role of institutional forces, such as discrimination, in determining labour market success.

Consider the following SLM model. The model has three central hypotheses. First, the labour market is permanently divided into two parts, each with its own characteristics and mode of operation. Second, institutional rather than market forces play the major part in the allocative and distributive mechanisms of the labour market, particularly in one of the segments. Third, access to one segment by labour market entrants is controlled, and mobility between the segments is restricted. Discrimination against certain groups is central to the controls and restrictions.

The labour market is dichotomised between a primary and a secondary segment. The former embraces firms with structured internal labour markets and jobs that are characterised by high earnings, good working conditions and employment stability. Within this segment there are opportunities for training and promotion, and the rules governing work are well established and administered fairly. The secondary segment embraces firms with open internal labour markets and jobs that are low paying, offer few fringe benefits, poor working conditions and involve menial and repetitive work. Firms are characterised by unstable patterns of employment, general skills, few opportunities for promotion and arbitrary management. This is a description of segmentation, but what are the causal mechanisms behind this dichotomy between firms and why do some jobs become good jobs and not others?

Technology is not the crucial distinction between primary and secondary firms. A significant proportion of the work in the economy could be performed in either segment. Basic technology is the same. Firms in the same industry will be in different segments. The occupational structures of primary and secondary segments are the same. Segmentation is thus not associated with skill levels or other such factors associated with the productivity of workers. However, firms will take different decisions about how to utilise and develop the available technology and once a particular technology has been adopted this will affect the way work is organised and whether the firm operates in the primary segment or not.

The crucial distinction between firms in the primary and secondary segments lies in the degree of non-competitive behaviour. In certain firms employers with monopoly power in product markets face organised labour with a bargaining position based as much upon historical precedent as upon current market conditions. Their interaction produces a code of rules and regulations governing internal organisation. The union wants employment security. The firm wants, and will pay for, stability and freedom from conflict. A system of labour organisation grows up within the firm which is bureaucratic, rigid, respected and in time strongly protected. Under these conditions the firm chooses to operate certain technologies which produce large scale units, high capital intensity, tasks requiring specific skills and heavily interdependent work activities. It naturally chooses, simultaneously, to operate structured internal labour markets, heavily based upon institutional mechanisms, custom and practice and continuous collective bargaining.

The source of the dichotomy within the labour market is thus the existence of firms' monopoly power and unions' bargaining power. The former arises from a relatively stable demand, barriers to entry in the form of differentiable products, specialisation in producer goods, predatory tactics by firms and permissive government policy. Many of the same factors are likely to encourage union growth and bargaining power, as do certain historical and local social forces. It therefore follows that, having chosen their technologies, firms in the primary segment tend to be simultaneously large, capital-intensive, able to exercise monopoly power in product markets and characterised by extensive unionisation. They are in general the longest established firms in any industry. Secondary segment firms are typically competitive, small scale, labour-intensive operations, providing little training and with low unionisation of their workforces. It is in the interest of secondary segment firms to maintain a flexible workforce. Basically jobs become good jobs if they are in non-competitive areas because non-competitive forces lead to favourable technological and institutional structures within firms.

Within this view of segmentation one could place particular stress upon the firm's position at the expense of the unions, or vice versa, even if both elements are necessary to the model. One might want to argue that firms take their decisions on technology and particularly the internal labour market, under extreme pressure from workers. It is thus union organisation which is the key to providing good jobs. Alternatively, one might argue that it is employers who lead in producing good jobs. It is part of a strategy to motivate workers but also to divide labour in order to make control easier. Segmentation of jobs is segmentation of the workforce, which reduces mutual interests and controls aspirations.

It is important to emphasise that the basis of an internal labour market is very different in SLM models to that portrayed in Chapter 8. The structured internal labour market that develops over time within a primary firm can best be explained by sociological rather than economic factors. Firms do not develop structured internal labour markets because of the fixed labour costs of the technology that governs their operations. Firms choose their technology according to their monopoly/union position. The fixed labour costs are a product of that decision and do not shape the nature of the internal labour market. Customary practices and historically determined norms dominate the operation of the internal labour market. They determine the relative position of each job, not simply in terms of earnings, training and mobility, but also in terms of status. It becomes very difficult for the firm to adjust to market forces. Changing the relative position of one job worsens other workers' positions in the hierarchy and they will resist the change.

The mechanisms that determine wages and allocate labour are quite different in the two segments. Primary segment wages and employment are determined within structured internal labour markets by rules and procedures which are unresponsive to economic factors. The wage a person receives depends not just upon his personal productive ability but on the wage associated with the job he does: a wage determined historically by labour market custom. Similarly, promotion will be determined through institutional rules, based for instance on seniority, rather than on personal merit.

In the secondary segment jobs can be very insecure, low paid and have few prospects. The segment is thus characterised by market employment instability, reflected in higher discharges, quits and absenteeism. This instability is enhanced by the menial nature of the work typically found in this segment. The low level of specific skills associated with the choice of technology means that employers have little incentive to encourage workers to develop stable employment patterns. Consequently the characteristics of individual workers are of little consequence to secondary segment employers who will not put much effort into distinguishing between applicants when hiring and promoting at any level but will act as if they are all of the same quality. Variations in productivity-related characteristics across workers in the secondary segment will consequently not be strongly reflected in variations in earnings. Wage structures in the secondary segment will be determined by aggregate supply and demand.

Each higher skill level within primary firms will contain more jobs and will be more heterogeneous than in secondary firms because of the importance of specific skills. But higher level jobs in primary firms will usually be filled internally. The only significant 'port of entry' is at the bottom. In secondary firms, on the other hand, there are ports of entry at every level. Workers in the primary segment rarely move between jobs because of their established position in the hierarchy. Workers in the secondary segment can and do move frequently between jobs inside the segment. They are trying to improve their position but are usually unsuccessful.

The SLM model not only distinguishes the two segments but also argues that movement between them is controlled and extremely limited. Primary workers would not choose and are rarely forced to move down. Secondary workers are not often allowed to move up. Mobility is restricted because secondary workers lack industry-specific skills given the low level of on-the-job training in their segment. But the lack of upward mobility primarily arises because of institutional and social barriers unrelated to human capital. The reason why secondary workers cannot get into the primary segment is not because they lack ability or productive potential, but rather because of the refusal of workers and employers in the primary segment to accept them into their work groups. In the social hierarchy of the workplace secondary segment jobs have low status and consequently those workers who fill them are socially inferior. Primary workers and employers will thus discriminate against them when hiring in order to maintain their own relative position in the socio-economic scale.

Mobility between the segments is also limited by the particular hiring requirements used by primary firms. The primary segment values and fosters stability and discipline and the development of 'good work habits'. Jobs in the secondary segment offer little incentive for workers to develop good habits and stable patterns of employment, whatever their personal inclinations, since the tasks involved are often physically hard, boring and repetitive. Consequently they display unreliability and require constant supervision. Since such characteristics are inconsistent with employment in the primary segment it becomes difficult for workers to transfer into the upper segment, the more so the longer they remain in the secondary segment. Firms will use work histories to decide between applicants and this will eliminate secondary workers. In the SLM model this is discriminatory because the majority of secondary workers would display good habits if they were put into the primary segment; and if the majority of primary workers were put into the secondary segment they would soon display bad habits. Work habits are characteristics primarily of jobs not of workers.

Certain groups of workers in the secondary segment can be singled out as having the least chance of achieving upward mobility. Women, older workers, racial and ethnic minorities are discriminated against. They are excluded not because they lack productive potential but because they are regarded as inferior labour, whatever their personal record in the secondary segment.

Since mobility across segments is restricted, any individual's lifetime income opportunities are crucially determined by whether he can get into the primary segment at the bottom level in the early stages of labour market participation. This will of course depend on the size and rate of growth of the primary sector. But discrimination plays a crucial role too. Young B workers will be excluded. And so, possibly, will be the very youngest market entrants who therefore have to enter the secondary segment and get their chance to move up only after a few years if, against the odds, they have a good record. There will also be discrimination on class lines whereby young people from lower social groups are eliminated from the reckoning. There will, no doubt, also be an element of luck in selection, given the limited information firms have to go on at this stage. Social capital and family connections will be of some value in the selection process.

The implications for B workers are particularly severe. Because they are excluded from mobility and restricted on entry, the proportion of B workers in the secondary segment, and possibly the proportion of the secondary segment that is made up of B workers, will become very large. The bad work habits of the secondary segment will become the bad habits of the B group as a whole, thus reinforcing prejudices. They, along with other lower class workers, are more likely to suffer low pay, low work attachment, low income, low social capital, which will inevitably combine to affect the chances of their children. Therefore, *ceteris paribus*, the relative position of B workers and lower-class families becomes cumulatively worse.

The SLM model provides a very different view of the labour market and consequently of labour market disadvantage to that of the traditional approach. First, the labour market is no longer seen as a continuum along which workers are spread with the disadvantaged at one end. The secondary segment is a distinct market, with its own characteristics and ways of setting wages and allocating labour. Second, and most important, the disadvantaged do not end up in the lower segment because they lack the human capital to work in primary segment jobs. Rather, institutional restrictions on job choice mean that some workers have access only to low status, low wage employment. This is particularly important for policy. It suggests that policies that aim to improve the productivity of disadvantaged workers will have little impact on the position of such workers. It is not lack of education or of the ability to undertake training that distinguishes secondary segment workers but rather their inability to gain access to good jobs. Nor does a general expansion in demand improve the position of secondary workers because this will usually increase the number of secondary rather than of primary jobs. In order to help those groups who do badly in the labour market, according to the SLM model, it is necessary to break down the barriers to primary segment jobs. This might be done in two ways: by subsidising the employment of disadvantaged workers or by the introduction of anti-discrimination legislation to encourage primary firms to employ disadvantaged workers. One can expect, however, since both workers and employers in the upper segment have an interest in maintaining a low status–low wage segment in the labour market, that a reduction in discrimination will be resisted.

An alternative strategy would be to change the nature of employment in the secondary segment. This could be done by minimum wage legislation, encouraging the development of trade unions and by subsidising on-the-job training. Again, vested interests in the maintenance of a cheap labour sector must be overcome. It might also be expensive if the secondary segment is operating according to market forces.

Another obvious strategy would be to encourage the growth of the primary segment. This might be achieved by encouraging greater concentration and larger work units and strengthening unionisation. The drawback here of course is that the primary segment is associated with lower consumer welfare and allocative inefficiency. The same result could be achieved by expanding the public sector since this is one of the principal employers in the primary segment. Again there are offsetting costs in the form of inefficiency, as well perhaps as distortions arising from an enlarged state share of total activity and growth in the relative size of the non-industrial part of the economy.

## 12.3 The empirical study of segmentation

Since the SLM model suggests very different policies to help the disadvantaged from those proposed by traditional theory, it is important that it be examined empirically. Several variants of the SLM model discussed here have been put forward and tested in the literature. But there are a number of common tests. The first looks for bimodality in the distribution of earnings or of any other measure of the goodness of jobs. The second assesses the relative importance of human capital variables in determining the incomes of primary and secondary workers. The third considers the extent and determinants of mobility from the secondary to the primary segment. Finally, circumstantial evidence can be examined to consider the extent to which minority groups of workers are over-represented in secondary jobs.

A strict interpretation of the SLM model suggests that the distribution of earnings or of any other index of the goodness of jobs should be bimodal, reflecting the underlying division of workers into two distinct populations. Cross-section empirical analysis suggests, however, that this is not the case. The estimated distributions are unimodal.

Perhaps the most common test of the SLM model uses regression analysis to examine wage determination processes in the two segments of the labour market. This involves, first, dividing workers into two groups to represent the two segments. Various criteria are used such as income or some measure of the social and economic status of the worker's occupation. Human capital earnings functions like those in Chapter 9 are then estimated for each group. Since abilities and constraints are the same for primary (p) and secondary (s) groups in Figure 12.1, both choose to invest in skills to the same level $S_1$ with expected returns $r_S$. But subsequent market experience produces returns of $r_S^s < r_S$. Productivity is simply not rewarded to the same extent in the secondary segment. So

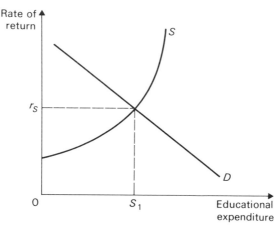

**Figure 12.1**

$$\left.\begin{array}{l}\log W^{\mathrm{p}} = \log W_0 + r_S S_1 + \displaystyle\sum_{i=1}^{n} a_i^{\mathrm{p}} X_i \\[2em] \log W^{\mathrm{s}} = \log W_0 + r_S^{\mathrm{s}} S_1 + \displaystyle\sum_{i=1}^{n} a_i^{\mathrm{s}} X_i \end{array}\right\} \qquad (12.1)$$

If the labour market is segmented, the estimated coefficients in the secondary segment equation should be significantly different from those in the primary segment equation. Estimates of the return to education and on-the-job training for secondary workers are generally lower than those for primary workers.

The earnings function test above can be extended by including additional variables that represent the institutional determinants of earnings emphasised by SLM models. One might then investigate the relative importance of individual productivity characteristics against institutional forces by comparing the relative importance of the two sets of determinants in the regression equation. The results indicate that structural factors are important determinants of earnings, but explain less of the variation in earnings than do individual characteristics.

The third test of the SLM model focuses upon the hypothesis that secondary workers face strong barriers to upward mobility which are independent of individual quality. A subsidiary hypothesis is that a worker's initial job will be the most significant factor affecting her future labour market success. Unfortunately, little empirical analysis of these hypotheses has been undertaken, the main reason being the scarcity of longitudinal data. What evidence there is casts doubt on a strict interpretation of the SLM hypotheses. In general there is more mobility between segments than the SLM model suggests, and even more important perhaps, human capital variables such as schooling are critically important to the probability of starting a career in the primary segment and to the likelihood of upward mobility. It is the case, however, that there are considerable differences between racial and ethnic groups. Coloured youths, for example, are less likely to start in a primary segment job than are equally productive white youths. The upward mobility of coloured workers appears to be unrelated to their education and training, suggesting significant discriminatory practices. Discrimination is clearly a significant though not an insurmountable obstacle to mobility.

The final piece of evidence SLM economists provide to establish that the labour market is segmented is mainly descriptive. It involves identifying the location of B workers in the labour market. Statistics show that a high proportion of female and coloured workers are employed in low wage jobs and industries that have the characteristics attributed to lower segment employment. Even after controlling for education and other personal characteristics, these groups have low earnings compared to those of the labour force as a whole. Studies of the economic position of these workers thus provide circumstantial evidence of segmentation. However, all such evidence is open to different interpretations and therefore does not allow firm conclusions to be drawn.

## 12.4 Future developments in labour market analysis

Let us consider whether the SLM model offers a sound basis for future developments in labour economics. There are several obvious weaknesses to the segmentation approach. First, the existence of only two segments so distinctly different seems hard to accept as a useful view of a complex, heterogeneous labour market. There seems little case for such extreme polarisation: the market contains firms lying along a continuum of monopoly power and unionisation; demand conditions are not dichotomised into stable and unstable categories;

technology, capital intensity, scale and division of labour are all matters of degree. One could increase the number of segments but then the criteria for segmentation become substantially more complex and arbitrary and the segments tend to lose their distinctive qualities. Second, the model rests on the numerical importance of the primary segment of the economy. There is little evidence of widespread structured internal labour markets. What evidence there is indicates the relevance of differences in technology and specific skills. Third, the idea that the skill characteristics of jobs and people in the two sectors are the same seems unreasonable. The occupational structure of primary firms will be much wider and more complex than in secondary firms. This is partly because it is very likely, as suggested in Chapter 9, that lower rewards to skills will induce secondary workers to invest less in them, so that in time they will be excluded from primary jobs by virtue of their inferior productivity. This does not necessarily mean that discrimination is irrelevant; it may simply take a different form. Fourth, *a priori* there seems a strong case for believing that the underlying technology of different industries is substantially different and that this will play a large part in producing differences in monopoly power and unionisation across the economy. Basic differences of technology will also mean differences in fixed labour costs which induce varied cost-minimising internal structures. Institutional factors are important, but there are very strong technological constraints. Fifth, the SLM rests on strong and widespread labour market discrimination. The available evidence on discrimination is not helpful. It appears to exist, but it is unclear to what extent. It could be concluded that discrimination outside the labour market and social forces are more important. The SLM model, despite the importance attached to labour market discrimination, offers little new insight into the mechanics of discrimination. The analysis is based primarily upon discrimination as a consequence of information problems within the labour market. This makes discrimination the product of cost-minimising efficient behaviour, which is inconsistent with the SLM model's otherwise institutionalist view of the labour market. We have noted in Chapters 4 and 8 that this is not an entirely satisfactory basis for modelling discrimination because it is within the ability of firms, and indeed in their interests, to check up on their preconceptions, to accumulate information and thus reassess prejudices as soon as events make them unprofitable. Empirical work has not yet been able to distinguish clearly between different models. Sixth, the concept of the structured internal labour market is perhaps taken too far. There is evidence to suggest that firms do recruit semi-skilled labour primarily from internal unskilled candidates, that firms do recruit some foremen from the semi-skilled, and that some technical supervisors do come from the skilled group but in all cases the length of the promotion ladder is very short and is travelled by only a few workers. Semi-skilled people only very rarely rise into skilled levels. Foremen and technical supervisors only occasionally rise into managerial positions. Few clerical posts lead by predetermined routes to managerial jobs. Seventh, the evidence suggests that a minority of workers do operate in jobs very much like those described as existing in the secondary segment. They are at the bottom of the hierarchy. For whatever reason they arrive there, they remain there because no-one finds it profitable to invest in them.

The evidence for the SLM model is very limited and not convincing. The model is extremely difficult to test with the data available to researchers. Fundamentally, it does not provide a clear basis for distinguishing primary from secondary jobs. The notion of a good job is complex and normative, and the distinction used in empirical work must therefore be somewhat arbitrary. Those tests that are available are far from conclusive. For example, the results for earnings equations which show different returns to education and quality variables between primary and secondary segments are not inconsistent with human capital theory. The latter argues that wages and quality are non-linearly related across individuals as in Figure 12.2(a) even if rates of return are all the same. To divide any sample in half on the basis of $W$ and to fit two linear relationships between $W$ and $S$ will necessarily show a different and lower response of wages to quality in the lower segment. Even if the logarithm of wages is used as the dependent variable, truncation of the data could seriously bias the results. In Figure 12.2(b) the observed values of log $W$ are distributed randomly about the true relationship, (TR), between log $W$ and $S$. Dividing the sample might flatten the estimated relationship for the lower group of observations far more than for the top group, com-

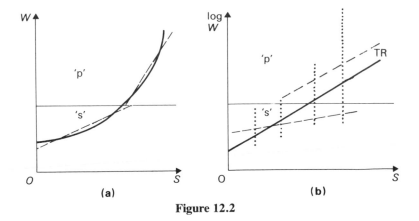

**Figure 12.2**

pared to the relationship estimated over the whole sample. The results may well follow from segmentation but may equally well arise because of the way the data are divided up by high and low incomes. The SLM model is very different from the conventional approach, yet all too often the tests conducted are of predictions that could come from either approach.

The SLM model may have serious limitations but it is also valuable in a number of respects. First, the model argues that discrimination, trade union activities and other institutional forces cannot simply be treated as relatively minor qualifications to an otherwise competitive economy as the traditional approach assumes: they are in fact central to understanding how the economy works. More research into these forces is required. We are aware that our theories of discrimination are problematic, trade union activities are complex and institutional forces intangible. Research will be very difficult given the problems of measuring key concepts. But further research into labour market discrimination as a consequence of inadequate information and stereotyping in hiring and job structuring is essential. There is also a strong case for further study of bargaining by relativities and of internal labour markets. The present state of analysis of non-competitive forces is far from satisfactory.

Second, the SLM model is based upon rigid segmentation within every level of productive activity. Whilst such segmentation can be overstated there remains a strong feeling that the labour market does contain groups of non-competing workers. There is a distinction between professional, managerial and administrative workers and the rest, a distinction very strongly associated with the possession of higher educational qualifications. There may not be the sharp dichotomy of the SLM model, but the distinction between certain job levels rather than within them remains a real one and one which is closely associated with enduring social stratification. There is also a very real distinction between the employed and the self-employed, with the interests of the latter better protected in an economic system which favours private enterprise.

Third, the SLM focuses strongly upon the distinction between jobs rather than that between workers: good jobs make good workers, not vice versa. There appears to be a valid and important point here, if not one that leads to the supremacy of institutional processes. In practice jobs differ because of technology. Technology will shape the job structure: it could produce many low level jobs and few higher level jobs; it could set rigid lower limits to the productivity of workers who can fill each job. Wages in jobs are thus set by the productivity required to perform them rather than by the productivity of the labour that fills them. Wages are attached to jobs not people. There could be many workers in low level jobs who are perfectly capable of performing higher level tasks but who get no opportunity. There could also be people unable to enter higher level jobs who would be prepared to accept a wage below the going rate for the job if it reflected their productivity.

Fourth, the SLM focuses attention on the experiences of individuals within the economy rather than on the behaviour of individual labour markets emphasised by traditional theory. It is important that both aspects be developed. Focusing upon individuals directs theory and research towards the cumulative forces of the labour market, the positive and negative feedback that alters each individual's chances of success with each successive decision. To research the feedbacks which operate through productivity, attitudes to work, and work habits, requires special data and techniques. Few longitudinal studies of cohorts of individuals in the labour market are as yet available, but their importance is clear.

Fifth, a central objective of the SLM approach is to explain the role of the labour market in determining the fortunes of people in poverty. The conclusion is that providing more education and skills will not remove the problems of low pay and unemployment. Whilst this conclusion may be too strong, at several stages in our analysis we have seen that the provision of education and training is not in itself enough to eliminate poverty. There is indeed a need to study the labour market experiences of marginal workers in order to define and assess specific labour market policies that will help this group: employment subsidies, higher state benefits, special counselling and so on.

Sixth, the SLM model highlights the problems of the many workers who are in bad jobs. Not only does this feed back to produce lower productivity, weak attachment to the labour force and so on, it also represents a negative element in workers' utilities, and a large one too given the proportion of non-sleeping time most people spend in market work. The SLM model is right to stress the importance of this. Whether greater unionisation is enough to remedy matters is, however, very doubtful if we are right that it is primarily technology and demand conditions that determine job characteristics. Where improving job content also improves workers' output there is no problem. The market can be trusted to sort things out. But instances of the 'Volvo effect' are likely to be rare. In most circumstances improving job quality will raise costs. Both competitive and non-competitive firms will favour low costs. Nowhere does society as a whole have the opportunity to choose. All individuals, as consumers, will impose low costs on others and favour, unsuccessfully, high quality jobs for themselves. The state has been accustomed to intervene only to set minimum standards of safety, working conditions and so on. One could wait for technological change to improve jobs but the signs are not promising. Change is slow, it may remove physical labour only to replace it by repetitive boring tasks, and it devalues traditional skills. Technological change may be associated with the relative decline of manufacturing, and there is much evidence to suggest that, by and large, jobs in the service sector are even less satisfactory. There is a pervasive pressure to increase the division of labour and therefore a genuine need for analysis and research of the alternatives.

Seventh, the SLM model offers a different perspective from that of traditional theory on how the labour market actually works. There is a significant amount of powerful non-competitive behaviour. The experiences of individuals in the labour market are shaped not primarily by their own actions but by the structure and dynamics of the economic system. In the SLM model the economy works according to criteria which are inconsistent with efficiency. Traditional policy assessments are thus inappropriate. The important issue is to improve distribution. Within this perspective the policy measures required to improve matters need to be and should be aimed at achieving structural changes. Whilst one may doubt the value or feasibility of expanding the primary segment, the central point persists that where structural forces are at work structural remedies are required. In several places during our analysis we have indicated how labour market outcomes can reflect and strengthen the class structure of society. There is a real need therefore to work out and evaluate radical policies to counter this process: policies which go beyond marginal reforms of the labour market and income maintenance to extensive redistribution of wealth, strong positive discrimination in favour of the disadvantaged, and further extensions to the spread of ownership and control of productive resources. The SLM model recognises the powerful vested interests which prevent reform. It counsels a more abrasive strategy to help the disadvantaged at the expense of the advantaged; switching state funds towards inner cities; student loans to increase the resources of selected sixth formers; measures to reduce the restrictive practices of workers' organisations, especially at higher skill levels; financial support redirected to workers' co-operatives and B group entrepreneurs; restrictions on private education; reforms to control streaming and stereotyping in schooling.

Whilst the SLM model does not really offer a viable alternative strategy for developing labour market analysis, it does urge widening of the traditional scheme of study. One could argue that this goes beyond the confines of what is currently thought of as economic analysis, that the data are simply not available, that labour economics is still a young subject, that important normative rather than positive issues are raised. There is of course every reason to pursue further the insights provided by developments of the traditional approach and thus, for example, to obtain more reliable estimates of the own wage elasticity of hours supplied. But it is also extremely important to consider the underlying structural determinants of labour market mechanics.

## Further Reading

### CHAPTER 12: THE LABOUR MARKET, EFFICIENCY AND DISTRIBUTION

N. Bosanquet and P. Doeringer, 'Is there a dual labour market in Britain?', *Economic Journal*, Vol. 83 (June 1973).

G. Cain, 'The challenge of segmented labor market theories to orthodox theory: a survey', *Journal of Economic Literature*, Vol. 14 (December 1976).

D. M. Gordon, *Theories of Poverty and Underemployment* (Lexington, Mass.: Heath, 1972).

R. Mayhew and B. Rosewell, 'Labour market segmentation in Britain', *Oxford Bulletin of Economics and Statistics*, Vol. 41 (March 1979).

J. Rubery, 'Structured labour markets, worker organisation and low pay', *Cambridge Journal of Economics*, Vol. 2 (March 1978).

# Index

ployment 300, inflation and 335ff;
natural rate of 311–14, 347ff, 351,
352; participation and 165–9; policy
measures and 298–301, 303–5, 306–8,
311–14, 315–17; price inflation and
308–9, 313–14; recurrent spells of
331, 333–4; search and 311, 314–16,
329–30, 332; social welfare function
and 304; specific skills and 330–1;
structural 304–7; trade unions and
311–12, 315; voluntary 309–17, 347;
wage dispersion and 312–13; wage
rigidity and 314–15
Unemployment benefits 318, 325,
326–8, 329–30; *see also* replacement
ratio
Unemployment – vacancy relationship
301–4, 306–8, 319–22, 325–7

Wage determination: ability and 273–4;
275; basic model 247–9; compensating
differentials and 248–9; discrimination
and 266–72; 277–82, 288; equality of
opportunity and 285–6; human capital
model 60, 249–59, 272–5; in segmented labour market theory 382–3,
385–6, 389; monopsony and 269–70,
283; trade unions and 258–66, 275–7,
286–7; uncertainty and 271
Wage dispersion: income inequality and
290; individual 252–3, 256–7,
259–60, 262–3, 268, 288; industrial
258–9, 263–4, 283–5; occupational
257–8, 263–4, 283–4, 287; poverty
and 290–2; unemployment and
312–13
Wage leadership 122